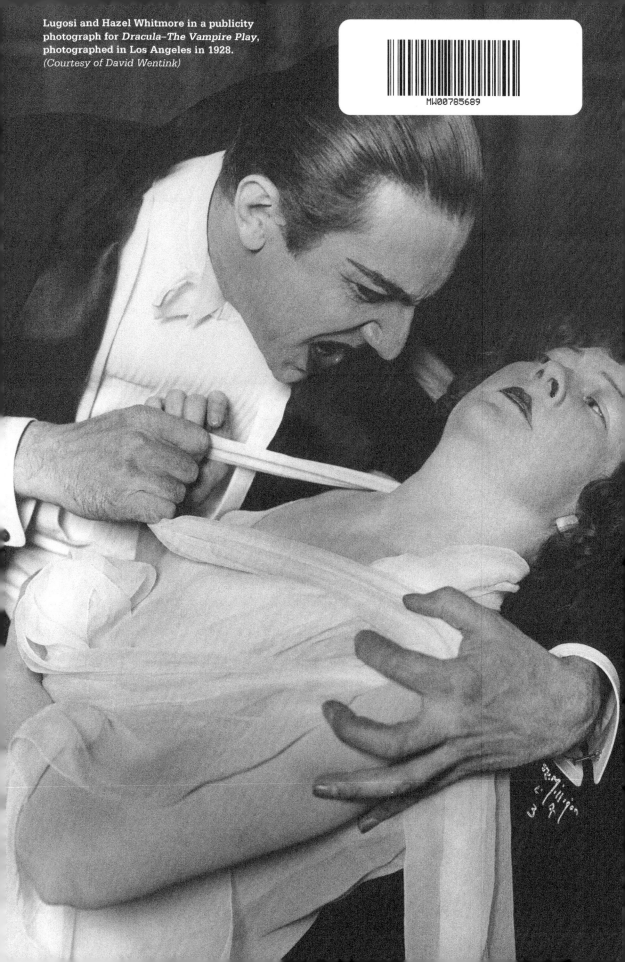

BECOMING
DRACULA
THE EARLY YEARS
OF **BELA LUGOSI**
VOLUME ONE

By Gary D. Rhodes and Bill Kaffenberger

Featuring photographs from the
collections of John Antosiewicz, Bill Chase,
Kristin Dewey, Roger Hurlburt, Dennis
Phelps, and David Wentink

Designed by Michael Kronenberg

Cover photo of Bela Lugosi and Hazel Whitmore in 1928 courtesy of David Wentink.
Back cover photo is the original movie poster for *Küzdelem a létért* (*The Struggle for Life*, 1918), aka *A leopárd* (*The Leopard*).

Printed in the United States

Published by BearManor Media
1317 Edgewater Drive 110
Orlando, FL 32804
books@benohmart.com

Unless otherwise noted, all photographs come from the collections of Gary D. Rhodes and Bill Kaffenberger.

Library of Congress Cataloguing-in-Publication Data
Rhodes, Gary D. and Bill Kaffenberger
Becoming Dracula: The Early Years of Bela Lugosi, Volume I / Gary D. Rhodes and Bill Kaffenberger

Includes bibliographical references and index
ISBN 978-1-62933-533-9 (hardcover)
ISBN 978-1-62933-532-2 (softcover)

1. Lugosi, Bela, 1882-1956.   2. Motion Picture Actors and Actresses–United States–Biography.
I. Rhodes, Gary D.   II. Kaffenberger, Bill.   III. Title.
PN2859.H86L834

Authors' Notes: Some images chosen for this book are of an imperfect quality, but they are reproduced herein due to their rarity and their importance to the narrative.

Dedicated to

Robert Cremer and Bela G. Lugosi

Lugosi as Dracula in 1930.
(Courtesy of Dennis Phelps)

To my friend Dick
Bela Lugosi

Introduction

"[T]he victim of the vampire becomes his
creature, linked to him in life and after death."
– Deane & Balderston, *Dracula–The Vampire Play*, 1927

"Life itself is a continuous process of vampirism."
– Manly P. Hall, 1927

Béla Lugosi became Dracula, even if he wasn't predestined to be Dracula. The process was both long (meaning that more than 47 years of his life passed before he signed a contract at Universal Pictures to star in *Dracula*), and relatively short (meaning the speed with which Horace Liveright cast him in *Dracula–The Vampire Play* on Broadway).

Either way, he lived more than a single lifetime before becoming the vampire onscreen. He had resided in four countries, married three times, and fought in the War to End All Wars. He acted onstage for nearly three decades and in films for nearly fifteen years before *Dracula* fascinated and frightened moviegoers in 1931.

Prior Lugosi biographies have spent relatively little space on the years we (re-) construct. By contrast, we offer 48 chapters that chronicle approximately 48 years, requiring this book to be published in two volumes. The first covers 1882 through 1920; the second covers 1921 through 1930. Each features relevant appendices.

Becoming Dracula is the result of decades of shared research that has taken us halfway around the world. Our trips to Hungary, Romania, Germany, and Austria, as well as to numerous American cities have been crucial, as digitized sources, while important, are dramatically limited. Far too many one-of-a-kind scripts, contracts, and documents of all kinds remain unavailable for viewing unless one visits the archives that hold them. Equally notable is the fact that an enormous number of publications, including city newspapers, languish on aging microfilms. Consider *Dracula–The Vampire Play* on Broadway. More than half of the New York newspapers that covered its opening are not digitized.

Digitized publications in Hungary would be vastly incomplete without a careful search of primary sources held at libraries in Budapest, Szeged, and elsewhere. We spent day after

LUGOSI BÉLA. Goszleth felv.
A Budapesti Szinház Jézus előadásán.

Lugosi in *A passiójáték* (*The Passion*).
Published in the January 5-12, 1913 edition
of *Színházi Élet*.

day carefully examining literally thousands of posters covering dozens of Hungarian towns and cities in an effort to uncover every Lugosi stage performance possible, opening doors while closing others, learning what venues he did and didn't play. And for Germany, page-by-page scrutiny of all film trade publications – some never even transferred to microfilm, let alone digitized – became a necessity.

Traditional research methods and digital exploration must merge, as the latter alone is fraught with limitations, if not troubles. Our marriage of both has resulted in an exhaustive compilation of literally thousands upon thousands of sources. As Hamilton Deane and John L. Balderston wrote in *Dracula–The Vampire Play* (1927), "The dust was somewhat deep, but we are used to dust in Transylvania."

Regarding our presentation of the information

Lugosi (left) in *Álarcosbál* (*The Masked Ball, 1917*). *(Courtesy of John Antosiewicz)*

BECOMING DRACULA

Lugosi in Hungary.
(Courtesy of Noémi Saly)

we excavated, a few notes are in order. For the sake of internal consistency, we spell Lugosi's first name as "Béla" from Chapter 1 through 25, which cover his years in Hungarian, German, and Hungarian-American entertainment. We opt for "Bela" for Chapters 26 through 48, the period in which was involved in English-language entertainment. Our rationale follows the predominant spelling in the press in the periods in question.

Also for the sake of internal consistency, we render the word "theater" with that spelling, even when articles or advertisements used the spelling "theatre." With regard to Hungarian and German titles and names, we privilege the original languages, giving English translations on the first occasion of their usage in each chapter. In addition to historical accuracy, we have opted for this approach given that most of the plays and films mentioned never actually had formal English titles.

We also rely on the original Hungarian and German spellings, including the given languages' approach to the use (or not) of uppercase letters in film and play titles. This extends to the titles of Hungarian newspapers and magazines, which – contrary to Hungarian film and play titles – were generally rendered on covers and mastheads with the first letter of each word being uppercase. Moreover, we should note that our use of diacritic marks and spellings

Lugosi in a publicity photograph for *99-es számú bérkocsi* (*Rental Car Number 99, aka 99*, 1918).

BECOMING DRACULA

of Hungarian words follows established grammatical norms, even when they are on occasion at odds with primary sources that we use. Misspellings and absent diacritic marks in the Hungarian and Hungarian-American press of the period were not uncommon.

Lastly, we would note that many of the images reprinted herein are of lesser quality, taken as they are from yellowing pages of aging publications. However, these are generally the only known copies and so – despite their poor condition – we include them due to their relevance and rarity.

We hope the result brings Lugosi back to life, not through vampirism, but rather through rigorous historiography. Here are his hopes and dreams, his challenges and setbacks. Here are his important roles and hitherto-unknown credits. And here is a story that has remained untold for too long.

In his novel *Dracula* (1897), Bram Stoker asked, "Is there fate amongst us still, sent down from the pagan world of old, that such things must be, and in such way?" In the film *Glen or Glenda* (1953), Lugosi firmly declared, "Dance to that which one is created for!"

But in this book, we avoid teleological arguments and conclusions. Whether Lugosi was fated to be Dracula we do not know. Perhaps; perhaps not. After all, despite being born in Hungary, most of his early years were far removed from vampires and horror. For the bulk of the 48 years we chronicle, Dracula played no role in the drama of his life.

Then Lugosi became Dracula onscreen in 1931. He would dress as the vampire for the rest of his 73 years, and, ever since then, Dracula has dressed as Lugosi. That is Lugosi's legacy, the source of his ongoing fame.

Our two-volume project is thus the story before the story. We are hopeful that it adds meaningfully to ongoing research into the world of Béla Lugosi.

Regény-Csarnok.

DRAKULA

Angol regény.

Irta: Bram Stoker.

Harker Jonathan naplója.

(Gyorsirással jegyezve).

I.

Május 3. Besztercze. Münchenből 8 óra 35 perckor indultam este. Bécsbe másnap reggel érkeztem; 6 óra 36 perckor kellett volna érkeznem, de a vonatunk egy órát késett.

Budapest csodálatos egy helynek látszott, ha a kevésből, a mit a vonatról és rövid sétám alatt láttam, itélhetek. Nem mertem nagyon messzire menni az állomástól, mert hogy későn is érkeztünk, meg nem biztam egészen az indulás pontosságában sem. A benyomásom az volt, hogy elhagytuk nyugatot és keleten vagyunk, a nyugati hidak egyik legremekjebbén, a mely itt a hatalmasan széles és mély Dunát fogja át, keresztül a hajdani török uralom tradicziói közé jutottunk.

Elég jókor indultunk és éjjelre Kolozsvárra értünk. A Royal-hôtelben szálltam meg éjszakára. Ebédre, vagyis inkább vacsorára csirkét ettem, a mely valamiféle piros borssal volt elkészitve, igen izlett, de roppant szomjas ételnek bizonyult. (*Megjegyzés.* A recipéjét megszereztem Minna számára.) A pincér hozzá intézett kérdésemre azt mondta, hogy ez *paprikás csirke* és minthogy ez nemzeti eledel, hát mindenütt megkaphatom a Kárpátok között. A csekély német tudományomnak itt is igen

Published in the *Budapesti Hírlap* on January 1, 1898.

Acknowledgments

The authors would like to extend their gratitude to the various archives, libraries, museums and universities that kindly offered assistance during the research phase of this project: the Alexander Library of Rutgers University of New Brunswick, New Jersey, the American Heritage Center at the University of Wyoming, the Andover-Harvard Theological Library of Massachusetts, the Antigo Public Library of Antigo, Wisconsin, the Annenberg Rare Book and Manuscript Library at the University of Pennsylvania, the Ardmore Public Library of Oklahoma, the Bancroft Library at the University of California at Berkeley, the Billy Rose Theater Division of the New York Public Library, the Bundesarchiv in Berlin, the Chicago History Museum Research Center of Chicago, Illinois, the Chickasaw Regional Library System of Oklahoma, the Cleveland Public Library of Ohio, the D. C. Public Library of Washington D. C., the Department of Special Collections at the University of California at Santa Barbara, the Deutsche Kinemathek, the Free Library of Philadelphia, the Harry Ransom Center at the University of Texas at Austin, the Hillman Library at the University of Pittsburgh, the Historical Society of Pennsylvania, the Howard Gottlieb Archival Research Center at Boston University in Massachusetts, the Hungarian Film Institute, the Hungarian Theater Museum and Institute of Budapest, Hungary, the Immigration and Naturalization Service, Interlibrary Loan at the University of Central Florida, the Kiplinger Research Library of Washington D. C., the Library of Congress of Washington, D. C., the Los Angeles Public Library, the Margaret Herrick Library of the Academy of Motion Picture Arts and Sciences, the Media History Digital Library, the Museum of History, Ethnography, and Fine Arts–Lugoj, Romania, the Museum of Performance and Design of San Francisco, California, the National Archives of the United States, the National Széchényi Library Theater History Collection of Budapest, Hungary, the New York State Historical Association, the Newark Public Library of New Jersey, the Pasadena Playhouse of California, the Pennsylvania Department of Education – Bureau of State Library, the Pest-Buda Restaurant of Budapest, Hungary, the Pickering Educational Resources Library at Boston University, the Research Service of the Budapest City Archives of Hungary, the San Diego Public Library of California, the Santa Barbara Public Library of California, the San Francisco Public Library, the Syracuse University Archives of New York, the University of Central Oklahoma, the University of Debrecen University and National Library, Arts and Sciences Library of Debrecen, Hungary, University of Pennsylvania Penn State Special Collections Library, and the University of Washington Libraries/Special Collections.

In addition, the authors would like to express their appreciation to the following individuals who have helped make this book possible: Carolyn Edgington Anderson, Tom Anker, Jerry Armellino, Dr. Bonhardt Attila, Leonardo D'Aurizio, Ellen Bailey, Wendy Barszcz, Marty Baumann, Scott Berman, Tom Brannan, Olaf Brill, Larissa Brookes, Duane Brower, John Brunas, Michael Brunas, Bob Burns, Joe Busam, Bart Bush, Petrina Calabalic, Paolo Caneppele, Jeff Carlson, Allison Carmola, Mario Chacon, Ross Clark, William Cornauer, Mária Cseh, Richard Daub, Kate Deeks, Frank J. Dello Stritto, Dorothy Demarest, Patricia Dew, Harald Dolezal, the late David Durston, the late Robert Ray Edgington, Ruth Edgington, Robert Edgington Jr., Michael Engel, Scott Essman, the late Philip R. Evans, the late William K. Everson, Elena Filios, Fabian Fuerste, Lawrence Fultz, Jr., Shawna Gandy, Cheri Goldner, Julio Gonzalez, Emily Goodrich, the late Richard Gordon, the late Gordon R. Guy, Steve Haberman, G. D. Hamann, Warren G. Harris, Betsy L. Hendrix, Dora Hicsik, Suzette Hinson, David J. Hogan, Suzanne Horton, Durham Hunt, Roger Hurlburt, the late Steve Jochsberger, Steve Kaplan, Amy Kastigar, Constance Kelly, Anthony Kerr, Nancy Kersey,

Eugene Kirschenbaum, Robin Ladd, Rosemary Lands, Sierra Lepine, Frank Liquori, Bill Lord, Steve McFarland, Lauren Martino, Jeremy Megraw, David Merlini, the late Linda Miller, D'Arcy More, Dejan Mrkić, Peter Michaels, Jean-Claude Michel, Mark A. Miller, Deborah A. Mitchell, the late Lynn Naron, the late Randy Nesseler, Ted Newsom, Dr. James P. Niessen, Scott Nollen, John Norris, Jim Nye, Chris O'Brien, Marcus O'Brien, Margaret O'Brien, Dennis Payne, Victor Pierce, William Pirola, William V. Rauscher, Mike Ravnitzky, Robert Rees, Kate Reeve, Jeffrey Roberts, Barbara L. Rothschild, Dr. Andrea Rozsavolgyi, Becky Scarborough, Bruce Scivally, the late Richard Sheffield, Joseph Shemtov, Samuel M. Sherman, Margaret Sides, Bettina Sinkó, Zoran Sinobad, Barb Smith, Don G. Smith, Lynette Suckow, Karin Suni, Vera Surányi, Graham Sutton, Dr. Andor Sziklay, László Tábori, Kirsten Tanaka, Dominika Tápai, the late Brian Taves, Maurice Terenzio, Mario Toland, Ádám Török, Nadine Turner, Elizabeth Van Tuyl, John Ulakovic, Judit Katalin Ulrich, Dr. Steven Béla Várdy, Jon Wang, Leo Wiltshire, the late Robert Wise, Laraine Worby, Valerie Yaros, Gregory Zatirka, and Péter Zsolt.

The authors would also like to offer their deepest thanks to a number of individuals who gave so much of their time and support that they proved crucial to this project's completion: the late Forrest J Ackerman, Gyöngyi Balogh, Matthew E. Banks, Buddy Barnett, Sidney Blackmer, Jr., the late Richard Bojarski, Tom Brannan, Olaf Brill, Kevin Brownlow, Mario Chacon, George Chastain, Ned Comstock, Michael Copner, Michael J. David, Jack Dowler, Edward "Eric" Eaton, John Ellis, Theodore Estes, Donald F. Glut, Michael Ferguson, Phillip Fortune, Beau Foutz, Fritz Frising, Christopher R. Gauthier, Robert Guffey, Lee Harris, Cortlundt Hull, Elena Kaffenberger, Dr. Michael Lee, Mark Martucci, Susan D. Mazza, Jerry McCoy, Lisa Mitchell, Tamara Nagy, David Nahmod, Constantine Nasr, Henry Nicolella, Donald Rhodes, Phyllis Rhodes, William Rosar, Noémi Saly, Dr. Robert Singer, Anthony Slide, Carter Smith, Billy Stagner, David Stenn, Elemer Szasz, Tamás Gyurkovics, and Glenn P. White.

Special recognition goes to the following: Dr. Mirjam Dénes for translating hundreds of Hungarian documents into English and providing many insightful comments and observations about Hungarian theater; Raymond E. Glew for assisting in our Budapest research; Dr. Ildikó Sirato, Edit Rajnai, and the staff of the National Széchényi Library Theater History Collection of Budapest, Hungary for their assistance in making available rare Hungarian theater playbills for our research; Mária Kórász and the Vasváry Collection at the Somogyi Library in Szeged, and Zsuzsa Köpsódi for her assistance in locating theatrical documents from the University of Debrecen University and National Library, Arts and Sciences Library of Debrecen, Hungary.

Likewise, we extend our deepest thanks to Bela G. Lugosi, Lynne Lugosi Sparks, and Lugosi Enterprises for their support and assistance; David Wentink for providing the amazing cover photo; John Antosiewicz, Bill Chase, Kristin Dewey, Roger Hurlburt, and Dennis Phelps for sharing photos from their collections; John Soister and Tom Weaver for Weaver for proofreading and providing insightful commentary on our rough drafts, as well as to Robert Cremer and Dr. Robert J. Kiss for proofreading and providing translations of several hundred German documents into English.

Likewise, we acknowledge the crucial contribution of Michael Kronenberg, who devoted much time to creating the stunning layout design for both volumes of this project, and Ben Ohmart at BearManor Media, who has been so supportive of our research.

Gary D. Rhodes
Orlando, FL

Bill Kaffenberger
Henrico, VA

Prologue

"At his own request, Bela Lugosi will go to the grave wrapped in the black cape of Dracula, the horror character in which he scored the greatest triumph of his long motion picture career." – Associated Press, August 18, 1956

Chapter 1

Legends

"Is it mad to tell deliberate lies to serve a purpose?
Lies that do not harm anyone? If so, then chalk this
down on the ledger under 'Mad.'"[1]
– Béla Lugosi

By the time Béla Lugosi spoke about lies and madness, he had been a professional stage actor for four decades. He had been in the movies for a quarter of a century. And he had been a horror film star for ten years, achieving fame in the title role of *Dracula* at Universal Pictures in 1931. He was a screen legend, and legends are those stories that are hard to verify.

Lugosi was born Béla Ferenc Dezső Blaskó to István and Paula Vojnits Blaskó in Lugos, a town in the Bánát region of Hungary, on October 20, 1882 (not 1884 or 1888, as he would occasionally claim during his years in Hollywood). His parents had married in 1858, his father being ten years older than his mother. His first name was profound, recalling as it did Béla I, Béla II, Béla III, and Béla IV, who ruled Hungary during parts of the 11th, 12th, and 13th centuries. And his surname Blaskó can be traced to at least as early as 1627. But one of Lugosi's ancestors did not found his hometown, nor was it named for his family, as he sometimes claimed.[2]

Lugos – now known as Lugoj and located in Romania since the end of World War I – dates to the fourteenth century; it had once served as a fortress town. At the time of Lugosi's birth, Lugos was situated in southern Hungary and was within the boundaries of the Austro-Hungarian Empire. The beautiful Temes River rolls through its heart.[3] In 1882, the town's population was roughly 16,000. Peasants brought their crops to market, just as they had for centuries. But some of the shops sold the latest in Viennese furniture, making Lugos very much the convergence of two time periods, the new and the old.

The town was also somewhat cosmopolitan, in part due to its active wine trade, and in part due to its diverse population, which included not only Hungarians, but also Germans and Romanians. Vibrant traditions of these cultures flourished, as did both the Roman Catholic and Greek Catholic churches.

At the time of Lugosi's birth, the Blaskó family lived at Number 6 Kirchengasse (Church Street), located on the Hungarian/German side of the river, the opposite being populated primarily by Romanians. It was a small, modest house, but strangely known to many eyes throughout the world. Given that it was located directly beside the Roman Catholic church where Lugosi was baptized, the Blaskó home appeared on more than one picture postcard.

Lugosi's proud Magyar ancestors had survived as farmers. His father István broke with family tradition to become a baker, his bakery located at the entrance to Kirchengasse. He later became a banker at the Lugos Volksbank, elected to its Board of Directors as early as 1879.[4] By 1892, he had become its vezérigazgató (Chief Executive Officer).[5] And he was the proud father of four children: Lugosi (the youngest), his two brothers, László and Lajos, and a sister named Vilma.

Lugosi's godparents were Ferenc Bayer (aka Ferencz Bayer) and his wife Vilma Küszer. Bayer and his brother were executors of the Német-Bogsáni takarékpénztár (Bogsán Savings Bank) in Lugos. Presumably István knew Bayer through their shared professions. During his life, Bayer also served as a judge and as vice-mayor of Lugos.[6]

The Blaskó family assumed an honorable place in the community, and lived – as a classmate of Lugosi's later recalled – "a normal bourgeois life."[7] They were not nobility, as later accounts would suggest.[8] Nor did his father own an estate, as Lugosi once claimed.[9] István was no Baron, and Lugosi was no Count.

But Lugosi likely did hear the name Dracula during his youth, in reference to Vlad III Dracula, aka Vlad Țepeș, aka Vlad the Impaler, the infamous 15th century Wallachian prince. Articles about him appeared somewhat frequently in the press, including once during the year of Lugosi's birth. This historic Dracula might well have been something of a legendary hero to the Romanians in Lugos, having fought so fiercely for their ancestors against the Turks. They would never have considered Dracula to be a vampire, nor would the Hungarians, though centuries earlier the Hungarians and particularly the Germans helped exacerbate tales of Dracula's cruelty. Most notably, Lugosi was Hungarian, and Dracula was not. It was King Matthias of Hungary that had in fact imprisoned Dracula in Visegrád from 1463 to 1475.[10]

During his youth, Lugosi might also have learned about Countess Erzsébet Báthory, aka Elizabeth Bathory, who had been accused of murdering hundreds of young women from 1585 to 1609. Though she avoided trial, the "Blood Countess" spent her last four years imprisoned in a room at Čachtice Castle, located in what was then Upper Hungary. Unlike Vlad III Dracula, Báthory was Hungarian. Legends that she bathed in blood to restore the beauty of her aging skin were well known, but she was not considered to have been a vampire at the time of Lugosi's childhood.[11]

Lugosi likely heard local tales of ritual exhumations, which were not uncommon in the

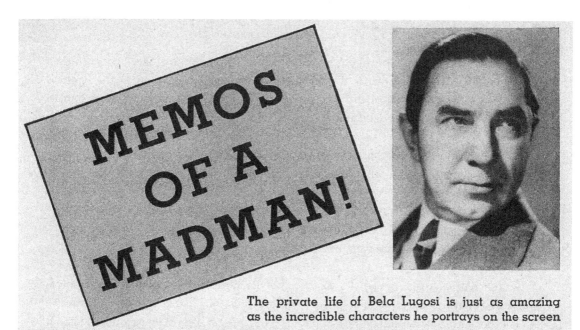

MEMOS OF A MADMAN!

The private life of Bela Lugosi is just as amazing as the incredible characters he portrays on the screen

"... *but am I mad?*
. . . living here, in the California sunshine, with my small son, the Little Bela, playing in the garden, with household sounds about, that seems a purely rhetorical question, more than a little absurd . . .

Yet my wife, a quiet girl, not of the theatre, crystal clear of mind and serene of spirit, admits that I have a strange power over her. The servants in our household, after they have been with us a while, tip-toe about. My wife's sister stayed with us for one year and, *for no accountable reason*, lost twenty-five pounds. She said it was because she could not rest.

My wife will tell you that she cannot rest, either, when I am in the house. There are strange vibrations in the house, she insists, when I am there. The only time she ever really relaxes, she says, is when she knows I am sleeping or when I am not there. She will tell you that I know what she wants and what she is thinking without her saying a word. Hearing this, people have accused me of psychic powers.

I do not claim any psychic powers beyond my belief in thought transference, telepathy, the power of suggestion which all who will may share. Which all who will *strongly enough* may share, I should add. Because it is my sure belief that if you have a very definite will, *you can impose it*. But to do so is an act of vampirism on one's self. For all of the faculties of the will, the mind, the emotions, the beat of the heart, the pulse of the blood, all the powers drained and concentrated into the will—then, it can be done.

One night we had a guest. I drink many vegetable juices. This night I had the juice of the beet. Our guest turned white and felt ill. Questioned, she laughed rather foolishly, said it had fantastically occurred to her that I might be drinking a *cocktail of blood!*

Exceedingly fond of Roquefort cheese,

I eat a great deal of it. One night I remarked my liking for it and was told, with a tremor in the voice of my dinner partner, that Roquefort is aged in *bats' caves* . . . was that, she wanted to know, half in fun but somewhat mordantly in earnest, *why I craved it . . .?*

I have what I consider reasonably normal fears of men. I am afraid of burglaries. When we are away from the house, the help must stay up until we return. We have four wolf-hounds who, at all times, guard our bedroom doors. There is a gun in every room in the house. There are lights burning in our house all night long. There is no dark in our house, ever.

Other men take similar precautions. Blood-hounds stalk the estate of Harold Lloyd. In Marlene Dietrich's house, iron bars protect the windows . . . and no one is surprised. Yet I have been told that I fear the powers of darkness because *I know, too well, what the powers of darkness may hold.*

I am afraid of dying. I am very much afraid of dying. But not of death itself. No . . . because now, in this concentrated time, with all the changes going on in the world, I would suffer to miss any of it. Yet it has been suggested to me, again half in fun, again sinisterly in earnest, that my fear of dying is because I know what it is . . . beyond.

I pick out everything my wife wears. I like to see her in simple things. I do not like exotic things on women. When we were first married, I stopped my wife from using make-up. I did it, she will tell you, very gradually and very delicately. First the lipstick . . . "do not use it," I said, "you have natural color in your lips, I like the natural color" . . . then the rouge, then the powder . . . I told her "when you wear make-up, you look just like the rest of them." I allow

As told to Gladys Hall

her to wear no jewelry and no perfume. I took the curls away from her face. I push her hair back of her ears all the time saying, "Now, this is the way you are the loveliest . . ." men like natural women, I submit, it is a natural instinct. But I have been told, *"Dracula* would not like exotic women, either . . . he would like young, fresh maidens . . ."

Up until our baby came, my wife was very anemic . . . "Strange" more than one person said, "strange that *you* should be anemic . . ."

The dogs are terribly important in our household. I talk with them like with people and those gifted with morbid imaginations read into this *what they choose to read* . . .

I never sleep by night. I read the nights through. I do not go to bed until somewhere between three and five in the mornings. I wake at midday. I have my breakfast at three in the afternoon. I read again until our dinner at 7:30. We may then go for a drive, my wife and I. I return and read the night through again. This has been my habit for many years. But it is suggested to me that I *dare not sleep*, that I am a creature of the night, that, by day, not only am I not awake but, perhaps, *not even alive* . . .

It is all a little monstrous. Sometimes it is a little funny. But it is also very interesting because it shows the power of suggestion of horror on the human mind. It is the explanation of why murder mystery books, front page murders, horror films are so enormously popular. People, *women especially,* are not repelled by horror, they are strongly and strangely attracted to it, and by it.

Bela Lugosi-Dracula: the two have become synonyms, virtually inseparable. Follow "Dracula," as I have done, with such pictures as "Chandu, the Magician," "Murder in the Rue Morgue," "White Zombie," "The Devil Bat," "The Son of Frankenstein," "The Raven," "The Phantom Ghost," [*Continued on page 87*]

From *Silver Screen* magazine, July 1941.

Bánát region, as well as folklore about ghosts and vampires. In Bram Stoker's novel *Dracula* (1897), Jonathan Harker explains, "I read that every known superstition in the world is gathered into the horseshoe of the Carpathians, as if it were the centre of some sort of imaginative whirlpool." In 1914, Dudley Wright's book *Vampires and Vampirism* claimed:

> The Hungarians believe that those who have become passive vampires in life become active vampires after death; that those whose blood has been sucked in life by vampires become themselves vampires after death. In many districts the belief also prevails that the only way to prevent this calamity happening is for the threatened victim to eat some earth from the grave of the attacking vampire, and to smear his own body with blood from the body of that vampire.[12]

Two different fan magazine articles about Lugosi described how Hungarians kept relatives who passed away indoors for days or longer to make certain they had died a "Christian death, and not the hideous-half-death of the vampires."[13] And in 1928, Lugosi told a journalist about the iron stakes that some Hungarians plunged through the hearts of the dead to "forestall any posthumous wanderings about."[14]

Mention of vampires in Hungarian literature appeared as early as 1786, when one book discussed how they "suck the blood of living people."[15] The Hungarian press printed many stories about supernatural vampires in the nineteenth century, including the year of Lugosi's birth.[16] Yet another, published near the time of the Hungarian Revolution, told readers a tale in which, "Intrigue left its hiding place, its blood-thirsty vampires struck at him, sucked his life out, and celebrated over the corpse with loud and dark, crow-like laughter."[17]

Lugosi told one journalist that his "training was received at the knee of his old nurse, and her fearful stories of ghosts and vampires made interesting bedtime tales...."[18] The locals believed in "resurrected creatures able to transform themselves

Lugosi as a young boy with his sister Vilma.

into huge bats."[19] On yet another occasion, contradicting his usual stories about his family, he said he never went to bed scared because he "came from a poor Hungarian family and there were too many of us in the house to be alone or to be frightened."[20] A third article claimed Lugosi:

> was, like all youngsters in that region, frightened out of his wits by peasant maids and nurses who talked by the hour of vampires, evil spirits, and the undead – those hapless mortals who only seem to die, but don't really pass away until a stake is driven through their hearts.[21]

Lugosi added that he never went into his family's cellar because it was full of bats. He saw them outdoors, too, at dusk.[22] So he said; so he allegedly said. As the Hungarian author Imre Madách wrote in *Az ember tragédiája* (*The Tragedy of Man*) in 1861, "In days of old, the world was mad/A dread of ghosts ev'n heroes had."

In Lugosi's youth, such folklore likely took up little of his time. Reminiscing on his childhood, he recalled:

> I was very unruly as a boy, very out of control ... Like Jekyll and Hyde, except that I changed according to sex. I mean, with boys I was tough and brutal. But the minute I came into company with girls and women, I kissed their hands; I kissed their hands again. With boys, I say, I was a brute. With girls, I was a lamb. Not madness, that, I submit. Rather, I like to think, the warrior and lover which are in every man... for men, the kill; for women, the kiss.[23]

Postcard of Lugos that shows the Blaskó home immediately to the left of the Roman Catholic church where Lugosi was baptized.

The Blaskó home, located at Number 6 Kirschengasse, Lugos. *(Courtesy of Florin Ieapan)*

Lugosi's father István Blaskó.

BECOMING DRACULA

Newspaper advertisement for the bank where István Blaskó worked.

On another occasion, Lugosi claimed he "earned his first money for holding a girl's pup while she sat on a park bench and kissed her sweetheart. [He] was seven years old at the time and all he remembers is that the dog seemed unusually strong and kept tugging at the leash and that the kisses were rather lengthy affairs."[24]

As for the "kill," it came in the form of the West encroaching on the East, in which Lugos children pretended to be Native Americans:

> As a small boy in my native town of Lugos, in southern Hungary, one of my most passionate pursuits was the acquiring of scalps! That is, we pretended they were scalps. In our town, we were half Romanians and half Hungarians. To show the superiority of the Hungarians, it was our habit to take the hats away from the Romanian boys, pretending they were scalps we took, like the American Indians. I had, at one time, 700 hats of Romanian boys. I gloated over them. They showed my superiority and leadership. I thought of them as scalps. But that can be ascribed, can it not, to the animal nature, the cruelty inherent in any small boy?[25]

Perhaps it was cruelty, as well as the penchant for small boys to exaggerate, to lie. In another interview, Lugosi claimed that he, the commander of the Hungarian boys, had collected 1,500 hats over the space of two years and sold them for "a lot of money."[26]

Unlike his older brothers, who attended the Lugos Roman Catholic Gymnasium, Lugosi, after attending grammar school, entered the Hungarian State Superior Gymnasium in 1893.[27] In his first and second years, he excelled only in music.[28] In his third and final year, he excelled in music and religion.[29] His entire report card for the 1895-1896 school year is as follows, with a "1" being the highest grade and a "4" being the lowest:

Behavior in Class: 2
Religion: 1
Hungarian Language: 3
Latin Language: 4
German Language: 3
History: 4
Biology: 2
Mathematics: 4
Geometry: 3
Physical Education: 3
Music: 1[30]

One classmate recalled that Lugosi was "a lively boy, a weak student, and pretty unruly."[31] Another said he "didn't want to learn or study."[32]

At times, his behavior conflicted with István's strict household, where the father's word was law. Lugosi later said:

I had a very severe father. A man who never punished me physically, but something in his way of looking at me and I would get stiff ... I had such respect for him ... I chilled with fear. It was he who gave me, I know, my knowledge that it

366. Lugosi népbank. — Lugoser Volksbank. — [1883—1913.] — **Az intézet üzlet-ágai. Elfogad:** Takarékbetéteket 4½%-ra. — **Kölcsönt ad:** Jelzálogra a becsérték feléig; bemutatandó: telekkönyv, becslevél, adókönyv. — **Leszámítol:** 2 aláirással ellátott 6 havi lejáratu váltókat 5½—8%-al. — **Előleget ad:** Értékpapirokra, az érték ³/₄-éig; terményekre az érték ³/₄-éig; arany és ezüstre az érték ³/₄-éig. — **Alaptőke:** 100,000 frt, — névre szóló 2,000 dib részvényben 50 frt befizetéssel. — **Részvényei ára** 1894 áprilisban frt: 60. — **Osztalékok** 1889—1893 frt: 4·50, 4, 4, 4, 4·50.(= 9, 8, 8, 8, 9%) — **Összforgalom** frt: 5.195,236. — **Betétemelkedés** + frt: 21,920. — **Takarékbetéti könyv-szám:** 361. — **Elnök:** Hatieg Titus. **Alelnök:** Marschofsky Árpád. **Vezérigazgató:** Blaskó István. **Aligazgató:** Schnitzer Adolf. **Igazgatósági tagok:** Gidófalvy Béla, Hegyesi Salamon, Horger János, Jcrga József, Németh Dávid, Pfeiffer Leonhart, Schreiber Antal, Schwarz Dávid. **Felügyelő-bizottság:** Stern Móricz, Szlabey György, Traunfellner Károly, Marschovszky Béla. **Titkár és fökönyvelö:** Pinkus Jakab. **Segédkönyvelő:** Hegyesi Hermann. **Pénztárnok:** Grau János. — **A magyar vagy német czéget** jegyzi: két igazgatósági tag együttesen. — **Alapszabályok:** 1883. január 14-én. — **F. évi közgyülése volt:** Február 25.

MÉRLEG.	1893. December 31.		BILANZ.	
Vagyon — Activa:	frt	Teher — Passiva:		frt
Készpénz — Cassabestände	8,116	Alaptőke — Stammcapital...		100,000
Váltó-tárcza — Wechselportefeuille ...	461,957	Tartalékalap — Reservefond		15.000
Kölcsönök jelzálogra — Hypothek.-Darl.	55,788	Betétek — Spareinlagen		159,771
Kölcsönök értékpapirokra és zálogra — Lombard	10,588	Visszleszámitolás — Reescompte		253,650
Kölcs. kötvényekre — Auf Schuldsch.	613	Hitelezők — Creditoren		5,581
Adósok — Debitoren	5,279	Különfélék — Diversi		655
Átmeneti tételek — Transitor. Posten..	1,793	Átmeneti tételek — Transitor. Posten		5,649
Ingatlano'k — Immobilien	3,549	Nyereség — Reingewinn		11,829
Fölszerelés — Geschäftseinrichtung.. ..	560			
Különfélék — Diversi	3,892			
	552,135			552,135

Record of Lugosi Népbank referencing István Blaskó. From *Magyar Compass*, 1894.

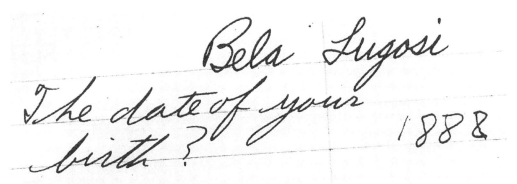

Bela Lugosi

The date of your birth? 1888

During his life in America, Lugosi answered a questionnaire in which he first wrote 1882 as the year of his birth, and then apparently changed it to 1888. *(Courtesy of Dennis Phelps)*

was not physical force which inspires the fear that makes me sick of soul so much as that which comes from the eyes, some subtle emanation from the personality as a gas that takes the strength from men's limbs.[33]

He also recalled an occasion when he was late for dinner after his father had already warned him about punctuality. István did not speak. "The courses were served," Lugosi explained, "to all but me. I did not get one mouthful to eat. When we were done, I was required to kiss the hand of my mother and my father, to thank them for the dinner, and to walk out. That was the kind of punishment he gave. It bit deeper than the lash."[34]

When he was approximately twelve years old, Lugosi might have left home, at least briefly. His classmate remembered:

[H]is father sent him to [Resica] to attend an industrial school where he learned to be a locksmith. Thus, our direct contact was interrupted, but I heard that he was not long in [Resica] and left school and stopped working as a locksmith.[35]

PULL HERE

BELA LUGOSI (Universal Pictures)

Born in Hungary, 1884, son of Baron Lugosi. Attended high school and Academy of Theatrical Art in Budapest and was first Lieutenant in the Hungarian Infantry. He is an accomplished musician and dancer. He is 6 feet, weighs 179 pounds, has dark blue eyes and dark brown hair.

OPEN HERE

Cigarette card of Lugosi featuring incorrect biographical information. *(Courtesy of Lynn Naron)*

István died on September 11, 1894, his death having been important enough to be reported in one of the Budapest newspapers.[36] This came not long after István lost the family savings in a financial deal gone wrong. He was dismissed from the Lugos Volksbank posthumously on February 24, 1895.[37]

Postcard depicting Lugos during the time of Lugosi's youth.

— 67 —

HARMADIK OSZTÁLY.

A tanuló neve, vallása	Magaviselet	Hittan	Magyar nyelv	Latin nyelv	Német nyelv	Történelem	Természettan	Mennyiségtan	Rajzoló mértan	Testgyakorlat	Román nyelv	Ének	Gyorsírás	Rendkívüli rajz
Aschenbrier József rk.	1	1	1	2	2	2	2	2	2	2	-	2	2	-
Bás János gkath.	2	2	3	3	3	3	3	3	3	2	2	2	-	-
Blaskó Béla rk.	2	1	3	4	3	4	2	4	3	3	-	1	-	-
Bock Győző gkel.	2	3	2	2	3	3	3	3	3	3	1	-	-	2
5 Dipold Imre rk.	1	1	1	2	1	1	1	1	2	3	-	1	2	-

Béla Blaskó school grades for 1895-96. Published in *A Lugosi M. Kir. Állami Főgymnasium IV-IK ÉVI Értesítője 1895-96.*

BECOMING DRACULA

Photograph of Resica in 1902.

Lugosi once said that he ran away from home before István's death, rather than after. But Lugosi's own school records disprove that story; they show that he remained in classes until the end of the 1895-1896 school year.[38] This would put his departure from Lugos, at the earliest, at least a year and a half after his father's death, when he was nearly fourteen.[39]

Lugosi claimed that he made his way to the mining town of Resica (now Reşiţa in Romania), walking all "300 miles" on foot.[40] The actual distance is only 54 miles, and there was rail service between the two. Whatever the real story, Lugosi reflected on his life in the city, including working in the mines:

> There, in the dark bowels of the earth, I did sometimes think I might go mad ... there we were subhuman men ... there I learned my horror, now of the darkness ... of the earth's deep darkness rather than the darkness of another world....

Postcard of Resica.

The railroad station at Szabadka from which Lugosi departed to attend his first Budapest theatrical audition. *(Courtesy of Dejan Mrkić)*

In time, I was promoted to be a riveter, making bridges ... then to the machine shop where they build four and five thousand horse-power machines ... there was something about the perfectionism of that giant machinery, functioning with the delicacy of a woman's breathing, that is also responsible for my passion for perfectionism today ... no, not madness, this, I say ... but method, a passion for method and for functional perfectionism.

When I was eighteen, I was promoted to assembling machines, putting them to work. I thought it was like being a god who has control over the fruits of the bowels of the earth ... to touch my hand to a button controlling machines of such vast horse-power gave me a feeling of maniacal strength ...

[My hands] ... it was my hands that won me the part of Dracula on the New York stage ... it is my hands people remark [on], often, shuddering ... it is my hands to which are ascribed unnatural powers ... if sobeit [sic] they have such powers, they did not acquire them in supernatural ways, but from gouging metals out of the earth, from pounding rivets into vast bridges, from controlling machines mightier by far than the men who made them ... the powers of darkness are not so powerful as these....[41]

Nevertheless, Lugosi the teenager tired of manual labor. He made the decision to move. Was he already eighteen, or was he perhaps younger? It is difficult to say.

Lugosi, seen in the center of the second row, during the period when he was an engineer's apprentice in Szabadka. *(Courtesy of John Antosiewicz)*

His destination was the town of Szabadka (now Subotica in Serbia), 162 miles west of Resica, the decision prompted by an invitation from his sister. By that time, Vilma had married Stefán Loósz. Together with Lugosi's widowed mother, they resided in Szabadka. Lugosi re-entered school in 1898, but scholarly success was out of reach. After a mere four months, he once again sought employment. He recalled:

> [My sister's husband] was a professor of a gymnasium. They felt very badly that I was in the class of those who work physically. ... For a time I worked as a skilled machinist in a railway repair shop. But this, too, was not clean work.

> I would come home with my hands and nails grimed with oil ... 'devil's hands' my sister would laugh, *not looking at them*.[42]

With help from his brother-in-law, Lugosi apparently found work in Szabadka as an engineer's apprentice.

But none of this was the life Lugosi wanted. According to a later account, he had once aspired to be a "highwayman."[43] In 1933, a journalist for the *Philadelphia Public Ledger* wrote: "By the time he had reached his 17th year ... Lugosi was determined to take up the stage as a career."[44] At roughly the same time, Bram Stoker published his novel *Dracula* (1897).

The title character explains, "Where ends the war without a brain and heart to conduct it? Again, when, after the battle of Mohács, we threw off the Hungarian yoke, we of the Dracula blood were amongst their leaders, for our spirit would not brook that we were not free." Like his historical forebear, the Dracula of fiction, the King of the Vampires, was certainly not Hungarian.

Lugosi would likely not yet have known about Stoker's *Dracula*. How much literature he even read at that time is unknown, though one account from Hungary suggests he wrote poetry as a young man.[45] And Lugosi had developed a fondness for the theater, even though – according to one quotation attributed to him – he had to "conquer" a lisp by practicing "exercises for the tongue."[46] He also recalled:

> Through the influence of my brother-in-law, the director of the little theater in the town asked me to come into the chorus. I went to the chorus, but never having done anything but manual labor, I was awkward. They tried to give me little parts in the plays, but I was so uneducated, so stupid, people just laughed at me. But I got the taste of the stage.

> I also got the rancid taste of humiliation. It was then I got, too, the knowledge of the main key to my character, the knowledge of which I have spoken; that I had the ability to focus my will, my mind, my body, my emotions, into one deep and driving channel.[47]

That drive caused him to write a letter to the Actors Guild in Budapest. Chalk down on the ledger the truth or the lies or both: The legend of Lugosi entered a new stage.

(Endnotes)

1   Lugosi, Bela, as told to Gladys Hall, "Memos of a Madman," *Silver Screen* July 1941.

2   Lugosi, Bela. "From My Life." *Los Angeles Evening Herald* 7 July 1928; Mackey, Joe. "Big Bad Bela." *Picture Play* July 1934; Shirley, Lillian. "Afraid of Himself." *Modern Screen* Mar. 1931.

3   After Lugos became part of Romania, the Temes River became known as the Timiş River.

4   *Központi Értesito˝* 1 Jan. 1880.

5   *Magyar Compass* (Budapest: Bróza Ottó Könyvnyomdája, 1892-93).

6   *Budapesti Közlöny* (Budapest) 15 Nov. 1883; *Budapesti Közlöny* (Budapest) 15 Nov. 1883; *Nemzet* (Budapest) 20 Mar. 1889.

7   Halász, Péter. "Dracula." *Amerikai Magyar Világ* (Cleveland, OH) 20 Apr. 1969.

8   See, for example: Hall, Gladys. "The Case of the Man Who Dares Not Fall Asleep." *Motion Picture* Aug. 1929.

9   Chrisman, J. Eugene. "Masters of Horror." *Modern Screen* Apr. 1932.

10   See, for example: *Magyarország és a Nagyvilág*, 1882 (18. évfolyam, 27-53. szám). [Vlad III Dracula was mentioned in the Hungarian press over 100 times during the 1880s.]

11   Treptow, Kurt W. *Vlad III Dracula: The Life and Times of the Historical Dracula* (Ia i: The Center for Romanian Studies, 2000).

12   Craft, Kimberly. *Infamous Lady: The True Story of Countess Erzsébet Báthory* (Self-published, 2009).

13   Wright, Dudley. *Vampires and Vampirism* (Philadelphia, PA: David McKay, 1914).

14   Quoted in Hall, Gladys. "Do You Believe This Story?" *Modern Screen* June 1935. Another example is Hall, "The Case of the Man Who Dares Not Fall Asleep."

15   Wait, Edgar. "Dracula Practices Mysteries Off Stage." *San Francisco Examiner* 26 Aug. 1928.

16   Theschedik, Samuel and Kónyi, János. *A paraszt ember Magyar Országban, Mitsoda és mi lehetne* (Pétsett, 1786).

17   See, for example: *Ország-Világ* 1882 (3. évfolyam, 1-19. szám).

18   *Pesti Divatlap* 27 May 27 1848. (1-28. szám)

19   "Bela Lugosi in *Arsenic* Here Friday Night." *Worcester Telegram* (Worcester, MA) 15 Mar. 1944.

20   Shirley, Lillian. "Afraid of Himself." *Modern Screen* March 1931.

21   Gardner, Hy. "Broadway Newsreel." *Brooklyn Eagle* 5 Apr. 1939.

22   Mok, Michael. "Horror Man at Home." *New York Post* 19 Oct. 1939.

23   Ibid.

24   Hall, "Memos of a Madman."

25   Wilk, Ralph. "Hollywood Flashes." *Film Daily* 2 July 1931.

26   Hall, "Memos of a Madman." For the sake of internal consistency, we have altered this article's spelling of "Rumanian" to "Romanian."

27   Mok, "Horror Man at Home."

28   *A Lugosi Róm. Kath. Magy. Főgymnásium értesítvénye az 1877-78 tanévről* (Lugos: Nyomatott Wenczely Jánosnál, 1878) and *A Lugosi Róm. Kath. Magy. Főgymnásium értesítvénye az 1879-80 tanévről* (Lugos: Nyomatott Wenczely Jánosn és Fiánál, 1880).

29   *A Lugosi M. Kir. Állami Főgymnásium értesítője az 1893-94 iskolai évről* (Lugos: Nyomatott Wenczely Jánosn és Fiánál, 1894) and *A Lugosi M. Kir. Állami Főgymnásium értesítője az 1894-95 iskolai évről* (Lugos: Nyomatott Virányi János Könyvnyomdájában, 1895).

30   *A Lugosi M. Kir. Állami Főgymnásium IV-IK évi értesitője 1895-96 iskolai év.* (Lugos: Nyomatott Virányi János Könyvnyomdájában, 1896).

31   Ibid.

32   Halász, "Dracula."

33   "Dracula war ein Lugoscher!" This article, published in a Lugoj tourist booklet, drew upon research

– including an interview with one of Lugosi's classmates – published in the 20 Aug. 1933 edition of *Krassó Szörényi Lapok*.

34   Hall, "Memos of a Madman."

35   Ibid.

36   Halász, "Dracula."

37   "(Gyászrovat.) Meghaltak." *Budapesti Hírlap* 14 Sept. 1894.

38   *Központi Értesito˝*, 1895.

39   *A Lugosi M. Kir. Állami Főgymnásium IV-IK évi értesitője 1895-96 iskolai év.*

40   It is possible that Lugosi briefly ran away from home during his father's lifetime, only to return soon thereafter.

41   Hall, "Memos of a Madman."

42   Ibid.

43   Ibid. Emphasis in original.

44   "Native of Hungary." *The Montgomery Advertiser* (Montgomery, AL) 3 Feb. 1944.

45   "Defaulting Romeo Gave Lugosi His Chance on Stage." *Philadelphia Public Ledger* 3 Aug. 1933.

46   Czigány, Lóránt. Írok. *Tehát Vagyok – Emigráns napjaim múlása, 1971-1981* (Budapest: Kortárs Könyvkiadó, 2005).

47   *Seattle Times* (Seattle, WA) 18 Oct. 1931.

48   Hall, "Memos of a Madman."

Lugosi
during the
early years
of his acting
career.

Chapter 2

Gathering at Baross Square

The great Hungarian playwright Imre Madách described the way the passage of time obscures people and events:

> While thou art fondly kissing,
> Dost thou not feel the soft and gentle breeze
> That plays about thy face, and fades away?
> Within a year, that dust is inches deep –
> A century hence, it reaches to the knee.
> In a few thousand years it will entomb
> Thy pyramids, and hide thy name in sand.

A century later, it is difficult to reconstruct Béla Lugosi's stage debut and his early years in the theater. His own memories conflict with surviving pages of newspapers and playbills, which are themselves imperfect and incomplete.

And yet, examining literally thousands and thousands of them causes the dust to rise, allowing some of the past to be excavated and exhibited to modern eyes.

Hungarian Theater in the Early 1900s

To understand Lugosi's dream of acting, as well as his training and early professional experiences, it is necessary to understand the Hungarian theater as it once existed. During the period from 1900 to 1919, when Lugosi was active in Hungary, the education of actors was rigorous and followed a relatively set pattern. As early as 1865, the Nemzeti Színház (National Theater) in Budapest established a training institution for actors. Over the years that followed, various actors and directors established their own private schools, regionally and in Budapest.

The Nemzeti Színház held auditions on average twice a year. Prospective actors traveled to

BUDAPEST — Baross-tér a központi pályaudvarral

Postcard depicting Baross Square in Budapest.

Budapest from throughout the country to audition. Well-known directors, actors and other important theatrical figures served as judges. Those who were successful would be offered a contract for an acting school, or, if they showed special talent, would immediately be given a contract with a Budapest or regional theatrical troupe. The latter sometimes traveled, but were often based in a particular city.[1] Unsuccessful candidates could return to audition again months later.

In addition to the training regimen, actors debated and adopted different acting styles. Lugosi would have encountered these from the start of his acting career. The Meininger Style was considered romantic naturalism. The Moscow Style emphasized the psychological. And then there was the Viennese Operetta Style, a very conservative approach to theater and acting. However, the new styles coming into vogue were the avant-garde, such as those championed by Max Reinhardt and Piscator. With their emphasis on physical movement, the avant-garde approaches inspired many Hungarian actors, directors, and production designers.[2] Nevertheless, the Meininger and romanticized realist styles were still favored by the provincial and traveling theater troupes.

These styles affected Lugosi's future characterizations. In viewing films as diverse as *Dracula* (1931), *White Zombie* (1932), *The Black Cat* (1934), *The Raven* (1935), *Son of Frankenstein* (1939), and *Ninotchka* (1939), one can almost see Lugosi choosing between naturalistic, realistic, and over-the-top acting styles, learned in his youth, carefully and thoughtfully tailored to the specific needs of a given role.

Beyond just acting styles, though, the Hungarian theater underwent significant change and conflict in the period from 1894 to 1922. Some in the theater community believed regional theaters offered the best acting even if they could not afford elaborate sets. And the Nemzeti Színház was beginning to lose its leading position to private competition from the Magyar Színház (Hungarian Theater), the Budapesti Színház (Budapest Theater), and the Vígszínház (Comedy Theater). Those theaters presented contemporary programs based on psychological realism. In addition, cabarets were coming into vogue, as were so-called "art theaters" with modern acting styles and staging to reach a new kind of audience.

Artwork showing Budapest nightlife in the period.

Members of traveling troupes, as well as those based in a single town or city, had to become familiar with a large array of plays. In most cases, the same actors performed a different play every evening. Occasionally, matinees presented a different play than the one staged on the same evening. Consecutive evenings might feature an opera, an operetta, a farce, a comedy, and a historical drama. Specific plays ranged from Shakespearean classics to new works by Hungarians like Ferenc Molnár.

In addition, troupes frequently performed a unique form of Hungarian theater called "vidéki játék," or "folk play." Closely related to "paraszt tragédia" ("peasant tragedy") and "paraszt vígjáték" ("peasant comedy"), these were quite popular at that time. They featured stock characters like the town mayor, the wealthy peasant, the poor peasant, the beautiful girl, the old maid, and so forth. Such productions included a wealth of unsophisticated jokes, often accompanied by music. They were designed to be simple entertainment, which made them somewhat comparable to American melodrama popular in the late nineteenth and early twentieth centuries.

Origins

The exact time and place of Lugosi's acting debut has been a continuing source of confusion and guesswork, with Lugosi and his biographers presenting conflicting stories. Lugosi allegedly claimed that, as a young boy, he wrote, produced, and acted in plays in a vacant warehouse in his hometown.[3] In another account, Lugosi told an interviewer that, in 1899, a member of a traveling theatrical company fell ill.[4] The company selected Lugosi as the actor's replacement, with his success being so great that he was able to overcome his

Two images of Lugosi, the young stage actor, from the same photo shoot.

parents' objections to him pursuing acting.[5] But by that year, his father was deceased. And for that matter, Lugosi later wrote that he never faced "parental objection" to his plans for a stage career.[6]

On another occasion, Lugosi told a very different version, claiming he joined a "small village theatrical troupe," but was dismissed after two weeks. "This happened twenty or twenty-five times," he added in what was at minimum an overstatement. "But each time, *I learned a little* ... each time I was humiliated I learned a little and my will was forged to whiter and whiter heat." He also said the humiliation became the impetus for him to start reading hours a day for ten years in an effort to educate himself.[7] "It was a cruel, heartless stage I invaded," he bemoaned.[8]

Another account has Lugosi debuting as a baritone in the chorus of a small theater in Szabadka and then appearing as a butler with another theater company in 1900 before moving on with them to Szeged.[9] However, Lugosi's earliest documented appearance in Szeged was not until 1903, which comports with an interview in which he claimed he made his debut at the age of twenty.[10] Yet another tale suggests that Lugosi, in his ambition to become an actor, appeared in amateur productions in 1901 and 1902 but did not undertake any professional acting until contracted by the Ferenc József Színház (Franz Joseph Theater) in Temesvár (now Timişoara in Romania).[11]

Confusion also surrounds the title of the play in which he first appeared. In 1923, he recalled:

BECOMING DRACULA

Postcard of Szabadka featuring the local casino. *(Courtesy of Dejan Mrkić)*

One day, when I was 16, it was announced that a stock company would present *Romeo and Juliet* – my favorite play – which I knew by heart, at the local playhouse. The whole town was disappointed when a rumor went about the morning of the performance that the play could not be presented because of the sudden illness of the leading man.

I saw my chance, went to the manager, and offered to play the part. He hesitated, but finally consented. He announced the change, and made preparations for a hasty departure after the performance, thinking that the crowd might be angry at him after seeing my acting. There, as you Americans say, I made my first 'hit,' and since then I have never left the stage.[12]

In 1932, when he was starring in *Murders in the Rue Morgue*, a Universal Pictures biography repeated the story that Lugosi made his stage debut as Romeo. A program for the 1945 play *No Traveler Returns* told readers the same. But this story seems to be incorrect.

Careful primary research undertaken in Hungary helps remove much dust, further revealing why Lugosi's stage origins have been so difficult to discern. For example, Béla Lugosi was *not* the only "Lugosi" on the Hungarian stage in the early twentieth century. Jenő Lugosi, Lajos Lugosi, and Dániel Lugosy were also professional actors. The fact that playbills sometimes credited talent by surname alone presents an initial problem, but one that can be accurately solved by extensive investigation of the theater troupe in question. This is all in addition to the fact that there were actually a few different people named Béla Blaskó in Hungary at that time. One of them was a confectioner in the town of Békés; another made news after committing suicide. In addition, Béla Földes wrote under the pseudonym "Béla Lugossy."

The theater in Szabadka circa 1901.

Separating Béla Lugosi from these other persons is not the only challenge, as Lugosi the young actor used a variety of stage names. While he usually retained his first name Béla, he was occasionally billed with the first names Dezső and Géza.[13] He also relied on various professional surnames, ranging from his family name Blaskó to Lugosi, Lugossi, Lugosy, and Lugossy. In a 1947 interview, he recalled, "I was obliged by [theatrical] custom to take a Hungarian name. My home town was Lugos, so I picked Lugosi, which merely means a resident of Lugos."[14]

Blaskó was originally a Slavic name, so his stated reason for using "Lugosi" (in any variant spelling) seems questionable. Perhaps it was a desire to distance himself from his past, helping him to claim he was born of nobility.[15] Perhaps, conversely, it was nostalgia for his youth. Or perhaps it was an effort to trade upon the familiarity of the other Lugosis, some of them better known at the time than he was.

At any rate, the choice of spelling "Lugosi" is another complicated issue. While at times Lugosi made conscious decisions on the matter, he was also at the mercy of theater troupes and, more clearly, the printers they hired to publish playbills. Different spellings of "Lugosi" can be seen on publicity for plays staged only days apart in the same town. Even more telling is that conflicting spellings sometimes appeared on the *very same playbill*.

Such was not unusual, though. On playbills of the era, the last letter of the following surnames often varied between "I" and "Y": Zoltán Szatmári, Ferenc Csepreghy, Dezső Malonyay, Sándor Garamszeghy, and Alfréd Deésy. Much the same could be said about how the Hungarian press varied in spelling the last names of a few of Lugosi's silent film costars, including Richárd Kornay (aka Kornai), Klára Peterdi (aka Peterdy), and Gusztáv Vándori (aka Vándory). The issue of spelling is also noticeable in the last names of some of his later costars in Hungarian-American theater, including Boriska Bozóky (aka Bozóki), József Kenessei (aka Kenessey), Gyula Szalai (aka Gyula Szalay), Frida P. Tábory (aka Tábori), and Erzsi Torday (aka Tordai).

Removing dust that is inches deep is not easy. However, one account of Lugosi's stage origins is likely the most accurate, in part because some of it is confirmed by other sources.[16] Theater historian Béla Garay was a contemporary of Lugosi's. Born and raised in Szabadka, he later worked in Újvidék (now Novi Sad in Serbia).[17] Relying on primary evidence, he wrote:

At the end of September 1901,[18] one of the deputies at a large ironworks plant [located in Szabadka] stood before the workshop supervisor and announced that he would no longer appear at work on the next day, as he traveled to Pest for the entrance exam at the Actors' Association. That young locksmith was Béla Lugosi.... He was a tall, slim, handsome, fine man with a pleasant voice and a sharp wit. He did as he had said. He traveled to the capital with the train at dawn. He had previously read in the newspapers that the Actors' Association holds an admission exam. He sent his application to them via mail and then he was informed about the date when he had to present himself.

Young men and women – aspiring actors and actresses – were gathering at Baross Square [in Budapest, at the Main Station for trains from the east], in front of the imposing palazzo of the Actors' Association from early morning. They were all waiting with excitement for the start of the exam. Béla Lugosi was among them, waiting for the moments which might influence his destiny.

The members of the jury were arriving one after the other, some by hackney coaches, some by fiacre and some by tram. There they were: Ede Újházi or 'The Master,' Sándor Somló, Teréz Csillag, Gyula Gál, the actors of the National Theater, and many theater directors were also present who wanted to pick some of the talented young ladies and gentlemen and employ them. All the arriving members of the jury were greeted - by the raised hats of gentlemen and by the coquettish glimpses or humble nods of ladies, all eager to make themselves noticeable.

Soon, the bell rang, indicating the start of the exam. Excited applicants appeared in front of the jury one after the other. Some left the room with cheeks rosy with happiness and some with a disappointed face. Béla Lugosi was among the smiling ones who surpassed them all and was admitted to the Association.

Lajos Pesti-Ihász, director of the theater in Szabadka, offered a contract to Lugosi already during a break in the exams, which he [Lugosi] signed happily. A couple of days later he appeared on the stage as a freshman in the Theater of Szabadka, in the town of Kalocsa where the theater operated during the summer months. They rehearsed the first play of the season there. The colleagues kindly welcomed the new actor, the young actors looked at the elegant gentleman with envy while the ladies cast admiring glances [at] him.

Already on his first day the play director Frigyes Ferenczy assigned to him the main role [*sic*][19] of *A sasok* [*The Eagles*], a comedy by Soma Guthi and Viktor Rákosi; later he received the main role [*sic*][20] in *Cyrano de Bergerac* and then the main role [*sic*] in *A bor* [*The Wine*], a peasant play by Géza Gárdonyi. He had a lot to learn, but he was eager to work, since he saw his dreams coming true in these roles.

For the winter season, he moved from Kalocsa to Szabadka, and he opened it with his debut in *A sasok* on 2 November 1901. The cast was

An early portrait of Lugosi the actor.

anticipated by the audience as well as by the press. Lugosi had success, both liked him. He had a tough season but by the time his contract ended he had a colorful repertoire and a lot of onstage experience.[21]

The September 1, 1901 edition of *Budapesti Hírlap* included a brief article announcing auditions for new actors under the auspices of the Theater Guild had taken place in Budapest. This is consistent with Garay's account. Fifty candidates auditioned in front of the Guild on that day. Though Lugosi was not specifically mentioned in the article, neither were any of the other 49.

That an amateur actor, or even someone with no experience, could apply for an audition with the Theater Guild in Budapest and then travel there by train was not at all unusual.[22] As previously mentioned, these auditions were generally held twice a year in Budapest and were open to everyone.[23] And this story is not unlike certain details of Lugosi's memories.[24] The 1927 playbill to *Dracula–The Vampire Play* mentions that, after going to Budapest, he was "placed in a stock company for training in theaters throughout [Hungary]." In another account, Lugosi recalled that he "went up to Budapest," after which he was "hired for a small village theatrical troupe."[25]

At any rate, evidence has emerged about what occurred next, Lugosi's work for Lajos Pesti-Ihász (1849-1912). Originally a lawyer and an actor, Pesti-Ihász became a producer in 1883, with his troupe working mainly in such towns as Békés and Kecskemét, as well as the Szatmár region (now Satu Mare in Romania).[26] The Pesti-Ihász troupe settled in Szabadka for the 1901-1902 season, but also supported a summer theater troupe in the nearby town of Kalocsa. Lugosi left Budapest after the auditions to start rehearsals later in September 1901 for what remained of the summer

Lugosi, allegedly from an appearance in Újvidék, Hungary in 1902. *(Courtesy of Dejan Mrkić and Roger Hurlburt)*

season. During his brief apprenticeship in Kalocsa, Lugosi reportedly appeared in a version of *A sasok*, staged in the town of Baja on October 12, 1901. By contrast, a 1910 article in *Színházi Újság* claimed that Lugosi's first role was as Tarján Gida in *A dolovai nábob leánya* (*The Daughter of the Nabob of Dolova*). Whichever it was, the Kalocsa summer schedule also featured the plays *San-Toy*, *Katalin* (*Catherine*), and *A svihákok* (*The Cheaters*).

Whether Lugosi appeared in all of those plays is unknown. The bulk of the roles he did get were likely small. Nevertheless, Garay's account could explain Lugosi's recollection of having starred in *Cyrano de Bergerac*, a role mentioned in the 1927 playbill for *Dracula–The Vampire Play* and in newspaper and magazine articles.[27] Lugosi even told one fan magazine journalist that he considered his portrayal of Cyrano to be "his best stage work."[28]

After leaving Kalocsa, Lugosi debuted at the Népszínház in Szabadka on November 2, 1901, in *A sasok*. A repeat performance was staged on November 19. Though one source claimed he performed a leading role, his name does not appear in the few surviving reviews. In fact, one theater critic declared: "Should Szabadka always be the preparatory school for novice actors?"[29] That remark could have been a veiled reference to Lugosi.

Over thirty other productions were staged in Szabadka during the season, many of which likely utilized Lugosi in small roles. Some of the productions – such as *San-Toy*, *Bánk Bán* (*Bán Bánk*), *A svihákok*, *A bor*, *New-York Szépe* (*The Belle of New York*), *Sárga csikó* (*The Yellow Colt*), *A kis szökevény* (*The Little Fugitive*), *A szökött katona* (*The Runaway Soldier*), *IV. László* (*László the Fourth*) and *Felhő Klári* (*Claire Felho*) – later became staples in Lugosi's regional career with other troupes.

Béla Garay wrote that Lugosi remained in Szabadka for at least part of 1902. No known documentation identifies the roles he played. However, regional theatrical reports in

Budapest newspapers of the time indicate that the Pesti-Ihász troupe presented *Katalin*, *Hannelé* (*Hannah*), and *Pillangókisasszony* (*Madame Butterfly*), among others in the early part of the year. And *Szamos*, a regional newspaper reported the troupe would be performing in the county of Szatmár around the end of February 1902.[30]

But Lugosi had left the troupe by then, returning to Budapest, where the next phase of his career has been entombed and hidden by the sands of time for far too long.

(Endnotes)

1   Kaffenberger, Bill. Email interview with Dr. Ildikó Sirató, Director, Országos Széchényi Könyvtár, Theater History Collection, Budapest, Hungary, 31 Dec. 2017. Information regarding Hungarian theater in this chapter resulted from this interview.

2   Ibid.

3   Lennig, Arthur. *The Immortal Count: The Life and Films of Bela Lugosi* (Lexington, KY: University Press of Kentucky, 2003).

4   This story has Lugosi at approximately age seventeen. In yet another version of events, Lugosi claimed that he was nineteen when he made his stage debut with a "stock company" that came to his hometown. See "Bela Lugosi: The Film Fiend Who Is Loved by Children." *Picture Show* 21 Sept. 1935.

5   "The Biography Box: Bela Lugosi." *New York Sun* 13 Jan. 1926. The same basic account appears in the pressbook for *The Prisoners* (1929). A copy of it is archived at the New York Public Library for the Performing Arts, Dorothy and Lewis B. Cullman Center.

6   Lugosi, Bela. "From My Life." *Los Angeles Evening Herald* 7 July 1928.

7   Lugosi, Bela, as told to Gladys Hall, "Memos of a Madman," *Silver Screen* July 1941. Emphasis in original.

8   Lugosi, "From My Life."

9   Cremer, Robert. *The Man Behind the Cape* (Chicago: Henry Regnery, 1976), and Rhodes, Gary D. *Lugosi, His Life in Films, on Stage and in the Hearts of Horror Lovers* (Jefferson, NC: McFarland, 1997).

10   Shirley, Lillian. "Afraid of Himself." *Modern Screen* Mar. 1931.

11   Lennig, *The Immortal Count*.

12   "Bela Lugosi, Young Hungarian Actor, Joins Washington Heights' Growing Artists' Colony." *The Home News* (Bronx, NY) 2 Sept. 1923.

13   Lugosi's full name at birth was Béla Ferenc Dezső Blaskó. The 15 Aug. 1911 edition of *Pesti Napló*, a Budapest newspaper, announced that Lugosi had signed a contract with the Magyar Színház in Budapest. Curiously, the announcement gave his name as Dezső Lugosi, a stage name that he was no longer generally using professionally at the time. Béla Lugosi was the only "Lugosi" contracted to Nándor Benedek's company in 1902. A playbill for *Aranykakas* (*The Golden Rooster*), performed on 7 Aug. 1902, lists him in the cast as Gezá Lugosi.

14   Adams, Marjorie. "Bela Lugosi Glad of Respite from Horror-Inspiring Roles." *Boston Globe* 17 April 1947.

15   One of Lugosi's school classmates noted that, once he became an actor, Lugosi began to claim he was born into nobility. See "Dracula war ein Lugoscher!" This article, published in a Lugoj tourist booklet, drew upon research – including an interview with one of Lugosi's classmates – published in the 20 Aug. 1933 edition of *Krassó Szörényi Lapok*.

16   In an interview for a Szeged theater magazine ("Üzenetek." *Színházi Újság* 30 Oct. 1910), Lugosi indicated that his first professional theater experience was with the Lajos Pesti-Ihász company in 1901 in Szabadka. Numerous subsequent Hungarian publications have reported the Pesti-Ihász connection. See, for example: "Ki volt Lugosi Béla?" *Délmagyarország* (Szeged, Hungary) 26 Sept. 1973. "Gróf Drakula: Lugosi Béla." *Film Színház Muzsika* (Budapest, Hungary) 4 July 1987; and "Emberi szörnyeteg." *Békés Megyei Hírlap* (Békés, Hungary) 19 Aug. 1992. Furthermore, a detailed calendar of the history of the city of Szabadka notes Lugosi's debut (under his given name Béla Blaskó) in *A sasok* on 2 Nov. 1901 (Hegedüs, Attila and Szép, Ferenc. *Szabadka (1700-1910)* (Szeged, Hungary: Dugonics András Piarista Gimnázium, 2008-2009).

17   Historian Dejan Mrkić, who organized a scholarly tribute to Lugosi in the town of Szbadka in December of 2011, has in his possession a copy of a Lugosi publicity photo supposedly taken during a stage residency in Újvidék around 1902. However, no primary resources are currently available to confirm that Lugosi definitely worked in that town.

18   It is likely that Garay has the correct month, but not the correct date. According to the 1 Sept. 1901 edition of the *Budapesti Hírlap*, the auditions were in fact held on that day. The newspaper claims fifty candidates showed up for the "jury" and apparently "the jury was very strict with defining the entrance level and the exam lasted until the evening."

19   Lugosi was probably not placed in a lead role; rather, being a new and inexperienced actor, he was likely cast in small or supporting roles.

20   Ibid.

21   Garay, Béla. *Színészarcképek* (Újvidék: Forum Nyomda, 1971).

22   Kaffenberger, Bill. Email interview with Dr. Ildikó Sirató.

23   Kaffenberger, Bill. Interview with Dr. Ildikó Sirató, 28 June 2017.

24   It must be noted that other aspects of Lugosi's accounts differ from Garay's.

25   Hall, "Memos of a Madman."

26   Schöpflin, Aladár, editor. *Magyar Színművészeti Lexikon: A Magyar Színjátszás és Drámairodalom Enciklopédiája* (Budapest: Az Országos Színészegyesület és Nyugdíjintézete, 1929-1931).

27   See, for example, Mitchell, Helen. "The Philosophy of Bela Lugosi – The Horror Man of Hollywood." *To You!* May 1935; Whitney, Dwight. "The World of Drama." *San Francisco Chronicle* 8 Aug. 1943; and Fried, Alexander. "Those Chilling Horror Roles!" *San Francisco Examiner* 15 Aug. 1943.

28   Mackey, Joe. "Big Bad Bela." *Picture Play* July 1934. [This article does claim Lugosi's appearance in *Cyrano de Bergerac* came at the Király Színház (Royal Theater) in Budapest. He could have played the role more than once, but there is no known documentation to prove it.]

29   Kalapis, Zoltán. *ÉLECTRAJZI KALAUZ II Ezer magyar biográfia a délszláv országokból* (Budapest: Forum Könyvkiadó, 2003).

30   "Legközelebbi újdonságok." *Szamos* (Szamos, Hungary) 23 Feb. 1902.

Lugosi in *The Black Cat* (1934). *(Courtesy of John Antosiewicz)*

Chapter 3

'Midst the Wild Carpathians

O n more than one occasion in the late 1920s, Béla Lugosi spoke to the American press about the difference between becoming a successful actor in the United States and Europe:

Getting a break in America is mainly a matter of luck... In Europe, conditions are quite different... There, a man craving a stage or screen career must prove his ability before he can expect any sort of consideration. When he proves that he really has the knack of acting, he may become a member of one of the small repertory companies, which tour the provinces. As his acting ability increases with years of training, he is shifted to larger companies and better parts....[1]

There he is not chosen as a particular type and doomed to follow that type during his professional career. He gains attention because he can create types rather than because he suggests a certain type. Therefore, he becomes versatile and almost equally artistic in a variety of dramatic expressions.[2]

When Lugosi mentioned "Europe," he was referring to Hungary and to his own professional experience.

On January 7, 1902, the Budapest magazine *Zenevilág* implied that Szabadka might lose its theatrical troupe after the current season. As was often the case, several theater directors were vying for the contract. A change of director or venue would have been a potential threat to Lugosi's continued employment; this could have been what prompted him to return to Budapest and audition there once again.

On the other hand, László Beöthy, then working with the Nemzeti Színház (National Theater) in Budapest – and later the director of the Magyar Színház (Hungarian Theater) who would give Lugosi his first major opportunity in that city in 1911 – had been the guest of the

Pesti-Ihász troupe the week of January 13-19, 1902.[3] Perhaps Beöthy saw something of merit in the young Lugosi and suggested he attend the upcoming national auditions. Or perhaps Beöthy's mere presence there planted the idea in Lugosi's mind.

In any event, on approximately March 27, 1902, Lugosi – using the name Béla Blaskó – auditioned before the judges of the National Actors Association General Council. He was in a group of 93 candidates. A Budapest theatrical reporter recounted the event:

> This year, too, youth aspiring for a stage career showed up before the examination committee in large numbers, but of course, in most cases, their ambition was bigger than their talent. Mindful of the latest regulations of the Ministry of the Interior, which encourages the committee to be more selective in order to keep control of the growing number of actors, the jury screened very strictly all who aspired for the glory of the stage.[4]

In a setback for Lugosi, the guild apparently felt his "ambition was bigger than his talent" as he became one of seventeen applicants placed into the category "Visszautasíttattak." It translates, alas, "the following people were not admitted."[5]

And so Lugosi returned to the regional countryside theaters, where he would appear in plays by many authors, including Mór Jókai (1825-1904). One of Jókai's most famous works was the novel *Erdély aranykora* (1852), published in England in 1894 as *'Midst the Wild Carpathians*. In it, Jókai describes the Romanian "Gradina Dracului," meaning the "Devil's Garden." Of the Hungarian countryside, he writes:

> In the dim, dismal distance still higher mountains appear, from which the stream plunges down in a snow-white torrent. The morning mists exaggerate the magic remoteness of the scene, and when at last you have reached the [highest] point of that remoteness, it is only to see before you a still more awful expanse, still more desolate mountain ranges, forming as it were an immense and uninterrupted ladder up to heaven.

> ... From time to time the rumbling of the storm is still heard faintly in the distance. Sheet-lightning flickers above the mountain crests, painting everything white for an instant. The lightning, like the night, can only give one color to this region – the one paints it white, the other black.[6]

It was through these regions that Lugosi traveled, grappling with the many challenges that actors of the period faced.

The Provinces

With the exception of Szabadka and Temesvár (now Timișoara in Romania), the theatrical troupes Lugosi joined – like Nándor Benedek's and György Micsey's – were not based in

Postcard of Lugosi the regional theater actor. *(Courtesy of John Antosiewicz)*

Postcard depicting the Nagybánya region.

single cities. Instead, they regularly moved from towns to villages and to small resort spas, sometimes in areas where the means of travel were less than ideal. The actors confronted other obstacles as well. For example, during performances in Zalaegerszeg in early June of 1903, Lugosi and the rest of Micsey's company suffered from poor attendance, with "very few people looking for tickets."[7] When the troupe moved on to Keszthely in the latter part of June, "people, horses and other things [disrupted] the enjoyment" due to the "arena" environment – much like an open-air bullring or amphitheater – in which the plays were staged.[8]

Given that many of the small towns did not have theater buildings or suitable arenas, the troupes sometimes staged plays inside restaurants or hotels, as was the case when Lugosi appeared as Feri, a waiter, in *Aranykakas* (*The Golden Rooster*) in August of 1902 at the Aranybárány étterem (Golden Lamb Restaurant) in Hátszeg (now Hațeg in Romania) with the Benedek company. Later, in Zalaegerszeg, the Micsey troupe performed in that city's Aranybárány étterem és szálloda (Golden Lamb Hotel and Restaurant). The hotel, the oldest in the town, was quite elegant, with plays being staged in a grand hall on the second floor.[9] Nevertheless, the local theater critic complained that the venue was hardly suitable, due in part to its lack of appropriate heating in the winter, and that the hotel itself was difficult for out-of-town patrons to find.[10]

Other problems plagued these troupes as well. As independent acting schools proliferated, an increasing number of actors flooded the regional theatrical markets seeking employment.

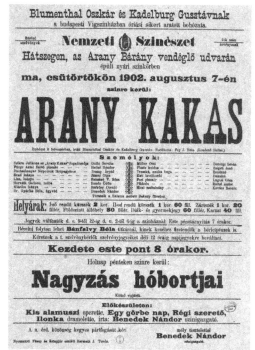

Note the two different spellings of the
Lugosi name on the very same playbill.
*(Courtesy of the Collection of Theater History at
the National Széchényi Library)*

Billed as Géza Lugosi in *Arany Kakas* (*The
Golden Rooster*, aka *Aranykakas*), a 1902
production by the Nándor Benedek Troupe.
*(Courtesy of the Collection of Theater History at the
National Széchényi Library)*

Not surprisingly, many of them were unable to secure employment in any given season.[11]
Those who found steady work were both talented and fortunate.

Nándor Benedek

When he returned to eastern Hungary after the disappointing audition in Budapest,
Lugosi might have briefly remained with the Pesti-Ihász troupe when it moved to the town of
Makó around June 1902. However, it is more likely that Lugosi had already contracted with
Nándor Benedek, who was working in Szilágysomlyó (now Şimleu Silvaniei in Romania) and
later Torda (now Turda in Romania) that same summer. Benedek, an actor born in Temesvár
in 1876, had started out in small troupes in the provinces. Shortly after what seems to have
been his only season as a company director, he immigrated to the United States to work for
a Hungarian theater foundation.

The Benedek troupe remained in Torda for a month before moving on to Hátszeg by early
August 1902. Surviving playbills make clear Lugosi's presence in that city. With the exception
of several months in Temesvár (September 1903 through May 1904), Lugosi would earn his
living during these years barnstorming from town to town until the autumn of 1908.

During his time with Benedek, Lugosi usually appeared in small or supporting roles. In
his first documented production for the troupe, *Aranykakas* (*The Golden Rooster*), a farce,
he portrayed a waiter. Curiously, Lugosi's billing varied wildly during the course of even
one month. For example, in August 1902, playbills show him as "Géza Lugosi," then "Béla
Blaskó," and then finally "Béla Lugosi." In one instance, for the historical drama *Kurucz Féja*

Postcard of the Nagybánya region.

Dávid (*Stubborn King David*), performed on September 6 in Szamosújvar, the *very same playbill* identified him as "Lugosi" and "Lugosy" for his two different roles. Despite previous claims to the contrary, this variance in his stage names would continue to some degree right up to and even beyond his arrival in Budapest in 1911, with one newspaper even touting the arrival of "Dezső Lugosi" at the National Theater.

Lugosi likely remained with Benedek's company until December of 1902, after which he joined György Micsey's company, which by then was operating primarily out of Nagybánya (now Baia Mare in Romania). Based on existing playbills, he was definitely active with Micsey by February of 1903; he could have joined Micsey as early as mid-December of 1902.[12]

F. György Micsey

F. György Micsey was born in Budapest in 1861 and died there in 1919. He worked primarily as a theater director in various towns in the Transylvania region. Later, he and his wife purchased and ran an open-air theater in a Budapest city park named Népliget (People's Park). His primary rival in Transylvania, at least for one season, was Nándor Benedek. The two waged a major battle at roughly the time Lugosi switched troupes. The details provide some insight into the intense competition for control of Hungarian theatrical circuits. In July of 1902, the *Budapesti Hírlap* wrote:

> On the 22nd day of this month many newspapers from the capital published a short article entitled 'Theater in Transylvania,' all of which were following a report sourced by the semi-official Hungarian Telegraph Office. These articles inform us that

BECOMING DRACULA

Postcard depicting Hunyadi Castle in Vajdahunyad.

the company run by director Nándor Benedek, and which momentarily operates in Torda, had a meeting and decided to send a complaint to the Minister of Interior and to the Association of Actors, because – based on their information – I was giving preference to F. György Micsey compared to other theater directors. The report says that Micsey booked all suitable places for performances during the summer and autumn, and he asked permission to hold performances outside his territory for the whole of September in Nagyenyed, Dés, Gyulafehérvár and Torda, and he did all this by using a letter of recommendation written by me.

First of all, I must declare that I did not provide director Micsey with any kind of recommendation letter, and he does not even need such a thing. Among the above listed cities Dés and Gyulafehérvár belong to the Transylvanian division, where – until his contract expires – only [his company] can hold theatrical performances, and where Nándor Benedek has nothing to do until September 1, 1903.

Furthermore, Micsey's contract has a clause in it which enables him to hold performances for a set period of time in three or four smaller Transylvanian towns, villages or spa towns, which are outside the division of Transylanian towns to which he was assigned, and he can do this if he acquires the permission of the local authorities. Thus, he had all the rights to apply for permission to perform in both Nagyenyed and Torda; and in case Nagyenyed gave him permission. That is his own lucky business and if Torda did not issue him one, again, that's his own unlucky business. That's it, and I think that the actors in the company of Nándor Benedek could spend their time more fruitfully if they were not having meetings about [those] things which are absolutely not their business.[13]

Perhaps Micsey's potentially larger circuit of towns had convinced Lugosi to switch troupes.

At any rate, Lugosi continued playing mostly small supporting roles with Micsey. One exception was the major supporting role of Marco Colonna in Maeterlink's drama *Monna Vanna*, on March 4, 1903, in the town of Déva (now Deva in Romania) and then at other stops along the circuit. He also received his first documented listing in a newspaper play review. The local critic for the Szatmár province mentioned his name in a review of *Kéz kezet mos* (*One Hand Washes the Other*) on May 4, 1903, indicating that Lugosi portrayed Baron Eberle.

Micsey's troupe remained in Nagybánya for at least part of January 1903 before moving on to Déva. After presenting Imre Madách's *Az ember tragédiája* (*The Tragedy of Man*) on February 13 in Déva and on March 20 and 23 in Nagyszeben (now Sibiu in Romania), along with other plays,

Postcard promoting Alois Berla and Carl Millöcker's 1878 comic operetta *Das verwunschene Schloss* (*The Enchanted Castle*).

Micsey's company moved on to Zalaegerszeg and Keszthely between March and June. Micsey's circuit also included the towns of Vajdahunyad (now Hunedoara in Romania), Kovászna (now Covasna County in Romania), Gyulafehérvár (now Alba Lulia in Romania), Szombathely, Székesfehérvár, and Veszprém.

It is notable that the troupe played Vajdahunyad, which is a small Transylvanian village home to Hunyadi Castle (aka Corvin Castle), where local legends claim Vlad III Dracula (aka Vlad Ţepeş, aka Vlad the Impaler) was once imprisoned. Lugosi appeared onstage only once in Vajdahunyad, at least during this particular tour. The production was of Alois Berla and Carl Millöcker's comic operetta *A boszorkányvár* (*The Castle of Witches*), which had premiered in Vienna in 1878 as *Das verwunschene Schloss* (*The Enchanted Castle*). Peasants see lights and ghostly figures moving around a deserted castle, believing it to be haunted. They also suppose an old woman living in a nearby forest is a witch. But in the end, the supernatural is explained away, as was the case in so many gothic novels and plays, as well as in later films, among them Tod Browning's *Mark of the Vampire* (1935) with Lugosi.

Yet another stop on the itinerary was Székelyudvarhely (now Odorheiu Secuiesc in Romania), where Lugosi played a small role in *A Notre Damei templom harangozója és*

Postcard depicting Temesvár at roughly the time Lugosi was there.

Eszmeralda, a szép cigányleány (*The Bellringer of Notre Dame and Esmerelda, the Fair Gypsy Girl*), a stage adaptation of Victor Hugo's 1831 novel *Notre-Dame de Paris* (*The Hunchback of Notre Dame*). Decades later, two different Hollywood studios considered casting Lugosi in the role of the hunchback: Universal in 1931 and RKO in 1939.

While in Székelyudvarhely during the second half of April 1903, the erratic billing methods for Lugosi became evident once again. During a three-week period, Lugosi was billed variously as "Lugossy" and "Lugossi." In addition, on several occasions when a double bill was presented, his name was spelled one way for the afternoon production and another for the evening show. In the case of *Aranylakodalom* (*The Golden Wedding*), presented on April 19, 1903, Lugosi, who had three different roles, was listed as "Lugossy" and "Lugossi" in different sections of the cast list for the play. Nevertheless, it is notable that the season advertisement for the troupe did promote him as being a "jellemszínész és szerelmes" ("character actor and lover").

By mid-July 1903, Micsey's troupe worked in the city of Siófok, remaining there until early August of 1903. Lugosi's tenure with Micsey likely ended there. By the time the troupe performed in Székesfehérvár in early September, Lugosi had signed with Ignác Krecsányi's troupe in Temesvár, only 43 miles from his hometown of Lugos.

Ignác Krecsányi and Temesvár

According to a 1910 biography published in the Szeged theatrical journal *Színházi Újság*, Lugosi "gradually won the sympathy of the directors, and after two to three years playing in smaller roles, he was given important ones." Lugosi's time in Temesvár is a testament to that fact. His eight months in the city were not only a welcome respite from the road, but were also marked by an increasing number of major supporting and lead roles. There is also the intriguing possibility that Lugosi attended a drama school during the day in Temesvár, paying for the training from his salary for performing at the Ferenc József Színház (Franz Joseph Theater).[14]

Ignác Krecsányi, Lugosi's stage director in Temesvár, had been born in 1844 and worked in the city since at least 1883. As was the case with so many of his colleagues, Krecsányi started out as an actor before transitioning to the production side of theater. He had a reputation for being willing to take a chance on younger talent, which may explain why he offered Lugosi a contract.[15]

Theater director Ignác Krecsányi, circa 1903.
(Courtesy of the Collection of Theater History at the National Széchényi Library)

During his residency in Temesvár, Lugosi appeared on stage at least 123 times in a variety of roles, many of them very small. In *Az ember tragédiája*, Lugosi played the minor roles of the Second Demagogue and Saint Just when the play was staged on November 1 and 2, 1903. And his role as the Second Man in *A regények* (*The Romanesques*), presented on October 29 and 30, 1903, was hardly more than a bit part.

That said, Lugosi also portrayed a significant number of major supporting roles, and even the occasional lead. For example, on October 22, 1903, Lugosi had the lead in Belasco's *Pillangókisasszony* (*Madame Butterfly*), the play on which Puccini would base his opera. Lugosi also appeared in such operettas as *San-Toy*, *Shulamith* (*The Shulamite*), *Bob herceg* (*Prince Bob*), *A két Foscari* (*The Two Foscari*), and a number of others.

And then, on December 28 and 29, 1903, there was George du Maurier's *Trilby*, featuring one of the great villains

The town theater in Temesvár.

Lugosi's first stage appearance in the city of Szeged. Published in *Szeged és Vidéke* on November 7, 1903.

Cast listing for what was likely Lugosi's final appearance with the Krecsányi Troupe. Published in *Magyar Színpad* on May 2, 1904.

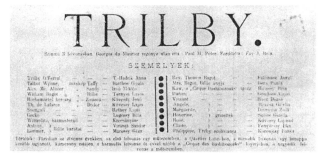

Published in the *Temesvári Színpad* on December 29, 1903.

of the stage, Svengali. Lugosi played a major supporting role as Gecko, with a local newspaper responding, "Béla Lugosi as Svengali's evil henchman was absolutely spellbinding."[16]

For reasons unknown, Krecsányi decided – for one set of performances only – to trade Lugosi for an actor from Szeged by the name of István Rédey. Thus, Lugosi, at age 21, traveled to Szeged to play the role of Imre Vas, a major supporting role in the play *Annuska*. In his two performances there, on November 7 and 8, 1903, Lugosi impressed the local critics. One reported that his "talent shines through."[17] Another called Lugosi "great."[18]

As far as can be determined, Lugosi completed his contract with Krecsányi by early May of 1904. By that time, a critic had written that Lugosi had "titillate[ed] women with a strong undercurrent of passion seldom experienced on the Temesvár stage."[19] A review of available playbills for the balance of 1904 and the entire year of 1905 show no evidence that Lugosi remained in Temesvár. Lugosi's first residency in a major Hungarian theater town had come to an end.

Budapest, Again

At the beginning of May 1904, Lugosi definitely accompanied Krecsányi's troupe to Budapest where Krecsányi had established an annual summer theater called Fővárosi Nyári Színház (Summer Theater of the Capital). There Lugosi appeared twice in the operetta *A kis szökevény* (*The Little Fugitive*), but afterwards was no longer listed as part of the troupe. By the time *A kis szökevény* had a repeat performance ten days later, on

Lugosi, (Lugossi, Lugossy, Lugosy).
— Béla. (Lugosy). gazdatiszt,VII, Hernád-u. 11,/a.
— Béla. szinész, VIII, kender-u 8.
— Gábor, rendőr, VII, Ilka-u. 35.
— Ignácz, (Lugossi), bád. üzletv.,VIII, Hunyady-u.3.
— József, bankhiv.,VI, Munkácsy-u. 27.
— Lajos, főv. hiv. szolga, II. csapláros-u. 10.
— Lajos, házmester, I, Maros-u. 7.
— Mihály. (Lugossy), hentes, VIII, práter-u. 66.
— Miklós. (Lugosy), haj. hiv.,VI,Podmaniczky-u. 79.
— Péter, (Lugossy), áll. hiv. VIII, kerepesi út 71.
— Róza. háztulajd., VI, Munkácsy-u. 27.

Evidence that Lugosi was working in Budapest during the 1904-1905 theater season. From the *Budapest City Directory* 1904/1905.

FÖLDMÜVES ISKOLAI

kiváló bizonyitványnyal, kellő gyakorlattal, 18 éves fiatal ember **magyar és oláh nyelv-ismerettel** gazdaságban szerény igények mellett megfelelő alkalmazást keres. Cim:

326   Lugossy Béla Gencs, (Szatmármegye.)   3—1

Classified advertisement for a *different* Béla Lugossy. From the *Gazdák Lapja* of November 17, 1905.

May 12, Lugosi had been replaced with an actor named Virányi.

Primary sources initially suggested that Lugosi left Budapest to work in the Károly Polgár Troupe during the next two theatrical seasons, 1904-1905 and 1905-1906.[20] After all, a number of theatrical historians have indicated Lugosi worked with Károly Polgár in such towns as Pécs, Nagybecskerek (now Zrenjanin in Romania), and Zombor (now Sombor in Serbia). (Some 35 years later, Universal Pictures announced *The Monster of Zombor*, an unmade horror movie of 1941 that would have costarred Lugosi with Boris Karloff.)

As all other seasons in Lugosi's countryside travels have been accounted for, it seemed likely that a contract with Károly Polgár would explain the "missing" seasons. However, recently discovered evidence directly contradicts that assumption, creating yet another mystery in Lugosi's life. Put another way, Lugosi – who didn't appear in *The Monster of Zombor* – might never have played the town of Zombor.

To begin, a review of the playbills for the 1904-1905 and 1905-1906 seasons for Nagybecskerek, one of Károly Polgár's major towns, shows absolutely no stage credits attributed to Lugosi. By contrast, the Budapest City Directory, covering May 1904 through April 1905, shows that Lugosi, occupation listed as "színész" (actor), was a resident for at least part of that 12-month period, living at Kender Street No. 8 in Budapest's District VIII. In a story published in *Színházi Újság* in 1910, Lugosi himself mentioned that he initially worked in Budapest after his season in Temesvár.[21]

However, other than the city directory, no specific references to him have surfaced in newspapers or theater publications for that period. There are several possible explanations. First, Lugosi might have remained with Krecsányi for the balance of the summer theater season but playing roles too small to be included in the cast listings of local newspapers or in the theatrical journal *Magyar Színpad*. If Lugosi did not remain with Krecsányi, it is possible he worked for a theater other than the Király Színház (Royal Theater), the primary venue for which cast listings were published in *Magyar Színpad*. Cast listings for the Magyar Színház (Hungarian Theater), the Nemzeti Színház (National Theater), the Várszínház (Castle Theater), the Magyar Király Operaház (Hungarian Royal Operahouse), the Népszínház (People's Theater) and the Vígszínház (Comedy Theater) generally did not appear in the journal. And newspapers usually only mentioned the main actors in their reviews.

So, Lugosi could have worked steadily at one or more of those theaters, even if in bit parts and crowd scenes. Consider what fellow Hungarian actor Mihály Várkonyi (Victor

Advance publicity for an unmade 1941 film with Lugosi and Karloff. *(Courtesy of Fritz Frising)*

Varconi) wrote in his autobiography about the Budapest of 1909: "The city of Budapest boasted over a dozen theaters, plus cabarets, student shows, operas, and touring companies. It was a glowing living Capitol of the Arts."[23] Várkonyi also recalled that a Shakespearean revival meant that actors could get paid for "appearing in the many scenes calling for crowd extras."[24]

Béla Polgár, circa 1932. (*Courtesy of the Collection of Theater History at the National Széchényi Library*)

Compounding the mystery is the fact that someone named "Lugosi" *was* listed as an actor in student plays presented at the Király Színház by the Szidi Rákosi Public School of Acting between February of 1905 and January of 1907. Several of them – specifically *Bob herceg, San-Toy, Gül Baba*, and *II. Rákóczy Ferencz Fogsága* (*Francis Rákoczi II in Captivity*) – were plays in which Béla Lugosi had already appeared at one time or another. However, reviews in the local newspapers make clear that *this* Lugosi was in fact the actor, singer, and comedian Jenő Lugosi.[25]

Further confusing the issue, a "Lugosi" was listed in the major productions staged at the Király Színház. Between December 9, 1905, and November 21, 1906, this "Lugosi" appeared in minor roles in the production of *Gül Baba* on 97 occasions and in *Bob herceg* twice; these were also plays in which Béla Lugosi had earlier appeared.

It is tempting to believe that *this* Lugosi was Béla Lugosi. However, the more probable explanation is that these are more credits of Jenő Lugosi, who received minor roles in major productions as a result of his training at the Rákosi school; he was clearly mentioned in newspapers in connection to several of these plays. It is also worth noting that this "Lugosi" did not appear in cast listings after November of 1906. By January of 1907, Jenő Lugosi had moved on to the Farkas Troupe, then presenting shows in Kassa (now Košice in the Slovak Republic).

As for Béla Lugosi, he may well have attended an acting school in Budapest during the 1904-1905 season other than Rákosi's. A statistical yearbook for the city of Budapest from that time shows a total of five acting schools in business, all established in the city prior to 1900.[26] In addition to Rákosi's, there was the Zoltán Horváth Preparatory School of Acting, the Solymosy Public School of Acting, the Acting School of the National Theatrical Association, and the National Royal Academy of Theatrical Arts.

This last school is particularly intriguing, as Lugosi later claimed in numerous interviews that he attended "the Royal Academy of Theatrical Arts in Budapest." The fact that the Royal Academy operated at a time when Lugosi was a resident might be important. Then again,

Lugosi playing multiple roles in the same play.
(Courtesy of the Collection of Theater History at the National Széchényi Library)

Lugosi with the Béla Polgár Troupe in 1907. *(Courtesy of the Collection of Theater History at the National Széchényi Library)*

the 1904-1905 yearbook for the Royal Academy does not list Béla Lugosi (or Béla Blaskó) as one of its students.

The following year, the mystery deepens. Lugosi is not listed in the Budapest City Directory published for 1905-1906. Likely this indicates he had moved, but where was he? One possibility is that he may have taken a non-theatrical job for a period of time. A Béla Lugossy, then residing in Gencs (now Ghenci in Romania), about 192 miles east of Budapest and 219 miles north of Lugos, ran an advertisement in a local newspaper in November of 1905:

> An 18-year-old man with Hungarian and Romanian language proficiency, with excellent certificate from an agrarian school, with sufficient work experience and with modest demands seeks for a suitable job in agriculture. Address: Béla Lugossy, Gencs, Szatmár County.[27]

Could this have been *the* Béla Lugosi? Probably not, unless he had for some reason removed five years from his age in an attempt to make the request more sympathetic.

Then, in March 1906, a locomotive driver or engineer named Béla Lugosi was injured in an altercation with another employee at a train station in Budapest.[28] While *the* Béla Lugosi certainly had worked in a railyard in Szabadka, there is no evidence that he was ever trained to drive a locomotive.

No, given his effort to succeed as an actor, it seems more likely that Béla Lugosi would have contracted with one of the at least 31 countryside troupes operating in Hungary at the time.[29] There are indications that he worked as an actor in Kolozsvár (now Cluj-Napoca)[30], but a thorough review of surviving playbills for this period has not yielded his name. The same lack of evidence occurs while searching other towns and cities where he logically could have been, including Pécs. Unfortunately, narrowing down where he might have worked is problematic due to the lack of surviving playbills and other publicity materials for some towns.

Playbill for the Béla Polgár Troupe in 1907. *(Courtesy of the Collection of Theater History at the National Széchényi Library)*

Béla Polgár

In either mid-August or early September of 1906, it is certain that Lugosi joined the Béla Polgár Troupe for the entirety of the 1906-1907 season. Born in 1860, Béla Polgár was the older brother of Károly Polgár. He started his theatrical career as an actor and later became a director and producer in a number of Hungarian cities.

In the fall of 1906, the Béla Polgár Troupe was working in the city of Békés, presenting *Helyre asszony* (*A Fair Woman*) on September 16, *Gül Baba* on September 17, *Csöppség* (*The Little One*) on September 18, *Drótostót* on September 19, and *A bajusz* (*The Mustache*) on September 20. The troupe probably moved on to other cities during the final months of 1906. *Pesti Hírlap* reported that Polgár's troupe was in Obecsen (now Bečej in Serbia) in January 1907, where it presented *A vig özvegy* (*The Merry Widow*), among other plays. Then, at some point in February, they relocated to Hajdúböszörmény.

Additional towns in Polgár's circuit included Nagykároly (now Carei in Romania), Nagyszalonta, Csongrád, Gyula, Kiskunhalas, Munkács (now Mukachevo in Ukraine), Sátoraljaújhely, Gyöngyös, Arad (now in Romania), Csanád (now largely in Romania), Bihar (now largely in Romania), Hajdú, Szatmár, and Kalocsa (where Lugosi had appeared in 1901). Those were in addition to Máramarossziget (now Sighetu Marmaţiei in Romania), located

BECOMING DRACULA

Playbill for a 1907 production with the Béla Polgár Troupe.
(Courtesy of the Collection of Theater History at the National Széchényi Library)

then in Máramaros County, where Lugosi's character Vitus Werdegast was imprisoned in the 1934 film *The Black Cat*. Lugosi would have appeared in plays in all of these towns.

On April 7, 1906, the *Iparosok Lapja* reported that Polgár put together a 36-person theater company, Érmihályfalvá, named after the town where it was headquartered. Over the next six or seven months, the troupe would stage productions in the "rural lowlands districts." Their repertoire included *Gül Baba*, *Milliárdos Kisasszony* (*Miss Millionaire*), *Tündérszép Ilona és A vasorrú boszorkány* (*Helena, the Fairy and the Witch*), *Csöppség*, *Berger Zsiga*, and *Helyre asszony*, as well as "various novelties."

Cast lists on surviving playbills indicate that Lugosi portrayed a number of leading roles and major supporting roles. He played the lead Jack Strahan in *Az igazgató úr* (*The Headmaster*), Daniló Danilovics in *A víg özvegy*, Lumpácius in *Lumpáciusz Vagabundusz,* and Richard Voysin in *A tolvaj* (*The Thief*). While he was still required to appear in minor roles, those became fewer and fewer in number.

During the summer of 1907, Lugosi once again traveled to Budapest to audition for the National Actors Association of Hungary. On approximately June 12, he passed the exams. But rather than being hired in Budapest or joining another troupe, by June 23, he had extended his contract with Béla Polgár for what turned out to be an additional season. Soon thereafter, the Polgár troupe had extended stays in the towns of Nagyszalonta, Csongrád, Gyula, Kalocsa, and Kiskunhalas.

Of this period, Lugosi's most important role was as one of the two male leads in Ferenc Molnár's famous play *Az ördög* (*The Devil*), which had just premiered in Budapest in April of 1907. Lugosi took the stage as János, the artist, in Kalocsa on October 31, 1907, with Béla Polgár playing the Devil. Though Halloween was not celebrated in Hungary at the time, the timing of the performance is still worth noting. Hungarians did honor All Saints' Day on November 1, praying for those souls in heaven, as well as commemorating November 2, praying for those souls who were still in purgatory and who might escape their graves. Along with cleaning and decorating tombstones, Hungarians often lit candles in cemeteries and inside their homes to guide souls to their destinations. A play like *Az ördög* would certainly have had particular resonance for audiences on the night of October 31. As its title character explains to a horrified character, "I am one who always comes at the right moment – I come from nowhere."

The troupe finished the year 1907 in Munkács, remaining in the city until near the end of February of 1908, performed briefly in the town of Kisvárda at the beginning of March, and then moved onto Sátoraljaújhely through April 12, even holding a benefit for the National Association of Countryside Journalists there.[31] Such benefit performances were not unusual for rural theater troupes. But a major highlight of Lugosi's stay in Sátoraljaújhely had nothing directly to do with his theatrical activities. A serious fire broke out in the town in late March. The local newspaper praised Lugosi for his actions as a volunteer rescue worker.[32]

The troupe then appeared in Gyöngyös and other towns during the balance of the regular season. Polgár also traveled a summer circuit in 1908, which began on Beregszász (now Berehove in the Ukraine) on May 11. However, Lugosi's tenure with the Polgár troupe apparently ended just prior to that date. Extensive reviews of plays performed in Beregszász, in which Lugosi had previously starred or had large supporting roles, made no mention of him.[33]

In any event, Lugosi's time with Béla Polgár came to an end in 1908, as he moved onto a new opportunity. Looking back on this period in later years, Lugosi claimed, "So, then, by the end of two or three years, I worked up to playing leading parts. I then went to a bigger troupe in a bigger town. Each week, each month, each year, a little higher, a little higher, a little higher!"[34]

In *'Midst the Wild Carpathians*, Mór Jókai writes, "The shadows of night have descended. Every living thing sleeps soundly. Love alone is wakeful." Lugosi would experience the love of audiences during the next, crucial phase of his acting career. The sheet lightning flickered brightly, illumining the night skies far beyond the mountain crescents.

(Endnotes)

1   Thomas, Dan. "The Film Shop." *Piqua Daily Call* (Piqua, OH) 7 Mar. 1929.
2   Untitled article. *Sunday Oregonian* (Portland, OR) 2 Sept. 1928.
3   "Színház." *Kecskeméti Friss Újság* (Kecskemét, Hungary) 11 Jan. 1902.
4   "Színház Zene." *Budapesti Napló* (Budapest, Hungary) 27 March 1902.
5   Ibid.
6   For the sake of internal consistency, we have altered the original spelling of "colour" to "color."
7   "Színészet." *Zalamegye* (Keszthely, Hungary) 14 June 1903.
8   "Szinügy." *Balatonvidék* (Keszthely, Hungary) 21 June 1903.
9   "The History of the Hotel – Arany Bárány Hotel." Available at http://aranybarany.hu/en/our-hotel/the-history-of-the-hotel/. Accessed 29 December 2017.
10   "Színészet." *Zalamegye* 21 June 1903.
11   In an article on regional theatrical contracts in the 5 Mar. 1903 edition of *Szatmári Hírlap*, theatrical companies were warned that fewer company directors were being granted licenses that year, which – along with the proliferation of actors without contracts – presumably created difficulties for provincial tours.
12   It would seem Lugosi did not join Micsey until mid-December 1902, if not later, as he does not

appear in any earlier list of troupe members. See: "Színészet." *Nagybánya és Vidéke* (*Nagybánya*, Hungary) 7 Dec. 1902.

13   "Irodalom és Művéset (Az erdélyi színészet)." *Budapesti Hírlap* (Budapest, Hungary) 25 July 1902.

14   "Üzenetek." *Színházi Újság* (Szeged, Hungary) 30 October 1910.

15   Mendel, Melinda. *Az Amerikai Magyar Színjátszás*. Doctoral Dissertation. (Târgu Mure , Romania: Universitatea de Arte Din Târgu Mureş, 2011).

16   "Krecsányi Ignác." *Magyar Színházművészeti Lexikon* (Budapest: Akadémiai Kiadó, 1994).

17   *Temesvári Színpad* (Temesvár, Hungary) 29 Dec. 1903.

18   "*Annuska.*" *Szeged és Vidéke* (Szeged, Hungary) 7 Nov. 1903.

19   "Színház." *Szeged és Vidéke* 8 Nov. 1903.

20   *Temesvári Színpad* 17 Feb. 1904.

21   See, for example: "Gróf Drakula: Lugosi Béla." *Film Színház Muzsika* 4 July 1987.

22   "Üzenetek." *Színházi Újság* (Szeged, Hungary) 30 Oct. 1910.

23   Varconi, Victor and Ed Honeck. *It's Not Enough to Be Hungarian* (Denver, CO: Graphic Impressions, 1976).

24   Ibid.

25   See editions published in 1904, 1905, 1906 and 1907 of these Budapest publications: *Budapesti Hírlap*, *Pesti Hírlap*, and *Pesti Napló*. Jenő Lugosi's name is included in reviews of the student plays staged by Rakosi's school, as well as in some productions at the Király Színház.

26   *A M. Kir. Kormány 1905, Muködéséről Az Ország Közállapottairól szlóló Jelentés és Statisztikai Évkönyv* (Budapest: Az Athenaeum Irodalmi és Nyomdai Rt. Könyvnyomdája, 1906).

27   Advertisement. *Szatmár* 17 Nov. 1905.

28   "Rendőrségi hírek." *Pesti Napló* 18 Mar. 1906.

29   The 8 Mar. 1905 edition of *Szatmárnemeti* (Szatmár, Hungary) reported "countryside troupes" were active in Miskolc, Puhó, Körmend, Csik-Gymes, Igló, Szeged, Kolozsvár, Kassa, Kecskemét, Temesvár, Szatmár, Facset, Debrecen, Győr, Rozsnyó, Székesfehérvár, Dombóvár, Radna-Lippó, Pécs, Békéscsaba, Szabadka, Balassa-Gyarmat, Zilah, Lugos, Nagyvárad, Bród, Szentes, Sopron, Versec, Kézdivásárhely, Arad, and Verbász.

30   Cremer, Robert. *Lugosi: The Man Behind the Cape* (Chicago: Henry Regnery, 1976). It should be noted that Lugosi could have played Kolozsvár in a year other than 1905 and 1906.

31   "V.H.O. Sz." *Pécsi Napló* (Pécs, Hungary) 30 Apr. 1908.

32   "Hírek." *Zemplén* (Sátoraljaújhely, Hungary) 1 Apr. 1908.

33   See "Jönek a színészek." *Bereg* (Beregszász, Hungary) 10 May 1908; "Színház." *Bereg* 24 May 1908; "Színház." *Bereg* 31 May 1908.

34   Lugosi, Bela, as told to Gladys Hall, "Memos of a Madman," *Silver Screen* July 1941.

Lugosi in an early
stage production.

Chapter 4

Well-Esteemed

"[Lugosi's] voice, appearance, and noble
zeal predestine him as a heroic lover."
– Debrecen theater critic

B y October of 1908, Lugosi signed a contract with Gyula Zilahy and thus began appearing onstage in Debrecen.[1] Zilahy, yet another actor-turned-director, was born in 1859. Early in his acting career, before eventually taking over the directorship of the troupe in Debrecen, he had played many of the same Hungarian towns that Lugosi would.

Lugosi's residency in the city marked the first time since Temesvár that he was able to remain in one place, free from the frustrations of a town for a day, or a week, or perhaps a month, before then traveling on to the next stop. At the time he moved there, Debrecen was the third largest city in Hungary after Budapest and Szeged, with a recorded population of over 90,000, nearly twice the size of Temesvár.[2] And Debrecen was an important cultural center. According to an account of its origins, the town's name meant "well-esteemed."

At one time the capital of Hungary, Debrecen was the location where the end of the Habsburg Dynasty was formally announced. While the city's first dramatic presentations reportedly occurred at an inn during the late 1700s, by 1908 plays had long been staged at the Városi Színház (Municipal Theater). Alfréd Deésy – with whom Lugosi would later collaborate on silent films in Budapest – worked as an actor in the city around the same time as Lugosi.[3] It was there that Lugosi was also able to act with such renowned Hungarians as Sándor Góth and Gyula Gál, with whom Lugosi later appeared in the film *99-es számú bercocsi* (*Rental Car Number 99*, aka *99*, 1918).

UDVÖZLET DEBRECENBŐL Piarz utca

Postcard of Debrecen from roughly the time of Lugosi's tenure in the city.

Lugosi might also have met Dracula for the first time in Debrecen, meaning the fictional vampire character. Bram Stoker's novel was translated into Hungarian and serialized in a Budapest newspaper in January 1898.[4] By May of that year, the Hungarian translation appeared in book form. It was popular enough to be reprinted twice over the next decade. The third edition appeared in 1909, while Lugosi was in Debrecen. Perhaps he had already heard of Stoker's *Dracula* before that year, but being in a city of Debrecen's size and cultural standing, he might well have seen the new edition at a nearby bookstore or read about it in local newspaper ads.

Lugosi could even have been aware that the association between the name Dracula and supernatural vampires was taking hold in Hungary, to the extent it provided a potent metaphor for journalists. In 1907, for example, one article compared a corrupt immigration agent to Dracula, making specific reference to

DEÉSY ALFRÉD

Postcard of actor-turned-director Alfréd Deésy.

Published in the *Budapesti Hírlap* on March 6, 1909.

Published in the *Sipulusz Lapja Kakas Mártón* on February 12, 1899.

Bram Stoker and to supernatural creatures who drink blood, in this case the "blood of a nation."[5] Only a stake through the heart could dispatch such villains, the journalist told readers. Comparisons of politicians to bloodthirsty vampires were hardly new: examples appeared in Hungarian newspapers repeatedly in key years of Lugosi's early career, whether 1901, 1904, or 1908, shortly before he moved to Debrecen. But the specific name "Dracula" was increasingly being used for similar metaphors.

Whatever Lugosi did or did not know about Stoker's Dracula, the character was extremely distant from his career, from the kinds of roles he played. What is particularly important is that Debrecen is where Lugosi first became well known as an actor. His time in Debrecen meant a significant increase in lead roles and top billing, particularly as Charles Moore in *A haramiák* (*The Robbers*), as Antonio in Shakespeare's *Velencei Kalmár* (*The Merchant of Venice*), as Manfréd in Byron's *Manfréd* (*Manfred*), as William Tell in *Tell Vilmos* (*William Tell*), as Adam in *Az ember tragédiája* (*The Tragedy of Man*), and as Romeo in *Rómeó és Júlia* (*Romeo and Juliet*). With these and other roles, Lugosi the romantic hero, sometimes the tragic romantic hero, began to emerge.

In the Hungarian film journal *Filmkultúra*, Anna Viola Szabó described Lugosi's time in Debrecen:

> He preferred playing a hero, most of all, a tragic and romantic hero; and according to critics, he really did his best in such roles, since in comedies of manners there is no place for spectacularly visible, pathetic feelings. Chatting pleasantly about nonsense, being present on the stage in such situations were not challenging to him; he accomplished these roles without an effort. 'He is talking as easily as if conversation was his profession' [said one critic] evaluating (and rather ambiguously) Lugosi in the role of a lancer captain.[6]

Debrecen theater critics regularly commented on Lugosi's emergence as romantic hero. Observing Lugosi in a number of roles, one of them wrote:

Lugosi as The Examiner in *A gyújtogató* (The Firebrand). *(Courtesy of Jon R. Hand)*

He is a young actor. He has not yet managed to show the full character and Hungarian power of the Lord [Zrínyi]; his art is not yet mature enough to do that. He can only achieve that level through much learning and immersion. Certainly, he has excellent [talent] for heroic roles, such as his figure, appearance, and voice. The latter one, however, has abandoned him here and there, and it needs thoughtful, further training....[7]

Typesetters might also have needed further training, as Lugosi's billing continued to fluctuate, with Lugosi, Lugossi, Lugosy and Lugossy being used on playbills in the city, and in a varying order that hardly suggests a conscious strategy.

Lugosi's first documented performance in Debrecen was in the role of Miklós Zrínyi in *Szigetvári vértanúk* (*The Martyrs of Szigetbár*), a historical drama by Hungarian playwright Mór Jókai, staged on October 6, 1908. He received mixed reviews, with one critic observing:

Béla Lugosy... is a talented actor; he recites well, but he gets tired quickly. In many scenes he appeared as a true Zrínyi, strong and firm. His physique is handsome, strong, his acting is satisfying, too, but he cannot always control his voice. By the way, this is a role in which one should not let his heart speak. In order to form an opinion on his

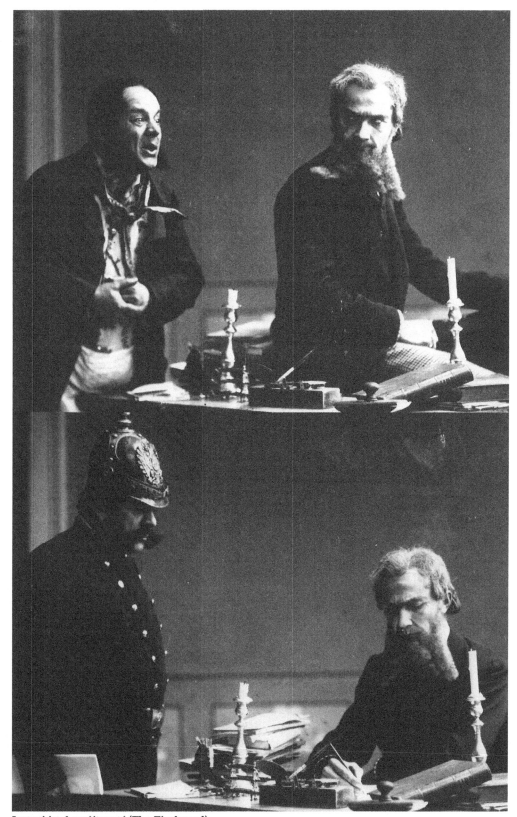

Lugosi in *A gyújtogató* (The Firebrand).

Postcard of the theater in Debrecen.

acting we must watch him in other roles, too.[8]

Another critic provided analysis of Lugosi's performance as well as predictions for his future:

> We must remember the acting of Béla Lugosy above all. He played Zrínyi's difficult role flawlessly, which is an almost impossible task these days. We do not want to criticize yesterday's performance in detail, but we would rather focus on his personal character in general...

> Lugosy is an actor with a handsome figure, a pleasant [voice] and a great intelligence. His gifts shine through in every move he makes. Whether his acting skills are equally developed or not, we will only see later. He was able to balance himself between the extremes of 'recitation' and 'talking.' Today's audience does not enjoy 'recitation' any longer, but 'speech' does not suit such a play, either.

> We predict a great future for this rather talented young man, whom Zilahy [the director] has chosen very well. This talented young actor spent a long time [acting in the provinces] and now making it on the unfamiliar stage in Debrecen will be to his advantage. His figure and voice were impressive, which will make him become one of the most beloved actors in Debrecen.[9]

Lugosi gets special billing as *Romeo in Debrecen* in 1909.
(Courtesy of the University and National Library of Debrecen)

Lugosi's next major opportunity came in November 1908, when he played the title role in Byron's *Manfréd*. The play opened on November 7 and was staged three additional times, on November 8 and 13 and December 15. The critic for *Debreceni Főiskolai Lapok* wrote:

The role of Manfréd was played by Béla Lugosi, who successfully dealt with this huge task. He is an intelligent and self-assertive actor who elaborated this difficult role with lots of study and conscience. His extraordinary talent mostly dominated three scenes, which are also the most beautiful in the whole poem.

One of them is the final monologue in the second scene of the second act ('We are all the fools of time and terror…'), which does not only compete with the famous monologue in Shakespeare's *Hamlet*, but the scenic interpretation of it might be even harder than that of Shakespeare's. The other ones are the dialogue with the abbot (Scene 1, Act III), and his fight against the demons, his titanic battle, his tragic protest in the final scene of Act III. The artistic abilities of Lugosi were most clearly visible in this final scene.[10]

The writer for *Debreceni Független Újság* had reservations about Lugosi's performance, but still recognized flashes of talent:

This [dramatic] poem was performed with great but awkward readiness last night in the theater of Debrecen … If we want to comment on Lugosi's performance, who played Manfréd, we must divide it in two. Manfréd, who struggles with the heavens, with youthful power and despicable passion was depicted pleasingly, sometimes with pure artistic quality. But he could not make the self-destructive, Hamlet-like Manfréd who constantly fights with himself come to life. In such situations he was dull, powerless, thrown back… and silent, an actor stumbling in cothurnus [a type of elevated sandal][11], who is happy to leave behind the passages with long and deep thoughts as soon as possible… The most valuable part in his Manfréd-study was his final battle with the devils.[12]

A third critic, however, had nothing positive to say about the performance, blaming Lugosi's youth and alleged inexperience for a lackluster performance:

... this young, undeniably ambitious actor is not yet mature enough to play the title role; with empty, muddled recitation he not only failed in bringing the beautiful thoughts of the play to the surface but he buried them even deeper. However, this is the management's mistake, which never takes into consideration the knowledge of the actors but it forces such tasks on members of the company, which often exceed their talents.[13]

Playbill with Lugosi as Manfréd in Debrecen in 1908.
(Courtesy of the University and National Library of Debrecen)

Lugosi's next significant part was another lead, as Adam in Imre Madách's *Az ember tragédiája*. First published in 1861 and compared at times to Milton's *Paradise Lost*, this poetic drama became one of the most important works in all of Hungarian literature. With its conflict between Adam, Eve, and Lucifer, the play continues to be staged in the 21st century. Debrecen was certainly not the first time Lugosi had appeared in the play; however, his past performances in the provinces had been in minor roles. Once again, critical reception varied:

Lugosi's Adam was such a patchwork. We have never seen Miltiades and Kepler destroyed to such extent by anyone playing Adam ever before. However, we definitely had to recognize some important skills in this actor, and we think we are right if we try to explain the unsuccessful performance on Sunday through Lugosi's misunderstandings. The basis of the fundamental mistake is that Lugosi portrayed Adam all through the play as a naïve, God-fearing, idle man who is lacking any kind of self-confidence, and who was just dropped out from Paradise ...

Today no one doubts that this perception is impossible. Lugosi's acting conveys an independent and modern interpretation of the role, through which he attempted to implement an unchanging personality with fixed ideas and values in the character he played. Despite enthusing over and then getting disillusioned with humankind in so many personas throughout the play, Adam remains the man who got expelled from Paradise, with the fears fueled by the lack of experience and with the timidity of the first man on Earth.[14]

In his performance as Adam, and in other roles in Debrecen, Lugosi relied increasingly on his voice and his gestures. Anna Viola Szabó wrote:

> One of the first assignments of Lugosi was the role of Adam after he signed his contract with the theater of Debrecen. With his performance he immediately split the crowd of critics in two, but there was a general agreement about 'the good-looking, talented young man' who, no doubt, had a bright future ahead of him. One of his critics praised him in the role of Adam as excellent, but we can hear hints of irony in his praise, when he writes: 'his voice, appearance, and noble zeal predestine him as a heroic lover!' – which is a rather surprising conclusion knowing the character of Adam. It is remarkable, however, that the critic recognized the most important and most powerful instruments of embodying a character as his voice and [the shape of the body and appearance]... In Lugosi's case those two characteristics were a given, and they cannot be earned by learning or practice.[15]

Despite perceived flaws in his interpretation of Adam, Lugosi apparently tried to modernize the role for changing audience tastes. As early as 1908, he was already showing a desire and an ability to do the unexpected with a role.

At the beginning of 1909, and for the duration of his Debrecen contract, the pace of Lugosi's workload quickened. During the first half of the 1908-1909 season, Lugosi's documented stage appearances numbered seventeen in nine different plays; those performances included two significant leading roles. The second half of the season saw Lugosi take the stage at least 69 times in 65 different productions. Leading roles in *Tell Vilmos*, *Rómeo és Júlia*, and *Az ember tragédiája* were balanced out with an increasing number of major supporting roles, the highest profile likely being as The Examiner in *A gyújtogató* (*The Firebrand*), which was presented seven times in Debrecen and then by the same troupe on five additional occasions in nearby towns.

Playbill with Lugosi as Armand Duval in Debrecen in 1910. *(Courtesy of the University and National Library of Debrecen)*

Lugosi even recited a monologue poem, *Hajótörés* (*Shipwreck*), as part of a bill of short specialty acts staged in Érmihályfalva in support of a performance of *A gyújtogató*.

Tell Vilmos premiered on January 22, 1909. The critical appraisal of his performance was not uniform:

> From the cast Béla Lugosi's performance is worthy of appraisal. He tried to solve the uneasy tasks of the title role with a noble ambition, but he did not entirely succeed. That he was unable to personify the man who loves freedom and loves his family until his death, can only be attributed to the actor's young age. His voice did not convey that warmth which can reach the hearts of the viewers. The audience appreciated his great effort, proving that he enthusiastically studied his role.[16]

Note the two different spellings of Lugosi's name on this Debrecen playbill from 1909. *(Courtesy of the University and National Library of Debrecen)*

In a rather unique approach, the playbill for the production had separate cast credits for each of the twelve scenes. Lugosi was billed as "Lugosi Béla" in all but the final scene, where curiously he was listed as "Lugossy Béla." Despite the differing reviews, the play was significant enough that Lugosi rated mention in one of the Budapest newspapers.[17]

After his first full season in Debrecen, Lugosi joined Zilahy's summer circuit in Nyíregyháza and Máramarossziget. He appeared in a number of productions that had already been staged in Debrecen, including what were to become signature roles for him at this point in his career, including Romeo and Adam. The troupe began performances in Nyíregyháza on the first of June 1909, remaining there until late July.

A June performance of *Rómeó és Júlia* received the following notice:

> We cannot say too many good things about the performance of *Romeo and Juliet*. Irén Huzella was acting the role of Juliet very suitably, though. She was girlish, she acted

sweetly, enchantingly, but her partner, Béla Lugosi, sputtered his role. Undeniably, he is an ambitious young man. His fault is the same as most young artists: when he is given heavy baggage, he tends to think that he can carry without varying his pace.

Young ardor, impetuous unruliness of boisterous blood: [these] are nice, but one should not forget that the speeding carriage might turn over too easily. We could only understand a couple of words, here and there, from Lugosi's overly fast monologues. 'In magnis et voluisse sat.' ('In great things, it is enough even to have willed.' – Propertius) – I would modify this proverb as follows: It is a mistake to aspire for big things in big projects.[18]

The troupe was in Máramarossziget by August 11, remaining there until at least August 31 before returning to Debrecen to prepare for the next season, which opened on September 29, 1909.

For his first production in the 1909-1910 season, Lugosi played the lead male role in *A tanítónő* (*The Lady Teacher*), a folk play written by Sándor Bródy.[19] The initial performance occurred on September 29, 1909. During this second season, Lugosi took to the stage at least fifty times between September and December in seventeen different productions, including the lead roles as Carl Moor in *A haramiák* and as the Hungarian Lord in *Bánk Bán* (*Bán Bánk*).

Between January and May of 1910, Lugosi appeared on stage at least 74 times in 31 different productions. He repeated his leading roles in *A tanítónő* and *Az ember tragédiája*. He also portrayed major roles like János in Molnár's *Az ördög* (*The Devil*), Antonio in Shakespeare's *Velencei kalmár*, Marc-Arrán in *Forradalmi nász* (*The Revolutionary Wedding*), and Armand Duval in Dumas' *A kaméliás hölgy* (*The Lady of the Camellias*, aka *Camille*).

Playbill from Debrecen in 1909. *(Courtesy of the University and National Library of Debrecen)*

Significant supporting roles increased as minor roles decreased. And many of Lugosi's reviews were quite positive, as in the case of *A haramiák* in 1909:

Schiller's classic drama was a box office hit even in the past, and the audience applauded with enthusiasm for the tirades of noble passions. The deeply intellectual, tastefully stylized acting of Béla Lugosi in the role of Károly Moor contained even more masculinity, and indeed more natural power, than what he was aiming for at the premiere. His serious ambition was met by the enthusiastic applause, which called him to the stage lights five times after the scene with his father.[20]

Yet another writer saw no negatives in Lugosi's interpretation and acknowledged his growth as an actor:

We must admit that the direction of the play is almost flawless, and this holds true to the quality of acting, too. Praise goes, first, to Lugosi, who, this time, played the role of Károly, the son of Maximilian, and he did it in a rather artistic way, showing refined nuances. Through his acting today we could clearly see how his talent grows.[21]

Lugosi's debut in *Bánk Bán* (*Bán Bánk*) on October 6, 1909, elicited praise from at least one reviewer:

We have not seen a better *Bánk Bán* for a very long time at the Debrecen stage. Lugossy played the title role with great intelligence and with a full use of his generous artistic talent. He played this difficult role, for which each word needs to be studied in depth, with superb elaboration, with dramatic intensity, and above all, with imposing intellect – the latter one making Lugossy an excellent dramatic actor.[22]

His appearance in *A kaméliás hölgy* on April 13, 1910 also received acclaim:

Béla Lugosi, a highly and often praised artist in our company, played the role of Armand Duval excellently. He was as perfect in simple conversations, as in those scenes when he feels cheated and he curses his loved one with a broken heart, or when he gets to know the truth and his action can no longer be overcome, and thus, he bends over his dying sweetheart with desperate pain: he played in all of these scenes in an equally excellent, thoughtful and delicately articulated way…

With all his recent perfor-

Playbill from Debrecen in 1909. *(Courtesy of the University and National Library of Debrecen)*

Folyó szám 224.   (C) bérlet utolsó.

Debreczen, 1910. évi május hó 14-én szombaton:

SZILAS FRIDA felléptével

Folt, amely tisztit.

Dráma 4 felvonásban. Irta : Echegaray.

Rendező: Zilahy.   **Személyek:**

Matilda	—	—	—	—	—	—	Szilas Frida	Don Justo	—	—	—	—	—	—	Kemény Lajos
Eszriqueta	—	—	—	—	—	—	Huzella Irén	Don Lorenzo	—	—	—	—	—	—	Mártonfi R.
Donna Concepcion	—	—	—	—	Szilágyi Berta	Julio	—	—	—	—	—	—	Kardos G.
Dolores	—	—	—	—	—	—	Sándori M.	Inas	—	—	—	—	—	—	Jászkürti
Fernando	—	—	—	—	—	—	Lugosi B.							

Kezdete 7½ órakor, vége 10 óra után, esti pénztárnyitás 6½ órakor.

Helyárak: Földszinti és em. páholy 9 kor. Földszinti családi páholy 15 korona. I. em. családi páholy 12 korona. II emeleti páholy 6 kor. Támlásszek I.—VII-ik sorig 2 kor. 40 fillér. VIII.—XII-ig 2 kor. XIII.—XVII-ig 1 kor. 60 fillér. Erkélyülés 1.20 fill. Állóhely (emeleti) 80 fill. Diák-jegy (emeleti) 60 fill. Karzat-jegy 40 fill. Gyermek-jegy 10 ̂yen aluli gyermekek részére 40 fill.

Playbill for Lugosi's last known performance in Debrecen.
(Courtesy of the University and National Library of Debrecen)

mances Lugosi confirms our long-standing statement again and again, that this great artist has a bright future ahead, and he is listed among the most talented and most outstanding, true artists in our company.[23]

Lugosi's farewell performance in Debrecen was as Fernando in *Folt, Amely Tisztít* (*The Stain That Cleans*) on May 14, 1910. The day before, a journalist wrote that, "the lovable heroic lover will say goodbye to our theater company on Saturday when he'll play in Echegaray's drama."[24] Lugosi then received yet another a positive notice:

Béla Lugossi, this actor marching towards his bright future, bade farewell to us last night. Our company loses an artist with great intelligence and with refined skills. With his never exaggerating, delicate acting, with his ever-tasteful performances, he caused great joy to the audience. His last role was that of Fernando in *The Stain That Cleans*. The audience applauded him with warm love various times. He received beautiful wreaths and bouquets from his friends, from the Csokonay Circle, from the Casino, from the students and from the lawyers.[25]

After the end of his second season in Debrecen, Lugosi once again spent the summer months in regional theater productions. From May 22 through June 29, 1910, he appeared in at least twenty productions in Nyíregyháza and Máramarossziget. During that time, a critic praised his latest performance in *Az ember tragédiája*: "the performances of Aranka Gazdy and Béla Lugossy were absolutely remarkable."[26]

Lugosi's popularity in the provinces and his important roles in Debrecen greatly enhanced his reputation. While the beginning of Lugosi's time in the city was marked by mixed reviews, critics almost uniformly praised him by the time of his departure:

It is worth mentioning regarding the future – although it might be too early to do so – that only two people leave the company [located in Szeged]: Kertész and Gizi Szőke, the latter one moves to Miskolc. The directorship has already found a superb substitute for Kertész, who is Lugosi from Debrecen. Nothing proves better than the farewell of the audience in Debrecen that he is an excellent artist: since Frici Tanay no one had received such a warm reaction from the public as Lugosi recently did.[27]

The Kertész mentioned was in fact Mihály Kertész, who achieved fame in Hollywood as Michael Curtiz, director of such films as *Angels with Dirty Faces* (1938), *Yankee Doodle Dandy* (1942), and *Casablanca* (1942). Lugosi would later cross paths with the talented actor-turned-director in Budapest.

But as of 1910, Lugosi left Debrecen for Szeged, the second largest city in Hungary. He was no longer an unknown supporting player of the provinces. He was the romantic, heroic lover of the stage. He was, at long last, "well-esteemed."

(Endnotes)

1   In her article "Kitűnő kvalifikációi vannak a hősi szerepekre – Lugosi Béla kultusza – debreceni szemmel," published in *Élet és Világ* (Debrecen: Déri Muzeum, 2007), Anna Viola Szabó states, "with the multitude of confusing data, the only thing which seems certain is that Gyula Zilahy employed the 27-year-old actor in Debrecen in the spring of 1908 to play the roles of heroic lovers." Lugosi probably signed in the spring of 1908 to perform in Debrecen for the next season. It is not likely that he moved to Debrecen until closer to the time of his debut there.

2   This calculation is based on 1910 population numbers.

3   Deésy worked off and on for the Városi Színház in Debrecen between 1906 and 1912. Although mostly acting and singing in operettas, he occasionally composed original music for productions, as with *Atalanta*, staged on 1 Apr. 1909. There is no available evidence that Lugosi and Deésy ever appeared in a play together but they likely crossed paths while Lugosi was there.

4   The *Budapesti Hírlap* (Budapest, Hungary) serialized Stoker's novel *Dracula* from 1 Jan. 1898 to 29 Mar. 1898.

5   "A drakula." *Budapesti Hírlap* 24 Mar. 1907.

6   Szabó, "Kitűnő kvalifikációi vannak a hősi szerepekre," quoting from the 4 May 1909 edition of *Debreceni Hüggetlen* Újság (Debrecen, Hungary).

7   Ibid, quoting from *Debrecen* (Debrecen, Hungary) 7 Oct. 1909.

8   "Színház." *Debreczini* Újság (Debrecen, Hungary) 7 Oct. 1908.

9   "Színház." *Debrecen* 7 Oct. 1908.

10   "Színház – Manfréd." *Debreceni Főiskolai Lapok* (Debrecen, Hungary) 15 Nov. 1908

11   The primary meaning of "cothurnus" here is an elevated sandal used in older stage productions, thus accounting for Lugosi "stumbling" on the stage. It can also mean an elevated style of acting sometimes used in classical tragedy.

12   Szabó, "Kitűnő kvalifikációi vannak a hősi szerepekre," quoting from *Debreceni Független Újság* (Debrecen, Hungary) 8 Nov. 1908.

13   Ibid, quoting from *Debrecen* 16 Dec. 1908.

14   Ibid, quoting from *Debreceni Független Újság* 1 Dec. 1908.

15   Ibid.

16   *Debrecini Újság* 23 Jan. 1909.

17   "*Tell Vilmos* Debreczenben." *Magyarország* (Budapest, Hungary) 2 Feb. 1909.

18   "Színház." *Nyírvidék* (Nyíregyháza, Hungary) 13 June 1909.

19   The literal meaning of "tanítónő" is "a female teacher." This distinguishes it from Lugosi's role in the play, which was that of a male teacher or "tanitó."

20   "Színház." *Debrecen* 4 Dec. 1909.

21   "Színház." *Debrecen* 3 Dec. 1909.

22   Szabó, "Kitűnő kvalifikációi vannak a hősi szerepekre," quoting from *Debreceni Független Újság* 7 Oct. 1909.

23   Ibid, quoting from *Debrecen* 14 Apr. 1910.

24   "Színház." *Debrecen* 13 May 1910.

25   "Lugosi Béla Búcsúja." *Debrecen* 15 May 1910.

26   *Város* (Debrecen, Hungary) 23 June 1910.

27   "Színház." *Békés* 10 July 1911.

Lugosi Béla

Postcard of Lugosi from his theater days in Hungary. *(Courtesy of John Antosiewicz)*

Chapter 5

Wherefore Art Thou?

"Borrow Cupid's wings and soar with
them above a common bound."
– Shakespeare

"Sweet thief of hearts! He is so charming
with his wonderfully blue eyes."
– Female fan commenting
on Lugosi in Szeged

D uring his life in America, Lugosi proudly remembered his stage career in Hungary, his triumph as Romeo, among so many other romantic roles. That success began in Debrecen, but it reached a plateau in Szeged in 1910, probably more than at any other point in his European career.

Szeged also became the place where women idolized him, onstage and off. He later recalled:

> During my years in the various troupes, there were long chains of love affairs. This is not stupid bragging. This was the life of a young and lusty actor in the provinces. It may be said 'but it is madness to keep count of the women in one's life … only vampires count their victims' … at that I can only shrug, 'Maybe.'[1]

As Romeo declares, "Love is a smoke raised with the fume of sighs." And sighs became common among Lugosi's female admirers.

Local newspapers heralded Lugosi's arrival in Szeged during the month of August 1910. At the beginning of September, playbills listed his name. Producer Áranka Ábray – who

Postcard of Szeged from the period when Lugosi was in the city.

had taken over the theater company after the death of her husband Lajos Makó in late 1908 – might have contracted Lugosi as early as the middle of January 1910.[2] The recently deceased Makó, a notable figure in Hungarian theater history, was born in Debrecen in 1854. He had started his career as an actor and expert stage swordsman in Budapest in 1877.

According to one account, Lugosi was scheduled to replace actor Jenő Krémer, who had moved on to a troupe in Sátoraljaúhely.[3] Another report indicated that he was replacing Mihály Kertész (Michael Curtiz).

With its population of approximately 96,000, Szeged was an important center of arts and education. The city was one of the most beautiful and modern in Hungary, having been rebuilt after a major flood in 1879. The Szegedi Városi Színház (Szeged Municipal Theater), a large, beautiful venue, served as home to productions featuring Lugosi.

He was generally billed as "Lugossy Béla" that season. His name appeared prominently on advertisements for his debut in *Rómeó és Júlia* (*Romeo and Juliet*) on September 2, 1910. While the company had quickly mounted what they saw as a suitable vehicle for Lugosi, apparently due to his success in it in Debrecen[4], the production was not without its problems. A writer for the Szeged press explained:

> The company has a new leading actor, Béla Lugosy, who had to be introduced. Thus, they pulled out the role of Romeo, an abundantly amorous figure. And the show is put across with the old, worn-out scenes and a newer, but even more worn-out stage direction that tells everything but consideration and meaning. We look forward to initiatives of bringing classics to life, but we really do not ask for such performances as this one.

SZEGED, 1910. I. évfolyam 2. szám. Péntek, szeptember 2.

MAI SZINLAP

MÜVÉSZETI ÉS SZÉPIRODALMI NAPILAP

| Szerkesztőség és kiadóhivatal telefonja: 836. szám. | ELŐFIZETÉSI ÁRA: házhoz hordva negyedévre 2 korona. Egyes szám ára 4 fillér. | Szerkesztőség, kiadóhivatal és nyomda KORONA-UTCA 15. SZÁM. |

Folyószám 2. Szeged, 1910. évi szeptember hó 2-án, pénteken: Bérletszünet.

Lugossy Béla bemutatkozása.

ROMEO és JULIA

Tragédia 5 felvonásban. Irta: Shakespeare. Forditotta: Szász Károly.

SZEMÉLYEK:

From *Mai Színlap* of September 2, 1910.

We want to say a few words about the new actor, too. We are still unable to formulate an opinion about his talent after today's performance. We found that he was diligently prepared with the text of the role. He learned it flawlessly and he recited it fluently, sometimes so fast that not all his words could be understood. Although youthful enthusiasm broke through his acting too strongly, we were unable to see the youthfulness of Romeo in his portrayal, the impetuous cravings and burning desire for youthful love. The audience (not too many people) applauded for the young actor, who, in other, more modern roles would preferably be able to utilize his acting qualities more favorably.[5]

A critic from nearby Csongrád also observed flaws in Lugosi's performance while still acknowledging his potential:

Only a few people came to the theater today despite the debut of the new member at the company: Béla Lugossy. ... Seemingly, Shakespeare on the stage becomes less and less attractive and full rows remain empty in the audience. Unquestionably, this fact had a negative effect on Lugossy, who seemed to lack enthusiasm. He is a good actor though, and his style of acting is modern. He committed a serious mistake today, but hopefully only today: he recited the dialogue for his role too quickly. Despite that, his pleasing voice still prevailed.[6]

Rather than a formal review, one local newspaper published a young lady's letter, which reads as follows:

Lali said that it was no problem, he came to the theater on account of me anyway, and to see Béla Lugossi, who is new here, and who came to replace [Mihály] Kertész. Lugossi is tall and handsome, but he appeared with an unshaved face and he spoke too fast, which is not a mistake, says Professor Horváth, if he'll kick the habit. Mama says he'll become a talented actor and that he plays well, but with a bit too many gestures. She says we'll watch him in a modern play, which is good, because we'll come back to the theater again. ... Lugossi will be introduced again, and he will introduce himself to me too, because Lali will make his acquaintance in the Royal Orpheum, and he will make sure we get to know each other, which will turn half of the town green with envy....[7]

Lugosi's Romeo had rapidly made an impact on at least some of the women in Szeged.

A week later, he portrayed János in Ferenc Molnár's *Az ördög* (*The Devil*). A newspaper editor later recalled that the performance "was really a flop that led to world fame ...":

Lugosi as Romeo in Szeged. Playbill from October 9, 1910. *(Courtesy of the Károly Somogyi City and County Library of Szeged)*

Portion of a playbill advertising Lugosi in Szeged. *(Courtesy of the Károly Somogyi City and County Library of Szeged)*

I was reviewing the play for a local newspaper and I gather that he was pretty nervous about opening night. He played a painter in the play but things didn't go well for him the first night. When he came out on stage during the first scene, he accidentally tripped over a piece of pipe and landed in a heap stage center. He knocked over the easel and the paint splattered all over his smock. Any other actor would have skipped town but not Béla. He just picked himself up and delivered his opening lines. The audience loved his courage and his performance so much that he became one of the most popular actors in Szeged.[8]

Lugosi's rapid dialogue delivery became a repeated complaint during the early part of the season. Less than two weeks after stumbling on the stage, when he appeared in *Amihez minden asszony ért* (*What Every Woman Knows*), a critic broached the issue again:

Béla Lugosi played the part of John. He was most convincing in Act 1. Here, he gave it a light touch. He skillfully visualized the poor, clumsy worker-apprentice, his pride and his stubbornness. However, he did not manage to convey the feeling of disaffection from Maggie, and the bitter flights of being lonely. Mostly, his speech is still fast and unchanging.[9]

A different critic proposed a possible explanation for what only seemed to be rapid delivery:

BECOMING DRACULA

I. évfolyam.   10. szám.   Szeged, 1910. október 30.

SZINHÁZI UJSÁG

SZINHÁZI ÉS MŰVÉSZETI HETILAP.

SZERKESZTŐ: Dr. LUGOSI DÖMÖTÖR.

Főmunkatársak | Szerkesztőség és kiadóhivatal:
Dr. Kornis Béla, Dr. Szekerke Lajos. | Kárász-utca 10. sz. ♦ Telefonszám 196.

Megjelenik vasárnap reggel teljes heti szinlappal.

Kiadja Ifj. ÁRVAY SÁNDOR könyvkereskedése SZEGED, Kárász-utca 10. szám.

Egyes szám ára 10 fillér.

Lugosi on the cover of the Szeged version of
Színházi Újság. Published on Halloween eve, 1910.

Szeged. Nyárai Antal a Szabin nők elrablásá-
ban bucsúzott a szegedi közönségtől. Az elmúlt
héten volt azonkivül Pajor Ágnes és Sümegi
Ödön bucsúfellépte is. A társulat e szezonbeli

Lugosi Béla, szeptember 1-től a Magyar-szinház tagja.

Announcement of Lugosi's hiring by the
Magyar Színház (Hungarian Theater),
published in *Színházi Hét* in May 1911.

At first, he was not understood
specifically because of his natural ways
of acting and his common speech.
Poor acoustics of the theater just made
it even harder. Furthermore, he has a
wonderful characteristic: he knows his
roles by heart. Now, in country theaters,
we are so much used to fake intervals,
during which the prompter whispers
to the actor the forthcoming text, that
the actor who knows his role by heart
sounds as if he were speaking way too
fast. I don't wish to overprotect him,
but surely those who saw him reciting
the role of the young delivery boy in
Amihez minden asszony ért and that of
the Captain Sender in *Bilincsek* [*Shackles*]
will share my opinion.[10]

Another journalist who also witnessed
Lugosi's performance in *Amihez minden
asszony ért* gave him a glowing review,
making no reference to the speed of his
delivery:

Béla Lugossy enacted the main
role in the play. He played exquisitely
the part of the man who misread his
own feelings and who was squirming
helplessly, his acting was straight and
true. He proved through this role that
his acting skills are outstanding.[11]

Best of all, noted Szeged writer Béla
Kálmány praised Lugosi at greater length
than probably any previous critic in any
town or city:

He has a handsome, intelligent face
and pleasant voice with a dark tonality.
His wits suit both, and he is imposing on

us with his nice locks of hair and velvet-like voice.

Béla Lugosy is an actor of the 20th century. He is a man in love when he plays a man in love. A fierce and unrestrained lover, and his aching heart almost breaks when he sees his Juliet dead, as Romeo. He speaks so humanely that when he says something very common, his speech leaves no trace, but when he expresses the great difficulties of human life with all its conflicts, he grabs the strings of our hearts and he stretches them until they tear...

Before he came to Szeged he was very successful already (the wreath ribbons made of silk to be found in his room are testimonials of his success). For actors in Debrecen, being honored by the Csokonai Circle is a decoration of the highest level: 'To the best Manfred ever.' Even Budapest-based newspapers were reporting on Lugosy, who, at that time was the only Manfred

Playbill for Lugosi's final performance in *Szeged* **before moving on to Budapest.** *(Courtesy of the Károly Somogyi City and County Library of Szeged)*

around. The classical repertoire of the Debrecen Theater heavily relied on [Lugosi]. They presented some plays by Shakespeare, and pieces by Madách, Goethe, and Byron.

We only saw him in the role of Romeo. A Romeo dying fiercely, beautifully, and deeply in love. We do not know the theater's plans for the future – only a few things are getting realized from the tentative program – but we would like to see him in the role of Manfred, Faust or Adam. His intelligent acting is not merely conceivable in roles close to his character. He is coping with the challenges of character roles, although, let me admit, that his Rozgonyi [in *A kard becsülete* (*The Honor of the Sword*)] is not a 40-year-old, cold, and cunning man.

There is a rumor about a theater director in Budapest wanting to hire Béla Lugosy. It is a pity for the Szeged audience, since they cannot understand why someone who received so few roles in Szeged so far, has to be moved to Pest. The director hiring him will make a good business for sure in the event he provides [Lugosi] with suitable roles. It is predictable that women will like him most, because women tend to appreciate his physical beauty more than the aesthetics of his acting.[12]

BECOMING DRACULA

During the 1910-1911 season, Lugosi took to the stage at least 163 times in a wide variety of productions. He truly became Szeged's leading and most popular actor. Gone were the bit roles and walk-ons, the insignificant supporting roles, at least for the most part. Now he assumed leading roles and major supporting parts. Along with Romeo, Lugosi portrayed such characters as János in *Az ördög*, John Shand in *Amihez minden asszony ért*, Count Armand Duval in *A kaméliás hölgy* (*The Lady of the Camellias*, aka *Camille*), Vronsky in *Karenin Anna* (*Anna Karenina*), the Archduke in *A*

Playbill for *Az ördög* (*The Devil*), performed in *Szeged* in 1910. *(Courtesy of the Károly Somogyi City and County Library of Szeged)*

sárga liliom (*The Yellow Lily*), and Count Danilo Danilovics in *A víg özvegy* (*The Merry Widow*), among others. And his performances spanned the full range of tragedy, drama, Hungarian folk plays, operetta, comedy and musical farce.

In an amusing aside, Lugosi terrified the audience during a performance of *A balkáni hercegnő* (*The Balkan Princess*), not by playing a vampire or other supernatural creature, but instead a "little scamp":

> Then, the dramatic-lyric hero appeared on stage… Lugosy, wearing a half-meter-long, more exactly a 49 and a half-centimeters-long necktie, which, I beg your pardon, had a

Balkan red color. He played a humoristic little role of a scamp, and he frightened the Balkan lords with his necktie. Unfortunately, he terrified the audience, too. What else shall we say?[13]

Lugosi received further praise after playing the title role in four performances of *A medikus* (*The Medic*) in the spring of 1911:

> Béla Lugosy, who appeared in the main role, created the character of the Medician in a

Published cast listing for *Amihez asszony ért* (*What Every Woman Knows*), performed in *Szeged* in 1910. *(Courtesy of the Károly Somogyi City and County Library of Szeged)*

The Szeged town theater.

strangely powerful way. His wrath was hovered over by poetry, his distress by comfort, and the indefinite, immature character he lent to the Medician predicted that he will not be able to commit sins. He only experimented with his own conscience. Later, his performance became much more mature than that of the premiere. The speech he addressed to the skeleton during the first and third acts was rather impressive, he was moving in the second act as well, while in the last act he depicted the struggle between father and son with real dramatic power.[14]

The troupe also made repeated use of Lugosi's singing voice, featuring him in at least thirteen operettas and folk plays with music. One popular operetta, *Narancsvirág* (*Orange Blossom*), performed three times in January of 1911, featured Lugosi in a romantic duet with actress Rózsi Felhő, whose character desires his kisses:

> I have thousands of suitors,
> Even more if I need more,
> All have quarrels,
> All have fights
> For my kisses.
> Today comes this one, tomorrow comes another one,
> Like spring comes after winter,
> All have quarrels,
> All have fights
> God knows why,

BECOMING DRACULA

:: KEDVENC VERSENY ::

I. *A kedvencverseny eddigi eredménye:*

Lugosy Béla	472
Felhő Rózsi	422
Várnay Janka	410
Kende Paula	394
Nagy Aranka	329
Tóvölgyi Margit	319
Lendvay Mici	253
Nyárai Antal	247
Almássy Endre	160
Csiky László	140
Fodor Ella	78
Békefiné	76
Pesti Kálmán	67
Sümegi Ödön	65
Mihó László	40
Juhászné	40
Békefi Lajos	39
Szücs Irén	34
Oláh Ferenc	22
Mezei Andor	20
Pécskai Vilmos	10
Virágháty Lajos	7
Anikó	5
Dobó Katica	5
Horváth Viktor	5
Rásó Ida	5
B. Almássy Julia	3
Koháry Pál	2
Koháriné	1

At one point, Lugosi topped the Szeged popularity poll, beating out all other actors and actresses combined. Published in *Színházi Újság* on March 12, 1911.

SZINHÁZI UJSÁG   19

Bérlet páros ¹/₃, páratlan ²/₃.

Pénteken és szombaton 1911. április 21. és 22-én este 8 órakor.

Ujdonság!   **A DÉLIBÁB**   Először!

operett 3 felvonásban, irta Sümegi Ödön, zenéjét szerzette Kun Richárd.

SZEREPLŐK:

Sirius király — — — Mezei	Ilma, a lányuk — — —	Békefiné
Narcis herceg — — — Békefi L.	Pomándy Béla — — —	Lugosy
Editha — — — Felhő R	Czésze) hivatalnokok	Virágháty
Brunó főudvarmester — Pesti	Luszter)	Koháry
Gorgon a herceg nevelője Baróthy	Guido. palotatiszt — —	Balogh J
Udvarhölgy — — — Rásó Ida	Irodaszolga — —	R Nagy
Petykó udvari bolond — Nyáray	Gépirókisasszony — —	Csige R.
Buchenheim Lipót — — Nagy D	I. Lakáj — — —	Pécskay
Kunigunda, a felesége — Juhászné	II. Lakáj — — —	Biró

Udvarbeliek. Vadonok. Irodaszemélyzet. Történik az I-ső felvonás Napkelet országban. A II-ik Budapesten. A III-ik Napkelet országban.

Published in *Színházi Újság* on April 16, 1911.

For all my little kisses,
God knows why.

Refrain:
Kiss me on my eyelids, Darling,
Kiss me on my lips, Darling,
The hour flies by fast,
Then someone else's turn comes.
Kiss my eyelids, Darling,
Kiss them, Darling, kiss my lips
Then leave, leave, leave me.[15]

Délibáb (*The Mirage*), a popular operetta performed four times in April of 1911, featured Lugosi and Dezső Nagy as a pair of marriage brokers, singing a duet about the pleasures and perils of their profession:

We are here,
Finally, at the finish line,
It was a long road
And a very tiring one.
We fiercely fought
Storms and winds
Till we arrived.
The noble goal
Of these good folks is
To find a husband and a wife.

Lugosi and colleagues, circa 1910. *(Courtesy of David Wentink)*

> If we succeed
> Even the Sun will brighten up,
> Since business is cardinal!
>
> Our business is arranging marriages,
> We are familiar with watching runaways,
> If end is good all is good,
> We will climb mountains and get through valleys,
> Our business is arranging marriages,
> If nothing else remains then run away,
> We will be the champions at the end,
> Wins the trick, wins the joke,
> Wins the cunning wit.[16]

Lugosi's talent with poetic dialogue and verse was not limited to the stage. He gave a recitation at a memorial for Lajos Makó on November 12, 1910, the second anniversary of the producer-director's death. Choosing a poem written by Sz. Vilmos Szigethy, Lugosi likely delivered it with much feeling and emotion:

> You believed that God sent us Art as His gift,
> You turned this house into a temple,

BECOMING DRACULA

Where pure hearts bring their offerings.
You were the guardian, and you'll stay here forever,
Your figure stands by the doorstep.
We bend our heads down, we take our sandals off.
Holy offering, float among us today,
When we light our candles dedicated to your memory![17]

In addition, Lugosi often lent his talents to other public appearances and celebrations. For example, along with poet Gyula Juhász, Lugosi was the main speaker in a "prologue" at a major event celebrating the Hungarian composer Franz Liszt.[18] Presented on May 13, 1911, the Liszt Ferenc Születésének Centenáriuma (Franz Liszt Birth Centennial) also featured famed Hungarian composer Béla Bartók in person playing a selection of Liszt works on the piano.[19]

Lugosi also continued to evoke strong passions from his female fans. Early in his tenure in Szeged, Lugosi himself made a request in a local newspaper, asking a reporter, "Let's make a deal! Please let me know the opinion – of women – about me."[20] The answer to his perhaps rhetorical question was evident in the many compliments later published in the local theatrical journals:

He is my favorite because he is so tall that one can only kiss him by climbing up a chair. Wow, that must be so… well… so tasty….

Darling, please make of yourself a photograph dressed like 'Prince Alexander' and send me a picture….

He must be terrific in the role of Adam!

Sweet thief of hearts! He is so charming with his wonderfully blue eyes. Not to mention his sweet dimply chin, oh! Sweet creature!

Ica, an enviable woman danced with him while I cannot even talk to him. Oh, my God![21]

[He has a] nice figure!

Beautiful Romeo.

Adorable Armand Duval.

He is my favorite because he was so sweet in *A sárga liliom*.

Have you seen him in the role of the Grand Duke? And you still ask? The knight of all ladies. These twenty pages have been sent to you by a charming little girl.

Sweet featherbrain.

Handsome boy.

I am envious about the actress playing the role of Judit.

Elegant Grand Duke....

No one is more handsome. [From] the beautiful women of Szeged.

Those who have seen him once cannot forget him. [From] a little girl from Szekszárd.

Your dancing girl from home, who has been thinking about you a lot, sends you 10 votes and thinks about you even more, most beautiful Béla![22]

Despite all the accolades, Lugosi was unable to put his unique spell on every female. A letter to the editor of a local newspaper conveyed what a few young women in the audience believed, that depictions of love on the local stage were unrealistic:

> Oh well! We are sick of Béla Lugosi already, and Tóni Nyárai sings to us in vain when we are banished from life. Because we want to know life! We attend high school because we are modern girls, and modern girls do not believe that the poet had not been thinking of the forbidden fruit when he had been writing what pure love was.[23]

Lugosi also occasionally ran afoul of critics, as in the case of his performance in *A víg özvegy*:

Thus, Lugosi, this lovable dramatic actor, played the role of Danilo. It is a pity that the ambition of his, which, in some respects is right, made him take such a false step. He does not know how to sing, or to play an operetta; his acting was disjointed and colorless. It is an unforgivable mistake

Bérletszünet.   Bérletszünet.

Szombaton, 1911. április 29-én este fél 8 órakor.
Biró Lajos előadása.

A sárga liliom.

Vidéki történet 3 felvonásban, írta Biró Lajos.

SZEREPLŐK:

A főherceg	— — — Lugossy	Bokor Adolf, kávés — — Pesti	
Thurzó Viktor, főhadnagy	Almássy	Czihás Péter, vállalkozó — Koháry	
Hessen Frigyes báró, főhad-		Rudas Béla, cipőgyáros — Balogh	
nagy	— — — Kállay	Zechmeister Mátyás, keres-	
Illésházy István gróf, főhad-		kedő	— — — R. Nagy Gy
nagy	— — — Virágháti	Zsivkovic János, bérlő — Nagy D	
Basarczy András, hadnagy	Sümegi	Rád János, főkapitány — Oláh	
Katolnay, ezredes — —	Mezei	A főispán — — — Baróthy	
A primadonna — —	Békefiné	Fiakkeros — — — Pápai	
Dr. Peredy Jenő, orvos —	Csiky	Emer — — — Várnay	
Peredy Judit, a huga —	Fodor	Náci — — — Nyáray	
Dr. Asztalos Kálmán, ügyvéd	Mihó	Lojzi — — — Pécskay	

Published in *Színházi Újság* on April 23, 1911.

from the director that he did not have enough force and expertise to stop [Lugosi] from experimenting, which, instead, should have been prevented....[24]

Nevertheless, Lugosi's confidence had grown to the point that on one occasion he responded to his critics. After hearing complaints that there were no high-quality performances in Szeged, he declared that "one must only look at [my] handsome figure and be convinced of the very opposite."[25]

To be sure, Lugosi continued to grow in stature during his stay in Szeged, particularly with the public at large. *Színházi Újság*, a local theater publication, ran a weekly "popularity poll." Surviving issues attest to Lugosi's popularity:

February 19, 1911	# 2 Male	# 4 overall
February 26, 1911	# 1 Male	# 5 overall
March 5, 1911	# 1 Male	# 4 overall
March 12, 1911	# 1 Male	# 1 overall
March 19, 1911	# 1 Male	# 2 overall
March 26, 1911	# 1 Male	# 3 overall
April 2, 1911	# 1 Male	# 3 overall
April 9, 1911	# 1 Male	# 2 overall
April 16, 1911	# 1 Male	# 3 overall[26]

Once he garnered the Number One Male Actor spot, Lugosi never lost it during the balance of his time in the city.

Near the end of the season, Lugosi also received particular praise from playwright Lajos Bíró, famed author of *A sárga liliom*:

Last week, Lajos Bíró held a conference in Arad – likewise in Szeged – before *A sárga liliom* was played. He said that, among theaters in the countryside, his piece was best performed in the theater of Szeged so far, and that's where the piece was also the most successful. This success – according to him – was achieved thanks to the outstanding acting abilities of Béla Lugosy. These few words, which Lugosy himself might happily want to record, are not mere words of appraisal, but a true evaluation of his acting abilities and theatrical intelligence.

Words of appraisal received from the author are of the highest rank for an actor. A character's personality, which has been conceived in an author's mind and which was born on the verge of dream and fantasy, is not often transmitted successfully through the eyes of another person. Béla Lugosy, whose fame has been spread across the country by Lajos Bíró and others, will join the Király Színház [Royal Theater] and the Magyar Színház [Hungarian Theater] under the directorship of László Beöthy, starting with next season. His admirers can say farewell to him during the premiere of *Anatol*.

I am not pleased to inform you about his departure. We would have liked seeing him more on the stage in Szeged. However, those who are invited to Budapest will certainly not stay in Szeged.

Unquestionably, Béla Lugosy can thank Szeged for much of his artistic development. This strong Hungarian city planted ambition, diligence, and self-criticism in his heart. Gradually, he left his bad acting habits behind. He kept fighting, analyzing other people's opinions, learning a lot, and practicing – and he found the real actor in himself.

His performance is not characterized by youthful ardor, but by knowledge, consciousness, reaching towards clear goals: they are pursuits of a strong man. Preparedness and background studies shine through all his roles, which are in harmony with his soul. This is the secret of his success. For actors of the countryside, these skills are inevitable. The actor must fill in the gaps left by the faulty direction, evoke the character of the author, and shape the character of the role at the same time.

Audiences in Szeged honored Béla Lugosy's pursuits with admiration. They understood each other, and so he rapidly became their favorite actor.[27]

Published in the *Dallas Morning News* on March 26, 1932.

Rumors that Budapest was interested in Lugosi came true. In March 1911, Imre Tóth arrived in Szeged to attend a performance of *A sárga liliom*:

Yesterday evening, Imre Tóth, director of the Nemzeti Színház [National Theater] in Budapest, watched *A sárga liliom* in the theater in Szeged. The scope of his visit was to find a *bon vivant* for the Nemzeti Színház. He picked Béla Lugosi, actor from Szeged, for this purpose. Certainly, there are only a few *bon vivant*-type actors across the country now. He could not have found any aspiring talent like Lugosi. Lugosi plays the role of the High Prince in *A sárga liliom* with such concentrated artistic quality that he did not leave any space for criticism. He recited the childish naïveté, the persistent stubbornness of the prince with utmost grace. He painted the ever-needy clumsiness of the sickly High Prince, his noble elegance, his charming ignorance with ever vivid,

BECOMING DRACULA

Lugosi dueling in one of his Hungarian silent films, possibly *Álarcosbál* (*The Masked Ball*, 1917).

but never too bright colors. Imre Tóth was impressed by Lugosi's acting yesterday.[28]

As his time in Szeged drew near a close, Lugosi continued to receive other accolades, with his admirers in the press using the spelling "Lugosi" rather than "Lugossy" or one of the other variants:

> Béla Lugosi, young actor in the cast, who will become a member of the Magyar Színház starting in the autumn, will say farewell to the public tomorrow in *Anatol*, which is the last piece to debut in this season, ending in two days' time. Béla Lugosi joined our theater only last September, but since then his acting skills made considerable development. He is a diligent, ambitious actor with a strong will and ability to learn. He is lucky to spend the early years of his career in the capital where he will have the opportunity to further develop his talents under the guidance of knowledgeable play directors. The audience liked him a great deal and encouraged him to accept challenges towards further success. Such successes were certainly made, and one can believe that the most successful period of his career is just about to come.[29]

Lugosi performed his final role in Szeged on May 20 and 21, 1911. He played Max in *Anatol*:

> The role of Max, Anatol's friend, was played by Lugossy rather skillfully. Lugossy, who is about to leave, was almost celebrated to death, of course, by the ladies (who gave him flowers and other, more useful gifts) in a demonstrative, enthusiastic, and ostentatious way. Not only does Lugossy have a nice figure, natural elegance, and lightness, but he also has talent, which hopefully will further develop in Budapest. I

emphasize the word 'but' because his latter quality seemed to be forgotten about amid the great celebration, during the enthusiastic farewell.[30]

The audience welcomed [Lugossy] with an ovation, applauded after each of his scenes, asked him to the front of the curtain many times and gave him as many flowers, wreaths, laurels and mementos as only prima donnas are likely to get. His farewell was full of enthusiasm, which testified that the young actor had many fans in the audience.[31]

Comes from Debrecen, goes to Budapest. Nevertheless, the year he spent in Szeged, while he self-controlled his own youth, means a lot in his personal development. His appealing looks were accompanied by excellent acting skills. His acting aims at providing acceptable, appealing role portrayals. Besides this, he explains the deeds of each character from a psychological point of view. In September, he will play on the stage of Magyar Színház in Budapest. We predict for him a great success. His qualities must find true expression there, too....[32]

Lugosi achieved great artistic and critical success in Szeged, success that paved the way to Budapest.

He had also made romantic conquests, as performer to audience, as lover to lover, and perhaps even as the other man. As the Devil declares in Molnár's *Az ördög*, "The real wife is the other man's wife." One account in 1932 claimed Lugosi fought seventeen duels with "jealous husbands, they say."[33] Robert Shomer recalled Lugosi saying that he had fought eleven duels in Hungary, adding "The only reason, I was told, that you fought a duel was if you were caught in somebody's bedroom with their wife."[34]

Whatever the number, some of Lugosi's duels could have taken place in Szeged, where he was indeed the romantic hero, onstage and off. Lugosi might have even become a better swordsman than Lajos Makó. But, as Romeo proclaims, and as suits Lugosi's piercing gaze, "there lies more peril in thine eye than twenty of their swords."

(Endnotes)

1   Lugosi, Bela, as told to Gladys Hall, "Memos of a Madman," *Silver Screen* July 1941.

2   "Vidéki szerződtetések." *Pesti Hírlap* (Budapest, Hungary) 12 Jan. 1910.

3   Sándor, János. "Szegedi Színjátszás Krónikája." Available at https://www.sulinet.hu/oroksegtar/data/kulturalis_ertekek_a_vilagban/a_szegedi_szinjatszas_kronikaja_a_koszínhaz_tort_1883_1944/. Accessed 12 May 2018.

4   "Színészet." *Békés* (Békés, Hungary) 11 May 1907.

5   "Színház – Rómeó és Julia." *Szegedi Napló* (Szeged, Hungary) 3 Sept. 1910.

6   "Romeo és Julia." *Délmagyarország* (Szeged, Hungary) 5 Sept. 1910.

7   *"Romeo és Julia." Szeged és Vidéke* (Szeged, Hungary) 3 Sept. 1910.

8   Cremer, Robert. "If It's Midnight – This Must Be Transylvania." *Famous Monsters of Filmland* 126 (July 1976).

9   "Színház – *Amihez minden asszony ért." Szegedi Napló* 21 Sept. 1910.

10 Kálmány, Béla. "Lugosy Béla." *Színházi Újság* (Szeged, Hungary) 30 Oct. 1910.

11 *"Amihez minden asszony ért." Mai Színlap* (Szeged, Hungary) 21 Sept. 1910.

12 Kálmány, Béla. "Lugosy Béla." *Színházi Újság* 30 Oct. 1910.

13 *"A balkáni hercegnő." Délmagyarország* 21 Nov. 1910.

14 *"A medikus." Színházi Újság* 5 Mar. 1911.

15 *"Narancsvirág." Színházi Újság* 22 Jan. 1911.

16 *"Délibáb." Színházi Újság* 23 Apr. 1911.

17 "Makó Lajos Szelleméhez." *Szeged és Vidéke* 14 Nov. 1911.

18 "Liszt-ünnepély." *Szegedi Napló* 14 May 1911.

19 "A szegedi Liszt- ünnepély." *Délmagyarország* 10 May 1911.

20 "Lugosy Béla." *Színházi Újság* 25 Sept. 1910.

21 "Lugossy Béla." *Színházi Újság* 4 Apr. 1911.

22 "Lugossy Béla." *Színházi Újság* 12 Mar. 1911.

23 "Szeged Összel – Leányok Nevében." *Szeged és Vidéke* 29 Oct. 1910.

24 "Kísérletek." *Délmagarország* 31 Mar. 1911.

25 *Színházi Újság* 19 Feb. 1911.

26 "Kedvenc Verseny." *Színházi Újság* 19 and 26 Feb., 5, 12, 19 and 26 Mar., and 2, 9 and 16 April 1911.

27 Kálmány, Béla. "Lugossy Béla." *Színházi Újság* 14 May 1911.

28 "Lugosi Béla és a Nemzeti Színház." *Délmagyarország* 16 Mar. 1911.

29 "Lugosi Béla búcsújátéka." *Szegedi Napló* 20 May 1911.

30 *"Anatol." Délmagyarország* 21 May 1911.

31 *"Anatol." Szegedi Napló* 21 May 1911.

32 "Lugosy Béla." *Színházi Újság* 21 May 1911.

33 Grandon, Robert. "Stars at Swords Points, All in Fun." *Dallas Morning News* (Dallas, TX) 26 Mar. 1932.

34 Quoted in *Lugosi: Hollywood's Dracula*. DVD. (Norman, OK: Spinning Our Wheels Productions, 2000).

Lugosi as Vronsky in *Karenin Anna (Anna Karenina)*. *(Courtesy of Jack Dowler)*

Chapter 6

Buda-Pest

In his play *Az ember tragédiája* (*The Tragedy of Man*) of 1861, Imre Madách wrote, "Winter and spring, each will find a place; Light and shadow will be near." In his epic novel *Anna Karenina* of 1878, Leo Tolstoy affirmed, "All the diversity, all the charm, and all the beauty of life are made up of light and shade." Light and shade, good and bad: this duality explains Lugosi's career in Budapest, a city itself comprised of two parts, two previous cities: Buda, on the west bank of the Danube, and Pest, to the east.

Before traveling to the capital city, Lugosi did have a remaining obligation after leaving Szeged. On May 22, 1911, he began a summer theater run in Gyula at the Erkel Ferenc Színkör (Ferenc Erkel Theater Circle). While there, he performed in at least twenty plays in the space of five weeks, many of them repeats from his Szeged season. He was Armand Duval in *A kaméliás hölgy* (*The Lady of the Camellias*, aka *Camille*) and the Archduke in *A sárga liliom* (*The Yellow Lilly*). And he was Count Vronsky in *Karenin Anna* (*Anna Karenina*).

He was generally billed as "Lugossy," but there were exceptions. He was "Lugosy" in *Zseni* (*The Genius*) on May 31, 1911, and "Lugosi" in *Sárga csikó* (*The Yellow Colt*) on June 4. The spelling of his name remained in flux, even if due to printers rather than his own strategy.

An amusing incident occurred during a production of *Othelló* (*Othello*) on June 17:

> We must mention Lugosi, too, who was handsome in the role of Cassio. To our regret, the performance was disturbed during the third act, by an outrageous, noisy intermezzo behind the scenes, which nearly caused panic in the crowded auditorium. As it turned out, a stand-in made a big jealous scene behind the sets. For his unprecedented behavior received the greatest possible, though much deserved punishment, namely, he was immediately dismissed from the company....[1]

Publicity called Lugosi's final major role in Gyula a "farewell performance."[2] The play, staged on June 27, 1911, was a comedy called *Bábjáték* (*Puppet Show*). A local critic responded:

[T]his old-fashioned, simple comedy was put on stage on Tuesday evening. Fifteen years ago, the audience must have watched it with great joy, but the theater-goers' refined taste does not find it witty, deep, or funny enough if we compare it to those pieces we are used to these days. Knowing the quality of the play, the performance was as good as it could be. Béla Lugossy is a talented actor and he will have a successful career alongside his artistic development.

He is not yet outstanding enough in those scenes which are filled with conversation. He played the role of Marquis Montklars [*sic*] in *Bábjáték* diligently, but he had performed much better in both *A sárga liliom* and in *Szent liget* [*The Sacred Grove*]. While he played excellently in the above two plays, in the one he chose as his [farewell]

Lugosi played Vronsky on the summer theater circuit in 1911 prior to moving to Budapest.

(Courtesy of the Collection of Theater History at the National Széchényi Library)

Gyulai Erkel Ferenc szinkör.

Ujdonság. Itt először. Ujdonság.

A t. bérlők felkéretnek, sziveskedjenek a **bérlet második felét** és a bérleti ösz-
szeg után esedékes 2 százalék pótdijat Dobay János könyvkereskedésében befizetni.

Bérlet 38. páros. Folyószám 47.

Kedden, 1911. évi junius hó 27-én szinre kerül
Lugossy Béla jutalomjátékául

BÁBJÁTÉK

Vigjáték 4 felvonásban. Irta: Pierre Wolf. Forditotta: Váradi Antal.

Személyek:

De Monclars Roger márki	—	**Lugossy Béla**	✖	De Jussyné	—	—	— Tóvölgyi Margit
Fernande, a felesége	—	Kende Paula	✖	De Lanceyné	—	—	— Szücs Irén
Ferney, Fernande nagybátyja	—	Nagy Dezső	✖	Durieux báróné	—	—	— Juhászné Ágnes
Nizerolles	—	—	Csiky László	✖	Brieyné	—	— Csikyné
Vareine Pierre	—	—	Oláh Ferenc	✖	Bonuiéres	—	— Mihó László
Valmont	—	—	Baróthy Antal	✖	Langeac	—	— Virágháty Lajos
Valmontné	—	—	Baróthyné Julia	✖	Trévoux	—	— Koháry Pál
Ganges herceg	—	—	Pesti Kálmán	✖	Szolga	—	— Ács Mihály

Történik napjainkban, Párisaan, az I., III., IV. felvonás De Monclars márkinál a II. Nizerollesnél.

Lugosi portrayed De Monclars in *Bábjáték* (*Puppet Show*), his penultimate performance in Gyula's summer theater series before moving to Budapest in 1911. (*Courtesy of the Collection of Theater History at the National Széchényi Library*)

performance, we can only say that he played his role fairly.[3] He received ovations, a rain of petals poured from the balcony, and from above, a wreath was sent off for him, while he also received two bouquets.[4]

Prior to moving to Budapest, Lugosi might also have appeared in a few productions in the town of Sopron, on the border between Hungary and Austria, but that has yet to be confirmed by primary sources.

Although Imre Tóth gave him the opportunity to appear at the prestigious Nemzeti Színház (National Theater) in Budapest, Lugosi apparently preferred the higher pay offered by the private theaters. He also probably believed he would have a better chance at immediately playing lead roles and large supporting parts. Due to the seniority system at the Nemzeti Színház, the older actors often were first in line for the better roles, regardless of their level of talent. Others, especially those newer to the roster, might have gotten the occasional lead, but usually they played smaller roles and even off-stage voices.

On August 15, 1911, the *Pesti Napló* reported that Lugosi had signed a contract with the Magyar Színház (Hungarian Theater) in Budapest, which had been founded by Szidi Rákosi and administered by her son László Beöthy. Curiously, the newspaper gave his name as Dezső Lugosi, which he was not generally using at the time.[5] Rákosi was one of the grand ladies of Hungarian theater, renowned as both an actor and a theatrical entrepreneur. Her son László had worked as a newspaperman before briefly heading the Magyar Színház and then taking over the directorship of the Nemzeti Színház in 1900. He resigned that position in 1902. Then he returned as director of the Színház in 1907, eventually buying it in 1916.[6]

Some biographers have claimed that Lugosi attended Szidi Rákosi's acting academy, either just prior to his September 1911 Budapest debut or earlier in his career, perhaps in the 1904-1905 or 1905-1906 theatrical seasons. However, the only documented reference to any Lugosi at Rákosi's academy was Jenő Lugosi, the actor, comedian and vocalist, who attended for approximately two years between late 1904 and early 1907. It seems previous writers have simply confused Jenő Lugosi and Béla Lugosi. This is easy to understand because theatrical trades usually billed Jenő simply as "Lugosi" while he was at the school. By contrast, newspaper reviews of his plays at that time definitively establish that this actor was Jenő Lugosi. Moreover, *Színházi Élet* later published a full roster of Rákosi's students.[7] Béla Lugosi is not listed, but Jenő Lugosi is.

MAGYAR SZINHÁZ.

Vasárnap este

Karenin Anna.

Dráma 4 felvonásban. Tolstoj regénye után irta Guiraud. Forditotta Góth Sándor. — *Személyek*:

Wronszky gróf	Lugosi
Karenin gróf.	Sebestyén
Oblonszky herceg	Kertész
Cherbatzky herceg	Réthey
Levin	Papp
Golinicseff	Tarnay
Tverskoj herceg	Kürthy
Szergius	Lakos
Karenin Anna	Báthori G.
Tverskoj hercegné	Csatay J.
Lydia Ivanovna	Zikó I.
Zsófi	Fábián C.

A VERY-puder használata folytán a bőrön felismerhetetlen zománc fejlődik.

I. felvonás. Wronszky gróf gárdatiszt mélyen szerelmes Karenin gróf feleségébe, Annába, de az asszony tisztességes marad.

II. felvonás. Wronszky keservében öngyilkos akar lenni. Anna elárulja magát, férje durván kérdőre vonja, erre Anna elzárkózik Wronszkyhoz.

III. felvonás. Wronszky és Anna boldogan élnek egy darabig Velencében és most visszatérnek Pétervárra abban a reményben, hogy Karenint majd válásra birják.

IV. felvonás. Karenin beleegyezett a válásba, de Wronszky már nem szereti Annát. Anna a vonat elé veti magát.

Lugosi's debut at the Magyar Színház (Hungarian Theater) is reported in this advertisement published in *Színházi Hét* for September 9-16, 1911.

As to being required to attend any acting academy before debuting in Budapest, it appears Lugosi was too busy with summer theater work to do so, at least until the end of June 1911. He was also well known as a regional actor. It seems unlikely that, after his successes in Debrecen and Szeged, he would have been required to attend any acting academy designed primarily for entry-level students.

Lugosi probably arrived in Budapest during the early part of July 1911 for a two-month preparation for the upcoming season. He resided first in Budapest's District VIII at No. 16 Déry Street on the Pest side of the Danube.[8] By 1914, he had moved to new quarters in District VII at No. 76 Rákóczi Street, also on the Pest side.[9]

When Lugosi arrived that summer, Budapest was still in its pre-World War I golden age and reigned as one of the most important cities in Austria-Hungary, in many ways the equal of the empire's co-capital, Vienna. In the census taken the year before, Budapest's population was 880,000.[10] By 1911, it had been for at least a decade "a modern city with first-class hotels, plate-glass windows, electric tramcars, elegant men and women [and] the largest Parliament building in the world...."[11] Electric street lights were rapidly replacing the old gaslights.[12] And then there were the Budapest women. Writer Gyula Krúdy observed:

> The city was blessed with its cult of women. The eyes of men trembled, the women were so beautiful: black-haired ones, as if they had come from Seville, and, in the tresses of the blond ones, tales from an Eastern sun were playing hide-and-seek, like the fireflies in the summer meadows.[13]

As a whole, the city population was a mix of Magyars, Jews, Slavs, and Germans. Its residents reflected a mix of respect for tradition in tension with new and liberal ways, the urban and provincial, the bourgeois with the feudal, all in a place "marked by rapid and even astounding change...."[14] It was indeed a modern and

Lugosi as Vronsky in *Karenin Anna* (*Anna Karenina*).

cosmopolitan city, no longer the "Buda-Pest" of old, but the "Budapest" of the twentieth century.[15]

According to historian John Lukacs, theater culture "ranging from the quality of the playwrights, the literary erudition of the directors, the efficiency of the stagecraft, and the excellence of many of the actors and actresses – was on a very high level."[16] Budapest was a city with not one major theater, but five: the prestigious Nemzeti Színház, the Magyar Színház, the Budapesti Színház (Budapest Theater), the Király Színház (Royal Theater), and the Vígszínház (Comedy Theater). The city was also home to the magnificent Magyar Királyi Operaház (Hungarian Royal Opera House).

Budapest thrived on both its artistic endeavors and its café culture. After the footlights dimmed, theatrical personnel gathered in the coffee houses. Writers, artists, actors, and intellectuals, even those with little or no money, practically resided at them. Sándor (Alexander) Korda once described the coffee houses as "universities" in which conversation formed an "essential part of Budapest's intellectual life."[17] Historian László Kontler wrote:

Lugosi as Vronsky in *Karenin
Anna* (*Anna Karenina*).

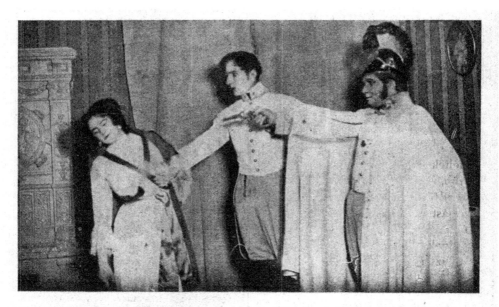

„Az élet szava." Az ominózus pisztolyjelenet. Az ezredesné — Haraszti Mici. Max — Lugosi.
Az ezredes — Kürthy. (A premieren ezt a szerepet játszotta Pártos.)   (Veres felv.)

As Max in *Az élet szava* (*The Call of Life*) at the Magyar Színház (Hungarian Theater) in 1911.
Published in *Színházi Hét* in October 1911.

[T]he quintessential 'second home' of the city dweller where he could expect to have polite company and spirited conversation, a game or two of billiards, chess or cards, or solitary immersion in the news of the wider or the closer world while refreshing himself with good coffee or just a glass of water, was the coffee house. Entire lives were spent talking politics, chatting, and disputing over artistic, literary, or everyday issues, or browsing newspapers and journals, even encyclopedias at these peculiar institutions, which numbered more than 600 in Budapest ... in 1896.[18]

Even without money, an actor could enjoy social life at these venues. As Mihály Várkonyi (Victor Varconi) recalled in his autobiography, Budapest "was famous throughout Europe for its spirit of generous acceptance and assistance in support of artists."[19]

At least in the short run, Lugosi's decision to sign with the Magyar Színház seemed wise. Beöthy had no qualms about placing Lugosi in a leading role for his Budapest debut, assigning him the part of Count Vronsky in *Karenin Anna*. The theater staged the play at least 21 times with Lugosi between its opening night on September 3, 1911, and its final performance on September 29, 1912. Also in the cast was future film director Mihály Kertész (Michael Curtiz).

Lugosi also starred in the major role of the Archduke in *A sárga liliom* on November 25, 1911. A decade later, a Hungarian writer in New York recalled the performance:

This piece was a great success in Budapest, which was played more than two hundred times at the Magyar Színház [during the theater's history]... Béla Lugosi's theatrical premiere in Budapest happened in this very play [sic][20]... Earlier, the same role had been played by Jenő Törzs, an all-time favorite of the audience of the Magyar Színház. There is no better proof of Lugosi's high-quality acting skills than the fact that he made such a great success after Jenő Törzs, that the audience did not let him go back to Szeged. ... This success turned him into such a phenomenon, that the Nemzeti Színház decided to contract him immediately [sic][21]... he worked at it until becoming one of the top actors in Hungary's most notable theater[22] thanks to his talent.[23]

Lugosi as Reginald Fairfax, with Lili Berky as Molly, in *A gésák (The Geisha)*, an operetta performed at both the Király Színház (Royal Theater) and the Magyar Színház (Hungarian Theater) between April and September of 1912. *(Courtesy of the Petőfi Literary Museum – Hungarian Theater Museum and Institute)*

During the autumn of 1912, Lugosi appeared in the play on eleven subsequent occasions.

Lugosi's greatest success during that first season in Budapest might well have been as Reginald Fairfax, the leading male role, in the operetta *A gésák (The Geisha)*.[24] After debuting on April 12, 1912, Lugosi and the show moved back and forth between the Király Színház and the Magyar Színház for 67 performances, likely due to Beöthy being the director at both venues. For the balance of his performances in the 1911-1912 season at the Magyar Színház, Lugosi never portrayed anything less than a major supporting role.

But then something strange happened. Lugosi's stage career appears to have come to a standstill after his September 29, 1912 performance in *Karenin Anna*. Except for a cabaret appearance at the famous Café Westend, there are no playbills or newspaper reviews that would indicate Lugosi acted at either the Király Színház or the Magyar Színház during the remaining months of 1912. He reportedly reopened negotiations with the Nemzeti Színház; however, at least by the autumn of 1912, those negotiations had not resulted in a contract.

Could Lugosi have appeared onstage as a bit player somewhere, or even an extra in a crowd scene? Though surely not his preference, that is possible. "It was wonderful training, hand in hand with wonderful success, because one day I played *Hamlet*, the next

Lugosi and the entire cast on stage in front of the set for *A gésák*. Lugosi is fifth from the left in the front row. Published in *Új Idők* on April 21, 1912.

I played a servant with three lines to speak," Lugosi once remembered, speaking about his time in Budapest.[25] And composer Gabriel von Wayditch, who left Budapest in approximately 1912, recalled seeing Lugosi as a "supernumerary, carrying a spear" in some play.[26]

No doubt Lugosi, with his passion for acting and his desire to work in the most prestigious theater in Budapest, was disappointed when negotiations stalled.

However, the delay opened the door for a different kind of passion, a role that would be as far removed from Dracula as any he would ever portray. Spring would overtake winter. Light would temporarily overcome the shade.

Closeup of Lugosi as Fairfax in *A gésák*. Published in *Új Idők* on April 21, 1912.

(Endnotes)

1   "*Othelló*." *Békés* (Békés, Hungary) 25 June 1911.

2   Despite *Bábjáték* being billed as his farewell performance prior to his move to Szeged, Lugosi did in fact appear in a supporting role in *A jómadarak* (*The Scoundrels*) on June 29, 1911.

3   When actors left one theatrical company for another one in a different town, they were ` often granted the favor of choosing the play for their final performance. The reviewer appears to be questioning why Lugosi did not choose a better play.

4   *"Bábjáték." Békés* (Békés, Hungary) 2 July 1911.

5   "A Magyar és Király-színház új tagjai." *Pesti Napló* (Budapest, Hungary) 15 Aug. 1911.

6   "Beöthy László." Magyar színházmuvészeti lexikonn (Budapest: Akadémiai Kiadó, 1994). Available at http://mek.oszk. hu/02100/02139/html/sz02/407.html. Accessed 14 July 2019.

7   "Rákosi Szidi jublileuma." *Színházi Élet* 26 Aug.-2 Sept. 1917.

8   *Budapesti Czim-és Lakásjegyzék.* (Budapest: Franklin-Társulat, 1913).

9   *Budapesti Czim-és Lakásjegyzék* (Budapest: Franklin-Társulat, 1914).

10   "Masses of People – The Development of the Population." *The World of the Habsburgs.* Available at https://ww1.habsburger. net/en/chapters/masses-people-\ development-population. Accessed on 14 July 2019.

11   Lukacs, John. *Budapest 1900: A Historical Portrait of a City and Its Culture* (New York: Grove Press, 1988).

12   Ibid.

13   Krúdy, Gyula, quoted in Lukacs.

14   Lukacs, *Budapest 1900.*

15   Ibid.

16   Ibid.

17   Korda, Michael. *Charmed Lives: A Family Romance* (London: Allen Lane, 1980).

18   Kontler, László. *A History of Hungary: Millennium in Central Europe* (New York: Palgrave Macmillan, 2002).

19   Varconi, Victor and Ed Honeck. *It's Not Enough to Be Hungarian* (Denver, CO: Graphic Impressions, 1976).

20   Lugosi had actually premiered in Budapest fifteen days earlier as Count Vronsky in *Karenin Anna*, also at the Magyar Színház.

5. Király-szinház. Magyar szinház.

(Igazgatóság : VII, király-u. 71. — Tel. 114—69 és VII, Wesselényi-u. 62. — Tel. 57—80.)

Igazgató : Beöthy László.
Titkár : Lázár Ödön.
Rendezők : Márkus László, Stoll Károly, Vajda László.
Karmesterek : Vincze Zsigmond, Marton Géza és Békési Ferencz.
Sczénikai felügyelő : Márkus László.
Ügyelők : Bérczy Géza, Karádi Elemér, Havy Lajos és Balázs Márton.
Gazdasági főnök : Leszkay András.
Gondnokok : Becsky Jenő, Zoltán Sándor.
Főpénztáros : Uhl Alajos.
Szinpadmester : Juhász József.
Díszmesterek : Mikolay János, Klein Béla.
Fővilágositók : Schlesinger Béla, Reinthaller Lajos.
Ellenőr : Czeglédy László.
Jogtanácsos : Marton Sándor dr.
Orvosok : dr. Salgó Ernő, dr. Torday Árpád, dr. Fleischmann Hugó.
Művésznők : Balogh Erzsi, Báthory Giza, Bera Paula, Csatai Janka, Erdei Berta, Fábián Czélia, Forrai Rózsi, Gerő Ida, Gombaszögi Frida, Halmi Margit, Kormos Ilona, Nagy Teréz, P. Tárnoky Gizella, Zala Karola, Tóth Irma, Váradi Erzsi, Zikó Ilma, Haraszti Miczi, Somló Emma, Lonrai Annie, Fedák Sári, Hudacsek Nelly, Berki Lili, Dobos Margit, Simonyi Maria, Somló Ilona, Soós Margit, Szegedi Erzsi, Dergán Blanka.
Művészek : Boross Endre, Csiszér Arthur, Dobi Ferencz, Gere Zsiga, Huszár Károly, Kertész Mihály, Kovács Andor, Király Ernő, Körmendy János, Kürthy József, Latabár Árpád, Z. Molnár László, Németh József, Papp Mihály, Pártos Dezső, Petheö Attila, Raskó Géza, Réthei Lajos, Rátkai Márton, Sáfrány Vilmos, Simai István, Szirmay Imre, Törzs Jenő, Tarnai Ernő, Tóth József, Toronyi Gyula, Thuróczy Gyula, Vágó Béla, Vándory Gusztáv, Hajnal György, Aszonyi László, Nádor Jenő, Lugosi Béla, Krasznai Elek.
66 tagból álló kórus, 12 tagból álló tánczkar és a Király-szinházban 38 tagu zenekar, a Magyar-szinházban 18 tagu zenekar, 25 nő és 25 férfi statiszta.

Company details for the Magyar Színház (Hungarian Theater) and Király Színház (Royal Theater), as published the *Budapesti Hírlap* of November 9, 1912. Note Lugosi is listed as a regular actor.

Lugosi in a photo taken circa 1913. *(Courtesy of David Wentink)*

21   Lugosi did not debut at the Nemzeti Színház in Budapest until over a year later when he portrayed Pontac, a minor supporting role, on January 5, 1913 in *A vasgyáros* (*The Forge Master*).

22   While Lugosi did become a favorite with some audiences in Budapest, he was by no means one of the top actors in the Nemzeti Színház. It would be more accurate to say that he was one of the most notable supporting actors as well as one of the highest paid newcomers to the Nemzeti Színház. Nevertheless, as his career progressed, he was given increasingly larger and major supporting roles as well as receiving lead roles more often than previously documented.

23   "A Lugosi-Elöadás a Legujabb Szenzációja Magyar Amerikának." *Színházi Újság* (New York) 1 Jan. 1922.

24   For a reference to Lugosi in *A gésák*, as well as a discussion of Japanese themes and art in opera and other formats, see: Dénes, Mirjam. "Shades of Japonisme in Hungarian Set and Costume Design by the Turn of the Century." in Tüskés, Anna, ed. *Hungary in Context. Studies on Art and Architecture in Hungary* (Budapest: CentrArt, 2013).

25   Lugosi, Bela, as told to Gladys Hall, "Memos of a Madman," *Silver Screen* July 1941. Emphasis in original. It is important to note that Lugosi appeared in *Hamlet* in Budapest, but never in the title role, at least so far as surviving documents and playbills indicate.

26   *Gabriel von Wayditch: The Caliph's Magician* (Musical Heritage Society: Oakhurst, New Jersey, undated). Some sources claim Wayditch left Budapest in 1911, but on his 1921 application for a US passport, Wayditch gave the year as 1912. Given that he was born in 1888, and that he even claimed to be conducting at the theater where he saw Lugosi, his anecdote, if true, must have taken place in 1911 or 1912.

Lugosi Béla

Postcard of Lugosi, the Hungarian stage actor. *(Courtesy of John Antosiewicz)*

Lugosi in a portrait probably
photographed in Budapest.

Chapter 7

The Passion

By the autumn of 1912, Lugosi's progress in the Budapest theatrical world was at a near standstill. Two months seemingly without work that year caused him to seek a unique role, one that would once again bring him to the attention of the Nemzeti Színház (National Theater). In mid-December 1912, a journalist told readers:

Since [Lugosi's arrival in Budapest], he was not as successful as anticipated; director Beöthy moved him to the Király Színház [Royal Theater]. He did not get a lead there either,[1] which caused certain conflicts between him and the theater, so next time he will appear on the stage of Budapesti Színház [Budapest Theater], under the directorship of Feld. ... The directorship of the Budapesti Színház chose Béla Lugosi for the lead [in *A passiójáték* (*The Passion*)].[2]

Contrary to the report, Lugosi had in fact played leading roles at the Király Színház and the Magyar Színház (Hungarian Theater). But those had come to an end. The Lugosi-Beöthy conflict might have resulted from Lugosi's desire for more leading roles, or perhaps from some other reason(s). At any rate, the Budapesti Színház cast him in what would become one of his most notable roles, Jesus Christ in *A passiójáték*.

Established in 1874 by director Zsigmond Feld on the Pest side of the city, the Budapesti Színház was originally known as the Fővárosi Városligeti Színkör (City Park Open Air Theater). Until 1899, the wooden-framed summer theater staged only German-language productions. Thereafter, the performances were exclusively in Hungarian. In 1908, at the cost of 250,000 crowns, Feld transformed the theater into a permanent stone structure that could operate year-round.[3] He used the venue primarily for operettas and low comedies. For him, *A passiójáték* was very much out of the ordinary.

By contrast, Passion plays had been a staple of theater drama since at least the 1600s. The most famous, performed every tenth year at Oberammergau, Germany was a memorial to both the life and suffering of Jesus Christ as well as to townspeople who had died during a plague in 1632.[4] This version emerged from a combination of a Passion play from the 15th century and a Reformation tragedy written in Augsburg, Germany by Sebastian Wild.[5] Lugosi's friend Lajos Bálint translated the text written by Father Hildebrand into the Hungarian language.

Previous Lugosi historians have credited the actor with a debut in *A passiójáték* at the Városi Színház (Municipal Theater) in Debrecen on or about April 15, 1916, for the Easter season. However, based on existing historical documents, this is an error, to the extent that there is now significant doubt that a Debrecen version with Lugosi ever took place. A playbill for an *entirely different play* exists for April 15, 1916, in the collection of the University and National Library of Debrecen, as well as for both the Western and Orthodox Easter weekends. A careful search of the published playbills for late 1915 through Easter of 1917 – which cover every day the theater there was active – do not show *any* performances remotely resembling *A passiójáték*. It is perhaps a comforting thought and a wonderful story, the possibility that Lugosi survived the horrors of World War I to portray the Prince of Peace in a triumphant return to Debrecen, but the available facts show that was almost certainly not the case. Indeed, the only known relationship between Lugosi and the play and Debrecen exists in the form of an original photograph that Lugosi kept of himself as Jesus; it is stamped Debrecen, but that could indicate nothing more than the location of where the photos were printed.[6]

As a large number of primary sources prove, Lugosi's debut in the play occurred in Budapest on December 21, 1912. A contemporaneous article describes how elaborate the production was:

Sublime sets which were designed for the Vienna Burgtheater, period dresses and machines for special lighting effects accompanying Pater Hildebrandt's grandiose work have already arrived in Budapest, and they are being assembled for the Budapesti Színház's stage under the surveillance of the Viennese scenic director. Parallel to the necessary on-stage constructions, the full renovation of the theater [where the audience is seated] is on its way, and thus, the splendorous stage will be in perfect harmony with the newly refurbished theater on the play's premiere ...

The directorship extended the number of heating machines so that in the future a mild, even temperature will fill in the theater. The uniquely large cast ... consists of 43 individual roles and on top of that another 110 people move on stage, which makes it one of the most monumental [productions] in terms of visuals, where all-new inventions of modern stage technology appear. The directorship of the Budapesti Színház chose Béla Lugosi for the lead, who has

Lugosi as Jesus Christ in *A passiójáték* (*The Passion*).

Lugosi in *A passziójáték* (*The Passion*), autographed to Lajos Bálint in 1913. *(Courtesy of Jon R. Hand)*

Published in *Délmagyarország* on December 13, 1912.

**Cast list and production details published in
Pesti Hírlap on December 29, 1912.**

been acting at the Magyar Színház until recently....[7]

The Budapesti Színházi is busy with the rehearsals of *A passziójáték*, directed by Aurél
[sic] Föld ... In response to the high interest towards *A passziójáték*, the directorship
of the theater releases tickets for the forthcoming dates from the start of next week,
which will be available at the theater's ticket office.[8]

Pesti Hírlap, a popular Budapest journal, published details for the production of *A
passziójáték* with Lugosi, which included full orchestral accompaniment:

The life, passion and death of Jesus.

Passion-play in 13 scenes, after the world-famous play from Oberammergau. Author:
Pater Hildebrand. Stage adaption by Oszkár Fronz. Translation by Lajos Bálint. Music
composed by José Bartoldy based on melodies by Bach and Haydn.

Entry into Jerusalem.
Betrayal of Judas.
Last supper.
Arrest of Jesus in the Garden of Gethsemane.
Jesus before Pilate.
Jesus before Herod.
In the robe of shame.
Crucify him!

Postcard of the Budapesti Színház, where *A passiójáték* (*The Passion*) was performed.

On Golgotha.

The crucifixion of Jesus.

Consumatum est.

The entombment.

The glorious resurrection and his ascension into heaven.[9]

The production with Lugosi was an unqualified triumph during the winter of 1912-1913, when it was staged 31 times. One critic declared, "The biggest and most deserved success was that of Béla Lugosi, who played the role of Jesus."[10]

Such publicity might have finally convinced Imre Tóth, the director of the Nemzeti Színház, to hire Lugosi. Indeed, Lugosi was still appearing in *A passiójáték* on January 5, 1913, the very day he debuted at the Nemzeti Színház in a minor role as Pontac in *A vasgyáros* (*The Forge Master*). He actually worked at both theaters until *A passiójáték* closed on February 2, 1913.

Lugosi's arrival at the Nemzeti Színház soon received two positive responses:

Published in *Budapesti Hírlap* on January 5, 1913. Lugosi debuted at the Nemzeti Színház (National Theater) in this play while he was still performing in *A passiójáték* (*The Passion*).

Lugosi in *A passiójáték* (*The Passion*).

Lugosi in *A passiójáték* (*The Passion*).

Imre Tóth recently employed a bunch of new, young actors who will [temporarily replace] the old actors on hiatus … Small roles have regularly been played by young and rather unskilled acting students so far, and the handsome newcomers will fill in these roles, among which some will not only be stand-ins at the theater, but will soon become artists who are capable of coping with more important roles, too. We have already introduced one of the new members, Béla Lugosi.[11]

The superb cast of the Nemzeti Színház has recently been reinforced with two new members. They are only new at the Nemzeti Színház though, since both are already old and dear acquaintances of the audience. It would be unnecessary to introduce … Béla Lugosi to the Budapest theatergoers… We got to know Béla Lugosi in the Magyar Színház some time ago, and recently he acted the role of Jesus in *A passiójáték* at the Budapesti Színház. … His performance proved that the Nemzeti Színház made a splendid acquisition by employing him. Thus, no doubt that the newcomers will soon be fitting into the experienced cast and they will become valued members of the community in their new home.[12]

Lugosi in *A passiójáték* (*The Passion*).

Nevertheless, Lugosi must have been disappointed with the Nemzeti Színház during the balance of 1913 and into 1914. Despite his success in *A passziójáték*, Lugosi played mainly small roles.

Between *A vasgyáros* and the summer break in early June 1913, Lugosi appeared in at least 21 additional productions. Ten roles were minor, and seven were average-sized supporting roles. Only two – Major Kadisa in *Az aranyember* (*The Golden Man*) and Gilbert Rivers in *A fogadott apa* (*The Adopted Father*) – could be considered major supporting roles. There is insufficient information to determine the size of his roles in the remaining two plays. As far as can be determined, there were no leads.

After the summer break, and for the balance of 1913, Lugosi appeared in at least twelve productions. Only two of those featured him in major parts, Malakov in *Bolondok tánca* (*Dance of the Fools*) and Lucien de Meré in *Az attaché* (*The Ambassador's Attaché*). The rest were small supporting roles.

Between January 1914 and the end of the season in mid-June, Lugosi appeared in at least thirty productions. Finally he was beginning to make an impact. Along with repeating his previous major roles in *A fogadott apa*, *Bolondok tánca*, *Az aranyember*, and *Az attaché*, he also played additional major roles like De Montegre in *A nők barátja* (*The Friend of Women*), Baron Várkövi in *Fenn az ernyő nincsen kas* (*The Tent is Up but There Is No Basket*)[13], and Jack Strahan in *Az igazgató úr* (*The Headmaster*).

Lugosi did receive a somewhat positive review for his significant part in *A nők barátja*:

> Today, Béla Lugosi appeared in a bigger role for the first time. He played De Montégre, the fierce lover from the mountains. He is a handsome figure with a warm voice, who had some great moments in the play, but they were only moments. Giving a half-caricature-like role to young actors is always problematic, since they do not yet possess such a level of self-sacrifice that would be necessary to make a laugh at themselves with dignity. Nevertheless, Lugosi is a promising [actor].[14]

Despite these advances, though, his remaining roles at the Nemzeti Színház in 1914 remained minor.

By contrast, the Magyar Királyi Operaház (Hungarian Royal Opera House) offered Lugosi a major dramatic role when it mounted a production of *A bethuliai zsidónő* (*The Jewish Woman*). The ballet opened on May 20, 1914, and was staged for an additional four evenings. There is

Szinházi műsorok.

	Magyar királyi Opera	Nemzeti színház	Várszinház	Vigszinház	Népopera	Király-színház	Magyar színház	Budapesti színház	Uránia-színház
Péntek — — —	Salome	Savitri. A lányom	–	Az ostrom	A sevillai borbély	Éva	A farkas	Passiójáték	A balkáni háboru
Szombat — — —	Lohengrin	Rosenkrans és Güldenstern	Az Erinnysek	Bella	Az igazgató ur	Éva	A farkas	Passiójáték	Az orsz. szin. akadémia zárodáss
Vasárnap délután	Tosca	Ármány és szerelem	–	d.e.: Mamsatos Poll, d.u.: Tatárjárás, este: Bella	Traviata	A mexikói sány Limonádé ezredes	A farkas	A veröshaju	–
Vasárnap este	Hoffmann meséi	Savitri. A lányom			Az igazgató ur	A minisztereinök	A vasgyáros		

Budapest theater schedule published in *Pesti Hírlap* on January 16, 1913.

BECOMING DRACULA

Kürthy György (Grantley Pelisse)   Paulay Erzsi (Portia)   Lánczy Margit (Antigone)   Lugosi Béla (Straham Jack)

Nemzeti Szinház. — „Az igazgató úr".   Wornitzer és Magyar felv.

LUGOSI BÉLA legujabb divatu elegáns ruháit „AZ IGAZGATÓ UR"-ban

HORVÁTH GYÖRGY URI SZABÓ DIVATTERME ☐ ☐ KÉSZITETTE ☐ ☐

VÁCZI-UTCA 36. SZÁM.

Published in the March 22-29, 1914 edition of *Színházi Élet*.

no evidence that Lugosi's character, Holofernes, was required to dance. Although he received good reviews, the overall production did not:

> The other two guest appearances and the reviews of them are very illuminating. One of them is that of Serafina Astafieva, who, after leaving Gyagilev's company, in her solo performance caused great disappointment to the Hungarian audience and critics. This fact highlights certain expectations, namely, that the artist should not only have a high level of technical knowledge, but also the ability of elevating her dance to an aesthetic value through the exposure of the human body, which is a characteristic of modernity. According to critics, Astafieva is a dancer not skilled enough, and her nakedness is meaningless.
>
> The failure was shared by the Operaház, given that it backed a substandard production with its full capacity, with all its dancers, and a full orchestra. This fact could not even be changed by the performance of the Hungarian partners of Astafieva, Ferenc Nádasi and Béla Lugosi, who received positive reviews.[15]

Lugosi, far right, as Baron Várkövi in *Fenn az ernyő nincsen kas* (*The Tent is Up, but There is No Basket*), a major role in a play staged in March of 1914. *(Courtesy of the Collection of Theater History at the National Széchényi Library)*

Színházi Élet, which had championed Lugosi after his successful run in *A passiójáték*, enthused over his performance:

> It is well known that the Operaház borrowed Béla Lugosi from the Nemzeti Színház for Madame Astafieva's ballet. … Lugosi, the young, promising artist not only excelled with his dramatic movements in the role of Holofernes, but he made a stir with his beautiful, tall and fair figure, too.[16]

Once again, as in Debrecen and as in Szeged, Lugosi impressed audiences as much with his looks and personal magnetism as he did with his acting skills, to the extent that the manager of the Operaház tried to lure Lugosi away from the Nemzeti Színház:

> Last time we mentioned that manager Sydow offered a contract to Lugosi. Now we can report positive news about this offer: Sydow is willing to employ Lugosi for 150 nights, paying him a hundred crowns for each night's performance and covering all his expenses. Béla Lugosi has not yet accepted his offer, but he takes it into consideration.[17]

Another scene from *Fenn az ernyő nincsen kas* (*The Tent is Up, but There is No Basket*) with Lugosi the second from the left. Published in *Új Idők* on March 15, 1914.

For reasons unknown, Lugosi did not sign the contract with Sydow. He remained with the Nemzeti Színház, probably due to its prestige.

But Lugosi could not have known that he would soon face a war much more discouraging than anything in his professional career, a war that would forever change his life and the entire world.

(Endnotes)

1   Lugosi played the male lead in *A gésák* (*The Geisha*) on many occasions in 1912.

2   "Lugosi Béla a Budapesti Színházban." *Délmagyarország* (Szeged, Hungary) 13 Dec. 1912.

3   "A Városliget Színházai." Available at http://mek.oszk.

Lugosi, standing behind the woman in the hat, in *A kölcsönkért kastély* (*The Borrowed Residence*). Published in the February 8-15, 1914 edition of *Színházi Élet*.

hu/02000/02065/html/2kotet/34.html and http://mek.oszk.hu/02100/02139/html/sz28/149.html. Accessed on 14 July 2019.

4   "History of the Passion Play." Available at https://www.ammergauer-alpen.de/oberammergau/en/Discover-History and-stories/Passion-Play/History-of-the-Passion-Play. Accessed on 30 Jan. 2019.

5   Ibid.

6   The photograph also bears the handwritten date of 1916. Primary research clarifies that the date is almost certainly incorrect.

7   "A passiójáték." *Az Újság* (Budapest, Hungary) 12 Dec. 1912.

8   "A passiójáték." *Színházi Hét* (Budapest, Hungary) 15-22 Dec. 1912.

9   "Budapesti Színház – Jézus élete, szenvedése és halála." *Pesti Hírlap* (Budapest, Hungary) 27 Dec. 1912.

10   "Passiójáték a Budapesti színházban." *Pesti Hírlap* 22 Dec. 1912.

11   "A Nemzeti új tagjai." *Színházi Élet* (Budapest, Hungary) 5-12 Jan. 1913.

12   "Ujak a Nemzetiben." *Színházi Élet* 5-12 Jan. 1913.

Fauszt (*Faust*): Lugosi's final documented performance prior to joining the military, from the June 14, 1914 edition of *Budapesti Hírlap*.

13   The significance of the title is that, when traveling merchants had no precious objects to display in baskets but, rather junk, they used a tent or covering on the carriage to conceal the poor state of their merchandise. This eventually became a proverb meaning someone who tries to show more than what he actually has.

14   "*A nők barátja.*" *Budapesti Hírlap* (Budapest, Hungary) 25 Feb. 1914.

15   Patonai, Anikó Ágnes. "Baletteloadasok a Budapesti Operahazban az elso vilagháború kitörése elott." Kappanyos, Andras, Ed. *Emlékezés Egy Nyár-Éjszakára* (Budapest: MTA Bölcsészettudományi Kutatóközpont, 2015).

16   "Astafieva asszonynak." *Színházi Élet* 24-31 May 1914.

17   Ibid.

Lugosi as a second lieutenant in World War I. *(Courtesy of John Antosiewicz)*

Chapter 8

The Great War

"No other treasure has the populace
than their own blood, which they
magnanimously, prodigally
shed for the fatherland."
– Imre Mádach

At the end of the 1913-1914 season, the Nemzeti Színház (National Theater) granted pay raises to a few select actors. Lugosi was one of them, his salary increasing from 1,000 to 1,600 crowns per month.[1] Nevertheless, Lugosi volunteered for service in the Hungarian military only two weeks after the outbreak of World War I. On August 15, 1914, the *Pesti Napló* reported that he was a Second Lieutenant in the Forty-Third Royal Hungarian Infantry of the Austro-Hungarian Army. For the time being, he was no longer an actor.

As a member of the Nemzeti Színház, Lugosi was exempt from military service. Why then choose so rapidly to join the army? Likely it was patriotism and a sense of duty, probably to fight for Hungarian peasants and laborers and an idealized "fatherland," rather than necessarily an obligation to the reigning Hungarian bourgeoisie or any potential dependence on Austria (or, for that matter, Germany, which was part of the Triple Alliance).

The Austro-Hungarian Empire, sometimes known as the "Dual Monachy," had formed in 1867, and had granted much autonomy to Hungary. Its ruler was the Austrian Franz Joseph I; the theater where Lugosi performed in Temesvár had been named for him. Following the assassination of the Archduke Franz Ferdinand, the heir apparent to the throne, the government declared war on Serbia in late July of 1914. Further declarations of war and military mobilizations came quickly, thrusting much of the world into turmoil.[2] It became the "war to end all wars."

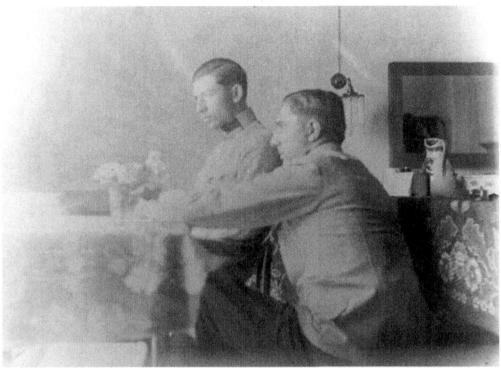

Lugosi and his friend Béla Rann in 1914, just before being deployed to the western front.

Lugosi might also have been spurred to volunteer for duty because of a woman. On at least five occasions in America, journalists reported a bizarre story about the "Woman with Yellow Eyes," whom Lugosi supposedly met on a vacation at the seaside resort of Abbazia, also known as Opatija.[3] The year was 1914, and if the vacation actually happened, it would have been in July, after the Nemzeti Színház season closed in June. Lugosi recalled:

> The first time I was introduced to her I broke out into a deathly cold sweat. My heart and pulse raced and then seemed to stop, dead. I lost control of my limbs and faltered in my speech. I was never happy in her presence. I felt always sick and dizzy and depleted. Yet I could not remain away from her.[4]

Articles on the subject variously claimed that she was a real vampire with pale skin and "tiny, pointed teeth, like fangs," or that she was a human vamp who maliciously inspired husbands to leave their wives.[5] In some accounts, she was nameless; in another, Lugosi knew her by first name alone, Hedy.[6] This woman, a non-Hungarian, allegedly gave Lugosi "the most exciting, the most mad experience" of his life.[7] She put her "mark" on him, emotionally even if not physically.[8]

These stories were fanciful, sometimes entering the realm of absurd vampire fiction. But Lugosi did allegedly say, "Only the fact that war broke out may have saved my mind." Perhaps in these tales a small degree of truth resides. Perhaps he had traveled to Opatija on

True Hollywood Ghost Stories

II---The Case Of The Man Who Dares Not Fall Asleep

By GLADYS HALL

MOLDERING grave-yards and shrieks in the night. The drip-drip-drip of blood. The odor of Death that comes from the secret places. A man with a pale green face and stretching hands. Ghouls. Unspeakable things. The worm that never dies.

A bloodsucker in human form —*Dracula!*

You have read the book, "Dracula"? By Bram Stoker?

You have seen the play of "Dracula"?

I have seen the—let us say the man, *Dracula.*

He is here. He is in Hollywood. He walks the streets by day with pallid face and preternatural hands. He works in the studios. He lunches at the Montmartre. He is to be seen in a forthcoming Corinne Griffith production, "Prisoners." Watch for him. Scrutinize his eyes.

By nights, he never sleeps. He never sleeps lest—but hush! S'h'h! This is another matter.

One I dread to tell lest this sleepless man—this man who cannot love as other men love—but hush! S'h'h!

You've never believed in vampires? You've thought them figments of disordered imaginations? Mordant fancies? You are wrong—there are vampires. In human form. Disguised by day. And dread beyond description by night. The fancy shudders away from the writing of such a tale. The flesh creeps and crawls. The little lonely human spirit whines in its thin envelope. It crouches in its pitiful lair and whines, as the banshee whines about the house of the newly dead.

ARE THEY EACH OTHER?

Dracula is Bela Lugosi.
Is Bela Lugosi *Dracula?*

Many men have from time to time been called male vampires. But Bela Lugosi is one in more than a figurative sense in the part which has made him famous—and fearful lest the fiction bring a dread reprisal upon him. Lugosi comes to the screen from playing the title rôle of "Dracula," the bat-like man who drew both blood and souls from his victims

Or is he himself the victim of a *Dracula* in—but of that, more later.

Bela Lugosi is intimately aware of vampires. For Lugosi comes from the town of Lugos, in Hungary. The black mountains of Hungary where dwelt Bram Stoker's awful hero. The black mountains where dwell those vampires who kiss human beings into a semblance of death. It is true. It is done. The mountain folk will tell you so themselves. It is done time and time again. Bela Lugosi has seen the very funerals of these vampired dead. And then, nights later, when they awaken in their dread resting places, the vampires who have marked them as their own—are waiting.

So often and so frightful is this practice that in the town of Lugos they keep their dead for days and sometimes weeks to make sure they have died the sweet death of the Church and not the horrible, half-death of the vampires.

I have said that Bela Lugosi comes from Hungary. No, no, no, he doesn't come from Hungary. He was driven from Hungary by a———. He fled the place, emaciated, a skeleton, drained of blood and nerve and sinew. He fled

(*Continued on page 86*)

31

Published in *Motion Picture* magazine in August 1919.

Gábor Ernő zászlós,   Zátonyi Kálmán zászlós,   Komáromi Pál hadapród,   Lugosi Béla zászlós
a Folies Caprice tagja.   a Vigszinház tagja.   a m. kir. Operaház tagja.   a Nemzeti szinház tagja.

Lugosi's military service honored in *Színházi Élét* on September 5, 1915.

vacation, and perhaps he had fallen in love with a woman who spurned him only days or weeks prior to the start of war. Perhaps.

At any rate, although support for the war was initially enthusiastic, the Austro-Hungarian Empire was ill prepared militarily. As historian Bryan Cartledge noted:

> The euphoria was short-lived. Successive defeats at the hands of the underrated Serbs and a disastrous campaign against the Russians in Galicia quickly brought home to the peoples of the Monarchy the harsh realities of modern warfare. Of all the combatants, Austria-Hungary was the least well prepared for war, partly because of the Hungarian Parliament's relentless opposition to increased recruitment to and expenditures on the common army without political concessions.[9]

The devastation on the battlefield and on the home front would have severe consequences to the country as a whole and to Lugosi as an individual.

Lugosi and his fellow soldiers were deployed to Galicia, a region that is now on the borderland of Poland and the Ukraine. Their campaign was disastrous. The objective was "to launch an offensive attack against Russian controlled Poland. Such a plan ended in a significant amount of deaths among the Hungarian army,"[10] with nearly two-thirds of the 100,000-strong fighting force being killed.[11]

Lugosi later found himself "promoted to ski patrol and sent to fight in the Carpathian Winter War."[12] Conditions there were extremely severe, with an estimated fifty percent death rate among the soldiers.[13] Octavian C. Taslauuanu, a Romanian officer who fought in the Carpathians, recalled some of the dreadful conditions that Lugosi and his fellow soldiers would have faced:

> The fighting in the Carpathians, because of the difficulties of the ground and the severity of the season, demanded the greatest effort and suffering of which our army

1. Gálosi Zoltán. 2. Gál Béla. 3. B. Baróthy József. 4. Kürthy György. 5. Gábor Ernő. 6. Leszkai András. 7. Loránt Vilmos. 8. Deréki János. 9. Krasznai Elek. 10. Csiszér Artur. 11. Lugosi Béla. 12. Thúry Elemér.

Lugosi's military service honored again in *Színházi Élét*, as published on December 24, 1916.

was ever capable. Those who have not taken part in it can have no idea of what a human being is capable ... Everything was wrapped in a mantle of snow, whose virginal whiteness soothed us and made our thoughts turn calmly to death, which we longed for as never before. The men dug coffin-shaped trenches, so that when in the evening I went to inspect them lying in these ditches covered with juniper, they looked to me as if they had been buried alive ... The men, despite the cold, lost no time in undressing to change their linen. I then saw human bodies which were nothing but one great sore from the neck to the waist. They were absolutely eaten up with lice.[14]

During his time in the army, Lugosi's experiences were nothing if not dangerous and disheartening. His stature as an actor at the Nemzeti Színház resulted in one of his injuries being reported in a Budapest newspaper.[15] And his stature as a soldier meant that at some point he was promoted to the rank of captain.

Lugosi was wounded at least twice: in the shoulder and in the thigh, and once with general head and body wounds caused by shelling and explosions. In 1936, an article also reported that he had been "gassed."[16] Then, in 1941, Lugosi claimed, "a bullet passed through my body and left me – *living*. Dracula, it has been pointed out to me, could not be killed by any means of Man!"[17] He also recalled seeing a "friend charge into a hail of machine gun fire. I [saw] his body slump over, suddenly changed from life to death."[18]

Just months after Lugosi rose to fame as a star at Universal Pictures, a newspaper recounted another of his wartime experiences:

He spent Armistice Day with his regiment, unable to get leave. But he did not care.

Gary D. Rhodes | Bill Kaffenberger

Lugosi in his officer's uniform. *(Courtesy of Bradley Wynn)*

Having fun with his fellow soldiers in World War I. Lugosi holds the bottle on the far right.
(Courtesy of John Antosiewicz)

His thoughts were still under the horror of what had occurred shortly before. His outfit had been under fire for four days, unable to get through to their own trenches. A traveling kitchen managed to creep up in their direction, and the men, ravenous from lack of food, made a rush for the wagon, oblivious of his warning.[19]

For a fan magazine article on movie stars who had fought in the war, Lugosi relayed further details of the same event:

I [saw] a group of men like dogs – tearing at the earth, looking for scraps of meat. ... There was a mad rush – discipline was forgotten. Those men, like animals, watering at the mouth, fought to reach the steaming pots. Then, a shell struck right in the midst of it all. Men, horses, and goulash flew in all directions. As soon as the debris cleared, those who were left, seemingly unmindful that other shells – hundreds of them – were whizzing overhead, got down on their hands and knees and grubbed in the mess for what they could find of the remains of the food.[20]

Twelve men died from enemy fire that day.[21] Of all of the stories printed in the magazine, Lugosi's was the most disturbing.

Along with vague mention of fighting near Serbia, Lugosi told another specific story to the press:

The Forty-Third on ski patrol. Lugosi is second-to-last in the middle row.

There was a moment I could never forget … We were protecting a forest from the Russians. All of us were cowering beneath huge trees, each man beneath a tree. A young officer, incautious, went a little way out of cover and a bullet struck his breast. I forgot the Russians were firing from their line with machine guns. Not a selfless man, I had one selfless moment… I ran to him and gave him first aid. I came back to my tree and found that it had been blown to the heavens, in heavy, crushing pieces. I became hysterical. I wept there on the forest floor, like a child… not from fear, not even from relief … from gratitude at *how God had paid me back for having that good heart*![22]

While recuperating in a military hospital, Lugosi reportedly convinced doctors that he was mentally unstable, thus securing his release from active duty.

Why did Lugosi want to leave the military? In his autobiography, fellow Hungarian actor Mihály Várkonyi (Victor Varconi) described the great disillusionment that many soldiers experienced:

I don't know if you can imagine the times – 1914, '15, and '16. Hungarians were suddenly called to National Service to fight with the Germans. None of us really understood it. We were told to serve with these great Prussian walruses who, by and large, we disliked, to go and kill people we never knew or held anything against. These new enemies were Russians, Slavs, and at least closer to us through bloodlines than the Germans. Yet we had to do it.

BECOMING DRACULA

Lugosi while recovering from his battlefield injuries.

... we were all under the ultimate command of the Germans. It was a rule of the time, a written order, that a Hungarian officer must always step aside, into the gutter if necessary, to let a German officer pass if the two were sharing the walkway. You can imagine how close this made us feel toward our German brothers.[23]

Lugosi spoke along similar lines, saying the First World War was a time "when the Hungarians hated their ancient enemy Germany and refused to fight on the Western Front against America and England."[24] He made that statement in the United States while American troops fought the Nazis, but it could have been his longstanding belief. War is always Hell. How much worse is it when a soldier fights for those he disdains?

Biographers have sometimes given March or April of 1916 as the date of Lugosi's release from military service.[25] But in a brief article about actors that served in the military, the March 25, 1916, edition of *Pesti Napló* strongly implied that Lugosi had been out of the service for some time.[26] On the very same day, the *Pesti Hírlap* confirmed Lugosi's long-term sick leave and his pending return to the Nemzeti Színház on April 1.[27]

The theatrical journal *Színházi Élet* reported Lugosi's homecoming in Budapest as triumphal:

We have been publishing a whole gallery of portraits in order to prove that a good actor can cope with all kinds of roles, even with that of the heroic soldier. We have a whole regiment of heroic actors who have achieved great success in different battlefields. It is true that many of them have paid a high price with their precious and young lives. That is why one feels a bit of an indecent joy whenever we hear that upon their honest duties, our beloved actors are back to their most prestigious vocation: the theater.

We happily announce here the name of Béla Lugosi, who in less than three years got himself into the favor of two different audiences in the capital city, just as he had been one of the most popular actors of the Hungarian countryside for a few years. After the Magyar Színház, he was quickly transferred to the Nemzeti Színház, where his outstanding qualities were soon evaluated with big roles.

However, the outbreak of war broke off this splendid young career for a good while, and on the first day of mobilization, Béla Lugosi was willing to do the hardest but perhaps the most important role. He fought for six months in the North and South. The elegant [and suave actor] turned into a bearded, mustached, grim soldier, who could be dreaming of the audience's applause only within the noise of machine guns.

In the sixth month, he got too close to one of those machine guns, whose noise is so much like applause, and heavily wounded, he was taken to a hospital in the capital. But after a few weeks spent there, he recovered and for the sake of variation, after the

Lugosi while recovering from his battlefield injuries. *(Courtesy of John Antosiewicz)*

Serbian and Russian fronts, he has recently been 'working' for many months on the Italian front.

Finally, it was his nerves which gave up working, for which he was hospitalized with serious illness. Now he is on permanent sick leave. What does a real actor do in such a situation? Will he be resting after two years of fatigue? No. Instead, he urgently requests a new job from his director. After all, it is quite clear that if someone's nerves are not healthy enough to listen to the noise of cannons, they can still listen to the applause of the audience, and instead of following higher commands they can successfully follow the instructions of the theater's director or those given by the director of the play.

So did Béla Lugosi, and of course, the Nemzeti Színház welcomed the talented artist who, before the war, had some great and valuable successes, promising for his future career. Lugosi, therefore, took off his military uniform and he even got rid of the winter jacket and Cossack fur-cap which he 'borrowed' from the Russians, in which he is depicted on one of the photographs enclosed here. He turned into a sleek, elegant, civilian man again, and the audience of the Nemzeti Színház will very soon be lucky enough to see him in this old and new form of his. Certainly, seeing him again will delight many who have liked Béla Lugosi in his pre-war performances, while he is much welcomed by the theater, too, where his colleagues got back an always honest, hard-working, useful and – especially – talented actor.[28]

Though it welcomed him back, the Nemzeti Színház did not give Lugosi any major lead roles to play.

And returning to civilian life did not mean the war left his thoughts. In 1936, he told an interviewer:

The world has had too much war, and so have I … I was twice wounded in the last one, the first time fighting the Russians in the Carpathian Mountains and next on the Italian front. I went into the war a lieutenant and I came out a badly wounded captain of infantry.[29]

As a reminder of that terrible time, he kept "a good luck charm … made from a Russian machine gun slug which wounded him during the world war."[30]

Lugosi's time in the service no doubt left him scarred in many ways, both physically and emotionally. Though the American Psychiatric Association did not recognize Post Traumatic Stress Disorder (PTSD) until 1980, it was merely the renaming of a condition long a part of human history.[31] The aftereffects experienced by soldiers due to the intense fighting during World War I, for example, resulted in the coining of the term "shell shock."[32] Two different articles – one published in 1936 and the other in 1944 – claimed Lugosi had suffered from shell shock.[33]

To what extent the war may have affected Lugosi is uncertain, but some things are known. It left him with damaged nerves in his leg, which in turn led to the sciatica and, eventually, the medically induced drug addiction that plagued him. But it also left him with a sincere and long-lasting empathy for war veterans. From performing in shipboard cabaret cruises and hospital concerts in support of wounded Hungarian veterans in post-war Budapest, to performing *Dracula–The Vampire Play* for the American troops during World War II, to visiting wounded war veterans during his summer stock performances near the end of his career, he never forgot the veterans. Or his own military service.

In Bram Stoker's novel *Dracula* (1897), the vampire count explains, "The warlike days are over. Blood is too precious a thing in these days of dishonourable peace; and the glories of the great races are as a tale that is told."

(Endnotes)

1   "Színház. Zene. Pletykálkodás." *Az Újság* (Budapest, Hungary) 28 June 1914.

2   Kontler, László. *A History of Hungary* (New York: Palgrave Macmillan, 2002).

3   Chrisman, J. Eugene. "Masters of Horror – Karloff and Lugosi." *Modern Screen* Apr. 1932.

4   Hall, Gladys. "Do You Believe This Story?" *Modern Screen* June 1935.

5   Hall, Gladys. "The Case of the Man Who Dares Not Fall Asleep." *Motion Picture* Aug. 1929.

6   Chrisman, "Masters of Horror."

7   Lugosi, Bela, as told to Gladys Hall, "Memos of a Madman," *Silver Screen* July 1941. Emphasis in original.

8   Finn, Elsie. "Beauty Hung a Hex Sign on Bela Lugosi." *Philadelphia Record* 9 Apr. 1944.

9   Cartledge, Bryan. *The Will to Survive – A History of Hungary* (London: Hurst and Company, 2006).

10   Pourclaux, Andrew. "Dracula in the Trenches: When Bela Lugosi Served in WWI." *Vintage News* Available at: https://www.thevintagenews.com/2018/10/21/bela-lugosi-served-in-ww1/. Updated on 21 Oct. 2018. Accessed on 12 Jan. 2019.

11   "The Real Terror In Transylvania – Bela Lugosi On The Eastern Front." Available at: https://europebetweeneastandwest.wordpress.com/2013/11/29/the-real-terror-in-transylvania-bela-lugosi-on-the-eastern-front/. Updated 29 Nov. 2013. Accessed 12 Jan. 2019.

12   Pourclaux, "Dracula in the Trenches."

13   Ibid.

14   "The Real Terror In Transylvania."

15   "Elesett és megsebesült önkéntesek." *Magyarország* (Budapest, Hungary) 16 Dec. 1914.

16   Harrison, Paul. "In Hollywood." *Wisconsin Rapids Daily Tribune* (Wisconsin Rapids, WI) 28 Feb. 1936.

17   Lugosi, Bela, as told to Gladys Hall. Emphasis in original.

18   Ergenbright, Eric. "The Man Who Knows Too Much!" *Screen Play* July 1932.

19   Tildesley, Alice. "13 Years Ago *Over There*." *Seattle Times* (Seattle, WA) 8 Nov. 1931.

20   Wilson, Harry D. "The Movie Heroes of the World War." *Motion Picture* Dec. 1931.

21   Tildesley, "13 Years Ago *Over There*."

22   Lugosi, Bela, as told to Gladys Hall. Emphasis in original.

23   Varconi, Victor and Ed Honeck. *It's Not Enough to Be Hungarian* (Denver, CO: Graphic Impressions, 1976).

24   Caldwell, Lily May. "Boogieman Bela Lugosi Here – But He Really Is a Nice Guy." *Birmingham News* (Birmingham, AL) 5 Feb. 1944.

25   The authors undertook great effort to obtain Lugosi's military records, both from Budapest and Vienna, but they were apparently lost years ago, making it difficult to determine the exact date of Lugosi's enlistment or discharge.

26   "Budapesti színészek a fronton." *Pesti Napló* (Budapest, Hungary) 25 Mar. 1916.

27   "A haretérről visszatért színesz." *Pesti Hírlap* (Budapest, Hungary) 25 Mar. 1916.

28   "Lugosi Béla." *Színházi Élet* (Budapest, Hungary) 2-9 Apr. 1916.

29   Hazen, David W. "Bela Lugosi Famous in Hungary as Actor Before Entering Movies." *The Oregonian* (Portland, OR) 17 Feb. 1936.

30   "Carries Slug for Luck." *South Bend Tribune* (South Bend, IN) 3 Jan. 1939.

31   Davidson, Jonathan R. T. M.D.; Stein, Dan. J., M.D., Ph.D.; Shalev, Arieh Y., M.D.; and Yehuda, Rachel, Ph.D. "Posttraumatic Stress Disorder: Acquisition, Recognition, Course, and Treatment." *The Journal of Neuropsychiatry and Clinical Neurosciences* (Durham, NC: Duke University Medical Center, Spring 2004).

32   Corvalan, Juan C., M.D. and Klein, David, Psy.D. "PTSD: Diagnosis, Evolution and Treatment of Combat-Related Psychological/Psychiatric Injury." *Missouri Medicine* (Jefferson City, MO: Missouri State Medical Association, July-Aug. 2011).

33   Harrison, "In Hollywood"; Finn, "Beauty Hung a Hex Sign on Bela Lugosi."

Publicity still of Lugosi in *The Black Cat* (1934).
(Courtesy of John Antosiewicz)

Chapter 9

Returned

Perhaps the closest the public will ever come to seeing the effect of World War I on Béla Lugosi is in Universal's *The Black Cat* (1934). In one of the opening scenes, Lugosi's character Vitus Werdegast recalls his time in the military and his life as a prisoner of war. Raw emotion from Lugosi's real-life experience informs his performance. "I have returned," he famously declares in a manner that might be as much about Lugosi's own life as Werdegast's.

During Lugosi's year and a half away from Budapest, other actors had moved up in the ranks. While he did not have to start from scratch when he returned to the Nemzeti Színház (National Theater) on April 1, 1916, it still took time to rebuild his career and regain momentum.

Despite the fact that the Nemzeti Színház never fully utilized his talents, his impact on Budapest audiences, particularly women, was positive. Reminiscing about her early work in the Hungarian theater, actress Oly Szokolay once said:

> I don't really remember with whom I fell in love the first time. Oh my God, it happened such a long time ago … but now I remember! It was Béla Lugosi, at the Nemzeti Színház. I was only 12 years old, but I was undoubtedly in love with him. I was playing the role of a slave girl who was his lover, and you can imagine how well I was playing that role. I even wanted to jump off from the second floor. For him. It lasted for a month. After that, I never fell in love with anyone. Instead, from that time on, people were falling in love with me.[1]

During the period from 1916 to 1919, Lugosi's profile with the Nemzeti Színház resumed its pace and continued to grow, but he was still assigned a considerable number of small supporting roles. For example, in *Az ember tragédiája* (*The Tragedy of Man*) on January 19, 1917 (and for an additional eleven performances that year), he played three minor parts; at

Lugosi, the Hungarian theater actor.

Lugosi and friends, circa 1916.

regional theaters, he had earlier portrayed the lead role of Adam.

Lugosi gradually received opportunities to showcase himself in larger roles, usually winning praise from the Budapest critics. On October 19, 1916, he played De Montegre in *A nők barátja* (*The Friend of Women*), repeating the same on several occasions in 1917. He also had a major supporting role in *Maria Magdolna*, which opened on May 19, 1917. Later that same year, he played the title role in *Árva László Király* (*Lonely King* László).

In 1918, Lugosi continued to show some measure of progress. He played an important supporting role as Kadisa in *Az aranyember* (*The Golden Man*), which opened on January 3. On April 7, he portrayed Armand Duval in *A kaméliás hölgy* (*The Lady of the Camellias*, aka *Camille*), a role well known to him from his regional theater days. After having portrayed Varville the first two nights, he took over Duval from such established actors as Károly Mihályfi and Árpád Ódry. At least one reviewer was impressed:

Béla Lugosi, the talented young artist of the Nemzeti Színház, played the role of Armand Duval... for the first time [in Budapest] yesterday afternoon. It was not a minor task... and we are glad to acknowledge that Lugosi solved the difficult task in an excellent way. His acting was powerful, masculine, disciplined and tasteful in dramatic outbreaks and most importantly: interesting all the while. The audience appreciated all the beauty of the new Armand Duval and applauded vividly for Lugosi during the whole performance.[2]

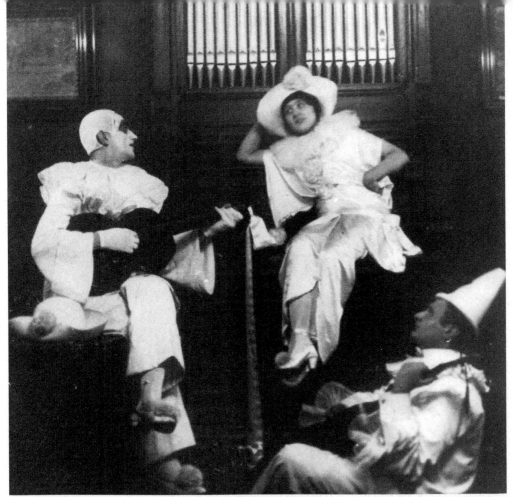

Lugosi in Hungary, appearing in some type of cabaret show.

BUDAPEST.   Nemzeti szinház. — Nationaltheater. — Théatre National.

The Nemzeti Színház (National Theater) in Budapest, from the era in which Lugosi played on its famed stage.

RÁKOSI SZIDI, VÁRADI ARANKA LUGOSSY BÉLA, LÁNCZY MARGIT
Nemzeti Szinház: Görögtüz.   *Papp Rezső fölv.*

Lugosi had a major role in *Görögtűz* (*Greek Fire*). Published in the May 12-19, 1918 issue of *Színházi Élét*.

In the case of *Árva László Király*, the lead actor took ill, thus providing Lugosi another chance to take over the main role from a popular older actor and make it his own:

Árpád Ódry's passing illness called Béla Lugosi to the front, who has been mostly in the reserve so far. Tonight, while playing the role of László Hunyadi ... the handsome, masculine actor with a pleasant voice proved that he will be suitable for similar, more prominent roles, too. In case the theater gives him the chance to polish his noticeably rusty abilities, to learn a more natural way of speaking, to make his movements smoother and his outbursts more tempered. Even in this style, his personification of Hunyadi was an interesting one, an independent character study which was quite different from [Ódry's], as if he had been overly conscious about its originality. The audience, which still fills up the rows of the theater each time the magnificent tragedy of Ferenc Herczeg is being played, welcomed Lugosi with delight, and applauded for him ... Her Royal Highness Princess Sophia and His Royal Highness Prince László, too, watched the performance from the royal box.[3]

In May 1918, Lugosi played a prominent role in the comedy *Görögtűz* (*Greek Fire*). Despite mixed critical reviews, Lugosi's favorite character type, the romantic lover, clearly showed through:

> The casting turned out to be unfortunate... The protagonists, Aranka Várady and Béla Lugosi are out of [place] in their roles. The one is incapable of convincing us about her artistic and feminine excellence despite her intelligent acting, and the other, being an elegant and pleasant stage figure, shows no trace of such a superior intelligence, which would be required by the character he plays.[4]

> Béla Lugosi has a handsome appearance, his dress-coat fits his slim figure as if it were cast on him, and the auditorium sighs aloud at his sight. But is there anyone who believes that this otherwise pleasing actor is a university

Lugosi with Szidi Rákosi in *Görögtűz* (*Greek Fire*). Published in *Vasárnapi Újság* on May 12, 1918.

professor from Geneva as a civilian? No. He remains a handsome, Hungarian heroic lover throughout the show. And the core of the role he plays is that he only pretends to be someone from the countryside, and under the surface, he is the professor of 'experimental psychology,' a European scholar from head to toe. No wonder when his true character is revealed, not only the characters of the play are astonished, but also we, the viewers, are as well, although we should have figured it out long ago, we should have believed it long ago.[5]

The success of the performance must be evenly shared between the author and the performers. First of all, Aranka Várady and Béla Lugosi, who played the lovers in a natural and casual way, with well-balanced acting.[6]

Then, later in 1918, Lugosi reprised his major role as De Montegre in *A nők barátja*.

Lugosi's tenure at the Nemzeti Színház became an important component of his Hungarian career. While true he never played the sheer number of leading roles that he had in Debrecen or Szeged, it is crucial to consider existing barriers that he had to face. The seniority system at the Nemzeti Színház meant that no actor, no matter how popular, would play lead roles

Lugosi Béla
A NEMZETI SZINHÁZ
TAGJA.

regularly unless they were among the longest-serving members of the company.

Though Lugosi would remain active at the Nemzeti Színház until he left Hungary in June of 1919, the number of his stage appearances, whether in supporting roles or the occasional lead, decreased noticeably. There were two primary causes. First was Lugosi's increasing involvement in union politics that eventually led to national politics. And then there was his work in the rapidly growing Hungarian film industry.

Lugosi not only tried to rebuild his career after his military service, but he also tried to construct part of it anew.

(Endnotes)

1   "Szokolay Oly." *Színházi Élet* (Budapest, Hungary) 11-17 Apr. 1926.

2   "Lugosi Béla." *Az Újság* (Budapest, Hungary) 9 Apr. 1918.

3   "Nemzeti Színház." *Budapesti Hírlap* (Budapest, Hungary) 14 Mar. 1918.

4   Schöpflin, Aladár. "Színház." *Vasárnapi Újság* (Budapest, Hungary) 12 May 1918.

5   Kosztolányi, Desző. *"Görögtűz."* *Pesti Napló* (Budapest, Hungary) 4 May 1918.

6   Keszler, József. *"Görögtűz."* *Az Újság* 4 May 1918.

Lugosi and Ila Lóth in a Hungarian silent
film, possibly *Leoni Leo* (*Leo Leoni, 1917*).

Chapter 10

Arisztid Olt

Béla Lugosi achieved his greatest fame as a film star at Universal Pictures in Tod Browning's *Dracula* (1931). During the early thirties, when Lugosi appeared in subsequent horror movies, Universal's logo featured an airplane circling the globe, flying higher and farther than even Charles Lindbergh could have dreamed. The image is wonderfully absurd, an enormous plane in outer space. But it speaks to the global potential of the cinema, as does the very name "Universal." Film could traverse borders, geographical and political, to inform and delight audiences everywhere on the planet.

Before the rise of the talkies, the international reach of the cinema was particularly evident. Silent films faced no language barrier. Intertitles could easily be translated and replaced, while the images remained the same. No dubbing was required. Here was pantomime that needed no translation. In Shakespeare's *As You Like It*, one character declares, "All the world is a stage." In the early twentieth century, all the world became a movie theater, with film directors in so many countries vying for their work to be screened internationally. One of them was the Hungarian Alfréd Deésy.

Deésy began his career as an actor in rural theater troupes. Finding his way to Budapest, he acted in several plays and films before turning exclusively to film directing.[1] Lugosi knew him from their days together in Debrecen; it was Deésy who convinced Lugosi to try film acting. On the one hand, some theater actors of the period looked down on the cinema. On the other, Lugosi's slow pace of advancement at the Nemzeti Színház (National Theater) may well have convinced him to take Deésy's advice in 1917.

By that time, the cinema had been a part of life in Budapest for two decades. Historian Gyöngyi Balogh noted:

> It was the famous Lumière Company which started to show films regularly from May 10, 1896, in the coffee house of the Hotel Royal in Budapest. The entrance fee

was 50 pence and there were several screenings daily. Within twelve months, other Budapest cafés had taken on cinematography and by 1897 other towns had followed suit. The subjects of the first café-projections were cheap, canned, international sensations featuring exotic landscapes, important events, comic scenes and famous beauties. However, in the first decade of the new century the Hungarian movie-theater business became independent and moving pictures started to be shown on their own, rather than as elements of variety shows.

The first non-newsreel Hungarian film, *A Tánc* [*The Dance*], directed by Béla Zitkovszky, was made at the Uránia Hungarian Scientific Theater, a venue opened in 1900 by the 'Uránia Scientific Society' so that its educational lectures could be

Advertisement for Star's 1917-18 season, as published in *Mozgófenykép Hiradó*.

illustrated by moving pictures. *Dance* was made to illustrate a lecture on dancing given by the well-known writer and politician, Gyula Pekár. It was shot on the roof terrace of the Uránia and featured stage stars of the period in short sketches.[2]

During 1907-1908, the term "mozi," meaning a "moving picture theater," came into common parlance.[3] The numbers of these establishments grew rapidly. Historian Zsolt Nagy observed:

By 1912 there were 270 permanent movie theaters in Hungary. By the eve of the First World War there were 108 cinemas in Budapest alone. The first Hungarian film studio, Hunnia, was built in 1911/12. ... Two of the first Hungarian narrative films or dramatic art films were the 1912 *Nővérek* (*Sisters*) and *Ma és holnap* (*Today and Tomorrow*). Others soon followed. By the end of the First World War there were over two dozen film studios at work and between 1914 and 1918, they released well over 250 pictures....[4]

The year 1918 became the peak period of production. Literary classics and bestsellers formed an important part of the source material used by filmmakers. Balogh explained:

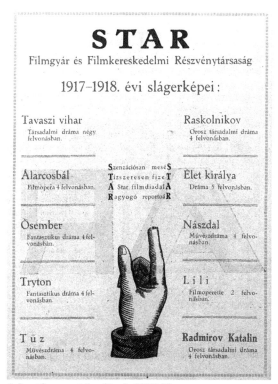

STAR

Filmgyár és Filmkereskedelmi Részvénytársaság

1917–1918. évi slágerképei:

Tavaszi vihar Társadalmi dráma négy felvonásban.	**Raskolnikov** Orosz társadalmi dráma 4 felvonásban.
Álarcosbál Filmopera 4 felvonásban.	**Élet királya** Dráma 5 felvonásban.
Ösember Fantasztikus dráma 4 felvonásban.	**Nászdal** Művészdráma 4 felvonásban.
Tryton Fantasztikus dráma 4 felvonásban.	**Lili** Filmoperette 2 felvonásban.
Tüz Művészdráma 4 felvonásban.	**Radmirov Katalin** Orosz társadalmi dráma 4 felvonásban.

Advertisement for Star's 1917-18 season, as published in *Mozihét Kino-Woche* in April 1918.

Apart from the dream-factory type of movies, 'literary films' were also very important. Hungarian silent film was more closely linked to world literature – as well as contemporary Hungarian literature – than the later sound pictures would ever be. The prestige of the new artistic genre seemed to be heightened if it was based on a recognized literary work. The [films] mainly used classics of the 19th century (writers and poets like Mihály Vörösmarty, János Arany, Mór Jókai, József Eötvös, Kálmán Mikszáth) or well-known contemporary writers (Zoltán Ambrus, Mihály Babits, Sándor Bródy, Ferenc Herczeg, Ferenc Molnár, Gyula Pekár). Prestigious films based on world classics were hardly a rarity (Andersen, Balzac, Victor Hugo, Émile Zola, Tolstoy, Chekhov, Gorky). ... films trying to attract huge audiences were often based on foreign best-selling books (Elinor Glyn, Gaston Leroux, Georges Ohnet).[5]

Despite the reliance on well-known literature, most Hungarian silent films did not find an audience in America. A reporter later spoke to Lugosi about this fact:

> [Lugosi] tells some interesting things about pictures in Hungary. There are about fifty producing companies there. And twelve of them make good pictures. They are not the type that register well over here, he says. They are behind the Germans in technique. The war left them in even a greater predicament as regards to equipment for production. They are beginning all over again where they had left off in 1914.[6]

And Lugosi was a part of that movement. During 1917 and 1918, he appeared in at least eight Hungarian silent features, as well as one short subject. These marked the beginning of his legendary film career.

The Star Film Company

The bulk of Lugosi's Hungarian screen roles took place at the Star Film Company. It was a major studio with output to match.[7] Located on the outskirts of Budapest, its facilities included ten major buildings.[8] Within the first eighteen months of operation, the company

Advertisement for Star Film players, as published in *Mozihét Kino-Woche* in 1918.

MŰVÉSZEK!

A Star filmgyár szinészei, bár egy-részük a legelőkelőbb fővárosi szin-házak ismert tagjai, egészen uj, in-ternácionális hangzásu nevekkel je-lennek meg a Star-filmeken és inter-nácionális szinvonalon álló játék-müvészettel — nem pedig más té-ren szerzett reklámmal — teszik értékessé filmalakitásaikat. A Star-filmgyár az első Magyarországon, amely állandóan szerződtetett saját társulatával játszat el minden sze-repet. Ez a magyarázata annak a stilszerü és kiváló összjátéknak, amellyel a Star-filmek már eddig is ☙ ☙ ☙ ☙ kitüntek. ☙ ☙ ☙ ☙

A Star-film müvészgárdájának névsora:

Góth Annie	Olt Aristid
Bársony Lilla	Dán Norbert
Korthy Myra	Turán Gusztáv
Peterdy Klára	Kurd Viktor
Hollay Camilla	Fiáth Robert
Maretta Rolla	Kornay Richárd
Loth Ila	Konrády Péter

STAR-filmgyár és filmkereskedelmi r. t.

Published in *Mozihét Kino-Woche* on July 22, 1917.

had amassed five million crowns in capital.[9] As for its onscreen talent, Star claimed they did not hire stage actors, but rather trained their own talent, believing that acting for the theater and the screen represented two very distinct styles.[10]

Here might be one reason that Star Film always credited Lugosi as "Arisztid Olt," which would at times be spelled "Aristid Olt." And then there is the possibility that the change of name was to make him sound less Hungarian, as part of an overall drive towards marketing the films in foreign markets.[11] That said, the name "Olt" was indeed known in Hungary, being the name of a river in the country. In 1918, *Színházi Élet* featured a curious short interview between Lugosi and actress Mariska Vízvári:

Mariska: 'You have such a bad name,' said the actress disapprovingly. 'Arisztid Olt.'

Béla: 'How could that be bad?' asked Lugossy in defense.

Mariska: 'Yes, it is very bad,' Vízvári went on. 'How dare they call a *bon vivant* 'Arisztid Olt' instead of calling him 'Arisztid Gyújt.'[12]

Here Mariska makes a good-natured joke, focusing on the Hungarian meaning of the word "olt." It means, "to put out the light, to snuff out a fire." The actress asks why he is not named "gyújt," which means the opposite, as in "to make a fire, to light a candle, to turn on the light."

Star Film's releases seem to have themselves lit a fire with the Hungarian movie-going public. The company presented a major preview of a number of its new productions in October of 1917.[13] Featured were *Tryton, Lili, Az élet királya* (*The King of Life*, aka *Élet királya*), *Álarcosbál* (*The Masked Ball*) and *Radmirov Katalin* (*Catherine Radmirov*).[14] One local writer observed:

The Star Film [Company], which is known to have been launched not so long ago, and which produces an unusually large number of films under the usual conditions in Hungary by the help of an even more unusually well-prepared personnel, held its official introduction in Hungary at the Uránia [Theater] last week, for three entire days, on Tuesday, Wednesday and Thursday.

These three days should be recorded as the starting point of the history of Hungarian movie production, which has an importance from the viewpoint of its European history, too. The six movies that were first introduced by the factory are all unique from the aspects of filmmaking, professional sacrifices, concept, design, and literacy All acknowledgments,

Ila Lóth, one of Lugosi's various costars at Star Film.

therefore, praise the willingness of the [company], its serious artistic leadership, especially the job done by Richárd Geiger [the head of the company], who stabilized the internationally [acknowledged] foundations of the factory with extraordinary skill. The giant complex, and the overall artistic execution of the plays, bear everywhere the intellectual seal of the surprising expertise and superhuman energy of Professor Tibor Rákosi, the managing director of the [company].

The factory's playwright, József Pakots, let his artistic taste shine through the [art of perspective representation in the design and painting of scenery for the films]. Alfréd Deésy, general director, produced an extraordinarily genius and inspired work, which makes him enter the league of the best movie directors of all time. The sensationally proportioned and beautifully made sets were designed by the artist-teacher István Szerontai Lhotka (Stefan Lhotka)". To sum up, the Star's three-day presentation provoked some sounds of surprise from the audience, in which the representatives of movie [studios], directors of traveling theaters, and many notable figures were seated...

Lugosi in *Az élet királya* (*The King of Life*, aka *Élet királya*, 1917). *(Courtesy of John Antosiewicz)*

All in all, everything that makes these movies into world-class productions praises the talents serving the artistic program of this Hungarian company.[15]

For its logo, the Star Film Company chose not an airplane in outer space, but instead placed their name inside a star. Over it looms a large bat.

Lugosi at Star

Lugosi's experience at Star was quite different than at the Nemzeti Színház. In one of his first films, Alfréd Deésy's *Leoni Leo* (*Leo Leoni*, 1917), he played the title role. In preparation, Lugosi reportedly asked a detective friend to take him on a brief research trip. According to the local press, fantasy met reality:

Among actors, the excellent Aristid Old [*sic*] prepares himself for his new roles with great ambitions. His all-time motto is: All things must be learnt after life, one must stay realistic. Now, knowing that one of his scenes in his new adventure movie, *Leoni Leo*, is situated in a thieves' nest, he asked a detective friend to take him to a notorious suburb for one night. The next day, [Olt] showed up with a bright face. 'Well, how did you succeed?', they asked him. 'Great,' he said happily. 'Imagine my luck. The villains played their roles so well that they managed to steal my gold watch!'[16]

In keeping with its strategy of adapting famous authors, Star had based the four-act film on George Sand's 1835 novel *Leone Leoni*.

Much the same was true of Deésy's *Az élet királya* (1917), which was based on Oscar Wilde's novel *The Picture of Dorian Gray* (1891), the well-known tale of a man who sells his soul to ensure that his portrait ages rather than himself.[17] Star made no effort to conceal the source material, with one 1917 advertisement in *Mozgófénykép Híradó* giving the film's title as *Dorian Gray*, rather than *Az élet királya*. Norbert Dán played Dorian Gray[18]; Lugosi played Lord Harry Watton, known in the novel as Lord Henry Wotton. One critic called the film:

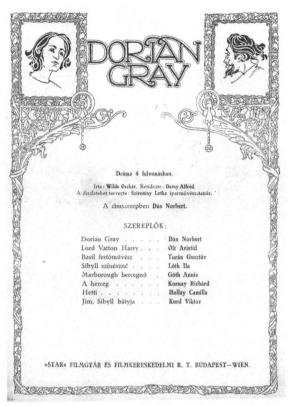

Published in *Mozgófénykép Híradó* in 1917.

… a great psychological drama … which was adapted on the screen by [screenwriter] József Pakots. This movie can be an interesting comparison with the German production on the same theme [Richard Oswald's *Das Bildnis des Dorian Gray* (1917) starring Bernd Aldor as Dorian], which has been introduced recently. The dramaturgy, the shocking psychological thread, and the exquisite interiors of the Hungarian [version] had an elemental effect on the audience. Here, two new male stars were introduced, Norbert Dán and Arisztid Olt.[19]

Another critic wrote "the role of Lord Watton was played by Arisztid Olt with an artfulness of the highest quality."[20] Yet another judged his acting to be "most noble."[21] Star previewed the film in October 1917 at the Uránia, with its premiere coming at Budapest's Corso Theater on January 21, 1918.

Álarcosbál (1917) marked yet another adaptation, this time of Verdi's opera *Un ballo in Maschera* (1859), which was itself based on Eugène Scribe's libretto for Auber's 1833 opera *Gustave III, ou Le bal masqué*. As in *Az élet királya*, Lugosi played the second male lead (René), with Norbert Dán again taking the first (Prince Mondero). After a preview in October 1917, the four-act film had a well-publicized premiere at the Corso on March 11, 1918. Reviews were again positive:

[This] large-scale movie-novelty, which is unparalleled in richness ... is a worthy pendant to the world-famous opera of the same title. As much as Verdi's opera, this large-scale, splendid Star production can touch the heart of the viewer, too. All the exotic beauty and warmth of the beautiful opera are incorporated in the scenes ... so that it really resonates with Verdi's music. The opera's shocking plot ... was adapted for the film so amazingly that it keeps our souls in constant excitement through four acts. The colorful and large-scale cinematography rivals with the grandezza of [Teatro alla] Scala in Milan. In it, all kinds of attractions are piled on top of each other. These include the secret council of the conspirators, the midnight meeting of the governor's council, the fantastic magician-cave of the fortune-teller, the unprecedentedly colorful, grandiose masquerade, the assassination of the governor, and the unveiling of the conspiracy.

Lugosi in *Az élet királya* (*The King of Life*, 1917).

The audience will hardly be able to take in all the beautiful, fascinating, lavish visuals and imaginative arrangement of the opera-based movie, which is due to the merits of director Alfréd Deésy. The visionary cobweb-scene, the tennis party and the scene of the conspirators are all directorial bravados. The [production] resembles a heart-crushing, feverish dream filled with lyric, music and poetic fantasy. Humanly deep is the tragedy of the heroine, which dissolves into silent idyll, through the heart's nobility. The complicated role of Amália, the heroine who continuously suffers, stuck in the middle of the competitions of men in love with her, was played by Annie Góth, with a touching delicacy. Aristid Olt conquered the spectators by his portrayal of the secretary's gorgeous, warm character. Norbert Dán enriched the interesting role of the governor with many noble features, while Oswald, the conspirator, was played with demonic effects by Róbert Fiáth.[22]

Another critic added, "The development of the drama had a shocking effect on the audience. ... A series of touching scenes was accompanied by the audience's sounds of [appreciation] and their constant applause."[23]

Lugosi in *Az élet királya* (*The King of Life*, 1917).

Lugosi then played the lead role of violinist Paul Bertram in Deésy's four-act feature *Nászdal* (*Wedding Song*, 1918, aka *A nászdal*). Ignác Balla and Nándor Ujhelyi's dramatic story finds Bertram living happily with his wife Sylvia and their child. Trouble brews when the pianist Izau (Károly Lajthay) falls in love with Sylvia (Klára Peterdi, aka Klára Peterdy) and unsuccessfully tries to seduce her. The two men duel, with Bertram killing his enemy and then hiding. The police capture Bertram, but mistakenly believe that he is Izau. While in prison, Bertram plays the wedding song he wrote for Sylvia. She recognizes it, and the case of mistaken identity is resolved. The married couple departs on a second honeymoon.[24] One critic praised the "rich scenic design" and "almost fairytale-like" quality of the production.[25] Another observed: "An incredibly subtle mosaic of episodes makes the sublime plot, which appears on the big screen through the classically artistic interpretation of Aristid Olt and the surprisingly nice acting of Klára Peterdi."[26]

Deésy also directed Lugosi in the lead male role of *Tavaszi vihar* (*Spring Tempest*, 1918). Period sources vary as to whether the film was four or five acts in length. The title of László Békeffy's original screenplay referred to the storm of emotions raging in the souls of people, particularly Adrienne (played by Myra Corthy). Episodes from her life unfold onscreen. One is that of the mother who abandoned her child, peeking inside the house where the child

Despite his change in costume and appearance, this still is also Lugosi in *Az élet királya* (*The King of Life*, 1917).

and its foster parents live. It is Christmas night, and the mother freezes to death. Other tales depict a concert scene, as well as the shooting duel of a husband and his wife's lover. A critic responded, "Star Studio releases a magnificent movie again, the novelistic plot, the beautiful scenography, and the splendid cinematography will make it a box-office hit."[27] And Lugosi "presented the role of the husband artfully and with dramatic depth."[28] Another reviewer believed that Lugosi "played the role … with dramatic, deep empathy and with delicate acting."[29] Here it seems Lugosi found himself playing the forlorn spouse, not the other man, as in his real-life duels.

Lugosi's final feature film at Star was Deésy's *Küzdelem a létért* (*The Struggle for Life*, 1918), aka *A leopárd* (*The Leopard*). Based on French writer Alphonse Daudet's 1889 play *La lutte pour la vie*, which had been staged at Budapest's Nemzeti Színház in 1894, this five-act drama featured Lugosi as Pál Orlay (Paul Orlay), the male lead (known as Paul Astier in the play). The Budapest theatrical journal *Színházi Élet* considered the film a major event and published a detailed overview:

> The grand style of 'tragedies of fate' is a characteristic of this colossal-sized drama. Human malevolence, the sacrifice of victims, the death toll of souls make it extremely exciting, shocking and powerful. The protagonist, architect Pál Orlay, is a follower of Darwin's dark theory, which argues that the strong man must clear weakness out of his way. This human beast takes its victims through his passion, so that he could [tower

Lugosi in one of the Star
films, probably *Leoni Leo*
(*Leo Leoni*, 1917).

Lugosi in *Álarcosbál* (*The Masked Ball*, 1917).

above everyone else]. A widow, a princess with a delicate soul, a sweet little messenger girl, and a wealthy baroness struggle [and] are captured by his demonic power. He walks [over] all of them, but at the very moment he approaches the princess with a poison cup in his hands, the deadly bullet of destiny reaches his heart.

This drama is full of excitement, tension, and wild passion. The scenic design is grandiose. The ancient, gothic halls of the prince's castle, the lush palm house full of passion, the romantic scenes in nature, the splendid hunting scene, luxury and depravation make this impressive drama realistic, which impresses, crushes, fascinates, and finally liberates the viewer. The main role is played by Annie Góth, the outstanding artist of Star. She plays with exquisite delicacy, with beautiful appearance, gestures, and poses, and a high level of empathy shines through all her acting. She was greatly liked and appreciated by the whole audience. Klára Peterdi showed her polished, artistically mature acting skills, too, while Ila Lóth touched the audience's feelings with the noble simplicity of her dramatic toolkit. In the male roles were Arisztid Olt and Ferenc Virág, both manifesting acting ability of great style.[30]

Along with his feature films, Lugosi also appeared in a two-reel short subject at Star with the title *A régiséggyűjtő* (*The Antiquarian*, 1918). A review in the local Budapest press observed:

After the almost unprecedented success of *Az élet királya* this week *A régiséggyűjtő* will

Lugosi in *Álarcosbál* (*The Masked Ball*, 1917).

make its debut at the Corso [Theater]. It is a new movie by Star, a comedy in two acts. The ingenious direction confirms the proven talent of Mihály Kertész [Michael Curtiz]. One can admire Kamilla Hollay's lovely impishness, and the cheerful appearance of Arisztid Olt, Norbert Dán and Miklós Ujváry in the main roles.[31]

Though produced in 1917, *A régiséggyűjtő* premiered in early 1918. It was Lugosi's only comedy film at Star.

The Phönix Film Company

Established on April 6, 1917, Phönix (Phoenix) launched after purchasing the Kino-Riport Film Company, including all its equipment and studios, then supplemented its equipment stock with purchases made mostly abroad.[32] The main office was located at 59 Rákóczi Street in Budapest's District VIII and the studios were at 10 Sziget Street.[33] Phönix was known for adapting Hungarian "bestsellers," novels, and dramas as the primary basis for their films; however, they occasionally filmed original screenplays as well.[34] Phönix remained successful until just after the end of World War I, but went into a slow decline, ceasing feature-length productions and struggling onward until closing on November 30, 1926.[35] At the time Lugosi became involved with them, Mihály Kertész was – as Alan K. Rode has noted – "executive producer with artistic control over all productions."[36]

Lugosi in *Álarcosbál* (*The Masked Ball*, 1917).

Lugosi at Phönix

In addition to his work for Star, Lugosi acted in two films for the smaller Phönix, both directed by Mihály Kertész. The first to be produced was titled *Az ezredes* (*The Colonel*, 1918), based on a three-act stage comedy of the same name by Ferenc Herczeg. Lugosi played the leading role in what became the last of his Hungarian films to be released. A Budapest critic wrote:

> The comic situations and laughable scenes of the extremely amusing piece were a great success. Béla Lugosi, Kläry Lotto, Zoltán Szerémy, and László Z. Molnár once again proved their great acting talent in the main roles and made a superb contribution to the success of the new movie. *The Colonel* was created by the best Hungarian studio, the Phoenix, and we can safely say that it can be proud of its latest hit.[37]

At four acts in length, *Az ezredes* premiered at the Omnia in Budapest on December 30, 1918.

Lugosi's second acting job at Phönix was *99-es számú bérkocsi* (*Rental Car Number 99*, aka *99*, 1918). Others in the cast were veteran actor Gyula Gál (with whom Lugosi had often worked at the Nemzeti Színház), Mihály Várkonyi (Victor Varconi, with whom Lugosi would later costar in the 1931 American film *The Black Camel*), and Lajos Réthey (who had played Svengali to Lugosi's Gecko in *Trilby* onstage in Temesvár in 1904).

OLT ARISZTID— PETERDY KLÁRA

Jelenet a „Nászdal" cimü Star-filmből. Bemutatják ápr. 3—15-ig a Corso-mozgóban.

Lugosi in *Nászdal* (*The Wedding Song*, 1918).

99 tells the story of a London police officer who visits a "millionaires club" and makes a wager that he can commit a crime that the police will not discover for at least thirty days.[38] Lugosi portrays one of the detectives involved in the wager. *Színházi Élet*, the premiere stage and film publication in Budapest, responded favorably:

> [*99*] will be introduced to the audience at the Royal Apollo Cinema, where it will open on August 31.[39] The script of the four-act criminal mystery with the strange title was written by Iván Siklósi, art director and dramaturge at Phoenix, whose imagination has made this high-quality motion picture interesting and valuable by adding his brilliant ideas for the scenario. We cannot reveal anything about the story, because the studio wishes it to remain a surprise. The movie's extraordinary plot is based on a brilliant idea. The ending of this captivating, complex and exciting movie will strike the audience with the power of sensation. Mihály Kertész directed *99* with amazing professional ability. Mihály Várkonyi, Zoltán Szerémy, Jenő Balassa, Béla Lugosi, Lajos Réthey and [Kläry Lotto] appear in the main roles, all of them giving their best this time, too.[40]

In a rather humorous case of continuity lapse in the film, another publication reported:

In one scene, [Gyula] Gál, the detective, stands in front of a door and hesitates, [wondering] whether he should enter or not. He holds a cigar between his teeth, three-fourths of which has already been smoked. The next scene (when the detective enters the room) was recorded only one day later. Both the director ... and Gál forgot about the details of the day before ... and the detective enters the room with a huge, lit cigar, of which no part is yet missing.[41]

In his book *Michael Curtiz: A Life in Film*, Alan K. Rode described another production anecdote:

URÁNIA
magy. Tudományos Színház

Szombat, vasárnap
junius 22-én, 23-án

a Star-filmgyár legujabb attrakciója

NÁSZDAL

dráma 4 részben.

Irták: **Balla Ignác** és **Ujhelyi Nándor.**

A főszerepekben

Olt Arisztid,   Peterdy Klára

és **Kornay Richárd.**

Előadások d. u. 5., 7. és 9 órakor. Vasárnap d. u. 2 órától kezdve. Jegyek előre válthatók d. u. 3 órától, vasárnap d. u. fél 2-től kezdve.

Published in *Délmagyarország* on June 22, 1918.

After the Phönix lab overexposed a reel of film during final production, the thirty-six-year old Lugosi proved more than a match in proud stubbornness with his director. In a typical on-the-set display of imperial brusqueness Kertész ordered Lugosi to do retakes to replace the ruined scenes. The actor, put off by Kertész's manner, refused and was excoriated in front of the entire company. Lugosi stalked off the set and did not return until Kertész agreed to apologize to him in front of the crew.[42]

Though produced after *Az ezredes*, *99* was the first of the two to appear on theater screens. It was successful enough that Phönix planned a follow-up entitled *77*, which would have featured the same London policeman character.[43] It appears, however, that *77* never went into production. Nevertheless, film historian István Nemeskürty notes that *99* and *Az ezredes* ranked among Kertész's most successful Hungarian films.[44]

The fact that Lugosi remained a stage actor at the Nemzeti Színház while appearing in these films gave rise to at least one amusing incident:

Lugosi, a funny man, showed up at the [Nemzeti Színház for a] rehearsal of *A*

Lugosi in *Tavaszi vihar* (*Spring Tempest*, 1918). *(Courtesy of John Antosiewicz)*

hadifogoly [*The Prisoner of War*] wearing a dress suit, a white tie and a cylinder. He was a few minutes late, for which he apologized to Hevesi, the director of the play. Everyone thought he must have attended a wedding in the early hours of the morning, since no one climbs out of bed and gets dressed in such a formal garment.

However, Lugosi attended the next rehearsal in the same, groom-like outfit, he even wore a white aster in his buttonhole. This second time curious onlookers could not help but stare.

'My work attire,' he said negligently, 'we shoot a movie in the mornings at Hűvösvölgy [a district on the Buda side called in English 'Cold Valley'].'[45]

Lugosi had thus become a star of stage and screen, one whose fame would eventually circle the globe much like the plane in Universal Pictures' logo.

That would all happen after he left Hungary, though. Likewise, his Phönix director Mihály Kertész would achieve his greatest successes in America. By contrast, most of their colleagues

BECOMING DRACULA

Részlet a **Küzdelem a létért** cimü 5 felvonásos filmdrámából

Advertisement for *Küzdelem a létért* (*The Struggle for Life*, 1918), aka *A leopárd* (*The Leopard*), as published in *Mozihét Kino-Woche* in 1918.

Lugosi in *Küzdelem a létért* (*The Struggle for Life*, 1918), aka *A leopárd* (*The Leopard*). *(Courtesy of John Antosiewicz)*

remained in Hungary, including Alfréd Deésy, who directed films there until 1947.

And then there was Károly Lajthay, Lugosi's costar in *Nászdal*. In 1921, when Lugosi was already in America, he directed *Drakula halála* (*Dracula's Death*), the first film to depict Bram Stoker's character. In the script (which Lajthay cowrote with Mihály Kertész), a madman (played by Paul Askonas) has delusions in which he believes he is the supernatural vampire.

Lajthay shot the film in Vienna and in Budapest. A Hungarian trade publication observed:

> Drakula *in person* – a phantastic creature, some kind of modern bluebeard – brings a new woman into his amazing castle, this new woman being played by Margit Lux. He stops at nothing in order to possess the woman: he summons demons and spirits and strange creatures to gain control over her, but then a cross around her neck comes into view... and Drakula, this wonderful, and at the same time mysterious creature, is dispelled by it.

> ... Since I might not be able to give away anything by admitting now that *Drakula* is a film, I will say that it is a film destined to become sensational, the plot of which must not be told due to the extraordinary excitement it conveys and the fact it will depend upon suspense when it appears on the screen.[46]

A screening of *Drakula halála* (also known at the time as *A vámpír násza/Marriage of*

PHÖNIX

MÜVÉSZEI

1917   1918

Published in *Mozihét Kino-Woche* on December 25, 1917.

the Vampire) might have occurred in 1921, but it was not released until 1923. For reasons unknown, the film quickly disappeared from theater screens. No evidence has yet surfaced that *Drakula halála* was ever re-released in Hungary, or that it was screened in any other country. Perhaps it was under another title, or perhaps not. The film seems to have vanished after the spring of 1923. By contrast, Lugosi did not.

Lugosi in a publicity photography for *99-es számú bérkocsi* (*Rental Car Number 99*, aka *99, 1918*).

BECOMING DRACULA

(Endnotes)

1 "Déesy Alfred." *Mozihét Kino-Woche* (Budapest, Hungary) 11 Nov. 1917.

2 Balogh, Gyöngyi. "History of the Hungarian Film, From the Beginning Until 1945." Available at https://filmkultura.hu/regi/2000/articles/essays/balogh.en.html. Accessed on 16 Jan. 2019.

3 Lukacs, John. *Budapest 1900 – A Historical Portrait of a City and Its Culture* (New York: Grove Press, 1988).

4 Nagy, Zsolt. *Grand Delusions: Interwar Hungarian Cultural Diplomacy, 1918-1941.* Doctoral Dissertation (Chapel Hill: University of North Carolina, 2012).

5 Balogh, "History of the Hungarian Film, From the Beginning Until 1945."

6 Untitled clipping. *The Morning Telegraph* (New York) 25 Feb. 1925

7 Nemeskürty, István. *Word and Image: History of the Hungarian Cinema* (Budapest: Corvina Press, 1968).

8 A photograph of Star's studio and its many buildings is archived in the collection of the Hungarian Film Institute in Budapest.

9 "A Star Művészgárdája." *Mozihét Kino-Woche* 2 June 1918.

10 Ibid.

11 Lugosi's name change was apparently not unusual for some of the other actors at the Star Film Company. Gyula Fehér used the pseudonym Róbert Fiáth and Lajos Gellért went by the screen name of Viktor Kurd. Those two cases also appear to be an effort to make the actors sound less Hungarian.

12 "Rossz Név." *Színházi Élet* (Budapest, Hungary) 15-22 Sept. 1918.

13 "Uj Star-filmek." *Pesti Napló* (Budapest, Hungary) 28 Oct. 1917.

14 In an advertisement published in *Mozgófénykép Híradó* on 18 Apr. 1918, *Az élet királya* is rendered simply as *Élet királya*.

15 Ibid.

16 "Két éve csinálnak magyar filmet." *Színházi Élet* (Budapest, Hungary) 26 Aug.-2 Sept. 1917.

CARY LOTTE—LUGOSI BÉLA
„99"
Phönix-film

Lugosi and Kláry Lotto in *99-es számú bérkocsi* (*Rental Car Number 99, aka 99, 1918*), as published in *Színházi Élet* for September 1-8, 1918.

Lugosi in *Az ezredes* (*The Colonel*, 1918).

17   Prior to being published as a novel in 1891, a shorter version of *The Picture of Dorian Gray* was printed in *Lippincott's Monthly Magazine* in 1890.

18   According to *Mozihét Kino-Woche* for 18 May 1917, Star's competitor, Phönix, had originally intended to film a version of the novel with actor Leopold Kramer in the leading role.

19   "Uj Star-filmek." *Pesti Napló* 28 Oct. 1917

20   "*Az élet királya.*" *Színházi Élet* 27 Jan.-3 Feb. 1918.

21   "*Az élet királya.*" *Mozihét Kino-Woche* 20 Jan. 1918.

22   "*Álarcosbál.*" *Színházi Élet* 10-17 Mar. 1918.

23   "Uj Star-filmek."

24   "*A nászdal.*" *Mozihét Kino-Woche* 7 Apr. 1918.

25   "*Nászdal.*" *Pesti Napló* (Budapest, Hungary) 9 Apr. 1918.

26   "Heti Müsor az Urániában." *Egri Újság* (Budapest, Hungary) 23 May 1918.

27   "*Tavaszi vihar.*" *Pesti Hírlap* (Budapest, Hungary) 21 Apr. 1918.

28   Review in *8 Orai Újság*, reprinted in *Mozgófénykép Híradó* 21 Apr. 1918.

29   *"Tavaszi vihar." Mozihét Kino-Woche* 21 Apr. 1918.

30   *"Küzdelem a létért." Színházi Élet* 21-28 July 1918.

31   "A néma tanu. *A régiséggyüjtő." Pesti Hírlap* 27 Jan. 1918.

32   "Phönix Filmgyár Rt." *Hangosfilm Filmenciklopedia.* Quoting from Andor, Lajta. "A magyar filmlaboratóriumok története 1901-1961-ig." *Filmspirál* 24; *Névjegyzék* A "Központi Értesítő", 1918 évi folyamának első feléről. (43. évfolyam, 1. félév); *Névjegyzék* A "Központi Értesítő", 1927 évi folyamának első feléről. (52. évfolyam); *Mozihét Kino-Woche* 8 Apr. 1917; and "A Phönix-filmgyár." *Színházi Élet* 7-14 Apr. 1918. Available at https://www.hangosfilm.hu/filmenciklopedia/phonix-filmgyar-rt. Accessed on 30 July 2019.

33   Ibid.

34   Ibid.

35   Ibid.

36   Rode, Alan K. *Michael Curtiz: A Life in Pictures* (University Press of Kentucky: Lexington, KY, 2017).

37   "Színház. Zene." *Az Újság* (Budapest, Hungary) 1 Jan. 1919.

38   *"99." Mozihét Kino-Woche* 15 Sept. 1918.

39   It seems that *99* did not play the Royal-Apolló until 12 Sept. 1918.

40   *"99." Színházi Élet* 1-8 Sept. 1918.

41   *Képes Mozivilág,* issue 1919/21.

42   Rode, *Michael Curtiz: A Life in Pictures.*

43   *"99." Mozihét Kino-Woche* 20 Oct. 1918.

44   Nemeskürty, *Word and Image.*

45   *Az Újság* 8 Sept. 1917.

46   "I Attended a Wedding." *Színház és Mozi* Jan. 1921.

„Star" Filmfabrik und Filmvertrieb A.=G. Wien VII.

Neubaugasse Nr. 25

Telephon 30485   Telephon 30485

Unsere Hauptdarsteller

Aristid Olt

Lugosi pictured on the cover of *Neue Kino-Rundschau* in 1917.

Chapter 11

Shadows

"I could see outside the dim, shadowy forms for
a moment before they entirely faded away."
– Bram Stoker, *Dracula*

"Last night I was in the Kingdom of Shadows," Maxim Gorky famously wrote after attending a Lumière film screening in 1896. "If you only knew how strange it is to be there," he added:

> It is not life, but life's shadow, it is not motion, but its soundless specter. ... It is terrifying to see, but it is the movement of shadows, only of shadows. Curses and ghosts, the evil spirits that have cast entire cities into eternal sleep, come to mind ....[1]

Gorky would not be alone in comparing the cinema to the spirit world. "A ghostly seance this, from first to last," Hunter MacCulloch claimed in his poem *At a Motion Picture Show*, published in 1911.[2]

So many metaphors for the cinema are possible, of course. Film theorist André Bazin spoke of "change mummified," for example. The images that flicker on a screen survive, even as the living persons depicted in them do not. "Film preservation" may thus have many meanings.

But what of those films that do not survive? Lost or destroyed, approximately fifty percent of the movies made before 1930 are gone. The numbers for Hungarian silent cinema are even starker. At the time of this writing, none of Lugosi's Hungarian films are known to exist, save for a brief fragment of *Küzdelem a létért* (*The Struggle for Life*, 1918), aka *A leopárd* (*The Leopard*).

In many cases, a film might be lost, but its content is refracted through synopses and critical reviews that do survive, as well as in other ephemera like publicity materials. Here

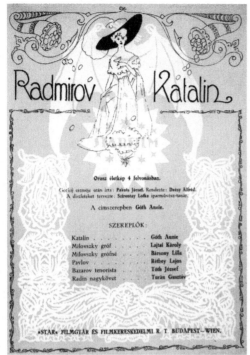

Published in *Mozihét Kino-Woche* on February 3, 1918.

Published in *Délmagyarország* on 26 April 1918.

is the nether region in which so many silent films reside. They do not exist, but can be understood, at least to a degree, through ancillary sources. Publicity stills for *London After Midnight* (1927) abound, even if the film is lost.

But then there are those cases where information quickly reaches its limit, if not conflict. Consider Alfréd Deésy's four-act Star feature *Radmirov Katalin* (*Catherine Radmirov*, 1918), which took its inspiration from Maxim Gorky's 1902 play *The Lower Depths*. Lugosi had appeared in the stage version on seven occasions in Temesvár during 1903 and 1904. The 1918 film version starred Annie Góth and Károly Lajthay, future director of *Drakula halála* (*Dracula's Death*, 1921). Trade announcements made no mention of Lugosi, nor did most period credits for the film. However, during the film's run at the Uránia Theater in Szeged in April of 1918, newspaper advertisements listed Arisztid Olt as being in the cast. A brief review in the April 25,1918, edition of *Délmagyarország* not only mentioned Olt and Góth, but also applauded their performances as being given "with their usual art."[3] By contrast, other reviews of the time mention Góth, but not Lugosi.[4]

It remains questionable if Lugosi was in the film. The cast did include such Star Film Company stalwarts as Lajos Réthey, Gusztáv Turán, and Richárd Kornay. Perhaps Lugosi was misidentified. Or perhaps not, as one critic who remarked on his appearance was based in Szeged, where Lugosi had made such an impression years earlier. And while he normally played the lead or second male lead roles at Star, it is possible Lugosi portrayed a smaller supporting role for *Radmirov Katalin*. After all, Star films sometimes featured more actors than the handful

Published in *Szeged és Vidéke* on April 26, 1918.

Published in *Mozihét Kino-Woche* on January 6, 1918.

who were credited. Lugosi might have appeared in this film; he might not have.

Then there is the case of Cornelius Hintner's Star feature *Lili* (1917), a comedy in four acts based on Hervé's 1882 operetta of the same name. In the film, Antoinine[5] is in love with René; her grandmother Lili unhappily discovers the couple kissing. She forbids them to be together. Antoinine soon finds Lili's old diary and reads about her early life and secrets. She learns that her grandmother was not allowed to marry her lover, a militia trumpeter named Plinchard. Instead she was forced to marry the Baron de la Grange. He later cheats on her with a chanson singer, leaving Lili despondent.

Lili is also tormented by the advances of the Baron's uncle, an old fool. In the meantime, Plinchard's heroic actions lead to his promotion to colonel. When he visits the town where the Baron lives, he first conquers Leona, and then secretly spends a night with the Baroness. That's where Lili's diary ends. Antoinine then learns that René is actually Plinchard's nephew. With Plinchard's help, Lili finally gives her blessing to the young couple.[6]

As late as September 1917, promotional materials for the film claimed that Arisztid Olt played Plinchard at both the younger and elder stage of his life. The same cast listings show Irén Barta and Klára Peterdi portraying Lili (apparently at different points in her life), with Gusztáv Turán as René and Ila Lóth (in her first major role) playing Antoinine.

But advertisements and reviews for *Lili*'s preview at the Uránia in Budapest in October 1917 show Gusztáv Vándori (aka Gusztáv Vándory) in the role of Plinchard/Tábornok.

Published in *Mozihét Kino-Woche* in 1918.

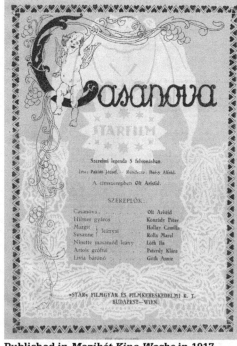

Published in *Mozihét Kino-Woche* in 1917.

Promotional materials in January 1918 repeated Vándori's name, and indicated that Ida Andorffy alone played Lili. Lugosi's name had vanished. Richárd Kornay's name appears on all of these materials, but his role switched from Saint Hypothese to the Baron. And a 1918 issue of the *Mozihét Kino-Woche* published a series of photographs that show Vándori as Plinchard. Lugosi did not appear in any of the images.

A contemporary review of *Lili* – which was screened for an unprecedented two weeks at Budapest's Corso Theater[7] – seems to confirm the changes:

> The first [film] of the second day had a charming, sunny, spring-like effect. *Lili*, a film [scripted] by Jenő Faragó, was based on the operetta of Hervé. In this movie, the audience was captivated by the warm and sensitive play of Ila Lóth, Ida Andorffy, Gusztáv Vándori, Richárd Kornai [sic] and Gusztáv Turán.[8]

What happened? No surviving documents explain the apparent changes, but Lugosi did not play Plinchard.

Nor did he portray Plinchard at an older age, once the character becomes the Tábornok (General). A surviving photograph clearly shows Vándori in uniform and wearing makeup to appear aged. That said, it is possible Lugosi played a different, smaller role in *Lili*. After all, an advertisement for it in Szeged did list Arisztid Olt's name, but that is probably a misprint stemming from the original advertisements. Unlike *Radmirov Katalin*, no critic reported seeing Lugosi in the film. The historical record is incomplete, but there is no compelling

Gusztáv Vándori as Plinchard at an older age in *Lili* (1917). *(Courtesy of the National Film Institute, Hungary)*

evidence that Lugosi appeared in *Lili*.

A third mystery arises with Alfréd Deésy's six-act feature *Casanova* (1918). In the autumn of 1917, advertisements published in Hungarian trades heralded Arisztid Olt as Casanova, the great lover. It seems the celluloid fulfillment of Lugosi the romantic lover and hero of the stage. The Szeged Romeo was now the Budapest Casanova. But when the film had its first screening at the Corso in September 1918, director Deésy received double credit: *he* was listed as Casanova.[9] As with *Lili*, something had apparently changed.

Various histories of Hungarian cinema – some written years prior to any book-length biographies of Lugosi – place him in the cast of *Casanova*, including *Magyar filmográfia* (Magyar Filmtudományi Intézet és Filmarchivum, 1962) and volume two of *Új filmlexikon* (Akadémiai Kiadó, 1973). But these likely relied on the early advertisements that named Lugosi in the title role.

While working on his book *Lugosi: The Man Behind the Cape* (Henry Regnery, 1976), Robert Cremer traveled to Hungary with Lugosi's fourth wife, Lillian. In the magazine *Famous Monsters of Filmland*, Cremer wrote:

> We drove over to the Hungarian Film Archive to see that rare Lugosi footage from *Casanova*. When I asked why there weren't more of Béla's films still in existence, I was told, 'It was tragic that so many of Hungary's early films were destroyed. Since so

Published in *Mozgófénykép Híradó* in 1918.

This ad, published in *Mozgófénykép Híradó* in 1918, credits Alfréd Deésy as the director and star of *Casanova* (1918).

many of our films were shown in Germany and their storage facilities were better than ours, we shipped many of our films to Berlin for better storage. ... This short piece of film is the only record of Béla Lugosi's Hungarian film career as far as I know.'

Then [film archivist Attila Szilágyi] ushered us into a screening room. The lights dimmed and *Casanova* flashed on the screen. A few minutes later, Lillian suddenly gripped my arm and whispered, 'That's Béla!' Sure enough, Béla was sitting on the edge of a marble bench romancing a young lady. There was no doubt in our minds that the world's most famous vampire possessed many talents that remained hidden by his snarling black cape. Tears welled up in Lillian's eyes as she watched Béla wooing the young maiden.[10]

However, others who have viewed the *Casanova* footage have not seen Lugosi in the surviving fragments. For example, playwright László Tábori watched it on two separate occasions, unable to pinpoint Lugosi in the film. In the 1970s, Dr. István Molnár, the director of the archive, commented that Lugosi did not appear in their archive's footage. In 2006, Gary D. Rhodes watched the same footage and also realized that it did not include Lugosi. It is possible that Cremer and Lillian in fact saw the surviving footage of *Küzdelem a létért* before it was properly identified. Or, perhaps more likely, the footage they screened went missing

　　　　　　　　　　　　　　　　　　BECOMING DRACULA

soon thereafter, which would also account for the discrepancy.[11]

In 1970, László Pánczél – an acquaintance of Lugosi's during his Hungarian cinema career – remembered viewing *Casanova* in 1918. He told researcher Jon R. Hand that Lugosi definitely appeared in the film, but not in a leading role. Here is a possible answer to all three of the movies described in this chapter: Lugosi appeared in them, but not in lead roles. That would explain why some viewers believed he was in these films, but he did not appear in their final credits. In fact, he may have appeared in yet other Star productions in small roles, not credited in contemporaneous sources. All that said, the only reason to believe Lugosi was actually in *Casanova* comes in the form of a memory of someone recorded over fifty years after that film's release.

Perhaps Lugosi appeared in one or two of these films, but not in all three. Or perhaps he was in none of them. Their current inclusion in any filmography must be accompanied with appropriate caution, particularly *Lili*.[12]

To appear in a movie might indeed result in a kind of cinematic mummification, but in Lugosi's case, this trio of films was long ago tomb-raided by a thief called Time. Their ghosts are too faint to be documented with precision. Their specters remain soundless.

(Endnotes)

1   Quoted in Leyda, Jay. *Kino: A History of the Russian and Soviet Film* (London: George Allen & Unwin, 1960).

2   McCulloch, Hunter. "At a Motion Picture Show," *Motion Picture Story Magazine* Mar. 1911.

3   "*Radmirov Katalin*." *Délmagyarország* (Szeged, Hungary) 25 Apr. 1918.

4   For example, see "*Radmirov Katalin*" in the 28 Mar. 1918 edition of *Egri Újság* (Budapest, Hungary). A review of the film in the 28 Oct. 1917 edition of *Pesti Napló* (Budapest, Hungary) likewise makes no mention of Lugosi.

5   Some period sources spell Antoinine as "Antoinin."

6   "*Lili*." *Mozihét Kino-Woche* 3 Feb. 1918.

7   "A *Lili* második hete a Corsoban." *Mozihét Kino-Woche* 22 Jan. 1918.

8   "Új Star-filmek." *Pesti Napló* 28 Oct. 1917.

9   Alfréd Deésy is credited as portraying *Casanova* in many contemporary reviews, not just in Hungary, but also Germany. See, for example, "*Casanova*." *Der Film* 30 Aug. 1919.

10   Cremer, Robert. "If It's Midnight – This Must Be Transylvania." *Famous Monsters of Filmland* May 1976. For the sake of internal consistency, we have altered the original article's spelling "Bela" to "Béla."

11   In a 31 Jan. 2020 email to Gary D. Rhodes, Robert Cremer recalled, "Lillian almost jumped out of her seat when she saw the footage. There was no doubt whatsoever that we did see [Lugosi] in the film footage that was shown; however, it must have been from another surviving fragment."

12   At least one Lugosi filmography has included *Diadalmas élet* (*Triumphant Life*, 1923), an obvious

error given its year of release and primary sources that discuss its production. Filmographies have at times also listed Lugosi as appearing in *Lulu* (1918). While not impossible given that it was a Phönix film directed by Mihály Kertész produced during the same time frame as when Lugosi appeared in *99-es számú bérkocsij* (*Rental Car Number 99*, aka *99*, 1918) and *Az ezredes* (*The Colonel*, 1918), no primary sources mention Lugosi's involvement in *Lulu*. Ads for *Lulu* in *Mozihét Kino-Woche* and in city newspapers listed as many as six actors, but not Lugosi. (See, for example, the advertisement in the 20 Sept. 1918 issue of *Szeged és Vidéke* [Szeged, Hungary].) The same is true of articles and critical reviews of the film. (See, for example: "A Phönix készülő filmjeiről." *Mozihét Kino-Woche* 9 June 1918" and "*Lulu és A mandarin*." *Pesti Hírlap* [Budapest, Hungary] 15 Sept. 1918.) It seems that earlier historians simply confused *Lulu* with *Lili* (1917). There is no known evidence to merit including *Lulu* in Lugosi filmographies.

A romantic scene from one of Lugosi's Hungarian silent films, probably *Leoni Leo* (*Leo Leoni*, 1917), *Álarcosbál* (*The Masked Ball*, 1917), or *Küzdelem a létért* (*The Struggle for Life*, 1918), aka *A leopárd* (*The Leopard*).

Chapter 12

"Baby"

"The most beautiful thing on earth is Ideal Love."
– Ferenc Molnár, *Liliom*

While his roles at the Nemzeti Színház (National Theater) did not generally live up to the promise of Debrecen and Szeged, Béla Lugosi's reputation as a Romeo continued in Budapest. But then he fell deeply in love with Ilona Szmik. And he was not interested in a brief affair.

Szmik's parents weren't quite upper class economically, but they were extremely well situated. Her father Lajos was a bank attorney; his own father had been a mine inspector. Lajos had been married twice, his first wife dying at a young age. His second wife, Ilona Voigt, was from a very old and noble Hungarian family.[1] Thirteen years separated their ages, and for the first seventeen years of their marriage there were no children. That changed in 1898, when Lajos was 50 and Ilona was 37: their daughter Ilona was born.[2]

As a child, Ilona had everything. Puppets and dolls and toys filled her room. She attended a prestigious Protestant school for girls. She studied French and German, as well as piano and voice. By the time Ilona was sixteen, she left school, wanting to see the world. Her parents agreed. She traveled, and then returned to enjoy the culture of Budapest.

Near the end of 1916, Lugosi met Ilona at a ball.[3] They quickly fell in love. "A very big love, a very big love for both of them. The biggest," Ilona's granddaughter Noémi Saly said.[4] And so, on June 25, 1917, they were married at Saint Anna's Catholic Church in Batthyány Square, on the Buda side.[5] Lugosi was nearly 35 and Ilona only 19. The existing wedding photo of the two together teems with happiness and love.

But Ilona's parents were not able to share in all of the joy. They had nicknamed her "Baby," and she was indeed their baby girl. Lajos had hoped for someone from Budapest's upper class to marry his daughter, not an actor from a small country town. Lugosi's affiliation with

A romantic scene from one of Lugosi's Hungarian silent films, probably *Nászdal* (*The Wedding Song*, 1918).

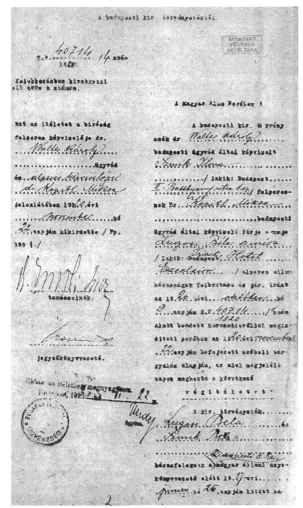

Detail from Ilona Szmik/Béla Lugosi divorce papers.
(Courtesy of the Budapest City Archives)

the Nemzeti Színház was another problem; Lajos knew how much the women in the audiences loved Lugosi, and he had heard rumors of affairs. But in the end, Lajos couldn't say no to Ilona's marriage; he had almost never told her "no."

After their wedding, Lugosi and his new bride went to Opatija, also known as Abbazia. There the newlyweds vacationed amongst the remains of medieval walls and the splendor of villas built by Hungarians in the nineteenth century. Why they chose to honeymoon in the city is unknown. It was the same location where Lugosi had allegedly met the "Woman with the Yellow Eyes" in 1914. And the wedding night was shocking for Ilona, who was not only a virgin, but also a young woman who knew nothing of sexuality.[6]

Prior to the marriage, Lugosi resided at District VII at No. 76 Rákóczi Street, on the Pest side. He had lived there before the war, and returned to the same residence in 1916.[7] After the newlyweds returned from Opatija, they stayed in a separate flat within the large home of Lajos Szmik at 1 Batthyány Street.[8] They were extremely happy, with Lugosi gaining more film roles and with Ilona staying at home. And Ilona's mother grew more and more fond of Lugosi. Of his first marriage, Lugosi later recalled:

> I tell you we were happy. Two people could not be more happy. I returned to my work with a fresh enthusiasm and the critics were most generous in their praise. My future seemed assured, and I loved Ilona as she loved me. We began to think of children.[9]

In 1918, Ilona's parents gifted her a house that they owned in Budapest's District VII, on the Pest side of the Danube near the city park. The notarized agreement provides the details:

A romantic scene from one of Lugosi's Hungarian silent films, probably *Tavaszi vihar* (*Spring Tempest*, 1918).

I. Since our daughter, Mrs. Béla Lugosi née [Ilona] Szmik, and her husband have been leading an independent household after their separation from us, the undersigned Lajos Szmik and his wife, Ilona Voigt, gift to our aforementioned daughter a three-story house and its legal rights (address: 44 Murányi Street, 7th district, Budapest) which holds the registry number 4280/5 in the land register no. 13167, and which is currently in our possession, with the purpose of easing the problems of their livelihood in the difficult circumstances of our time. We also agree that the name of our daughter should be appearing in the land register as the owner of the estate without our further hearing.

We, donating parents, however, stipulate that as long as one of us is still alive, our gifted daughter can dispose of or pledge the property in question only with our consent. So, at the same time with the registration of our daughter's name in the land register as the owner of the property, we also want to record the above described ownership limitation. After the death of both parents, this restriction will be cleared.

We gift to our daughter this house, which, at the time the last property tax was [levied], was estimated to be worth [approximately 190,340 crowns]. Condition of the gift giving is that she will take over the commitments of paying back the loans pledged on this house....[10]

Our daughter becomes owner of the house from 1 January 1919, and from then on, all benefits and incomes of the property will belong to her, but she must bear all the burdens related to house ownership and those of the above described mortgage payments, too.

II. I, Mrs. Béla Lugosi, née [Ilonka] Szmik, accept my parents' gift as described in the previous section with the restrictions set out there, and I commit myself to the due repayment of the mortgages listed in the previous point and to the payment of the public taxes related to the house.[11]

Esküvő. Vettük a következő értesítést: Lugosi (Blaskó) Béla a Nemzeti Szinház tagja, néhai Blaskó István, a Lugosi Népbank vezérigazgatójának és ómoraviczai Vojnits Paulának fia, f. hó 25-én d. u. 7 órakor vezeti oltárhoz a II. ker., Batthyány-téri Szt. Anna templomban Szmik Babyt, Szmik Lajos udv. tanácsos és Voyt Ilona leányát. Budapest, 1917. jun. hó. II. Batthyányi-utca 1. sz.

Published in *Nagybánya és Vidéke* on July 1, 1917.

Marriage photo of Lugosi and Ilona Szmik.
(Courtesy of Noémi Saly)

Lugosi's father-in-law, Lajos Szmik. *(Courtesy of Noémi Saly)*

Ilona and her parents signed the document on December 30, 1918. But Lugosi did not. He was given no legal ownership rights to the house.

Perhaps the particulars of the arrangements suggest growing tension between Lugosi and the Szmiks. Speaking with one fan magazine, Lugosi claimed the "Woman with the Yellow Eyes" unexpectedly returned, appearing in a front row seat at the Nemzeti Színház. The magazine added, "From that moment, Lugosi's interest in his wife waned."[12] But such stories were largely fictitious. There seems little doubt that Lugosi was a devoted husband, deeply in love with his "Baby."

Lugosi's home life was becoming tense, but the reason stemmed not from another woman. In late 1918, his career was evolving from stage and screen into politics. That he began to move in Communist circles disappointed the Szmiks, if not in the beginning, then certainly later, when it cost Lugosi his homeland.

(Endnotes)

1   Rhodes, Gary D. Interview with Noémi Saly, 24 May 2006.

2   Information on Ilona Szmik and her family comes from Noémi Saly, Szmik's granddaughter.

3   A fan magazine article later claimed that Ilona was a "society girl who had come to cheer the wounded." See Chrisman, J. Eugene. "Masters of Horror – Karloff and Lugosi." *Modern Screen* Apr. 1932.

4   Rhodes, interview with Saly.

5   "Esküvő." *Nagybánya és Vidéke* (Nagybánya, Hungary) 1 July 1917.

6   Information on Lugosi and Ilona's wedding night comes from Rhodes, interview with Saly.

7   *Budapesti Czim-és Lakásjegyzék* (Budapest: Franklin-Tarsulat, 1916).

8   Saly, Noémi. "The Mysterious Baby – The First Wife of Dracula." Available at: https://magyarnarancs.hu/narancsszem/a-rejtelyes-babi-90618. Accessed on 10 Dec. 2019.

9   Chrisman, "Masters of Horror."

10   With regard to loans, the rest of this sentence reads: "one of which was requested on 8 November 1895, was registered on no. 21382/1895 and the sum of which equals to (36,000) thirty-six thousand forints, that is, (72,000) seventy-two thousand crowns, the other one was requested on 12 November 1917, annotated by Károly Rónay royal notary in deed no. 697/1917 and was registered on no. 12566/1917, and the sum of which equals to (30,000) thirty thousand crowns. The former debt, including interests now equals with 51,592.66 crowns, the latter one including interests equals with 29,782 crowns, the sum altogether is 81,376.52 crowns, that is, eighty-one thousand three hundred seventy-six crowns and 52 pence. The share of monthly debt payments must be paid back to the [United Budapest Capital Savings Bank] on the due date."

11   Rónay, Károly közjegyző iratai (Notary Public). *Case No. 642 1918 Notarial Deed. Available in Catalog Reference HU BFL VII.153 1918 0642 at the Budapest City Archives, Budapest, Hungary.*

12   Chrisman, "Masters of Horror."

Opposite page: Lugosi standing in the front row, third from left, in Opatija (Abbazia).

Lugosi in one of his Hungarian
silent films, probably *Az élet
királya* (*The King of Life*, 1917).
(Courtesy of John Antosiewicz)

Chapter 13

The Count

Béla Lugosi had left the military in early 1916, but he had not left the Great War. No one could, not even if they were on the Hungarian home front, where food and fuel became scarce. Wages fell by up to forty percent. Thousands of wives and children of soldiers became destitute.[1] Of 1918, Hungarian actor Mihály Várkonyi (Victor Varconi) later recalled:

> Budapest had become a teeming, strife-torn city. The history, tradition and beauty were buried under the weight of returning war veterans and refugees. Men returned from battle with no glory, no pride; only the bitter taste of defeat and missing limbs. The innocent peasants were forced to leave the ruined remnants of their former peaceful countryside and come face to face with a totally new environment: the reality of a hostile confused city of violence and despair.[2]

The city witnessed regular strikes and protests against the war, a war that was being waged far more for the Kaiser in Germany and the Emperor in Vienna than for the poor in Hungary.[3]

Lugosi had emerged from the working classes. Like so many artists, including writer Ferenc Herczeg, in whose plays Lugosi had often acted, Lugosi cared deeply about them. The Armistice of November 1918 ended the war and the Habsburgs, but not the major problems in Hungary. Instead, the post-war period hurled the country into chaos.

And Lugosi chose to do something about it.

The Body Politic

Exactly when and how Lugosi first became involved in labor issues and politics remains unclear. The working classes had begun to organize in *fin de siècle* Hungary. Miners in Resica waged a major strike in 1897, at roughly the same time Lugosi worked in them. If he didn't participate, he surely heard the news.

Trade unions for each occupation grew in number during the first years of the twentieth century, including those for actors.[4] One source claimed that Lugosi had been instrumental in the creation of the Actors' Federation in 1907 to counter ill treatment by theater managers in the Transylvania circuit. Perhaps this is true, but no known primary documentation confirms it.[5]

It is evident that Lugosi became active in theater politics by January of 1914.[6] According to an article in *Színházi Élet*:

A birói minősités. A Nemzeti Szinházban a mult héten alakult meg az uj szinpadi törvényszék, amelynek hatásköre — mint ismeretes — késési, fegyeimi és hasonló ügyekben merül ki. A biróválasztás a fiatal generációnak kedvezett, amennyiben többek között Kürthy György, Horváth Tutyu, Hajdu Pepi, Lugosi is bent vannak a biróságban. A megválasztottak azóta rendkivül komor arccal járnak-kelnek a színháznál, mindössze Horváth Tutyu engedi meg magának azt a passziót, hogy birótársát, Hajdu Pepit ugrassa.

An article regarding Lugosi's election to the tribunal of the Nemzeti Színház (National Theater). Published in the January 11-18, 1914 issue of *Színházi Élet*.

In the Nemzeti Színház [National Theater], a new stage tribunal was set up last week, which focuses, as is well known, on delays, on discipline issues, and on similar cases. Elections favored the younger generation, with the court now including György Kürthy, Tutyu Horváth, Pepi Hajdu and Lugosi. Since then, the elected ones have been walking up and down the theater with extremely grim faces....[7]

In the spring of 1914, Lugosi apparently passed the exam to be accepted for the autumn term at the Budapesti Királyi Magyar Tudományegyetem (Budapest Royal Hungarian Academy), not in theatrical arts, but rather as a law student. Though other persons at times used the name "Béla Lugosi," none of them seem to have lived in Budapest in 1914. And so, the student-to-be was likely Lugosi.[8] Perhaps his brother Lajos, an attorney, inspired him. Perhaps he was growing tired of being cast in small roles at the Nemzeti Színház, or perhaps he saw a legal education as the route to formal political positions, whether in actors' unions or otherwise. He even would have been able to study part time and continue his acting career. All that said, Lugosi did not finally attend; registering for military service in World War I prevented him from doing so.[9]

Nevertheless, by January of 1917, Lugosi was deeply involved in theater politics. An article in *Pesti Napló*, one of Budapest's prominent newspapers, described the problem:

It is high time to have a closer look at the relationship between these actors and their employer, the state. This closer observation is worth some trouble. We can learn lessons, which beg loudly to be shared in public, anyway. One must, at last, say that the state is extremely frugal with its actors, the actors of the Nemzeti Színház have the lowest wages in Budapest; furthermore, many of them must fight with inhumane deprivation. This is such a shame which cannot be eased, not even if one turns as red as a beetroot.

... We talk about the populous group of *minorum gentium*, who cannot even dream about a living suitable for a human being, or not even about fair poverty. Many notable members of the Nemzeti Színház receive only inhumane deprivation as a payment for their work. It is as true as it sounds impossible. Let sentences be substituted by real examples. Let us take as an example a *bon vivant* who performs in major roles. This person earns a wage of 3200 crowns at the Nemzeti. One paragraph in his contract says that it is his responsibility to acquire a suitable costume for all modern roles he plays. A basic calculation reveals that in one season he has to have at least two garments sewn and two pairs of shoes be [repaired]. He puts on a new plastron [a form of undergarment worn under the costume] for each of his performances, and he

Count Mihály Károlyi.

throws away a collar after each night, as they become unusable after the performance since the makeup applied on the actor's neck makes them discolored. He cannot buy all these things from his full salary since there is no such thing as a full salary: he pays 10% for his pension, pays the taxes, too, and then, the state is so narrow-minded that it makes the actor pay for the revenue stamp of both copies of his contract. The contract, which will be owned by the state – the other party to the contract – bears the revenue stamp which the actor paid.

... Thus, the actor gets only 152 crowns in hand to live on.[10] He must pay the yearly rent of his flat/house and provide enough money for his family for an entire month. And he has to heat the home. And, in case his dress-coat is not elegant enough for the role of the Marquis, he might be accused of violating the contract. The case of the female cast members is even more complex, who, based on the contract, must

Lugosi with a group of unknown colleagues in Hungary.

acquire everything which is vital for a modern toilette. Shoes and stockings, pension and taxes, rent and gate-tax[11]: they barely have enough left to eat. This information is rather ungentle, but I hope the ladies will excuse us for discussing this private segment of their lives.

This is not all. There are twelve members in the cast who have contracts for stand-ins, but one paragraph of their contract says that, when it is necessary, they must be willing to play smaller roles, too. This 'necessity' is omnipresent, of course, and these people are regular actors. Their yearly salary is 1,800 crowns. They have a monthly wage of 150 crowns, for rent, for food, for living. They should also be responsible for having their own costumes, but the theater does not dare to require this anymore. As a silent agreement they can borrow their garments from the costume collection of the theater, but they can hardly borrow shirts, shoes, stockings, ties and gloves. Thus, they have to purchase these items from the money which remains from their 150 crowns after having paid the rent and food expenses. Such actors are Sándor Szőke, László Szőke, Ákos Ónody, Lajos Szatmáry, Zoltán Oláh, László Fehér Ö., whose names are well-known for the public from the many playbills on which they appear. These people

BECOMING DRACULA

can only dream (an unreachable dream) of Gyula Fehér's salary, which is as high as 3600 crowns, or that of Béla Lugosi or László Gabányi, which is 3200 crowns[12], or that of Teréz Nagy or Mária Kelemen, which is 3000 crowns.

The above listed members received a 20% raise during the war. Then, after working through those two war years, they requested advance payments, signed promissory notes and danced a *Danse Macabre* on the margin of total bankruptcy. And for what is this 20% worth? They receive 360 crowns on a monthly basis instead of 300 crowns. Those who received advance payments during the two terrible years receive 170 crowns for living.

Director Imre Tóth would like to pay a decent salary for his employees, with no effect. He does not take part in those affairs, which are being carried out in the Ministry of Culture, by the two state theaters, based on the opinion of Count Miklós Bánffy, Government Commissioner. The Count could not even imagine that shoveling snow pays better than being an actor at the Nemzeti. A day-laborer shoveling snow earns the same 360 crowns per month, but he is not obliged to own a dress-coat.[13]

Lugosi earned more than many of his colleagues, a fact that speaks to his success at the Nemzeti Színház, even though longer-serving members of the company usually received better roles due to the seniority system. Nevertheless, he was still concerned about the pay of coworkers making less money. And he seems to have looked not to Count Bánffy to solve the problem, but instead to Count Mihály Károlyi, the direct descendant of a Transylvanian prince.[14]

The Count

During October 1918, the Austro-Hungarian Empire began to fall apart. Just before the end of the war, Count Károlyi, a pacifist and a Marxist, became prime minister. He knew the war was lost even before it officially ended on November 11.[15] Károlyi and the newly formed national council thus proclaimed an October Revolution. Within weeks, an independent Hungarian Republic was born.[16] Károlyi became President of the coalition government, which functioned as a bourgeois democracy. It promoted universal suffrage, the secret ballot, freedom of the press, and land reform.[17] And Károlyi led by example, giving away his vast land holdings to peasants.

Károlyi looked to artists and intellectuals for assistance. For example, playwright and screenwriter Lajos Bíró – who had so praised Lugosi's work in *A sárga liliom* (*The Yellow Lily*) in Szeged – became a foreign diplomat in the new government.[18] And Károlyi gave Sándor (Alexander) Korda the position as commissioner of film production. Korda had published Hungary's first film journal, *Pesti Mozi*, before launching *Mozihét Kino-Woche* in 1915; *Mozihét* often covered Lugosi's films in 1917 and 1918.[19] By 1915, Korda directed his first feature film and then took over operation of the Corvin film studio in Kolozsvár, Transylvania. He was

Lugosi, actor-
turned-activist.
(Courtesy of John
Antosiewicz)

Szakszervezetünk megalakulásának története

Irta: LUGOSI BÉLA

Közvetlen az 1918. évi októberi forradalom előtt a IV. kerületi választókerületi pártszervezetben, melyhez tartoztam, olyan feszült és izzó volt már a hangulat, hagy elérkezettnek láttam az időt az ország szinésztársadalmának osztályharc alapján való megszervezésére, szakszervezetbe tömöritésére és proletáröntudatra ébresztésére. Tudtam, hogy itt csak felvilágositásra és szocialista nevelésre van szükség, mert a szinésztársadalom eddig a szocialista ideologiától csak azért állott távol és hogy mint müvész csak azért nem volt szocialista, mert társadalomtudománnyal nem foglalkozott. Elkápráztatta a fény és sok szines hazugság, ami körülvette. Tehát nyomoruságán keresztül kellett emberi öntudatát és a szocializmus iránti érdeklődését felrázni. Hogy ez sikerült, hogy a szinészrabszolga egyáltalán eszmélni is merészelt, nagy része volt ebben az 1918 októberi forradalomnak és annak a körülménynek, hogy

Andor. A szabadszervezet sürgősen előkésziti az érdekeltek nagygyülését*.

Azonban a várt, gyors megszületését a történtek dacára nehéz vajudások előzték meg. Széleskörü ellenmozgalom, a Fővárosi Szinészszövetség kétségbeesett állásfoglalásával kapcsolatban kizárátásom kilátásbahelyezése stb., mig végre 1919 február elején az Operaház egész testülete, forradalmi lendülettel, belépett a Magyarországi Közalkalmazottak Szövetségébe és megalakitotta a Müvészeti Szakosztályt. Ami ezután következett, az már csak egy, a biztos siker tudatában és a forradalmi hangulat hatása alatt történő győzedelmes hadjárat volt. A Közalkalmazottak Szövetségébe való belépést ennek vezetősége Ascher, Radványi és különösen Lévai elvtárs tették lehetővé. Mozgalmunkat a legnagyobb szeretettel támogatták és az ő védőszárnyaik alatt sikerült is a szervezkedés alapját lerakni. A

Excerpt from *Színészek Lapja*, published on May 15, 1919.

the key figure in Hungary's film industry.

It is hardly surprising that such figures as Korda took part in the new government. As Zsolt Nagy observed, the war left "more than physical devastation in its wake":

> The experience of war also led to a cultural and intellectual crisis as intellectuals and artists struggled to make sense of their new reality, a nexus of the new and the old. On the one hand, the world was rapidly transforming through technology. The distances between people were shrinking thanks to discoveries and inventions in communications and transportation. On the other hand, many questioned the direction in which humanity was going....[20]

Marxism provided an attractive answer to many artists in Hungary, among them music composer Béla Bartók and film director Mihály Kertész (Michael Curtiz).[21]

Lugosi is another name that must be added to that list. The scholar N. F. Dreisziger wrote:

> Like most of his fellow actors, Lugosi began his career under circumstances in which his self-esteem and ambition far exceeded his professional income. He felt that he was exploited and he never forgave his country's elite for the poverty he had to endure as a young man, even though by the time he had entered his mid-thirties, his career as an actor ... appeared assured. His passion and sympathy for the underpaid young members of his profession spurred him to political action during Hungary's post-war revolutions in 1918-1919....[22]

Lugosi's political action began in earnest within the framework of Károlyi's government. While still working at the Nemzeti Színház, Lugosi became heavily involved in union organization. By December 2, 1918, the old Actors' Association was folded into the new Free Organization of Theater Employees. Lugosi was part of a group that "thought that the aims of the Actors' Association had been too few...."[23] He then joined a ten-member committee to "summon an urgent meeting of the stakeholders" to form an organization "based on class struggle."[24]

In a letter to the editor of *Pesti Napló*, Lugosi attempted to explain the goals of the new group:

Published in the January 5-12, 1919 edition of *Színházi Élet.*

This union is not the opposition, including those who were dissatisfied with the Association of Actors in [Budapest], but the union of theatrical employees from all over the country who want to unite under the flag of socialist ideas, regardless of the Association of Actors in [Budapest], which does not want to enter the Social Democratic Party. I could not reveal my relation to this party until the revolution, since I was a state employee.[25]

Lugosi then published a lengthy statement that gave a detailed account of the establishment of the union:

Right before the revolution of October 1918, the mood was so tense and glowing in the constituency of the 4th district, in which I belonged, that I felt the time had come for the unification of actors in our country on the basis of class struggle, to bring them into a union and to help the awakening of their proletarian consciousness. I knew that no more but a little enlightening and socialist education was necessary, because actors had so far been absent from the socialist ideology, and such artists had not become socialists only because they were not studying the social sciences. They were dazzled by the light and the many colorful lies around them.

So, we had to shake up their human consciousness and their interest in socialism through their own misery. The fact that this operation was successful, and the actor-slaves dared finding their consciousness at all, was a great achievement of the revolution of October 1918, and by the self-proclaimed proletarian members of the Opera... Thus, the agitation found the most productive soil there, all the more so because comrades Jenő Landler and Albert Király, fully aware of their socialist prestige, listed such serious reasons in their presentations that some of my colleagues started to support all further agitation with utmost conviction...

However, the anticipated, fast birth was not preceded by labor, despite the events mentioned above. A far-reaching counter-movement was started, and I saw the prospect of expulsion because of the desperate commitment of the association of Actors of

BECOMING DRACULA

the Capital, etc., when finally, at the beginning of February 1919, the whole staff of the Opera entered the Hungarian Association of Civil Servants with a revolutionary momentum, and established its Art Division. What followed was a victorious campaign with the certainty of success and in a revolutionary mood Entry to the Association of Civil Servants was facilitated by its leaders ... They greatly supported our movement; we managed to lay the foundations of the organization under their protection. The community of actors is fully aware of this selfless help.

In the meantime, we managed to convince the majority of the members of the Nemzeti Színház, the most exploited actors of the country, of the pressing need of the Union, so they immediately joined the members of the Opera. The call for the movement and information-spreading were successful in the countryside, too....[26]

Rather than merely recite a Dies Irae, Lugosi believed in action, and responded enthusiastically in order to improve the lives of his fellow actors.

Lugosi later said that he had served as one of Károlyi's "lieutenants," and that he became "minister of the theater" as a result of his achievements and his "adherence to Károlyi's cause."[27] In 1931, a journalist referred to him as a former "cabinet minister" in Károlyi's "brief revolutionary government."[28] Those claims were largely exaggeration, it seems. How well Lugosi knew Károlyi during the end of 1918 and early 1919 is hard to determine. The two maintained an active correspondence during World War II that implies a longstanding familiarity, even friendship. But that was long after both men had left Hungary, long after the Count had been deposed, long after his coalition government had fallen apart.

(Endnotes)

1   Lukacs, John. *Budapest 1900 – A Historical Portrait of a City and Its Culture* (New York: Grove Press, 1988).

2   Varconi, Victor and Ed Honeck. *It's Not Enough to Be Hungarian* (Denver, CO: Graphic Impressions, 1976).

3   Hanák, Péter, editor. *The Corvina History of Hungary: From the Earliest Times to the Present Day* (Budapest: Corvina Books, 1991).

4   Ibid.

5   A thorough search of Hungarian newspapers uncovered no references to any activity during 1907 regarding the Színészek Szövetsége (Actors' Federation).

6   The December 29, 1912 edition of *Népszava*, a Budapest newspaper aligned with the Hungarian Social Democratic Party, lists a "Béla Lugosi" as being one of several individuals elected to an executive board at a Social Democratic Party meeting. It should not be automatically assumed that *this* Lugosi was the actor Béla Lugosi. More than likely it was not. The report related to an organization in the town of Arad, around 266 miles distant from Budapest. Lugosi was deeply involved in the production of *A passiójátek* (*The Passion*) by late December 1912. He would hardly have had time for this level of political involvement in the distant town of Arad. As stated in Chapter 2, there were other persons named Béla Lugosi living in Hungary at the time.

7   "A birói minősités." *Színházi Élet* (Budapest, Hungary) 11-18 Jan. 1914.

8   *A Budapesti Királyi Magyar Tudományegyetem Almanachja az MCMXIV – MCMXV Tanévre.* (Budapest: Kir M. Tudományegyetemi Nyomda, 1915). The subsequent editions of the almanac for 1915-1916, 1916-1917 and 1917-1918 also record "Béla Lugosi" being registered *only* for that single semester in the autumn of 1914.

9   Lugosi's registration at the school, even though it was in legal studies, might account for why he later claimed to have attended the Royal Academy of Theatrical Arts in Budapest.

10   This article also includes the following calculations of an actor's expenses:

     After all, one can easily calculate how much subsidiary expenses must be paid after a yearly salary of 3200 crowns, that is, after a monthly wage of 266.67 crowns.

     10% for pension 26.67
     Revenue stamps 3.33
     Tax 12.—
     6 plastron cleanings per month 7.20
     Monthly installment for costumes 41.67
     Monthly installment for shoes 20.—
     Makeup and other smaller expenses 4.—

     114.87

11   Gates of residential buildings were closed at night, and those who entered late or left early had to pay the "kapupénz" or "gate tax" to the housekeeper as compensation for waking him up. This could be considered roughly the equivalent of tipping the doorman.

12   Though Lugosi's salary was at the high end of what was paid to non-seniority actors in 1917, it was still not quite a living wage due to the out-of-pocket expenses required of theatrical personnel.

13   "Színház, művészet – Az állam művészei." *Pesti Napló* (Budapest, Hungary) 11 Feb. 1917.

14   Károlyi, Michael. *Memoirs of Michael Karolyi: Faith Without Illusion* (New York: E. P. Dutton, 1957).

15   Károlyi was not alone in his view that the war was lost. On October 17, 1918, István Tisza declared, "We have lost the war" to the Hungarian Parliament. See Hanák, *The Corvina History of Hungary*.

16   Hanák, *The Corvina History of Hungary*.

17   Ibid.

18   Korda, Michael. *Charmed Lives: A Family Romance* (London: Allen Lane, 1980).

19   Kulik, Karol. *Alexander Korda: The Man Who Could Work Miracles* (New Rochelle, NY: Arlington House, 1975).

20   Nagy, Zsolt. *Grand Delusions: Interwar Hungarian Cultural Diplomacy, 1918-1941.* Doctoral Dissertation (Chapel Hill: University of North Carolina, 2012).

21   Hajdu, Tibor. *The Hungarian Soviet Republic* (Budapest: Akadémiai Kiadó, 1979).

22   Dreisziger, N. F. "Émigré Artists and Wartime Politics: 1939-45." *Hungarian Studies Review*, Vol. XXI, Nos. 1-2, Spring-Fall 1994.

23   "Színházi Alkalmazolttak Szabad Szervezete." *Pesti Napló* 4 Dec. 1918.

24   Ibid.

25   Lugosi, Béla. "A szocialista színészek." *Pesti Napló* 6 Dec. 1918.

26   Lugosi, Béla. "Szakszervezetünk megalakulásának története." *Színészek Lapja* (Budapest, Hungary) 15 May 1919.

27   Wait, Edgar. "Dracula Practices Mysteries Off Stage." *San Francisco Examiner* 26 Aug. 1928.

28   "Chandler and Lugosi." *Dallas Morning News* (Dallas, TX) 9 Mar. 1931.

Lugosi during the late 1910s.

Chapter 14

The Red Danube

"Enough of words; the time for action has come."
– Béla Kun

I n the months immediately following World War I, so much was wrong, and so little could be done about it. As historian László Kontler has written, "There was probably no political force in Hungary at that time that would have been able to answer all of the conflicting interests and expectations in these turbulent times."[1]

Post-war negotiations with the Triple Entente went particularly badly. Count Mihály Károlyi, who was known as being somewhat pro-West, attempted to represent Hungary's plans for reconstruction, but the victors were uninterested. He had no direct say in their plans for Hungary, including alterations to territorial borders that would mean, among so many other changes, Béla Lugosi's hometown of Lugos became part of Romania. Károlyi later wrote, "The French government conceived the bright idea of presenting us with their famous ultimatum, thus definitely stabbing Hungarian democracy in the back."[2] Károlyi's government was becoming weaker and weaker, just as someone else was looking stronger and stronger.

As Bennett Kovrig recounted, "The energetic [Béla] Kun arrived in the midst of this chaos like a whirlwind."[3] Like Lugosi, Kun had fought in Galicia against the Russians. The two might have met there, but it would have been extremely unlikely, given the sheer number of troops. Once captured in 1916, Kun and his fellow soldiers served time as prisoners of war in Russia, where they became fervent communists. Kun even fought in Russia's October Revolution in 1917.[4] His commitment and ability to organize impressed even Lenin, with whom Kun became friendly.[5]

Returning to Hungary in November 1918, Kun formed a communist party. Bolstered by widespread discontent, its membership quickly reached 40,000. Kun gave up to twenty

Béla Kun.

speeches a day; his comrades published pamphlets and staged debates.[6]   Strikes became commonplace in January 1919.[7]   Kontler noted, "Károlyi's own party evaporated."[8]   The government coalition failed.

As of March 21, 1919, Kun took control of Hungary in a bloodless revolution. The Hungarian Soviet Republic was born. It was a "dictatorship of the proletariat."[9]   Industries were nationalized. Schools replaced courses on religion with those on socialism. While Kun was not particularly charismatic, he possessed an ability to find compromise between his hard left ideals and the less extreme views of the Social Democrats who aided him.[10]

And he drew encouragement from many Hungarian artists. Novelist Zsigmond Móricz, whose literature focused on peasants, supported the Kun government. He wrote:

> Communism, which naïve dreamers feared ... will bring about a splendid era of the genuine flourishing of the individual ... Now begins a true, happy, really human life.[11]

A large number of artists and intellectuals actively participated in Kun's government, including film theorist Béla Balázs. Indeed, many members of the film industry supported the new government. In his family memoir, Michael Korda explained:

> [Sándor Korda (Alexander Korda) and Lajos Bíró] both accepted appointments to the Communist Directory for the Film Arts, established by the Council of Commissioners, where they were joined by a well-known actor from the National Theater ... who later achieved world-wide fame in the role of Dracula....

Hungarian film production was now nationalized, under the overall direction of

Lugosi (fifth from left) attends a street demonstration in Budapest in May 1919. *(Courtesy of Jon R. Hand)*

Béla Paulik, a political commissar, who proceeded to set up a cumbersome bureaucracy to plan and carry out a vastly ambitious film program.[12]

The film business fascinated Kun, who grasped its potential for promoting communist ideals, as well as his own regime. Under his government, the industry produced 31 films in the space of approximately four months.

Kun made certain that the May Day parade in Budapest on May 1, 1919 was filmed. Mihály Kertész (Michael Curtiz) directed the production, which was released as an entry in the newsreel series *Vörös Riport-Film* (*Red Report Film*).[13] Béla Lugosi might be seen among those film personnel who are marching.[14] But he would play a far bigger role in the theatrical world of Kun's government.

Private theaters became nationalized, as did cabarets and music halls. Mihály Várkonyi (Victor Varconi) later said, "That wonderful institute, the [National] Theater, never changed. Nothing, not even wars and revolt, could upset the functioning of that unique national monument." But he also recalled, "The National Theater received directives from the Central Committee telling what performances to give and where to give them." Várkonyi was himself ordered to give a "recital of revolutionary poetry for the people."[15] And the singing of *The Marseillaise* and the *Working-Men's International* had to start and/or end every performance.[16]

Lenin noticed Kun's emphasis on such matters, causing him to question: "What sort of dictatorship [of the proletariat] is this you've got, socializing the theaters and musical societies? Do you really think that this is your most important task now?"[17] Apparently Kun did.

Within ten days of Kun taking charge, Lugosi held an important position in the new government.[18] That he was chosen for this position so promptly suggests that he already knew many communists and agreed with their agenda, at least in some measure. After all, Lugosi was a communist party member, and probably had been during the Károlyi period.[19]

In turn, Kun would have been well aware of Lugosi's successful union efforts, which seemed ever the more successful in the days leading up to the Kun revolution. In March of 1919, Lugosi had been instrumental in organizing a protest march of actors and other theatrical employees. That occurred just after he made a fiery speech at a Budapest conference of industry activists.

In a March 7, 1919 letter to the editor of the *Népszava*, the official newspaper of the Social Democratic Party, only two weeks before Kun took power, Lugosi detailed his agenda regarding a centralized government organization that would socialize all Hungarian theater:

> From an economic point of view, our goals are to solve the financial problems of employees at state theaters without making it too exhausting a solution for the state. Why? Because private theatrical enterprises which have as few personnel as [does] a quarter of

Az ország színészetének államosítása.

Miért és hogyan kell megoldani az államosítást.

Ennek céljai — gazdasági szempontból — az állami színházak alkalmazottainak gazdasági helyzetét rendezni anélkül, hogy ez az államot megterhelné. Mert míg a magánszínházi vállalkozások negyedrész személyzettel, hasonló befogadó képességgel mint az állami színházak, milliókat hoznak évente a fővárosi színházvállalatoknak és a vidéki színházigazgató vállalkozók összességének, mint munkanélküli profitot, addig a nagyszemélyzetű állami színházakra az állam évente milliókat ráfizet. Ha tehát az ország összes színházai alkalmazottainak fizetése, minden színházi kellék, ruha, szerelvény központi gyártása az állami színészet központot terheli is, ezzel szemben az ország összes színházának minden jövedelme a központ pénztárát illeti. Ezen művelet végrehajtása, fokozva a színpadi összkellékek egységes, központi, házi gyártásával és nagybani beszerzésével, a kiegyenlítő hatást, a kiadás és bevétel közt, a legrosszabb esetben sem téveszti el.

Kulturális, politikai és pedagógiai szempontból, hogy a színészet az állam kezében országosan szervezve és központilag irányítva visszanyerje eredeti hivatását és ne cél legyen, hanem ismét eszközze válhasson: az igazi kultúra, az irányított népnevelés és nemes szórakozás eszközévé.

Művészi szempontból, hogy azáltal, hogy a megreformált állami akadémiák, kérlelhetetlen szigorral, csak képzett és tehetséges hallgatóknak adhatnak képesítést — amely képesítés egyedül szolgálhat jogcímül az országos színészetnél való működésre —, hogy a kiváló tehetségű hallgatókat az állami támogatásban részesíti, hogy a meglévő, gyönge tehetségű színészek az országos szervezetben más alkalmazást is nyerhetnek; elérhető a művészi színvonal emelkedése.

A portion of Bela's "Respect the Actor" letter from *Népszava* of March 7, 1919.

the state theaters, and which have the capacity of accommodating almost as many spectators as a state theater can, earn millions of profit a year for the directors of private theaters in the capital and for those in the countryside, while the state pays millions a year for the maintenance of state theaters with a large number of employees. Therefore, although the salary of all actors in the country, and the making of all theatrical props, costumes, and machinery would mean a financial burden for the National Center of Theater, its central bank would be sustained by the united income of all the theaters in the country. This operation, which would be even more accentuated by the central production or large quantity purchase of unified sets and props, would not be able to fail the balance between incomes and expenses, not even in the worst of situations.

From a cultural, political and pedagogical point of view, our goals are for theaters to get back their original meaning, thanks to a central, state-run management, so that theater can recover its original function as a medium rather than as an aim: a medium for true culture, for the guided education of people and for noble entertainment.

From an artistic point of view, our goals are that reformed academies can issue a degree only to those who were both highly educated and talented pupils, and such degrees will be the only type that will be accepted by national theatrical institutions. Furthermore, pupils with an outstanding talent will be supported by the state and less talented actors can also find positions within the union, which do not necessarily mean that they will have an acting career. By doing so, a rise in the average performing quality can be reached.

From a social point of view, our goals are to raise the standard of living for theater employees and to guarantee its high standard; to fight unemployment by increasing the number of theaters as much as possible and by providing enough space for all spheres of society with an interest for culture, which, in consideration of the centralized supply system for human workforce and materials, is not at all improper from an economical

Handwritten and signed letter from Lugosi reporting on union activities. (*Courtesy of the Hungarian National Archives*)

point of view, either. Further goals are the provision of social care on a co-operative basis, to transform the sick leave and pension system into state-run policies, and to guarantee artists the best possible remuneration (in accordance with their literacy, talent, and utility) so that outstanding artists who are representative of the culture of our people can live a suitable lifestyle to their positions. Moreover, we aim that all theatrical costumes be made at the theaters' expense, theatrical staff have their own federation with distinct sections, have their own cultural association, home, and co-operative.

The majority of theaters in this country are in the hands of municipal governments. Similar to the case of school buildings, if the state wants to use theaters for adequate purposes, the local community cannot charge for it, since access to their use has been provided in the past, too, free of charge, with a little financial contribution in return. The state theater buildings do not have to be [socialized] anyway, so what is left to be done is the conversion of only those three remaining theater buildings in the whole country which are located in the capital and which belong to the property of legal entities, the conversion of which will not cause a problem for the state in case the recognition of the owners' income level stays moderately low.

At the moment, the props and costumes of theaters belong to the possessions of entrepreneur directors. These goods can be taken stock of and accessed upon presentation of invoices. If negotiations were not successful, the entrepreneur should be provided with an interest rate corresponding with the estimated price of the goods, which lasts until the factory responsible for theatrical goods starts up. After that, entrepreneurs and the state must agree upon a fair price. These entrepreneur-directors would be employed suitably afterwards.

Lugosi Béla feladata

A fővárosi szinészek szövetsége megszünt, tagjai beléptek a Fővárosi Szinészek Szakszervezetébe, mely művészeti szakosztályát képezi a Magyarországi Közalkalmazottak Szövetségének. Fenti szakszervezet a f. hó 27-én vidéki szinészek szakszervezetévé átalakuló Országos Szinészegyesülettel; az Országos Zenészszövetség, mint szakszervezettel; a Szinházak Műszaki Személyzetének Szakszervezetével megalapitotta a Szinházi Alkalmazottak Szervezetének Országos Szindikátusát. A Szindikátus szervezője Lugosi Béla, akit a Nemzeti Szinházból a közoktatási népbiztos szabadságolt, hogy a szinházak kommunizálásánál kapcsolatos teendőkben közreműködjék.

Published in the March 3-April 5, 1919 issue of *Színházi Élet.*

The theatrical companies of the countryside would be managed by the center, and governed by an independent artistic director and an economic director. All props (sets, technical equipment, costumes, wigs, accessories, etc.) would be made by, transported by and exchanged by the center.

In my view, this solution would provide a moral gain for actors and a financial gain for the state.[20]

Lugosi soon headed the National Trade Union of Actors, which was established on March 17, 1919. Three days later, his extensive directives for the union appeared in a proposed agreement:

The trustees delegated by the representatives of the Organizations, which were established due to the class struggle, listed below, are hereby founding the National Union of the Organizations of Theater Employees.[21]

1. Goals of the Union are:

a. To unite all theater employees in organizations connected to the institutions they are employed by, and to coordinate the collaboration of the above organizations sharing common interests.

b. To decide upon the necessity of the foundation of new theaters or eventually upon the necessary functioning of the ones already existing.

c. To create a job reporting center providing services free of charge and to make it compulsory for all members of the Union to register in it.

d. To establish an election system within theaters, to transfer management of theaters to the Union and to establish new theaters.

e. To establish a central pension office through uniting the already existing pension funds.

f. To provide maintenance/supplies based on co-ops.

g. To establish welfare institutions and cultural centers.

h. To update the art and technology of theaters.

2. Rights and Obligations of the Organizations within the Union:

a. They can ask for support from the Union in order to implement their decisions, which were made with respect to their inner autonomy.

b. They can unconditionally ask for support to strengthen and develop their local organizations.

c. They have to accept decisions of the Union, which concern the interests of all employees and they have to act accordingly.

d. They have to contribute financially to the expenses of the Union in proportion to the number of their members.

3. Actions of the Union:

a. To discuss and decide upon initiatives of general interest.

b. Are to be accepted and realized by the organizations.

c. In case the actions of the Union are not accepted and realized by certain organizations, the Union can inhibit the rights of those organizations.

d. The Union will deny solidarity with those organizations which place requests that are unlawful or unfair.[22]

Despite his increasing involvement in politics, Lugosi continued to remain somewhat active at the Nemzeti Színház (National Theater). Between January 2 and March 28, 1919, he took to the stage at least twenty times in six different plays. During those three months, he would play only one small supporting role, that of Lodovico in Shakespeare's *Othelló* (*Othello*). Otherwise, he appeared as Sarsy in *Bagatelle* and as The Prince in *Sancho Panza királysága* (*The Kingdom of Sancho Panza*), both in January. In February, he reprised his role as King László in *Árva László Király* (*Lonely King Laszlo*). The month of March brought Lugosi's final known Hungarian stage appearances. He portrayed Lucentio in Shakespeare's *A makrancos hölgy* (*The Taming of the Shrew*). Then, on March 28, as Baron Leitmaritz in an ensemble cast for *A fekete lovas* (*The Black Rider*), Lugosi appeared on the Hungarian stage for the very last time.

The halt to his stage appearances in March of 1919 was not by accident and was not intended to be permanent. But with the new union established, Lugosi wasted no time in attempting to implement his plans. He formally requested a leave of absence from his responsibilities as an actor at the Nemzeti Színház. In a March 20, 1919, letter to the Minister of Arts, Lugosi wrote:

Typed and signed letter from Lugosi to the National Union of Actors. *(Courtesy of the Hungarian National Archives)*

> I would like to report to you that I finished the organization of the theater employees in the country. I united all individual organizations under the National Union of the Organizations of Theater Employees. Organizations within the Union are the following: Organization of the Actors (and Actresses) in the Capital, the National Organization of Musicians, the Organization of Theatrical Technical Staff and the Organization of Actors in the Countryside.
>
> I am asking my Comrade, that you, as Minister of the Arts, release me from the Nemzeti Színház temporarily, and to give me an assignment so that I can contribute to the formation of the Union, and that I can realize my earlier plans to such extent and in such a way that corresponds to your orders and to the timing you dictate.[23]

Lugosi did in fact receive permission to be released on a temporary basis from the Nemzeti Színház on March 27, 1919.[24] That was a mere six days after Kun took control of the country. The timing was no coincidence.

Examining these various documents prepared in the days leading up to the Hungarian Soviet Republic helps clarify why Kun would have wanted Lugosi to serve in his government. As scholar N. F. Dreisziger observed:

> The advent to power of the communists under Béla Kun in March 1919 discouraged some of Lugosi's not-so radical minded colleagues, but it did not stop him from continuing his activities. He soon became the secretary[25] of the National Trade Union

Lugosi (front row, fourth from left) at a political demonstration in 1919.

of Hungarian Actors and he used his position to denounce the 'exploitation' and 'corruption' that, in his view, actors had been subjected to by the 'private capitalist managers' and 'the state' before the revolution.[26]

In meetings held on April 13 and April 17, 1919, actors across rural Hungary joined with their Budapest colleagues to establish the Hungarian Actors Trade Union. More than 1,000 people involved in the rural theatrical troupes reportedly attended to support it.[27] During the second meeting, Lugosi proposed that Rudolf Pajor, a delegate from the Socialist Party of Hungary, be approved as the editor of the union's journal. Pajor had praised the union, proclaiming, "new life and new opportunities wait for Hungarian art."[28]

Then, on April 25, Lugosi issued a letter to the Public Education Commission, announcing the establishment of a new arts council.[29] He wrote:

> When we provide information about the foundation of the above institution – the members of which were elected purely based on artistic points of view and irrespectively of any political relation reserved by the government of our socialist union – we ask the Commissioner of Public Education to consult the opinion of the art council during the management of all future issues related to theater. The art council is eagerly willing to help in all future issues.[30]

Lugosi thus became responsible for helping unemployed actors to find work. One of them, named Katalin Berendy, was advised:

Béla Kun.

... we cannot meet your request (for immediate employment at a specific theater). Since all theaters have become state institutions and there is no priority among the theaters, to whichever theater you'll be admitted, your placement will only be formally linked to that specific theater, as each actor or actress's artistic talents will occasionally be employed at the theater where they are needed at that very moment.

For this reason, please contact the Secretary of the Actor's Union, Comrade Béla Lugosi (36 Kertész Street, Budapest) from 5 to 6 p.m., who will record you in the list of unemployed actors and he will also help you in other ways."[31]

Lugosi also judged actor auditions in Budapest, which were very similar to those he had failed years earlier. As one notice explained:

Theater choir singers are wanted. Various theaters from Budapest search for a great number of choir singers with a good voice and sharp ears. Applicants for the exam shall contact the Secretary of the Actor's Union, Lugosi, at Fészek-klub [Nest Club]. Those with previous experiences will find themselves in an advanced position.[32]

Then he sat on a panel of nine judges to audition 250 unemployed actors looking to be hired by one of the rural theater troupes.[33]

Lugosi took his duties very seriously. They included bringing renewed attention to the plight of theatrical workers. In one of his published letters, he declared:

Respect the actor because he offers you his soul![34]

One can often hear from comrades, indeed even from those in a leading position, that the actor is not a proletariat. Let's face this opinion. Since we cannot suppose maliciousness from anyone, we can only attribute this wrong opinion to the complete ignorance of those who say it. What is the truth, then? Even in the past, ninety-five percent of actors were more proletarian than the most unskilled laborers, because, in most cases when actors took off their decorative costumes after the performance, they faced worry and misery. And either they had been crawling under the burden of

Lugosi in *Küzdelem a létért*
(*The Struggle for Life*, 1918),
aka *A leopárd* (*The Leopard*).

various ad hoc jobs – hence they could not correspond to their artistic calling, or were forced to beg from friends, to accumulate debt, or to prostitute themselves. And they endured, bearing the suffering, humiliation, and extortion, in order that they could act and get new roles, without which it was not worth living.

They were extorted by the private capitalist directors as well as by the state. The former ruling class kept actors in ignorance through telling them lies, it corrupted them financially and morally, and finally, it threw stones at actors for the sake of its [the ruling class's] own sins. And the starved and humiliated actors were forced to push the chariots of the former ruling classes, with grinding teeth. The price of their devotion for acting was martyrdom. What would have happened to acting in the past, if it had not been in the service of the former ruling classes? If actors wanted to remain actors, they were forced to stand in the service of the [ruling] class, which somehow assured their existence. The whole working society was forced to stand in the service of the ruling class the very same way. They were equally corrupted. Actors, however, managed to conceal their own misery by wearing some rather colorful rags. This fatal misunderstanding might have been caused by this fact.

And now that proletarians are free, they cannot deny the benefits of [the] proletariat from actors, they cannot let actors down, they cannot leave them in insecurity and misery by not acknowledging them as brothers. Because the new society is built on truth, and this would be injustice. When I am revealing these sore wounds to you, I am performing a duty.[35]

Lugosi was no mere lackey or dupe or administrative secretary; he headed a major department and announced his beliefs publicly.

As head of the union, Lugosi signed at least one order of major proportion, an edict that prohibited Kun's Red Army from entering actors' homes to confiscate their clothing.[36] This was a highly important issue at the time, as the military was commandeering a portion of the wardrobe of every man in Budapest for the benefit of disbanded soldiers.[37] Lugosi was trying to protect actors, even placing them above other citizens. Or perhaps he was mindful that, in this transition period, they sometimes still had to rely on their own wardrobes for their costumes. Whether it was fair or not, though, Lugosi's input on such a major issue proves he wielded a degree of power within the government.

And yet it was a government that quickly became despised, at least in many quarters. It was not the "true, happy, really human life" that Zsigmond Móricz had anticipated. Priests, clergymen, and monks could no longer vote. And the new regime printed worthless money on white paper, leading those who could to horde the older "blue" money. Mihály Várkonyi later remembered:

It was like a city under siege. The diet consisted almost exclusively of the sauerkraut that had flooded the country with the Germans during the war. On rare and happy occasions a few potatoes could be bought, but only if you had Blue money to exchange.

Worse still was the fate of Kun's enemies. Kontler recorded, "Besides common murders of actual or alleged enemies by the 'elite' detachments, some 120 death sentences were meted out by the tribunals for political reasons."

Kun's "Red Terror" was very real, and very horrific. As someone who lobbied for minority rights, Lugosi likely despised that side of Kun's government, though he did not resign.[38] He was a communist party member, and he was a socialist. Ilona Szmik later claimed that he "compromised himself seriously" during the Kun government.[39] That said, Lugosi may have felt similar to Sándor Korda, who joined the new regime even while preferring the approach of Count Károlyi. It is difficult to say. Questions here are better than answers, as the latter are only speculative.

At any rate, Lugosi and his fellow artists in Budapest learned that communism idealized and communism realized are two very different matters.

(Endnotes)

1   Kontler, László. *A History of Hungary: Millennium in Central Europe* (New York: Palgrave Macmillan, 2002).

2   Karolyi, Michael. *Memoirs of Michael Karolyi: Faith Without Illusion* (New York: E. P. Dutton, 1957).

3   Kovrig, Bennett. *Communism in Hungary: From Kun to Kádár* (Stanford: Hoover Institution Press, 1979).

4   Hoensch, Jörg K. *A History of Modern Hungary: 1867-1994*, second edition (London: Longman House, 1996).

5   Anderson, Richard. *The Red Aristocrats: Michael and Catherine Karolyi* (Brattlesboro, VT: Amana Books, 1991).

6   Kovrig, *Communism in Hungary*.

7   Kontler, *A History of Hungary*.

8   Ibid.

9   Hoensch, *A History of Modern Hungary*.

10   Hanák, Péter, editor. *The Corvina History of Hungary: From the Earliest Times to the Present Day* (Budapest: Corvina Books, 1991).

11   Quoted in Hanák.

12   Korda, Michael. *Charmed Lives: A Family Romance* (London: Allen Lane, 1980).

13   Cunningham, John. *Hungarian Cinema: From Coffee House to Multiplex* (London: Wallflower Press, 2004).

14   Footage from *Vörös Riport Film (Red Report Film,* 1919) appears in Florin Iepan's documentary *Le*

Vampire déchu (*The Fallen Vampire*, 2007).

15   Varconi, Victor and Ed Honeck. *It's Not Enough to Be Hungarian* (Denver, CO: Graphic Impressions, 1976).

16   Kaas, Baron Albert and Fedor De Lazarovics. *Bolshevism in Hungary: The Béla Kun Period* (London: Grant Richards, 1931).

17   Quoted in *Szabad Nép* (Budapest, Hungary) 21 Jan. 1949.

18   "Lugosi Béla feladata." *Színházi Élet* 30 Mar.-5 Apr. 1919. [Translated by Elemer Szasz.]

19   Rhodes, Gary D. Interview with Noémi Saly. 24 May 2006.

20   Lugosi, Béla. "Levél a szerkesztőnek." *Népszava* (Budapest, Hungary) 7 Mar. 1919.

21   Although different individuals referred to the National Trade Union of Hungarian Actors, the Hungarian Actors Trade Union, or the National Union of the Organizations of Theater Employees, they were all apparently speaking about the same organization.

22   Lugosi, Béla. *Proposal for Organization of a Theatrical Union* 20 Mar. 1919. Available in Archives V, Item 27, Number 67532, Year 1919 at the Hungarian National Archives, Budapest, Hungary. The agreement also contains the following organizational information: "The Union consists of five members sent by each organization, it has [blank] members altogether. The members of the Union elect a secretary and paralegal within themselves each year. The secretary of the Union can represent the Union only in the presence of a delegated Union member. The Union must approve the measures of the secretary. Agreements can be made only with the solid vote of all Union members. The above agreement is valid for two years."

23   Lugosi, Béla. Letter to Hungarian Minister of the Arts, 20 Mar. 1919. [Available in Archives V, Item 27, Number 67532, Year 1919 at the Hungarian National Archives, Budapest, Hungary.]

24   "Lugosi Béla feladata."

25   While the word "secretary" is an apt English translation of the name of Lugosi's post, it does not convey the importance of the position, unless thought of in the same way as, say, "Secretary of State."

26   Dreisziger, N. F. "Émigré Artists and Wartime Politics: 1939-45." *Hungarian Studies Review*, Vol. XXI, Nos. 1-2, Spring-Fall 1994.

27   "A színészek szakszervezeti közgyülése." *Az Újság* (Budapest, Hungary) 13 Apr. 1919.

28   "Színház és Zene." *Pesti Hírlap* (Budapest, Hungary) 18 Apr. 1919.

29   The members of the council were Lajos Bálint, Imre Pethes, Arpád Odry, Margit T. Halmy, Arthur Somlay, József Gábor, Gyula Csortos, Márton Rátkai, Emil Fenyvessy, Gyula Hegedüs, István Szentgyörgyi, Gyula Decséry, László Márkus, István Kernes, Sándor Hevesi, Vilmos Szilágyi, János Doktor, László Vajda, Anna Medek, Kálmán Csathó and Jenő Törzs.

30   Lugosi, Béla. Letter to the National Union of Actors, 25 Apr. 1919. [Available in Archives V, Item 10, Number 90700, Year 1919 at the Hungarian National Archives, Budapest, Hungary.]

31   Kelemen. Letter to Katalin Berendy, 11 Apr. 1919. [Available in Archives V, Item 10, Number 53838, Year 919 at the Hungarian National Archives, Budapest, Hungary.]

32   "Színházi karénekesek jelentkezése." *Pesti Napló* 6 Apr. 1919.

33   "Kétszázötven színész vizsgáju." *Az Est* (Budapest, Hungary) 18 Apr. 1919.

34   In the past, Lugosi biographers have translated this word as "love." We have chosen, however, to accept the recommendation to translate it as "respect." The Hungarian word "szeret" has multiple possible meanings. This word can be translated as "love," as in loving one's spouse or close family members and close friends. One can also use "szeret" when expressing positive feelings, such as respect toward a supervisor, a favorite food, a favorite film character, and so forth. Based on a careful reading of the text, "respect" seems to be closest to the meaning Lugosi intended.

35   Lugosi, Béla. "Levél a szerkeszt nek." *Népszava* 8 May 1919.

36   Abstract from the Order of the District Captaincy of the Red Army on 14th of May Current Year, No. 18, Clothing Confiscation. Signed by Béla Lugosi. 22 May 1919. [Translated by Elemer Szasz.]

37   Kaas, Baron Albert and Fedor De Lazarovics. *Bolshevism in Hungary: The Béla Kun Period* (London: Grant Richards, 1931).

38   After John Norman of the Office of Strategic Services interviewed Lugosi about Hungary in 1945, he made the following note: "Minority rights, [Lugosi] said, should be protected. (I could not help detecting a certain nostalgia for Transylvania as he related the history of that area.)" See: OSS FNB HU-731. Office Memorandum from John Norman to DeWitt C. Poole *Conversation with Bela Lugosi in San Francisco on 1 March* 3 Mar. 1945 [Available in the US Office of Strategic Services, Foreign Nationalities Branch Files, 1942-1945, National Archives.]

39   Quoted in Saly, Noémi. "The Mysterious Baby – The First Wife of Dracula." Available at: https://magyarnarancs.hu/narancsszem/a-rejtelyes-babi-90618. Accessed on 10 Dec. 2019.

Lugosi in Budapest, the city he had to flee in 1919. *(Courtesy of John Antosiewicz)*

Chapter 15

Escape

"If you put your ears on the track, you can
hear [the train] go all the way to Vienna."
– Ferenc Molnár, *Liliom*

Béla Kun did not prove capable of ruling Hungary in the turbulent, post-war period any more than Count Károlyi had. His attempts to negotiate with the Triple Entente failed.[1] During the summer of 1919, it became clear that Kun's government was in major trouble.[2] Romanians soon tried to take control of the country. Separately, opposition forces led by Admiral Miklós Horthy gathered in Szeged and made their way to Budapest. They constituted a "White Army" trying to eliminate the "Red Terror." Mihály Várkonyi (Victor Varconi) recalled:

The Communist Regime was not long for Hungary. The people constantly joked about which day the red balloon would burst. Finally, the White Army laid siege to Budapest, [and] prepared to depose the Communists once and for all. The Communists did not want to leave.

While Béla Kun fled to exile in Russia, units of two armies battled for possession of Budapest, street by street. The fighting lasted a few days. One day the Reds would occupy a street, the next the White Army.[3]

In July 1919, Kun had issued a decree compelling military service in the Red Army, but to little effect.[4] He also hoped to receive military aid from Lenin, who would likely have helped. But the Soviet Union's army was then encountering trouble in the Ukraine.[5] The

Postcard of Vienna in 1919.

result: Miklós Horthy assumed control of Hungary at the beginning of August 1919. The Hungarian Soviet Republic had lasted only 133 days.

Those who supported Kun's government, particularly those serving in it, were immediately subject to imprisonment or even death. The White Terror was more brutal than the Red Terror. John Cunningham wrote, "Anyone who participated in the revolution was in danger of being rounded up and, at best, imprisoned, while many were summarily executed."[6] For example, Horthy had Sándor (Alexander) Korda arrested and jailed in October 1919.[7] That was even before Horthy rode victoriously into Budapest in November.[8] Film director Sándor Pallós suffered an even worse fate, being tortured to death.[9]

Many others fled to Vienna, specifically because Austria granted them political asylum.[10] Béla Kun initially went to the city, prior to moving to Russia.[11] So did many of his comrades. Those in the arts also rushed to Vienna, among them Mihály Kertész (Michael Curtiz) and – after being released from prison – Sándor Korda.[12] Though Lenin believed some of the Communists in Kun's government had been "sincere," he condemned many of them as traitors who were too "fainthearted" to stay in Budapest and fight for the "dictatorship of the proletariat."[13]

Kun had actually looked to Vienna for assistance as early as June 1919, when he sent emissaries to the city in an effort – as Bennett Kovrig has written – "to drive the Austrian Communists into an uprising on June 15."[14] Lugosi apparently took part, at least to the extent of converting Viennese actors to the cause. A newspaper article published in July 1919 claims:

A further proof for the heightened political activism of the Hungarian Bolshevist

Regime in Vienna is the fact that the actor Béla Lugosi, who was a member of the Nemzeti Színház [National Theater], was sent to Vienna with the mission to campaign for support of Bolshevism among the actors and technical personnel of the Vienna theater. Lugosi, who is insignificant as an actor, implemented the Bolshevization of the Budapest stages. Since the implementation of the system, the Actors' Guild has been in steady decline, because the least important person in the choir receives the same salary as the actor in the leading role. Lugosi attempted to win over the Viennese stage personnel to his cause and has access to considerable funds in order to influence particularly the less prominent actors and personnel in order to promote the conversion of the Viennese Theater to Socialism.[15]

Painting of Vienna from a 1919 postcard.

Lugosi, likely accompanied by his wife Ilona, might have only stayed a few days in the city. There is an indication that he was there around June 21, 1919, shortly after the failed uprising.[16]

But this trip presumably occurred before it became necessary for him to actually flee Hungary, which would not have been until late July, if not August. Lugosi and his wife could have stayed in Vienna from June onward, fearing the end of the regime, but this would place him in a very different and much earlier timeline than everyone else who fled, to the extent he might have been seen as fleeing from Kun. That course of events thus seems highly unlikely. Instead, he probably returned to Hungary after the June trip to Vienna, only to escape to the same city weeks later.

Whether it was in late July or August or even thereafter, Lugosi did become – as Ilona's granddaughter Noémi Saly has said – "afraid. He was genuinely afraid for his life."[17] Journalists reported the same; in 1936, one reported that Lugosi had "fled for his life."[18] Lugosi himself told an interviewer that he left Hungary "suddenly" to "avoid being shot or hanged."[19] Saly added:

> [Lugosi and his wife] were helped to cross the borders by human smugglers: my grandmother was carried through the swamp of the Fertő lake [Neusiedler See, at the border of Austria and Hungary] on the back of a well-knit peasant. My great-grandparents only learned of their escape afterwards.[20]

According to another account, the Lugosis hid under a mound of straw in a wagon that

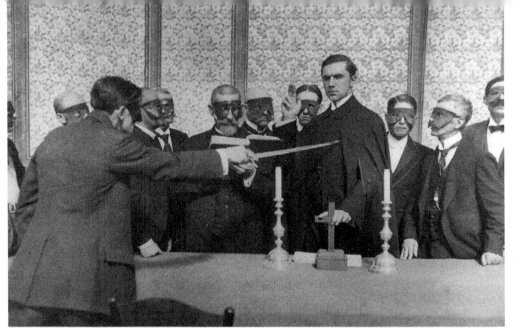
Lugosi in *Álarcosbál* (*The Masked Ball*, 1917).

took them to a plane, which took off just in time to evade capture. If there is any truth to these stories, they would have occurred after Kun's regime collapsed on August 1, 1919.

Once relocated, Lugosi would likely have spent time at Vienna's Filmhof Café, where many Hungarian ex-pats gathered to talk. Perhaps some of them believed they could return to Budapest once things settled down.[21] They probably discussed the need to earn money, which would not have been particularly difficult. Film studios in Vienna hired some Hungarians, in part because Hungarian films were often screened in Austria, and even shot at Austrian studios. And most people in Budapest at the time spoke some German.[22] That meant the possibility of playing roles in the Viennese theater.

Could Lugosi have worked onstage in Vienna, if not in some unknown film or films? Certainly that is possible. No documentation has yet surfaced, but in a 1935 interview, Lugosi claimed to have worked in Austria.[23] Regardless, the city would not have seemed as wonderful as it once was. As Michael Korda wrote in his family memoir:

> Defeat had eroded the social conventions that had made Vienna seem gay and charming, exposing disagreeable realities. Austria was reduced to a tiny state with a huge capital city, rather as if Paris were the capital of Switzerland. Austrian agriculture could not produce enough to feed the capital, so the farmers hoarded their produce. Austrian industry was almost nonexistent, since most of the Empire's factories had been in Bohemia, which was now the separate – and hostile – country of Czechoslovakia. The collapse of Austria's currency had led to rampant inflation, in which the savings of the middle class, together with their pensions, insurance and dreams, were instantly erased.[24]

The end result was that life in Vienna was hardly the oasis that Lugosi and his wife Ilona probably desired. Noémi Saly even believes Ilona suffered a miscarriage during this period.[25]

Deeply upset with Lugosi's "communist activities," Ilona's parents persuaded their "Baby"

Lugosi in one of his
Hungarian silent films.

Lugosi in one of his Hungarian silent films, possibly *Álarcosbál* (*The Masked Ball*, 1917).

to return to Budapest and divorce Lugosi.[26] Ilona believed they would die without her.[27] Lugosi claimed that he wrote her numerous letters "every second day," but never got an answer. Ilona's parents did not pass on the letters to her.[28]

The first divorce hearing took place at the Fifth District Court of Budapest on July 17, 1920, many months after Ilona returned from Vienna. An additional filing was made on October 9, 1920, prior to a final hearing in November of that year. The legal papers imply that Ilona never left Hungary with Lugosi, despite the fact that she had definitely lived with him for a time in Vienna. Pertinent details are as follows:

> The Royal Court of Budapest passes the following judgment upon suitor Ilona Szmik (address: Budapest, II. district, 1. Batthyány str.), represented by Dr. Károly Walter, lawyer from Budapest and upon defendant, her husband, Béla Lugosi, actor (address: Trieste, Hotel Excelsior), represented by Dr. Miksa Kopitl, lawyer from Budapest, in regards of the termination of their marriage … which decision is based on the lawsuit … filed on 9 October 1920, and on the hearing which took place on 22 November 1920.

> The Royal Court of Hungary announces the termination of the marriage between Béla Lugosi and Ilona Szmik, which was pronounced in the presence of the Hungarian

BECOMING DRACULA

State Registrar of Budapest's II. district on 25 July 1917, based on the fault of the defendant ... and it declares the defendant guilty....

No child was born from their marriage.

JUSTIFICATION

I. In this case the Royal Court is competent on the basis of [Hungarian law].

II. The suitor applied for the divorce because she had been left by her husband intentionally and without any legitimate reason on the 20th day of June 1919 and, despite the court's request, he [did not] return.

III. The content of the suit is the same as the suitor's previous claim to the defendant, who interrupted the marriage and communion at the above mentioned date, which, despite the judicial decision issued for that reason, has not been recovered by him since then, as stated in the certificate ... issued by local authorities.

Ilona Szmik and her second husband, Imre Francsek. *(Courtesy of Noémi Saly)*

Since the defendant did not claim in the lawsuit that he had a legitimate reason for leaving his spouse, the Royal Court cancels the marriage between the litigants... The marriage ended because of the defendant's [actions], for which he was found guilty.... The suitor expressly waived her legal claim for litigation costs....[29]

The marriage officially ended on November 22, 1920. In December of that year, after having burned most photos and letters from Lugosi, Ilona married for the second time.[30] The groom was Imre Francsek, a reputable architect who was closely associated with the mayor of Budapest. Like Lugosi, he was very handsome. But that was where the similarities ended. Francsek was everything Lajos Szmik wanted for his daughter, everything that Lugosi was not. Financially and socially, Francsek provided Ilona things that Lugosi couldn't. He was also able to live and work in Hungary without fear of any reprisal.[31]

Lillian Arch, Lugosi's fourth wife, later said of her husband and Ilona, "that one was a love-match."[32] Curiously, the *Budapest Address Directory* for 1922-1923 still listed "Lugosi, Béla, színész [actor] as residing at Batthyány utca 1 in District II." But by that time he had been away from Hungary and Ilona for a few years. His first wife and his home were lost to him. In fact, he may have had an affair in Vienna shortly after Ilona left him; the heirs of a woman in Vienna named Trudy once auctioned some liqueur glasses that Lugosi allegedly gave to her.

Ilona's granddaughter Noémi Saly remarked that, once returning to Hungary was no longer tenable, Lugosi firmly set his eyes on America.[33] Lugosi even hinted at this in an interview given in the mid-1930s:

> When I crossed the Hungarian border, I thought I could start a new life in the West. I was determined to change countries and to blow up my bridges behind me.[34]

But first he had to obtain enough financial resources for the journey, and that was apparently not possible in Vienna. And so he journeyed to Germany.

In Molnár's *Liliom*, the title character tells Ficsúr, "The [train] that just puffed past us – it goes all the way to Vienna." Ficsúr asks, "No further?" Liliom responds, "Yes – further, too." The script then suggests a "pause."

(Endnotes)

1   Kovrig, Bennett. *Communism in Hungary: From Kun to Kádár* (Stanford: Hoover Institution Press, 1979).

2   Kaas, Baron Albert and Fedor De Lazarovics. *Bolshevism in Hungary: The Béla Kun Period* (London: Grant Richards, 1931).

3   Varconi, Victor and Ed Honeck. *It's Not Enough to Be Hungarian* (Denver, CO: Graphic Impressions, 1976).

4   Kovrig, *Communism in Hungary.*

5   Ibid.

6   Cunningham, John. *Hungarian Cinema: From Coffee House to Multiplex* (London: Wallflower Press, 2004).

7   Kulik, Karol. *Alexander Korda: The Man Who Could Work Miracles* (New Rochelle, NY: Arlington House, 1975).

8   Lukacs, John. *Budapest 1900: A Historical Portrait of a City and Its Culture* (New York: Grove Press, 1988).

9   Cunningham, *Hungarian Cinema.*

10   Kontler, László. *A History of Hungary: Millennium in Central Europe* (New York: Palgrave Macmillan, 2002).

11   Lukacs, *Budapest 1900.*

12   Kulik, *Alexander Korda.*

13   Kovrig, *Communism in Hungary*.

14   Ibid.

15   "Der Neue Ungarische Delandte." *Neues 8 Uhr Blatt* (Vienna, Austria) 18 July 1919.

16   "Complications around the communist deeds of the two actors named Lugosi – One Lugosi betrayed the counter-revolutionists of Buda, while the other Lugosi encouraged actors to revolt." *8 Orai Újság* (Budapest, Hungary) 2 Feb. 1920. The article states that Lugosi left Hungary on 21 June 1919.

17   Rhodes, Gary D. Interview with Noémi Saly, 24 May 2006.

18   Harrison, Paul. "In Hollywood." *Wisconsin Rapids Daily Tribune* (Wisconsin Rapids, WI) 28 Feb. 1936.

19   Shirley, Lillian. "Afraid of Himself." *Modern Screen* Mar. 1931.

20   Saly, Noémi. "The Mysterious Baby – The First Wife of Dracula." Available at: https://magyarnarancs. hu/narancsszem/a-rejtelyes-babi-90618. Accessed on 10 Dec. 2019.

21   Though he went to Italy rather than Vienna, Count Károlyi believed he would only have to live in exile for one year (as opposed to his wife, who thought it would be three months). Instead, it became 27 years. See Karolyi, Michael. *Memoirs of Michael Karolyi: Faith Without Illusion* (New York: E. P. Dutton, 1957).

22   Lukacs, *Budapest 1900*.

23   Barnes, Eleanor. "Bela Lugosi to Produce Here, First Film is *Cagliostro*." 17 Sept. 1935.

24   Korda, Michael. *Charmed Lives: A Family Romance* (London: Allen Lane, 1980).

25   Rhodes, interview with Noémi Saly.

26   Saly, "The Mysterious Baby."

27   Rhodes, interview with Noémi Saly.

28   Sinclair, John. "Master of Horrors." *Silver Screen* Jan. 1932.]

29   Béla Lugosi/Ilona Smik Divorce Documents. Available in Catalog Reference HU BFL – VII.2.c – 1920 – 40714 at the Budapest City Archives, Budapest, Hungary.

30   Saly, "The Mysterious Baby."

31   Rhodes, interview with Noémi Saly.

32   D'Arc, James D. *Oral History Interview Donlevy, Lillian Lugosi, 1912*, 20 May 1976. Available at L. Tom Perry Special Collections, Harold B. Lee Library, Brigham Young University, Provo, UT.

33   Rhodes, interview with Noémi Saly.

34   Lugosi, Béla, quoted in *Californiai Magyarság* (Los Angeles, CA) 9 Nov. 1934.

Bela Lugosi, the wrongly
accused Hungarian actor.
(Courtesy of John Antosiewicz)

Chapter 16

The Strange Case of Janos "Bela" Lugosi-Buchter

"The darker the night, the brighter the stars."
– Dostoevsky, *Crime and Punishment*

L ike others who fled when the Kun regime collapsed, Béla Lugosi never returned to his homeland. Not geographically, at least. In terms of the language, culture, and food, Lugosi would later try to recreate Hungary in other places, including New York and Los Angeles. As a result, it was as if he hadn't completely left. Here is a situation known to so many emigrants.

But it was also true in another respect, one suited as much for detective fiction as for a biography.

To begin, the Horthy regime investigated known and suspected communists in the theater community. On January 20, 1920, an officer of the Budapest Branch of the Hungarian State Police wrote:

> As part of the investigation I showed up at the apartment of Jenő Balassa, which is situated in Katona József str. 39, where I asked him about the case. He denied that he has ever been a communist and states that he has always been against it, he has always been telling his actor colleagues about his lack of support for communism, and that he has already been denounced for this several times, but there is no firm basis for accusation. He denies the charges raised against him in the report.

> I asked Arthur Fehér, member of the [Comic Theater], address: 19 Wesselényi str., about the same matter. I did not succeed in interrogating Béla Lugosi, who is currently in Berlin. I also managed to interrogate József Kürthy, member of the Nemzeti Színház

[National Theater], address: 1 Páva street, Gyula Fehér, address: Rökk Szilárd str. 6., Jenő Horváth, address: 58 Dohány str. and Béla Salamon, member of the Orfeum, and they all deny that they were dangerous communists, since the goal of the Actors' Association was to interfere in the destruction of the theater by communists.

Then I continued the investigation regarding the above-mentioned people's case, but I found [no new evidence]. Until now I have not found any proof that they were guilty.[1]

By the end of the month, an official from the State Prosecutor's Office terminated the investigation of Lugosi and others, stating, "I did not succeed in proving they are guilty."[2]

But that decision did not end the lingering effects on Lugosi's reputation from his participation in the Kun regime. There was no end in sight in the hunt for Kun sympathizers. And thus the story becomes particularly bizarre.

Investigation cover sheet. *(Courtesy of the Budapest City Archives)*

In October 1919, a medical student named Gyula Rémi sent a letter to the headquarters of the Hungarian State Police Department in Budapest. Its contents led to Béla Lugosi being confused with someone named "Detective Lugosi":

Witnessed at the Headquarters of the Hungarian State Police in Budapest, 8 October, 1919, Gyula Rémi, a Budapest-born, 22-year-old Roman Catholic medical student (address: 8th district, 8 József körút, 3rd floor, 3.), states the following:

On July 2, 1919, two political investigators, Sándor Oravecz and Lugosi (deputy leader of the 32nd investigation unit), arrested me on suspicion of incitement, and took me to the Houses of Parliament. On August 3, I was released from the prison at Markó Street and knowing that these two detectives resided in Astoria, I informed the state police on August 5, but nobody came to Astoria ... In a few days Oravecz and Lugosi moved to the Metropol hotel, from which they soon disappeared.

I received the attached letter this morning, showing that Oravecz is in Fiume [now Rijeka in Croatia]. I ask that the Police in Fiume be told that they must arrest Oravecz and Lugosi, too – in case the latter one also resides there. It is possible that they used my name during their flight, since they have all my personal files.

Oravecz was a military deputy, then he voluntarily joined the terrorists.[3]

The true identity of "Detective Lugosi" was János Lugosi-Buchter, also known as "Béla Lugosi-Buchter." To make matters more confused, Lugosi-Buchter was an actor.[4] At a given point, he may have intentionally tried to be mistaken for the real Béla Lugosi.

At any rate, those prosecuting Gyula Rémi's case mistakenly identified Béla Lugosi as "Detective Lugosi." A document dated January 10, 1920, illustrates the increasing gravity of the situation: "For further action, I transfer the files of Béla Lugosi and Sándor Oravecz, communists, since they are currently staying in Fiume."[5] Further complicating matters, Sándor Oravecz, with whom Béla Lugosi was now wrongly considered a partner in crime, mailed a death threat to Gyula Rémi, which said in part:

The letter of July 21, 1926 that closed the investigation. *(Courtesy of the Budapest City Archives)*

Motto: A sure sign of your death.

I inform His Excellency, Remi, my friend, you bastard, you beast, that you did not stay quiet when the [revolution] happened. You know that I know everything, so I also know that what you said you were about to do is not going to happen. As far as I know you, you are too much a coward to dare doing it.

But you know I'm not a coward but a determined man, and that I'm going to go to Hungary and then you're in my hands. I'll kill you or I'll die, but I guess you'll be the first [who dies]. Anyway, you know I'm writing this letter to you so that you know you won't have a peaceful moment while I'm here, yet again I warn you, you dog, to shake with fear, because if I make a pity for your life then I will put out your two eyes.[6]

Lugosi in *Álarcosbál* (*The Masked Ball*, 1917). *(Courtesy of John Antosiewicz)*

A later report from the Hungarian State Police underscored the shady and violent character of the individual with whom Béla Lugosi was now incorrectly linked:

> According to the inhabitants of 6 Tátra street, that man [Oravecz] lived in the same house in a requisitioned flat until the collapse of the regime, he wore his dreaded leather jacket all the time and he threatened all with his continuous referencing to the revolutionary court, and he was careful to stop inhabitants acting against the orders of Kun and his companions.[7]

Separate from these matters, on November 1, 1919, an official of the Hungarian State Police in Budapest identified Béla Lugosi as a detective in the office of the 32nd Regiment, who "maintained a permanent connection with the terrorists."[8] But the same official contradicted himself by adding: "Since neither Rémi nor others were able to provide more details about Oravecz and Lugosi, I could not find out more about their identities or their place of residence."[9] The final document came in the form of an arrest warrant, in which the investigator pledged to find the suspects, who were supposedly hiding somewhere in Serbia. He vowed that he would "contact all the judicial and administrative authorities and ask them to investigate, arrest them, deliver them to the prison of the closest court or tribunal, and to inform the Budapest Public Prosecutor about it."[10]

BECOMING DRACULA

Thus, an arrest warrant was mistakenly issued for *Béla Lugosi* rather than the actual perpetrator, *János "Béla" Lugosi-Buchter*.[11]

These were two very different people of course, but the confusion did not help Lugosi's reputation in the local newspapers. Eight months after his departure from Hungary, the press suggested that it was Béla Lugosi, rather than Lugosi-Buchter, who was accused of the crime.[12] With Lugosi himself out of the country, some of his fellow actors, family members, and in-laws may well have believed what they read. Here might be yet another reason Lajos Szmik urged his daughter Ilona to return to Budapest and divorce Lugosi. And here might be why he was officially dropped from membership in the Nemzeti Színház (National Theater) in December of 1919.[13]

Though the Hungarian State Police ended its investigation, the Budapest Royal Criminal Court undertook its own inquiry. Various court documents outline concerns about Lugosi's activities during 1918-1919, beginning with a letter from one investigator dated May 17, 1920:

> I send you the investigative files against Béla Lugosi (Blaskó) in order to ask you to ascertain the suspect's place of residence. In case you find him, he must be heard out, otherwise please provide us with his description of person by urgent posting, so that we can attach it to the already existing files.[14]

The ongoing investigation resulted in several reports. The first was issued on February 9, 1921:

> Name and Personal Data: Béla Lugosi (Blaskó), 38 years old, Roman Catholic, born in Lugos, resident in Budapest, married, can read and write, has no notable property, has a clean record, actor.[15]

> Crime Type with Sections of Law Related to it, Time and Place of Crime: ... continuously committed provocation... violation of personal freedom....

> The Starting Date of Provisional Detention: Fugitive.

> Short Description of the Underlying Facts: Béla Lugosi (Blaskó), as a member of the working and military councils in the second district, constantly praised communism and proletarian dictatorship during meetings at the Fészek Club and at the Nemzeti Színház, saying that people must stick by these ideas, while he smeared the bourgeoisie. Moreover, he denounced a man named Kálmán Takács, as a counter-revolutionist, who was condemned for 2 years of forced labor by the Revolutionary Tribunal, and who also was imprisoned for more than 3 months.

> Opinion of the Royal Prosecutor: Based on the supporting investigative

documentation, suspect had been actively involved in the destructive work preparing the dictatorship of the proletariat. He had disbanded the Association of Actors and organized the Union of Actors. He was a member of the Central Soviet [government] and during the entire length of the dictatorship he was constantly abusing the civic class, and he praised communism and [Kun's] dictatorship. Moreover, he denounced the counter-revolutionaries he knew, making useful service for communism. After the fall of the dictatorship of the proletariat he escaped abroad and has been away from Hungary since then. Conversely, he is convinced of communism and as such he is a dangerous person to the legitimate order of state and society. Thus, I do not recommend him to [receive] grace.[16]

This investigative report shows that, even as late as 1921, official documents still merged facts about Lugosi-Buchter with Béla Lugosi, as if they were one person.

The Council of Grade of the Royal Criminal Court in Budapest received all of the relevant documents on February 17, 1921. The response was negative:

I inform you ... regarding the criminal case against Béla Lugosi (Blaskó), who is suspected of committing the crimes of continuous provocation and violation of personal freedom, that, according to the Minister of Justice's transcript ... dated March 1, Béla Lugosi (Blaskó) was not recommended for grace....[17]

Lugosi in *Leoni Leo* (*Leo Leoni*, 1917).

ORAI 8 ÚSÁG

Bonyodalmak a két Lugosi-szinész kommunista üzelmei körül.

Az egyik Lugosi árulta el a budai ellenforradalmárokat. — A másik Lugosi a szinészeket forradalmárositotta.

— Saját tudósitónktól. —

Newspaper article that exonerated Lugosi from the false charges. Published in *8 Orai Újság* on February 20, 1920.

The investigations continued, but on April 21, 1921, a chairperson at the tribunal wrote, "The letter of investigation issued against [the] suspect ... has so far failed to produce results and the investigation has been terminated."[18] The Court was thus advised to halt the proceedings on May 31, 1921:

> The Court must stop the process against Béla Lugosi (Blaskó), a 38-year-old, Roman Catholic person, who was born in Lugos and who is an actor, who has been accused of having committed the crimes of continuous provocation according to Article 172 (2) of the Penal Code, and defined in Article 19 of law no. 4. XIII, 1912, and violation of personal freedom, according to Article 323 (2) of the Penal Code, defined in the last paragraph. The procedure must remain stopped until the subject is found, and the Court must set the legal costs of the procedure, which are due to be assigned to him.
>
> Rationale:
>
> On 13 July 1920, the Royal Prosecutor's Office issued a letter of investigation against the aforementioned defendant ... This did not lead to any result. The Investigating Magistrate has fulfilled section 472 of BP. The procedure must therefore be stopped until the defendant has been found.[19]

Over five years later, on June 21, 1926, the Royal Criminal Court issued the following judgment:

> The Court terminates the criminal proceedings against Béla Lugosi (Blaskó) ... based on the limitation period set out in Article 106 of the Criminal Code, furthermore, the Court withdraws the letter of investigation ... Legal costs of the procedure are assigned to the Treasury ... The Criminal Court did not take any action, or make any decision against [the] suspect, which, according to Article 108 of the Criminal Code

could have interrupted the limitation period of the case after the issuance of the court order on 21 January 1921. Since the limitation period of the prosecution procedure has expired … the procedure had to be terminated and the letter of investigation had to be withdrawn.[20]

That same year, Hungary awarded general amnesty to all exiled citizens. And so Lugosi was no longer subject to arrest in Hungary, either for his own actions or those of Lugosi-Buchter.

Far more than the courts or police, a specific journalist exposed the confusion between the two men. In a February 1920 article for *8 Órai Újság*, he essentially exonerated the real Lugosi:

> The indictment against the 23-year-old actor, János Lugosi-Buchter, born in Kisvárda, which has been published recently by the State Prosecutor's Office, sheds new light on the ever-evolving tell-tale about Béla Lugosi, a communist, who used to be an actor at the Nemzeti Színház, and which story has been spreading fast among artist circles of Budapest during the communist regime.
>
> Béla Lugosi, against whom an arrest warrant was issued by the Attorney-at-Law of the Budapest Criminal Court, had been the secretary of the Actors' Union during the outbreak of the proletarian dictatorship, and in this position, he was propagating the [Hungarian] Soviet Republic most eagerly both within the acting circles and towards the wider public. The actors at the Nemzeti Színház drew apart from him, [and his] presence became more and more unpleasant in those acting circles already during the regime; then he became so unsupportable during the days of counter-revolution around 21 June [of 1919] that, after the fall of the terror, he fled from the capital without saying farewell to anyone and went to Berlin.[21]
>
> Lugosi's artist colleagues were against his passionate agitations, but his downfall was caused mainly by some news, which said that he committed deeds against his honor for the sake of the [Hungarian] Soviet Regime and betrayed the counter-revolutionary movement. According to the news, which was initially spreading in secret, but which got stronger day by day, Béla Lugosi had betrayed the counter-revolutionary association run by János Takács and 16 other citizens from Buda, by reporting them to Jancsi, supreme commander of the Red Watch. He and some 'terror boys' captured János Takács and some of his fellows in the apartment of the movement's leader on Zsigmond Street, and he delivered them to the Revolutionary Tribunal. The counter-revolutionists, after being tortured in various ways by the Lenin-boys in the dungeons of the Parliament, were condemned to 5, 10 or 15 years of penal labor.
>
> The above indictment of the public prosecution's office now raises awareness of the

Lugosi in Budapest.

embarrassing case and exempts the communist-minded Béla Lugosi to the extent that he can only be charged with agitation within the actors' unions and in public, but he is not guilty of betraying the counter-revolutionary movement of the citizens of Buda.

In fact, it was not János Takács, the leader of the counter-revolutionary movement, who introduced his plans to Béla Lugosi, former artist of the Nemzeti Színház, but the [sympathetic] citizens of Buda who entrusted János Lugosi-Buchter with their secret. That person was an actor, too, and a political detective working for the 32nd Red Army under the regime.

János Lugosi-Buchter was the traitor of the Buda counter-revolutionary movement, and again it was him who arrested János Takács and several of his companions at Zsigmond Street. After the fall of the dictatorship, Lugosi-Buchter was arrested by the state police on August 9 [1919] and he was escorted to the state prosecutor's office, where he has been in custody ever since....[22]

But the case of mistaken identity was not so easy to clear up. In October 1919, an anti-communist newspaper accused Lugosi of causing someone named "Major Bódy" to be evicted from his own house, thus causing Bódy great financial damage.[23] The charge was never proven. The real culprit was presumably Lugosi-Buchter.

Even in the non-political realm, Lugosi's reputation was sullied. In March of 1923, newspapers in both Szatmár and Budapest reported the arrest of a scam artist and beggar, real name János Ilniczky. Using multiple false IDs, Ilniczky developed a scheme to take money for goods and services that were never provided. Upon his arrest, using one of those false IDs, he tried to convince the police officers that he was the real Béla Lugosi.[24]

For the rest of his life, particularly his years in the United States, the real Béla Lugosi wisely downplayed his relationship to the Béla Kun regime. Serving in a communist government would have won few friends in America. When asked, Lugosi tended to focus on Count Károlyi, never mentioning Kun. On more than one occasion, Lugosi eliminated Kun from history by implying that Horthy's White Terror ended Károlyi's regime. In 1931, for example, Lugosi claimed:

When the war ended, the revolution in Hungary took place. Count Károlyi seized the government, and because I was a friend, he gave me a ministerial post. Soon the royalist party regained control, and where they could find a Károlyi adherent they hanged or shot him.

... It was the post-war penalty for being on the wrong side of politics. I'm told they use the same method in Chicago occasionally. Well, I didn't want to be 'taken for a ride.'[25]

In another interview, he said much the same, with a syndicated columnist reporting, "when Károlyi's government enjoyed its brief regime, Lugosi was Minister of the Theater." All of that came to a swift end due to a "monarchical party" that seized power.[26]

Of course Lugosi had indeed been a member of the communist party, and had served in the governments of Count Károlyi and – with much greater authority – Béla Kun. He had given speeches and he had led a communist union. He had even tried to sway actors in Vienna to the cause.

But Lugosi was not a terrorist or a traitor. He had threatened no one; he physically harmed no one. Along with so many notable artists, he fled Hungary. Unlike the others, he became an unwitting character in a real-life film noir. Allegations against Lugosi-Buchter defamed him, and then haunted him for many years. Though some of his later critics would have despised Lugosi's involvement with communism, the most virulent among them seem to have been swayed by rumors about Lugosi-Buchter, a villain whose capture did not completely restore Lugosi's reputation.

If there was any justice at all, it was that Lugosi was far from the reach of the Horthy government when the wrongful efforts to arrest him occurred, forging a new life and career in another country.

(Endnotes)

1   Letter to Budapest Branch of the Hungarian State Police, 20 Jan. 1920. Available in Catalog Reference HU BFL 638 f, 1/1920-IV-13-915 at the Budapest City Archives, Budapest, Hungary.

2   Notification from the Budapest Branch of the State Prosecutor's Office, 31 Jan. 1920. Available in Catalog Reference HU BFL 638 f, 1/1920-IV-13-915 at the Budapest City Archives.

3   Rémi, Gyula. Letter to the Headquarters of the Hungarian State Police Department in Budapest, 8 Oct. 1919. Available in Catalog Reference HU BFL VIII-18-d-1920-13/603-I-0096029 Lugosi Béla, 1920.

4   "Bonyodalmak a két Lugosi-színész kommunista üzelmei körül." *8 Órai Újság* (Budapest, Hungary) 20 Feb. 1920.

5   Letter to the Public Prosecutor's Office in Budapest, Undated. Available in Catalog Reference HU BFL VIII-18-d-1920-13/603-I-0096029 Lugosi Béla, 1920.

6   Oravecz, Sándor. Letter to Gyula Rémi, Undated. Available in Catalog Reference HU BFL VIII-18-d-1920-13/603-I-0096029 Lugosi Béla, 1920.

7   Report to the Hungarian State Police, Budapest, 22 Oct. 1919. Available in Catalog Reference HU BFL VIII-18-d-1920-13/603-I-0096029 Lugosi Béla, 1920.

8   Szőke, József. Report to the Hungarian State Police, Budapest, 1 Nov. 1919. Available in Catalog Reference HU BFL VIII-18-d-1920-13/603-I-0096029 Lugosi Béla, 1920.

9   Ibid.

10   Arrest Warrant, Budapest Prosecutor's Office, 29 Jan. 1920. Available in Catalog Reference HU BFL VIII-18-d-1920-13/603-I-0096029 Lugosi Béla, 1920.

                                              BECOMING DRACULA

11   "Bonyodalmak a két Lugosi-színész kommunista üzelmei körül."

12   The 1 Feb. 1920 edition of *Friss Újság* (Budapest, Hungary) claimed that "...Béla Lugosi and Sándor Oravecz ... were political investigators at the time" and guilty of the violation of the personal freedoms of Gyula Rémi.

13   *Az Est* (Budapest, Hungary) 12 Dec. 1919

14   Magoss, Károly. Letter to Budapest Royal Criminal Court Headquarters, 17 May 1920. Available in Catalog Reference HU BFL VII-18-d-1920-13/3769-I-00960217 Lugosi (Blaskó) Béla, 1920.

15   By the time of this report, Lugosi was no longer married or residing in Budapest.

16   Magoss, Károly. Order of the Ministry of Justice, Budapest Royal Criminal Court, 9 Feb. 1921. Available in Catalog Reference HU BFL VII-18-d-1920-13/3769-I-00960217 Lugosi (Blaskó) Béla, 1920.

17   Ibid.

18   From the Chairperson of the Tribunal. Letter to the Criminal Court in Budapest, 21 Apr. 1921. Available in Catalog Reference HU BFL VII-18-d-1920-13/3769-I-00960217 Lugosi (Blaskó) Béla, 1920.

19   Magoss, Károly. Letter to the Accelerated Five-Member Council of the Royal Court, 31 May 1921. Available in Catalog Reference HU BFL VII-18-d-1920-13/3769-I-00960217 Lugosi (Blaskó) Béla, 1920.

20   Eltzenbaum, Mayer. Letter to the Royal Criminal Court in Budapest, 21 July 1926. Available in Catalog Reference HU BFL VII-18-d-1920-13/3769-I-00960217 Lugosi (Blaskó) Béla, 1920.

21   As Chapter 15 explains, Lugosi went to Vienna prior to Berlin. Though he visited Vienna in June 1919, he may have not fled to that city until after the fall of Kun's government some weeks later.

22   "Bonyodalmak a két Lugosi-színész kommunista üzelmei körül."

23   "Színészek a kommunizmus alatt." *Tolnai Világlapja* (Budapest, Hungary) 4 Oct. 1919.

24   "Rendörkézen a soknevü szélhámos." *Friss Újság* 16 Mar. 1923; "Elfogtak ogy vakmer szélhámost." *Magyarország* (Budapest, Hungary) 16 Mar. 1923.

25   Shirley, Lillian. "Afraid of Himself." *Modern Screen* Mar. 1931.

26   "Notes on the Passing Show." *Dallas Morning News* (Dallas, TX) 9 Mar. 1931.

Lugosi in *Hypnose: Sklaven
fremden Willens* (*Hypnosis:
Slave of a Foreign Will*, 1919).

(Courtesy of John Antosiewicz)

Chapter 17

Babylon

"I am a camera with its shutter open,
quite passive, recording, not thinking."
– Christopher Isherwood, *The Berlin Stories*

When Lugosi arrived in Berlin during September of 1919, the city was on fire, ablaze, not from flames, but from what Mel Gordon has described as "Voluptuous Panic."[1] After the Great War, the Weimar Republic rose up from the ashes of a defeated nation and the abdication of Kaiser Wilhelm II. As Peter Gay has observed, Weimar was an "idea seeking to become reality."[2] With it came massive inflation, food shortages, and the shame of the Treaty of Versailles. Despite these troubles, or perhaps because of them, Berlin descended into decadence.

Here was the world that spawned Sally Bowles and Mr. Norris. Its avatar was Anita Berber, who simultaneously scandalized and tititlated Berlin with her celebrations of "Depravity, Horror, and Ecstasy," so often performed nude and fueled by copious amounts of cocaine.[3] And its adherents were legion, to the extent that cocaine, morphine, and opium were readily available.

Nightlife featured prostitutes and clubs catering to various sexual orientations and fetishes. Erotic revues and literature were all the rage. As Gordon noted, "Wild sex and all-night antics could be made anywhere. In private flats, hotel rooms, and rented halls, drug parties and nude 'Beauty Evenings' were constantly announced and held."[4]

Sex and vice were rampant, including in the cinema. Richard Oswald directed such 1919 films as *Prostitution* and *Anders als die Andern* (*Different from the Others*), the latter co-written with "sexologist" Magnus Hirschfeld. Citing such movies as Otto Rippert's *Hyänen der Lust* (*Hyenas of Lust*, 1919) and Karl Grune's *Aus eines Mannes Mädchenjahren* (*A Man's Girlhood*, 1919), and

DER VAMPYR

Vertrieb für die ganze Welt: Filmhaus Bavaria, München, Kaufingerstr. 2. Tel. 14269.
Tel.-Adr. „Bavariafilmhaus.“

Published in *Lichtbild-Bühne* on July 12, 1919.

drawing on such studies as Curt Moreck's popular 1926 book *Sittengeschichte des Kinos* (*History of Cinema's Morals*), Siegfried Kracauer chronicled a vogue for movies that focused on "matters of sex life with an undeniable penchant for pornographic excursions."[5] Most of them focused on heterosexual desires, including extramarital relations, burlesque strippers, and juvenile delinquency. Certainly these films were not pornographic as in later, 20th and 21st century definitions of that term, but they were suggestive, risqué, lurid, and sensationalistic.

Published in *Lichtbild-Bühne* in August of 1919.

Lugosi, Bèla, W 30, Eisenacher Str. 118.
Lützow 84 64
Lugscheider, Elise, Schneiderin, Kaiser-Friedrich-Str. 238. Neukölln (786)
Lugschütz, Frau S., Rentiere, Wilmersdorf, Berliner Str. 11. 12. Uhland (40 35)
Luhde, Adolf, Ingenieur, Konkordiastr. 23. Spandau (507)

Lugosi as listed in the Berlin telephone directory for 1920.

Lugosi – who would have been well aware of these movies due to their popularity – transitioned into the German film industry with relative ease. To begin, Lugosi spoke German. He had heard the language from his childhood, growing up in the Hungarian/German side of his hometown Lugos. Many persons in Budapest spoke the language as well; for that matter, German was the official language of the Austro-Hungarian government.[6] As Jonathan Harker says in Stoker's *Dracula*, "I found my smattering of German very useful here; indeed, I don't know how I should be able to get on without it."

Another reason Lugosi rapidly found work in Berlin was because of the recent importation of Hungarian films, including several of his own. Ufa released the 1918 Phönix films *Az ezredes* (as *Immer noch toller*) and *99-es számú bérkocsi* (as *99*). Thanks to Saturn-Film, German audiences also saw *Az élet királya* (1917) as *Die Spur seiner Sünden*; *Álarcosbál* (1917) as *Der Maskenball*; *Tavaszi vihar* (1918) as *Der Roman einer geschiedenen Frau*; and *Küzdelem a létért* (1918, aka *A leopárd*) as *Der Fluch der bösen Tat*.[7]

The third reason that Lugosi found work in Berlin resulted from good timing. Eichberg-Film, headed by director Richard Eichberg, produced movies featuring Lee Parry (Eichberg's wife), Violette Napierska (aka Violetta Napierska), and Bruno Decarli. But Decarli – who had notably starred in Robert Wiene's *Furcht* (*Fear*, 1917) – founded his own company (Decarli-Film Kommanditgesellschaft/Decarli-Film Limited) in mid-1919. Eichberg was thus in need of a new male star.[8] Lugosi's biography in the 1920 German publication *Film Magazin* specifically mentioned that Decarli's departure opened the door for him.[9]

Lugosi's first film for Eichberg was *Hypnose: Sklaven fremden Willens* (*Hypnosis: Slave of a Foreign Will*, 1920). In it, he portrayed the evil hypnotist Professor Mors. The subject matter would return when Lugosi starred in *Dracula–The Vampire Play* on Broadway, as well as in such films as *Dracula* (1931), *White Zombie* (1932), *Abbott and Costello Meet Frankenstein*

(1948), and others. And when he recounted the fantastical and allegedly autobiographical story of the "Woman with the Yellow Eyes," Lugosi claimed he knew "something of hypnotism," which that female vampire had used on him.[10]

Hypnose premiered at the Schauburg-Lichtspiele near the beginning of 1920. In *Film-Kurier*, a critic wrote:

> In the hands of a 'wise one' suggestion takes on ennobling power; in the hands of an 'evil one' crime and death. This is the motto for the new Eichberg film in 6 acts. And this reveals the content of the film: The evil one uses suggestion and crime and death are fast on its heels. The subtitle *Sklaven fremden Willens* offers a further exclusion [of suggestion's use for good purposes].

Bruno Decarli.

The film is totally suspenseful and reflects the most outstanding film technology using all the means at its disposal. It would be helped by applying the 'editor's scissors,' reducing the 6 acts to just 5. However, it must be asked whether it should only be judged on the basis of filmmaking. The film reflects the stamp of its director: Richard Eichberg. As he is wont to do, he has focused entirely on the sensational and special effects. And in this regard he celebrates a triumph. It's a real shame for the film, but only in this way can the film achieve the strong impact on the movie-going public that is its goal.

Another person who must be given credit is the cameraman, Joe Rive, who has delivered camera work in photographic and technical terms that is so beautiful that it could scarcely be surpassed.

The leading actress Lee Parry performs exquisitely and her dress is refined in taste. Violette Napierska apparently did not get a role in the film that suited her. Bela Lugosi, straight out of Budapest, is a welcome newcomer – he possesses decided talent, but must guard against exaggeration.[11]

Published in *Lichtbild-Bühne* in 1919.

Lee Parry.

On the same bill was Robert Misch's short film *Die tugendhafte Tänzerin* (*The Virtuous Dancer*, 1920), in which Wanda Treumann "undresses ... and shows her cute legs."

Within two weeks of *Hypnose*'s premiere, a change of title became necessary. An article in *Deutsche Lichtspiel-Zeitung* explained the problem:

> The Neue Berliner Film Co. is at pains to stress that the Eichberg-Film production *Sklaven fremden Willens*, currently playing its debut engagement at Berlin's Schauburg-Lichtspiele theater, is not the movie *Hypnose* starring [Austrian mentalist and clairvoyant] Erik Jan Hanussen, for which it has acquired the distribution rights throughout Germany. It has requested that the Schauburg-Lichtspiele eliminate all references to the originally announced title *Hypnose*.[12]

Eichberg complied, with the film subsequently known solely by its subtitle, *Sklaven fremden Willens*. Nevertheless, it was at the vanguard of a number of German features about hypnosis. After both versions of *Hypnose*, audiences saw such fictional films as *Der Funkenruf der Riobamba* (*Distress Call from the Riobamba*, 1920) and the documentary *Versuche in Hypnose* (*Experiments in Hypnosis*, 1921).

Lugosi's next film for Eichberg was *Der Tanz auf dem Vulkan* (*The Dance on the Volcano*,

Lugosi in *Hypnose: Sklaven fremden Willens* (*Hypnosis: Slave of a Foreign Will*, 1919).

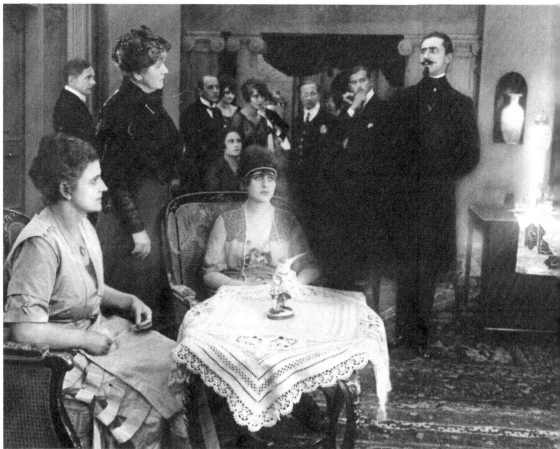

Lugosi in *Hypnose: Sklaven fremden Willens* (*Hypnosis: Slave of a Foreign Will*, 1919). *(Courtesy of John Antosiewicz)*

1920), which was released in two parts, *Sybil Joung* (*Sybil Young*) and *Der Tod des Großfürsten* (*The Death of the Grand Duke*). Shortly before the film's release, *Film und Brettl* told readers:

> Whoever only knows the beginning of this dramatically moving plot of the film *Der Tanz auf dem Vulkan* also knows that the events must develop with unsuspected suspense. If nothing else, Richard Eichberg knows how to create gripping events in social life and produce wonderful moving images with a sure hand. As the female leads he chose the beautiful blonde Lee Parry [and] Violette Napierska.... The interplay of these two very different women, which has already been greeted with lively interest, has again been welcomed by those who love the art of the silent film and know well how to judge it with appreciation.[13]

Following *Der Tanz auf dem Vulkan*'s premiere at the Ufa-Filmpalast in late February 1920, a reviewer declared:

> Richard Eichberg has unquestionably provided proof of his immense talent as

Lugosi (far right) in *Der Tanz auf dem Vulkan* (*The Dance on the Volcano*, 1920).

director of this two-part cinematic work. Film scenes with a wonderful effect unfold without interruption (although it becomes apparent that he is less at home with interior scenes). Naturally the cinematic work possesses everything that provides the director with the opportunity for strong cinematic effects. The large-scale dance scenes in the ballroom, which are certainly not easy to master technically, are first-rate. The fire in the ballroom, the image of the pogrom, the scenes of the conspirators and the filmed sequences in the limestone mountains have a thrilling effect. The plot is full of action and in that respect does justice to the medium of film.[14]

The *Deutsche Lichtspiel-Zeitung* added, "The large-scale production, which merely constitutes a prelude to Part Two, possesses all the qualities of a good commercial picture with international potential."[15] That prediction proved correct; a condensed version of *Der Tanz auf dem Vulkan* was released in the United States in 1921 under the title *Daughter of the Night*.

The American print survives in the collection of the George Eastman House; Lugosi helped film historian William K. Everson identify its German title in 1954.[16] Though truncated, its running time reveals lavish sets and costumes, as well as generally strong performances. The emotions Lugosi reveals onscreen provide the clearest surviving glimpses of him as the romantic hero during his European career.

Lugosi's third film for Eichberg was an "adventure story" written by William Merkel

Lugosi in *Der Tanz auf dem Vulkan* (*The Dance on the Volcano*, 1920).

and Arthur Teuber called *Der Fluch der Menschheit* (*The Curse of Humanity*), which was also released in 1920 in two parts, *Die Tochter der Arbeit* (*The Daughter of Labor*) and *Im Rausche der Milliarden* (*Intoxicated of Billions*, aka *Im Milliardenrausch*).[17] The film is lost, but a few frames survive. An industry trade announced:

> Eichberg's new adventure film is playing at the Schauburg [Theater]. No doubt there's a large audience (to which I don't belong) that demands movies of this type and leads to them being produced. This is the audience that thinks the inverted word order in the intertitles represents 'ejjukated writting style.' The opening of the picture is characteristic: a close-up of the director and the star – the entire film is equally atavistic – and then the intertitle, 'Back into childhood I dream myself...'[18]

The film's convoluted plot told the story of Anne Marie Theißen (i.e., Theissen), who inherits a vast fortune and mining operation after her husband dies. Her new lover Meindel works "tirelessly on a great invention." Lugosi played the malicious villain Mälzer (sometimes rendered as Maelzer). A period plot synopsis described just how much of a "bad guy" he was:

> The mechanic Mälzer, who lodges at her parents' place and was the first who aroused feelings of love in Anne Marie, has worked his way up to the position of technician

Lugosi in *Der Tanz auf dem Vulkan* (*The Dance on the Volcano*, 1920).

through tireless diligence and is now employed at Theißen Mining as a mine inspector. She sees him again for the first time deep under the surface of the earth. His love for her flames up again and now – following the death of Theißen – he attempts to exert his prior power over her again. However, she rejects his advances with pride and has him removed from his position at Theißen Mining.

Mälzer's love turns to fervent hate. He becomes a leader of the workers, agitator, rabble rouser and a willing tool of an emissary from a foreign country who wants to destroy the invention of Meindel which would have given his people a [head start].

Every evening at 8:00 p.m. the results of the boring machine are registered in the test facility. Not only these results must be destroyed, but also Meindel himself, who has just returned, with those results. Mälzer constructs a machine that he connects to the high voltage power lines and by means of electronic ignition should blow everything to smithereens at the appointed time. But fate would determine otherwise.[19]

BECOMING DRACULA

Oscar I. Lamberger
offers

ELEANOR PARRY
IN
"DAUGHTER
OF THE
NIGHT"

*The Dramatic Sensation
of Two Continents
A Thrilling Story of Love
and Adventure.*

Presented by
L. & H. ENTERPRISES inc.
NEW YORK   *By arrangement with Joseph P. Lamy*

Advertisement for the American release of *Der Tanz auf dem Vulkan* (*The Dance on the Volcano*, 1920). Published in *Exhibitors Trade Review* on November 19, 1921.

Another character touches the high voltage power line, which causes the facility to explode earlier than planned, and Mälzer with it. By contrast, Meindel and Anne Marie "belong to each other as fate had determined, forever, so that they can build a new life for themselves together."[20]

Positive reviews of *Der Fluch der Menchheit* appeared in *Lichtbild-Bühne* and *Der Film*.[21] The latter told readers that Lugosi's performance "merit[ed] praise." *Der Film* also drew attention to Joe Rive's "uncommonly good" cinematography, and praised Eichberg's "generally pleasing and successful" direction, despite the fact he allowed "minor bits of clumsiness" to "slip in along the way."[22]

Lugosi made at least one other film for Eichberg, *Ihre Hoheit die Tänzerin* (*Her Highness, the Dancer*), though its release was initially banned by censors, who became powerful beginning in May 1920 as a backlash to the type of sex films that Kracauer and others chronicled.[23] The surviving report claims:

> The film displays all characteristics of a smut/trash film. It races from one suggestive scene to another – such as: the sabotaging of the wire and the fall of the tightrope walker (female); her performance in the revue; and the duke's attempted seductions. ...

> ... [S]uch distorted images of human experiences must lead to a degeneration of the general public's moral sensibilities which can be equated with a corruptive impact. This corruptive impact cannot only be identified when immoral actions are portrayed which encourage imitation or create an unhealthy atmosphere, but also when, in the case of smutty literature and smutty films, situations that only occur rarely in normal life and do not involve totally degenerate people, are characterized as the most significant experiences and the most pervasive fates of people and thus are thrown together in order to provide entertainment for the masses, totally distorting the values of such events by exaggerating their appearances but remaining completely empty in content.[24]

Gary D. Rhodes | Bill Kaffenberger

Published in *Lichtbild-Bühne* on June 19, 1920.

Gamsa-Citograph G. m. b. H. (Gacifilm)

Die Frau im Delphin

Emilie Sannom   Béla Lugosi
Magnus Stifter   Ernst Pittschau

Published in *Film-Kurier* on February 5, 1920.

An advertisement for Eichberg's 1919-1920 season implied that Lugosi was in a trio of other films: *Jettatore* (*The Jinx*), *Sünden der Eltern* (*Sins of the Parents*), and *Nonne und Tänzerin* (*Nun and Dancer*).[25] All three were definitely produced. If Lugosi actually appeared in any of them, it was probably just *Nonne und Tänzerin*, as Bruno Decarli starred in the other two.[26]

Why Lugosi did not star in any subsequent Eichberg films is unknown. But he certainly worked for other film companies, including Emelka (Münchener Lichtspielkunst AG), appearing in its film *Das ganze Sein ist flammend Leid* (*The Whole of Being is a Flaming Misery*, 1920), a four-reel drama directed by Ottmar Ostermayr and costarring Fritz Greiner, Ernst Rückert, and Alice Matay. Its plot – based on a 1902 short story by Gustav Meyrink, who famously wrote *Der Golem* (*The Golem*, 1913/1914) – features two brothers who "destroy each other because of the heartlessness of a beautiful woman." According to *Lichtbild-Bühne*, the film's premiere was "was greeted to a large extent with high regard by critics...."[27]

Much more notably, Lugosi starred in *Die Frau im Delphin* (*The Woman in the Dolphin*, 1920, aka *Die Frau im Delphin oder 30 Tage auf dem Meeresgrund/The Woman in the Dolphin, or, Thirty Days on the Ocean Floor*), a "Sensations-Großfilme" produced by Gaci (Gamsa-Film und Citograph GmbH). Karl Freund – who would later shoot *Dracula* (1931) – was the cinematographer.[28]

One of Lugosi's costars was Ernst Pittschau. He had played Lord Henry Wotton in Richard Oswald's *Das Bildnis des Dorian Gray* (*The Portrait of Dorian Gray*, 1917), the very same role that Lugosi played in Alfréd Deésy's adaptation of Oscar Wilde's novel, *Az élet királya* (*The King of Life*, 1917, aka *Dorian Gray*).

The plot of *Die Frau im Delphin* was far more outlandish than *Der Fluch der Menschheit*, with its mix of action and science fiction not dissimilar to some American film serials. Shooting at the studio began in late January 1920 (or perhaps the beginning of February) and finished by mid-February, after which the cast headed to the coast to "complete the technically and artistically difficult on-location photography."[29] An industry trade published the following advance publicity:

> It's just after midnight. The sounds of a waltz, ballrooms, the upper crust, the eccentric billionaire, the beautiful woman, an insane bet – in short: adventure films. They have enjoyed a steadily increasing popularity with the public, which follows the exciting events, developments, the nearly utopian happenings in a downright suggestive suspense.

Lugosi in *Die Frau im Delphin* (*The Woman in the Dolphin*, 1920).

The film *Die Frau im Delphin* will represent a new record in this genre with a smorgasbord of unbelievable thrills that can be adroitly woven into this film genre. Under the direction of Arthur Brenken [aka Arthur Kiekebusch-Brenken], the actors and actresses Emilie Sannom, Magnus Stifter, Ernst Pittschau and Bela Lugosi contend with one another for the 'palm of success' – a diamond of immeasurable value is the object of the struggle as is the possession of the beautiful Ellinor, who is snatched away right from under the billionaire's nose at the last minute by a resourceful reporter. A submarine, airplane, automobile – in short, all modern conveyances are in the service of the film. Accidents, crashes, thefts, in short everything that will mesmerize the audience. You will tremble and marvel.[30]

One serialization of the film's story gave details about Lugosi's character Tom Bill, the "king of burglars" who at times pretended to be a jeweler named Amundsen:

'Go to hell!' – The safecracking tools fly into the corner as Tom Bill stands up, breathing heavily, and wipes the sweat from his brow. With every energetic move he makes, the king of the burglars' entire musculature remains taut. Acting on an impulsive decision, his sinewy hand grasps the blowtorch – throwing out bright illumination as its spitting, melting flame travels down the safe door. Like molten lava, the white-hot metal drips unwillingly onto the floorboards of jeweler Amundsen's private office – Tom Bill is in top form! *Brrrrr!* The telephone is ringing! 'This is the

BECOMING DRACULA

Lugosi in *Die Frau im Delphin*
(*The Woman in the Dolphin*, 1920).
(*Courtesy of John Antosiewicz*)

Published in the *Leipziger Volkszeitung* on January 6, 1921. *(Courtesy of Robert J. Kiss)*

Villa Gordon calling! To speak with the jeweler Amundsen!' – A wry smile forms   on Tom Bill's lips – 'This is Amundsen speaking! What's up?' – 'Gordon here! I'd like you to come over to my villa to appraise the quality of a valuable diamond. My racing car will pick you up!' – 'All right, I'll come!' – Silently, Tom Bill empties Amundsen's safe. Outside, the engine of a zippy Renault purrs. – With elegant composure, Tom Bill steps out from 'his' villa. Inwardly, he is laughing uproariously! - - - -[31]

At a given point in the film, Ellinor awakens from a "deathlike sleep" to learn that Tom Bill has disappeared with the diamond. By that point, he has learned the "secrets of a pneumatic chamber permitting travel between the submarine and the ocean surface." Ellinor pursues him, and the diamond is temporarily lost in a submerged buoy.[32] Tom eventually manages to sell a "marvelous reproduction" of the diamond to an American billionaire (Magnus Stifter). The two men have cheated one another, as the billionaire has paid Tom in "expired banknotes."[33]

Lichtbild-Bühne reported, *"Die Frau im Delphin* was extremely successful at a showing in Nuremberg for the press and prospective distributors on November 3 [1920] that was on a par with the success following a showing in Northern Germany. The well-executed night photography and the acting of Emilie Sannom earned admiration from the audience."[34] A review in the newspaper *B.Z. am Mittag* claimed:

Two unknown German women. Photograph from Lugosi's own collection.

The publicity drum has been beaten so relentlessly for *Die Frau im Delphin* that experience led one to approach it with a sense of skepticism. However, one was happy to be proved wrong by the movie's premiere at the 'Lichtspiele Unter den Linden 21' theater. A script that remained clear and concise throughout as it competently wove detective story elements into the adventures of a billionaire. The direction and sets are in many regards exemplary!

The heavy outlay in order to realize cinema's limitless possibilities had also not been in vain. The photography is quite excellent, with several sequences employing artificial lighting or shot at nighttime particularly successful! The standout among the performers is Emilie Sannom as Miss [Windford]. She possesses an outstanding technique that is all her own. Her expressive acting and sharply delineated gestures spare the need for copious disruptive explanatory intertitles. Likewise, the acting of Magnus Stifter as the billionaire (looking strikingly similar to [Hans] Mierendorff) and of Ernst Pittschau as the journalist with detective skills – for whom our entire branch gives thanks! – is both naturalistic and impressive.[35]

The wild story became one of the most heavily advertised and most financially successful of Lugosi's German films.

As for the wild Berlin nightlife, Lugosi may or may not have explored it. His personal photo collection did contain at least two images of topless German women, whom he presumably knew. And he definitely had a torrid romance with his Eichberg costar Violette Napierska. In a poem to her, Lugosi wrote:

Slumber envelopes your beautiful face
And a dream grips your soul in embrace;
I will guard you.

You are my dream every night, every day,
And regardless of where you might stay,
I will seek you.

Then, when you want to forget all the
world,
And fly to my arms like a bird,
I will love you.[36]

Their adoration was mutual, and was even apparent onscreen. In a review of *Der Tanz auf dem Vulkan*, a critic chastised them: "Ms. Napierska and Mr. Lugosi should avoid so much exaggerated ogling at each other."[37]

Lugosi's eyes could be as erotic as they were hypnotic. In the midst of a modern Babylon, rife with sex and drugs, the movie camera had recorded Lugosi repeatedly – "its shutter open, quite passive, recording, not thinking," as Isherwood wrote – capturing glimpses of one of his love affairs.

Violette Napierska.

(Endnotes)

1   Gordon, Mel. *Voluptuous Panic: The Erotic World of Weimar Berlin* (Venice, CA: Feral House, 2000).

2   Gay, Peter. *Weimar Culture: The Outsider as Insider* (New York: W.W. Norton, 1968).

3   Gordon, Mel. *The Seven Addictions and Five Professions of Anita Berber* (Venice, CA: Feral House, 2006).

4   Gordon, *Voluptuous Panic.*

5   Kracauer, Siegfried. *From Caligari to Hitler: A Psychological History of the German Film* (Princeton, NJ: Princeton University Press, 1947).

6   Steed, H. Wickham. *A Short History of Austria-Hungary and Poland* (London: Encyclopaedia Brittanica Company, 1914).

7   In *Film Magazin* (Berlin: Reinhold Kühn, 1920), the Lugosi "Darsteller" biography mentions that Saturn-Film also distributed *Nászdal* (1918) in Germany.

8   Untitled. *Lichtbild-Bühne* 26 July 1919; "DeCarli-Film." *Der Film* 26 July 1919; "Decarli-Film." *Der Kinematograph* 27 Aug. 1919.

9   "Béla Lugosi." *Film-Magazin.*

10   Chrisman, J. Eugene. "Masters of Horror – Karloff and Lugosi." *Modern Screen* Apr. 1932.

11   *"Hypnose." Film-Kurier* 4 Jan. 1920.

12   Untitled. *Deutsche Lichtspiel-Zeitung* 10 Jan. 1920.

13   *"Der Tanz auf dem Vulkan." Film und Brettl* Feb. 1920.

14   *"Tanz auf dem Vulkan." Lichtbild-Bühne* 6 Mar. 1920.

15   "Münchener Erstaufführungen." *Deutsche Lichtspiel-Zeitung* 13 Mar. 1920.

16   Rhodes, Gary D. Interview with William K. Everson. 1985. See also Everson, William K. Letter to James Card, 18 Aug. 1953 and Everson, William K. Letter to James Card, 27 June 1954. [Archived in a file on *Daughter of the Night* at the George Eastman House.]

17   Untitled. *Deutsche Lichtspiel-Zeitung* 21 Aug. 1920.

18   *"Der Fluch der Menschheit." Lichtbild-Bühne* 18 Sept. 1920.

19   *"Der Fluch der Menschheit." Erste Internationale Film-Zeitung* 12 June 1920.

20   Ibid.

21   *"Der Fluch der Menschheit. II. Teil." Lichtbild-Bühne* Sept. 1920.

22   *"Der Fluch der Menschheit." Der Film* No. 39, 1920.

23   With regard to the restoration of film censorship, see Kracauer, *From Caligari to Hitler.*

24   The record of the first submission to the Berlin censor of *Ihre Hoheit die Tänzerin* is dated 10 Nov. 1922. There are three records for resubmissions, dated 14 Nov. 1922, 11 Jan. 1923 and 16 Jan. 1923, with the latter awarding the film (which had been recut) an 'adults only' certificate.

25   Advertisement. *Der Film* 18, 1919.

26   Given surviving cast lists, if Lugosi did appear in *Nonne und Tänzerin*, it would have been a small role.

27   *"Das ganze Sein ist flammend Leid." Lichtbild-Bühne* 11 Sept. 1920.

28   "Aus dem Glashaus." *Film-Kurier* 5 Feb. 1920.

29   "Aus dem Glashaus." *Film-Kurier* 29 Jan. 1920; Untitled. *Lichtbild-Bühne* 14 Feb. 1920.

30   *"Die Frau im Delphin." Film und Brettl* Feb. 1920.

31   Ibid.

32   *"Die Frau im Delphin." Illustrierte Film Woche* 11, 1920.

33   *"Die Frau im Delphin." Illustrierter Film-Kurier* 14, 1920.

34   Untitled. *Lichtbild-Bühne* 13 Nov. 1920.

35   Quoted in "Vier Sensations-Großfilme." *Film Kunst* 1920.

36   Quoted in Cremer, Robert. *Lugosi: The Man Behind the Cape* (Chicago: Henry Regnery, 1976).

37   *"Tanz auf dem Vulkan." Lichtbild-Bühne* 6 Mar. 1920.

Lugosi in Europe, circa 1920.

Chapter 18

Expressionism

"Du musst Caligari werden!
(You must become Caligari!)"
– *Das Cabinet des Dr. Caligari*

Demons, phantoms, and killers stalked Weimar cinema, traversing through dark shadows on angular, bizarre sets, at times visible only through distorted camera angles and optical effects. But of all the monsters unleashed in these films, none was more potent or terrifying than the mysterious workings of the human mind.

Though the term "Expressionism" did not come into common usage until 1913, two prior schools in Germany founded the movement: *Die Brücke* (*The Bridge*) in 1905 and *Der Blaue Reiter* (*The Blue Rider*) in 1911.[1] The style not only influenced paintings, but also architecture, sculpture, music, literature, theater, and motion pictures. However widespread "sex films" were during Lugosi's time in Berlin, the most stylistically groundbreaking films of Weimar cinema were Expressionist.

In 1919, theorist Kasimir Edschmid explained Expressionism by pronouncing, "the chain of facts: factories, houses, illness, prostitutes, screams, hunger, does not exist; only the interior vision they provoke exists."[2] In August 1919, *Der Kinematograph* offered another definition:

> Expressionism – or the expression of art – means the projection of the experiences of the artist outward, whereas in contrast impressionism visualizes how the external experiences of the artist impact him personally. While impressionism remains the last offshoot of naturalism, expressionism forsakes any true depiction of the external world. …

Published in *Lichtbild-Bühne* in February 1920.

The expressionistic film could, naturally, forgo every passing thought and content to a far broader extent. Through the interlacing of images and the copying of images, one over the other, perhaps even in different ratios to one another as well as through the possibilities of special effects that could be incorporated into images, film technology is in the position to portray everything of a dreamlike, visionary and surreal nature better than any other art for the eyes – better than painting, stage theater, not to mention sculpture.[3]

By the time of this article, Expressionism had already begun to infuse the cinema, notably in such films as Robert Reinert's *Nerven* (*Nerves*, 1919) and Franjo Ledić's *Angelo, das Mysterium des Schlosses* (*Angelo, the Mystery of the Castle*, 1919), as well as in Fritz Freisler's Austrian-made *Der Mandarin* (*The Mandarin*, 1918).

Of course, the breakthrough Expressionist film that gained international fame was released after all of those, *Das Cabinet des Dr. Caligari* (*The Cabinet of Dr. Caligari*), which premiered at Berlin's Marmorhaus-Lichtspiele on February 26, 1920. That was the same day the Lugosi film *Der Tanz auf dem Vulkan* (*The Dance on the Volcano*, 1920) premiered at the Ufa-Filmpalast (aka Ufa-Palast am zoo). An advertisement for it in *Berliner Tageblatt* was much larger than the one for *Caligari*.[4] But *Caligari* quickly became dramatically more famous.

Directed by Robert Wiene and starring Conrad Veidt, Werner Krauss, Lil Dagover, and Hans Heinrich von Twardowski, *Caligari* became one of the most important landmarks in film history, a cinematic monolith, a totem of Expressionism.[5] In January 1920, *Film-Kurier* told readers:

> Before having a look into this new world, one is skeptical. One cannot s u d d e n l y imagine the asymmetrical lines and the triangular and quadratic figures of modern art in this space; one supposes a doubling up on the improbable. This is particularly alienating in the reality of cinematography. But the impression drives away all doubt.[6]

A few days after the film's release, *Der Kinematograph* observed, "The sickly aberrations of a demented mind find expression in the contorted, strangely fantastic images raised to the highest power."[7] And Siegfried Kracauer believed that *Caligari*'s screenwriters "must have

Lugosi in Berlin circa 1920. Seated with him are Paul Sydow and Serafina Astafieva.

been driven by one of those dark impulses which … sometimes engender true visions."[8]

Béla Lugosi would have been well aware of Expressionist art and cinema. It is difficult to believe that he did not watch *Das Cabinet des Dr. Caligari* in Berlin in 1920, if only because of its enormous fame and impact. Likewise, he would have known about *Caligari*'s immediate successor, Robert Wiene's *Genuine* (aka *Genuine: A Tale of a Vampire*, 1920) and possibly about Karl Heinz Martin's two films, *Von morgens bis mitternachts* (*From Morn to Midnight*, 1920), and *Das Haus zum Mond* (*The House of the Moon*, 1920). Here was a world, as Patrice Petro has written, of "nightmare states, claustrophobic atmosphere, and unstable identities."[9]

Invoking the subtitle of F.W. Murnau's *Nosferatu* (1922), Lotte Eisner has rightly referred to some Weimar films as "Symphonies of Horror."[10] Horror themes well suited Expressionism, and vice versa. Lugosi was in Berlin during the release of Richard Oswald's *Unheimliche Geschichten* (*Eerie Tales*, 1919), which starred Conrad Veidt and Anita Berber, Weimar's diva of debauchery.

Lugosi's direct participation in Expressionism came in F. W. Murnau's *Schrecken* (*Terror*, 1920), aka *Der Januskopf* (*The Head of Janus*). It was based on Robert Louis Stevenson's novella [*The*] *Strange Case of Dr. Jekyll and Mr. Hyde* (1886), and starring Conrad Veidt, fresh from his fame in *Caligari*. The triumvirate of Lugosi-Murnau-Veidt working together on an Expressionist horror film: here is the stuff that dreams and nightmares are made of.

Schrecken ranks among the most sought-after of lost films, a phenomenon that gives

Schrecken

von **Hans Janowitz**

In den Hauptrollen:

Conrad Veidt

Magnus Stifter / Margar. Schlegel
Regie: **F. W. Murnau**

SIRIUS-FILM
BERLIN SW. 48
Friedrichstr. 19.
Fernsprecher: Moritzplatz 388
Telegramm-Adresse: Siriusfilm

Published in *Lichtbild-Bühne* on June 5, 1920.

rise to much excitement (the tantalizing possibilities of how great it might be) and to much anticipation (of its recovery, resulting from persistent but baseless assumptions that it resides in some private collection or Russian archive). Contorted, strangely fantastic images become raised to the highest power. The yearning for what cannot be seen results in assumptions shrouded as facts. For example, despite assertions to the contrary, *Schrecken* was never released in the United States as *Love's Mockery*; as period reviews prove, that was in fact the American-release title for Murnau's *Der Gang in die Nacht* (1921).[11]

Margarete Schlegel.

But of all the cinematic ghosts that haunt *Schrecken*, perhaps the most curious is Lugosi's participation, which has likely been overstated in previous literature. The nature of his role remains in question, but a comprehensive review of primary sources strongly implies that it was minor. Ironically, he is thus generally absent from the production history and critical response to his most famous silent film, and the only one that probably deserves the adjective "horror."

At the time he directed *Schrecken*, Murnau was then at an early point of what became an illustrious career in Germany and America; he had directed only three prior features. Hans Janowitz provided the screenplay. At that point, given his co-authorship of *Das Cabinet des Dr. Caligari*, Janowitz was perhaps better known than Murnau. Veidt assumed the dual roles of a Jekyll-Hyde character. Playing opposite him was Margarete Schlegel, a stage ingénue and protégée of Max Reinhardt's Deutsches Theater in Berlin.

Exactly when Murnau shot *Schrecken* is hard to determine. One published production calendar suggests a start date of late February 1920, but – given that the hiring of cinematographer Karl Freund was not reported until March 6 – it might have been shortly thereafter.[12] Very little is known of the production, though one industry trade later claimed, "[Veidt's] barber had to undergo training to be able to take his shaggy hair and turn it into something fashionable," thus helping obtain the illusion of a distinguished man who transforms into [an] ugly fiend.[13]

It is tempting to believe that the production company, Lipow-Film, used a title other than Stevenson's to conceal the unauthorized use of his story. Perhaps that was the case, but an advertisement published in *Film-Kurier* at the end of April 1920 clearly says "Dr. Jekyll und Mr. Hide [*sic*]" under the title *Schrecken*.[14] The same is true of a full-page ad published

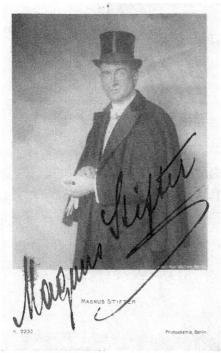
Magnus Stifter.

in *Lichtbild-Bühne* at the end of May 1920, one that correctly spelled the name "Hyde."[15] In addition, a surviving lobby card printed by Lipow-Film shows *Dr. Jekyll and Mr. Hyde* listed in smaller letters underneath *Schrecken*.

Lotte Eisner later called *Schrecken* a "sort of transposition of Stevenson's *Dr. Jekyll and Mr. Hyde*," and so the alterations may have been as much to create a new story as to infringe upon the old.[16] Narratives about doubles had deep roots in German literature, as well as in its feature films, such as Max Mack's *Der Andere* (*The Other*) and Stellan Rye's *Der Student von Prag* (*The Student of Prague*, 1913). At any rate, the surviving script for *Schrecken* specifically refers to a Dr. Jeskyll [*sic*] who lives in London. He purchases a bust at an antique store; it has two faces, one beautiful and one horrible. Here is the duality of man, the good and the evil.

The statue obsesses Jeskyll, who attempts to give it away. When that fails, the statue is auctioned, but Jeskyll buys it back. In his script, Janowitz wrote:

Dusty, cobwebs, dark. The room gives off an atmosphere of horrors and memories that make Jeskyll shudder. He hurriedly undoes the parcel, looks at the face, and utters a cry.

Cross-fade to the grimace of the satyr. Jeskyll hastily puts the statue back in its old place and rushes from the room.[17]

A period synopsis adds further insight into the experiments that Jeskyll makes as a result of his obsession:

This latter has created a chemical solution that instantly effects such separation within whoever consumes it, so that he is either left lurching around as a crippled, repulsive villain; or else dedicating himself to his usual charitable deeds. – Dr. [Jeskyll] calls his other self – Mr. [Hyde]. And, in this form, perpetrates one heinous act after another. – Murder, brutality, rape; all committed by [Jeskyll's] subconscious. But so long as he takes the antidote, then everything fades away like a bad dream.

The quiet scholar conducts experiment after experiment into this mystery, hoping to provide documentary evidence to substantiate his claims, which have otherwise merely elicited pitying smiles from his peers. But this evidence eludes him. And in the long run, his body proves unable to handle all the experiments. After a while, habit alone causes him to start transforming into the arch-backed, dreadful figure of [Hyde], even without consuming the elixir. His will no longer his own, but instead controlled by other forces, his body – and he himself – are ruined. The power of addiction! He is lost to life, and can only scuttle around furtively in the shadows.[18]

Though Janowitz's script does not provide acting directions for Dr. Jeskyll, it does include fascinating visual descriptions, to which Murnau added his own handwritten notes. For example, for the film's important nightmare sequence, Janowitz wrote:

BERLIN SW. 48

FRIEDRICH-STRASSE 16   Aufgang 11, III Treppen
                        Fernsprecher: Moritzplatz 10 642

SPEZIAL-LABORATORIUM

für individuelle

Entwicklung von Negativen

und sorgfältigste

Anfertigung der Mustercopie

Published in *Lichtbild-Bühne* in February 1920.

> Dr. Jeskyll in black pyjamas, sitting in a deep armchair, thinking. Sad thoughts. Anxiety. Behind him, against a dark background, appears the terrible head of Hyde. It hypnotizes him, and he follows it.[19]

At this point, Murnau suggests, "To begin with, just enormous eyes," an image that echoes similar imagery in *Das Cabinet des Dr. Caligari* and anticipates the same in later films like *White Zombie* (1932). Then Janowitz describes:

> Dark background still: slowly, as if materializing out of the mist, the square in front of the strange house appears. Hyde and the little girl run on in opposite directions and collide with one another. The incident in sequence 11 [in which Hyde tramples on a child and beats it with a stick] is repeated several times. Both figures are multiplied and Hyde tramples on the child more and more brutally.[20]

Murnau's notation insisted, "Enormous shadows!" From there, Janowitz wrote:

> Jeskyll appears near them, desperate but drawn there in spite of himself. Checks keep flying out of his hand, one after the other, towards the crying child. The checks

Lugosi (far right) in *Der Januskopf: eine Tragödie am Rande der Wirklichkeit* (*A Tragedy on the Border of Reality*). *(Courtesy of Richard Bojarski)*

dissolve in mid-air and disappear. Hyde grows more and more furious, and the children disappear under his feet as if he were stamping them into the ground. In his fury, he suddenly throws himself on Jeskyll, raising his stick in his hairy claws. Jeskyll staggers back. Quick fade.[21]

Murnau's alterations called for the multitude of Hydes to chase Jeskyll "towards the camera." At that point, the Hydes "combine to form one single horrific figure."

Lipow (in conjunction with Sirius-Film) held a trade preview of *Schrecken* in late April 1920. *Lichtbild-Bühne* and *Film-Kurier* praised the film, drawing particular attention to Conrad Veidt's performance. Both publications clearly refer to its characters by the names Jekyll and Hyde (rather than "Jeskyll" and Hyde), with *Film-Kurier* adding that *Schrecken* was "modeled after the world famous novel by Stevenson."[22]

The film apparently had another screening in June 1920. That month, a critic for *Neue Kino-Rundschau* declared it "belongs to the best that German film art has produced. The direction by F.W. Murnau is a textbook example and Konrad [*sic*] Veidt gives an unsurpassed masterly performance."[23]

Lipow-Film struck a "worldwide" distribution deal with Decla-Bioscop, a result of the previews and the favorable response to them.[24] When *Schrecken* premiered at Berlin's Marmorhaus-

Lichtspiele on August 26, 1920, it had a new title, *Der Januskopf,* as well as a subtitle, *eine Tragödie am Rande der Wirklichkeit* (*A Tragedy on the Border of Reality*).[25] The reason is unclear. Knowing that Lipow had freely used Stevenson's title in earlier publicity, perhaps Decla-Bioscop was concerned about legal liability.

After all, the character names had also changed from Dr. Jekyll and Mr. Hyde to Dr. Warren and Mr. O'Connor (repeatedly rendered in one industry trade as "O'Conner").[26] However, that change might have happened earlier. When *Filmwelt* reviewed the film under the title *Schrecken* and praised Veidt's performance as a "masterpiece of makeup and acting," it specifically used the character names Warren and O'Connor.[27]

The change of title to *Der Januskopf* is fascinating for other

Published in *Lichtbild-Bühne* on May 29, 1920.

reasons. For one, it places emphasis on Janus, the Roman god of duality who was usually depicted in statues as having two faces. That in turn creates something of a double meaning in the word "kopf," which in German means "head" as well as "bust," the result conjuring literal and figurative meanings for the statue that brings about Dr. Warren's downfall.

After the film's premiere, industry reviews were overwhelmingly positive. *Lichtbild-Bühne* wrote, "Let it today be noted that the film scored a great success on account of its breathtaking suspense, and that Conrad Veidt is to be heartily congratulated for his unsurpassable, masterful performance." *Der Film* called it "fabulously suspenseful," with "superb" acting and "excellent" cinematography.[28] *Erste Internationale Film-Zeitung* went even further:

> This newest motion picture released by Decla-Bioscop somewhat recalls its precursors *Caligari* and [Richard Oswald's] *Kurfürstendamm* [1920, which starred Conrad Veidt]; and yet, this hint of familiarity is really the only thing that the films have in common. Generally speaking, one can say that this new drama is equal to *Caligari,* and even outdoes it in a few gripping scenes. This may be attributed not least to the performance of lead actor Conrad Veidt, who has never before been seen in such a … difficult role, which – purely in its outward, physical aspects – places great demands on him. Hans Janowitz, drawing on an English source, has here furnished a well-thought-out, lucid screenplay. …

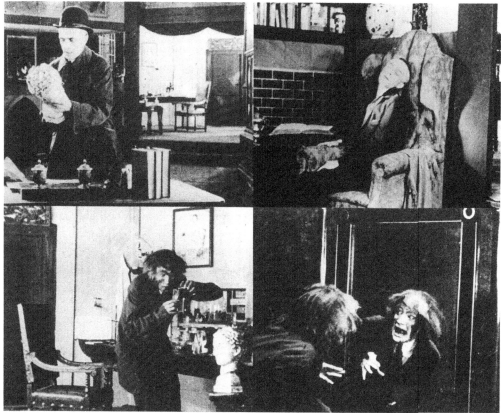

Conrad Veidt in *Der Januskopf* (1920).

As concerns the performances, everything here is first rate. Director F.W. Murnau – possessed of a distant, all-seeing eye, a tasteful sense for the pictorial and a strong, steady directorial hand – allowed the actors to give all that they were able. In particular Conrad Veidt, who has completely outdone himself – and all his previous performances – with this role. As Dr. Warren, admittedly, he delivered his familiar characterization of a 'sensitive type.' But what he achieved as O'Conner [*sic*] is the most excellent work one has yet seen from him, with even the tiniest nuances imbued with realism and naturalism. In this, he was supported to the utmost extent by the fine cinematography of Karl Freund and [Carl] Hoffmann.

... The sets are imposingly and tastefully designed, but suffer – alas – as a result of some occasional unsharp photography. Neither effort nor expense has been spared....[29]

Der Kinematograph agreed, believing the film was "gripping from beginning to end. The transformations that occur right on camera are a technical masterpiece with consummate impact. In this case film is superior to the stage." Its reviewer added, "Among the excellent photographic images of richly designed sets, the blue-tinted street scenes at night were particularly striking and the in-studio filming had particularly beautiful lighting effects."[30]

While *Film-Kurier* offered praise for Veidt, its critic worried about *Der Januskopf*'s appeal:

A film for the movie-going public? We doubt it. However good it is. The exaggeration of the gruesome elements (without psychological necessity and the counterbalance of 'good') and the catastrophic discord in which the film must end, given the somewhat complicated nature of the plot – which is finally resolved somewhat circuitously at the end of the film – do not correspond to the desires of the movie-going public for lighter film fare. The film will find its audience among exclusive circles; others will only see the sensational elements in the film....[31]

Film-Kurier was perhaps overly concerned, as German newspaper critics heralded *Der Januskopf*:

The writer has conceived his 'tragedy on the border of reality,' as he himself terms it, with great skill. Director F.W. Murnau has accommodated the writer's highly fantastic ideas well. Conrad Veidt in the lead role delivers a deeply poignant performance.[32] – *Berliner Tageblatt*

Conrad Veidt portrayed a human being who can turn into another entirely at will, and the frequently highly accomplished trick realization of his metamorphosis proved captivating. The film becomes a little gem on account of having Veidt in the lead role. This double part reveals him as a screen performer of worth.[33] – *B.Z. am Mittag*

Confined within everyday settings, the uncanny comes over all the more explosively... Conrad Veidt plays the dual role with astounding versatility... In addition, the photographic detail and use of lighting are excellent.[34] – *Berliner Börsen-Courier*

Conrad Veidt offered an exemplary artistic tour de force in his fulfillment of this rewarding task, and wholly earned the heavy applause he received.[35] – *8 Uhr-Abendblatt*

After a lengthy hiatus there is once again a Veidt movie that dignifies his name... A fantastic subject matter, the dichotomy between good and evil, effectively distilled into pure form and depicted in a highly suspenseful, often outright uncanny manner.[36] – *Berliner Börsen-Zeitung*

Its highly fantastic action, which veers into crime-story territory, remained thoroughly gripping to the very end... Conrad Veidt portrayed this fantastic creation (Dr. Henry Warren) with great artistic flair.[37] – *Berliner Lokal-Anzeiger*

A strong impression was left by the new Decla-Bioscop film *Der Januskopf* which debuted at the Marmorhaus. ... A fantastic theme, 'a tragedy on the border of reality.' Within which context it was thrillingly played out and logically resolved. ... The film has been ably directed by F.W. Murnau, is technically excellent, and over and above this brilliantly acted. Conrad Veidt takes on the leading role, and his performance is unheard-of in its poignancy. Youthful Margarete Schlegel is without question an asset to the cinema.[38] – *Neue Berliner 12 Uhr Mittags-Zeitung*

Fears that *Der Januskopf* would not resonate with audiences might have been incorrect. According to *Lichtbild-Bühne*, the film "has achieved widespread success, which we had predicted...."[39]

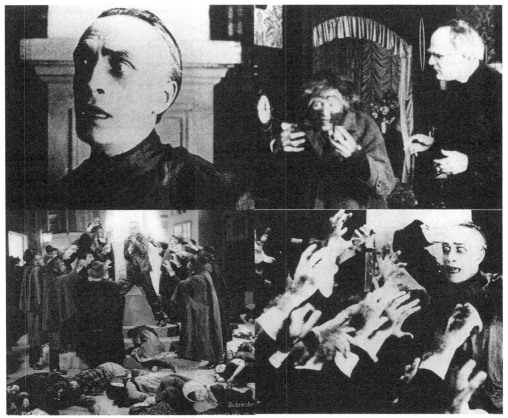

Conrad Veidt in *Der Januskopf* (1920).

No review seems to have mentioned Lugosi, though, which likely indicates his role was small. Film historians in years past have suggested that he played Dr. Warren's butler, which could be correct. But one surviving photograph shows Lugosi seated while Veidt stands, and Lugosi is not dressed like a butler. Based on other photos, the characters are at Dr. Warren's home. The second surviving photograph shows Lugosi at a table in what appears to be a pub. Beside him sits Veidt as Mr. Hyde/Mr. O'Connor. Lugosi is extremely well dressed and definitely does not appear to be a butler.

And so the question arises, might Lugosi have actually played some other role? Quite possibly. Given that *Der Januskopf* is a lost film and the surviving script evidently evolved during the shoot, the answer is unknown.

Other questions abound. How Expressionist was *Der Januskopf*? Surviving publicity stills do not show the distorted sets of *Caligari*. Some contemporary writers spoke of the two films as similar, but that could have had more to do with their narratives than aesthetics. Nevertheless, Expressionism was conveyed in Weimar cinema by means other than distorted sets, building *Stimmung* (mood) through lighting, shadows, acting styles, and even artwork and fonts on silent film intertitles.

It is true Murnau's surviving films are not particularly Expressionist, but as Eisner has identified, a duality was present in his style, which featured a "predilection for oscillating between reality and unreality." He was "at the one and same time an Expressionist writer and a poet of the *Kammerspiel* (chamber play)."[40] Murnau himself said, "I like the reality of things but not without the fantasy; they must dovetail."[41]

For example, Murnau's *Der letze Mann* (*The Last Laugh*, 1924) is not Expressionist, but when its lead character is drunk, the images he sees are certainly Expressionistic. Likewise, perhaps Dr. Warren's nightmare was Expressionistic. Indeed, however much he was steeped in other styles, such as German Romanticism, Murnau may have been more susceptible to Expressionism at an early stage in his career and in the immediate aftermath of *Caligari*. Here we should consider again Murnau's own comment on Janowitz's script: "Enormous shadows!"

However much or little it was influenced by Expressionism, *Der Januskopf*

Published in *Der Kinematograph* on September 12, 1920.

was probably terrifying. One need only consider Murnau's subsequent films to understand that potentiality. Of his *Faust* (1926), for example, Eisner declared, "No other director, not even [Fritz] Lang ever succeeded in conjuring up the supernatural so masterfully...."[42]

Nowhere in Murnau's filmography is that statement truer than with *Nosferatu* (1922), his unauthorized adaptation of Bram Stoker's *Dracula*. It is not an Expressionist film, but it bears some stylistic influence of the movement, including in the depictions of certain cityscapes and landscapes. *Nosferatu* also lives up to its subtitle *eine Symphonie des Grauens* (*A Symphony of Horror*). In it, Max Schreck – whose last name, similar as it was to *Schrecken*, evokes notions of fright and terror – portrays Graf Orlok, a variation on Stoker's Dracula character, not only in name, but also in appearance. Schreck's vampire remains the only lasting challenge to the icon of Lugosi's Dracula.

By the time that Murnau directed *Nosferatu*, Lugosi had already left Germany, just as he had left Hungary before Károly Lajthay directed *Drakula halála* (*Dracula's Death*) in 1921. There is no reason to suspect that, had he stayed in Berlin, Lugosi would have ever worked with Murnau again, let alone on *Nosferatu*. After all, he was indeed a minor player in *Schrecken*, a shadowy form in an Expressionist cinema of shadows.

As for audiences in Germany, they continued to enjoy films with horror themes, despite *Film-Kurier*'s fears to the contrary. In 1922, *Die Filmwelt* wrote, "Films about the spiritualistic, occult and hypnosis are all the rage at present."[43] According to *Der deutsche Film in Wort und Bild*:

The possibility of using photographic tricks to 'stage' occult and spiritualistic experiments will continue to furnish moviemakers with subject matter for esoteric films that serve to familiarize the general public with – and frequently cause them to reflect upon – these issues. Naturally, these feature films have nothing to do with scientific investigation into the area of the occult.[44]

The following year, *Die Filmwelt* added, "today one can prophesize about the great future for the ... fantastic film."[45]

Thanks to German directors working in America, Lugosi would later appear in Hollywood movies with Hans Heinrich von Twardowski of *Caligari* and Alexander Granach of *Nosferatu*.[46] Whether they reminisced about Weimar cinema, Expressionism, or characters like Dracula is unknown.

But more important would be the future of the "fantastic film," with German Expressionism becoming a major influence on the American horror film of the 1930s. Demons, phantoms, and killers would stalk Hollywood cinema, traversing borderlands and creating new shadows.

After all, Karl Freund, one of *Der Januskopf*'s two cinematographers, would shoot Tod Browning's *Dracula* (1931), in which Lugosi finally portrayed the title character onscreen.

(Endnotes)

1   Willett, John. *Expressionism* (New York: McGraw-Hill, 1970).

2   Quoted in Eisner, Lotte. *The Haunted Screen* (Berkeley: University of California Press, 1969).

3   "Der expressionistische Film." *Der Kinematograph* 13 Aug. 1919.

4   Advertisements. *Berliner Tageblatt* 26 Feb. 1920.

5   Twardowski was also known as "Hans Heinz von Twardowski."

6   "Expressionismus im Film." *Film Kurier* 6 Jan. 1920.

7   "*Das Cabinet des Dr. Caligari.*" *Der Kinematograph* 3 Mar. 1920.

8   Kracauer, Siegfried. *From Caligari to Hitler: A Psychological History of the German Film* (Princeton, NJ: Princeton University Press, 1947).

9   Petro, Patrice. *Joyless Streets: Women and Melodramatic Representation in Weimar Germany* (Princeton, NJ: Princeton University Press, 1989).

10   Eisner, *The Haunted Screen*.

11   "*Love's Mockery.*" *Film Daily* 4 Nov. 1928.

12   "Februar." *Lichtbild-Bühne* 6 Mar. 1920.

13   Proskauer, Martin. "*Schrecken.*" *Film-Kurier* 29 Apr. 1920.

14   Advertisement. *Film Kurier* 20 Apr. 1920.

15   Advertisement. *Lichtbild-Bühne* 29 May 1920.

16   Eisner, Lotte. *Murnau* (Berkeley: University of California Press, 1973).

17   Eisner, *Murnau*.

18   *"Der Januskopf." Erste Internationale Film-Zeitung* 33-34, 1920.

19   With regard to the Janowitz script and its translation, we acknowledge a great debt to Eisner's *Murnau*, from which these excerpts are taken.

20   Ibid.

21   Ibid.

22   Proskauer, *"Schrecken;* "Der Literarische Film." *Lichtbild-Bühne* 1 May 1920.

23   *"Schrecken." Neue Kino-Rundschau* 19 June 1920

24   *"Der Januskopf." Erste Internationale Film-Zeitung.*

25   *"Der Januskopf." Lichtbild-Bühne* 28 Aug. 1920.

26   *"Der Januskopf." Erste Internationale Film-Zeitung.*

27   "Neue Filme." *Die Filmwelt* 15,1920

28   *"Der Januskopf." Der Film* No. 36, 1920.

29   *"Der Januskopf." Erste Internationale Film-Zeitung.*

30   *"Der Januskopf." Der Kinematograph* 5 Sept. 1920.

31   Fredrik, L.K. *"Der Januskopf." Film-Kurier* 27 Aug. 1920.

32   Quoted in Advertisement. *Deutsche Lichtspiel-Zeitung* 18 Sept. 1920.

33   Ibid.

34   Ibid.

35   Ibid.

36   Ibid.

37   Ibid.

38   Ibid.

39   *"Der Januskopf." Lichtbild-Bühne* 28 Aug. 1920.

40   Eisner, *Murnau*.

41   Quoted in Ibid.

42   Eisner, *The Haunted Screen*.

43   "Spiritistische Filme." *Die Filmwelt* 1922.

44 "Hypnose and Occultismus im Film." *Der deutsche Film in Wort und Bild* 17 Feb. 1922.

45 "Der phantastische Film." *Die Filmwelt* 16, 1923.

46 Lugosi and Twardowski appeared in William Dieterle's *The Devil's in Love* (1933). Lugosi and Granach appeared in Ernst Lubitsch's *Ninotchka* (1939).

Lugosi (far right) in *Der Januskopf*. *(Courtesy of John Antosiewicz)*

BÉLA LUGOSÍ

BERLIN=CHARLOTTENBURG, Eisenacher Straße 118

Fernsprecher: Kurfürst 7260 und Lützow 8464

Lugosi as pictured in *Film-Magazin* (1920).

Chapter 19

The Wild West

"He played his part, too, like a man,
for I saw him the next day, with
thirteen scalps on his pole."
– James Fenimore Cooper,
Leatherstocking Tales

Weimar cinema was as multifaceted as it was multivalent. For aesthetes and stylists, Expressionism was its greatest achievement, but German moviegoers usually viewed (and in many or even most cases preferred) other types of film. Drawing on the likes of Oskar Kalbus, film theorist Siegfried Kracauer observed how many genres achieved popularity during and immediately after the war, ranging from Italian epics to comedies. He also noted:

The success of American Westerns was particularly sweeping. Broncho Bill[y] and Tom Mix conquered the hearts of the young German generation, which had devoured, volume after volume, the novels of Karl May – novels set in an imaginary Far West and full of fabulous events involving Indian tribes, covered wagons, traders, hunters, tramps, and adventurers.[1]

Indigenous production of westerns also became an important component of German film.[2] In July 1920, for example, an advertisement heralded *Texas Fred*, released as *Texas Freds Brautfahrt* (*Texas Fred's Search for a Bride*), and its cast, which included Max Schreck, the actor who became Graf Orlok in F.W. Murnau's *Nosferatu* (1922).[3]

Béla Lugosi participated in many of the popular German film genres from the time of his arrival in Berlin. During 1920, along with the films discussed in Chapters 17 and 18, he acted in at least seven films for three different companies, the plots ranging from detective and adventure tales to westerns based on the literature of James Fenimore Cooper. Within months, he thus became an Arab and an American, a hero and a villain, a cowboy and an Indian.

Published in *Der Kinematograph* on August 15, 1920.

Dua-Film

Lugosi appeared in at least two films for Dua-Film GmbH, which were likely shot in the spring or early summer of 1920.[4] In August of that year, *Der Kinematograph* explained:

> Under the auspices of [Dua], a film production company was founded that is focused on the production and distribution of detective and adventure films. In the next couple of days the third film in the 'John Hopkins' series and, in addition, the first film in the Nat Pinkerton detective series will appear. Screenplays by Jane Bess. Directed by Wolfgang Neff.[5]

Lugosi would become a part of both film series, presumably at Wolfgang Neff's request.

The first was probably *Der Sklavenhalter von Kansas-City* (*The Slaveholder of Kansas City*, 1920).[6] It was the third production by Neff and screenwriter Jane Bess to feature the heroic American detective John Hopkins, who battled a "vampire" criminal named George Corvin. The prior two films in this series bore the title *Apachenrache* (*Apache Revenge*, aka *Apachen-Rache*), with the first bearing the subtitle *In den Krallen des Vampirs* (*In the Vampire's Clutches*).[7] The second installment featured the subtitle *In den Krallen von Gg. Corvin, dem Ausbrecher-König* (*In the Clutches of Geo. Corvin, King of Escapes*, 1920).

Der Sklavenhalter von Kansas-City became the third installment. It was also referred to as *John Hopkins III*, with the overarching *Apachenrache* title eliminated, adopted as it was by another, non-Dua-Film series. Josef Reithofer played John Hopkins; Lugosi played George Corvin. At minimum, what this means is that Lugosi played a character explicitly referred to as a vampire in the two prior entries, if not also in the third.

Granted, here the term "vampire" is being used not to describe a supernatural creature, but rather a skilled criminal, of the type most famously seen onscreen in Louis Feuillade's serial *Les Vampires* (1915-16), but also in such earlier films as *Vampires of the Coast* (Pathe, 1909), *The Forest Vampires* (Domino, 1914), *Vampires of the Night* (Greene Features, 1914), and *Vasco, the Vampire* (Imp, 1914).

Nevertheless, for the first time, Lugosi the actor became Lugosi the vampire. Or perhaps, given the dearth of contemporary information on the first two installments, *Der Sklavenhalter von Kansas-City* was Lugosi's third onscreen portrayal of the (admittedly non-supernatural)

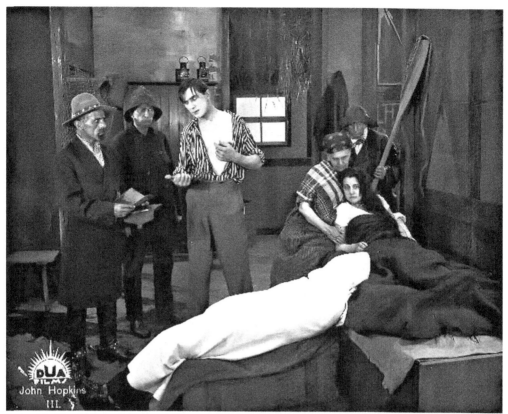

Lugosi in *Der Sklavenhalter von Kansas-City* (*The Slaveholder of Kansas City*, aka *John Hopkins III*, 1920/21).

vampire. In other words, it is not impossible that *In den Krallen des Vampirs* and *In den Krallen von Gg. Corvin, dem Ausbrecher-König* also featured him as George Corvin. This is speculation, but there is as yet no credible information on who played Corvin in those two films, and Lugosi was in Germany when they were produced.

Lugosi also played a gang leader in *Nat Pinkerton im Kampf* (*Nat Pinkerton in Combat*, 1920), specifically in the first released part, *Das Ende des Artisten Bartolini* (*The End of the Performer Bartolini*). Trades largely ignored the Dua productions of 1920, unfortunately, but the following production anecdote about the second Nat Pinkerton film, *Diebesfallen* (*Criminal Traps*, which did not star Lugosi) might give insight into the kinds of stunts and action seen in the first film, particularly given that rooftop train scenes were apparently a hallmark of Neff/Bess productions:

> Last Sunday Eberswalde was the scene of daredevil train stunts – leaps from one moving train to another, struggles between a detective and criminal on the roofs of trains traveling at breakneck speeds and an extremely risky fight on the front of a locomotive. A crowd of people formed columns along almost the entire stretch used by the trains during the shooting. ... Wolfgang Neff was the director, who calmly

Lugosi in *Der Sklavenhalter von Kansas-City* (*The Slaveholder of Kansas City*, aka *John Hopkins III*, 1920/21). *(Courtesy of John Antosiewicz)*

accomplished the most difficult moments [in filming].[8]

As for *Nat Pinkerton im Kampf: Das Ende des Artisten Bartolini* with Lugosi, on August 6, 1920, German censors approved it for exhibition, the same day they approved *Der Sklavenhalter von Kansas-City*. And yet it seems that both of Lugosi's Dua-Film productions had limited theatrical runs. They were probably the least viewed of all of his German films.

Ustad-Film

Receiving far more attention than Dua was Ustad-Film, which its president Fritz Knevels formed in order to adapt stories written by the beloved German novelist Karl May (1842-1912). Indeed, "Ustad" is a reference to the character of that name in May's four-volume *Im Reiche des silbernen Löwen* (*Kingdom of the Silver Lion*), published between 1898 and 1903.[9] One of Ustad's co-founders was Frau Dr. Marie Luise Droop. She had known Karl May, who dedicated his 1909 story *Merhameh* to her. And together with her husband Dr. Adolf Droop, she headed the Karl May Association.[10] In March 1920, *Der Kinematograph* reported:

The Karl May publishing house in Radebeul near Dresden has announced that the

Lugosi in *Der Sklavenhalter von Kansas-City* (*The Slaveholder of Kansas City*, aka *John Hopkins III*, 1920/21).

Ustad Film Dr. Droop & Company, Ltd., has been authorized as the sole production company for the filming of a series of Karl May films. Interested cinematographic circles are hereby warned by Frau Dr. Droop not to use these materials for which she holds the copyright and in particular not to 'adapt' episodic material from Karl May as such attempts will result in punitive action by the courts.[11]

Warnings from Droop were not random. The William Kahn Film Company had just announced that it had "free adaptations" of Karl May stories in pre-production.[12] The Karl May publishing house thus took that company to court in the spring of 1920.[13]

In June of that same year, Ustad – already eyeing the international market – distributed a trilingual brochure that announced the first five Karl May films: *Old Shatterhand*, *Die Todeskarawane* (*The Caravan of Death*), *Bei den Teufelsanbetern* (*Among the Devil Worshippers*), *Auf den Trümmern des Paradieses* (*On the Ruins of Paradise*) and *Vom Stamme der Verfluchten* (*From the Tribe of the Damned*).[14]

Ustad began with *Auf den Trümmern des Paradieses*, which Droop produced and co-adapted.[15] *Der Kinematograph* described its plot as follows:

Lugosi in *Der Sklavenhalter von Kansas-City* (*The Slaveholder of Kansas City*, aka *John Hopkins III, 1920/21*). *(Courtesy of John Antosiewicz)*

The epic film provides an overview of the history of Islam climaxing in the murder of Hussein, the last grandson of Mohammad. Tronier Funder of the Royal Theater in Copenhagen portrays the unfortunate Caliph who dies of thirst along with his entourage just steps away from the Euphrates River. ... The plot takes place in part on the ruins of the Tower of Babel.[16]

Headlining the cast were Carl de Vogt and Meinhart Maur, who played two roles. As *Lichtbild-Bühne* indicated, "Since both of [Maur's] characters appear simultaneously on the screen, director Josef Stein will use interesting special effects for this purpose.[17] The female lead was Kläry Lotto (aka Clairy Lotto), who had costarred with Lugosi in *99-es számú bérkosci* (*Rental Car Number 99*, 1918).

Working with artistic consultant Gustav Knauer and cinematographer Joseph Rona, Josef Stein shot *Auf den Trümmern des Paradieses* in the summer of 1920.[18] An industry trade reported:

[The] Ustad Film Company is cranking out their first Karl May film in the Johannisthal. What May's glowing imagination alluded to as novel, Frau Dr. Droop has translated into the language of film. Her manuscript, on the other hand, has been transposed into film narrative by the original Turkish director Muchzsin Bey [aka

Lugosi in *Der Sklavenhalter von Kansas-City* (*The Slaveholder of Kansas City, aka John Hopkins III*, 1920/21).

Lugosi in *Nat Pinkerton im Kampf* (*Nat Pinkerton in Combat*, 1920).

Muhsin Ertuğrul]. The entire cast is engrossed in their roles with true enthusiasm. It is immediately clear that the colorful, adventurous romanticism comes naturally to the actors. Meinhart Maur speaks animatedly about the tasks that challenge him in his role and doesn't allow the fun to be spoiled by the tremendous heat that – in his extraordinarily genuine costume bristling with weapons – can only be endured with a great deal of effort. Carl de Vogt is also quite colorful in his decorative Oriental [costume]. Ernst Stern has built a Mosque with a haunting power. ...

One cannot mention Johannisthal without a mention of the cafeteria. It is impossible to keep it secret. What Mr. Senftleben offers by way of ice-cold refreshments against the immense heat is also an artistic experience![19]

The shoot had ended by July 25, 1920, if not sooner.[20] Lugosi's participation was recorded in the trade press only once, and his role is unknown.[21]

Auf den Trümmern des Paradieses played Dresden in October 1920 before premiering in Berlin on November 5.[22] *Der Kinematograph* told readers:

Now the first Karl May film has been launched in the Motivhaus [movie theater] Whoever expected Indian and Wild West scenes in this film will be immediately disappointed. Eager readers of May will surely know that the prolific and well-known

BECOMING DRACULA

Lugosi in *Nat Pinkerton im Kampf* (*Nat Pinkerton in Combat*, 1920).

writer gathered his material from all corners of the globe – and perhaps those tales that are less well known and play outside the purview of the Indians theme are not at all his worst. ...

The film has several good qualities – above all the beautifully clear photography as well as the landscape scenes, the ruins on the Euphrates, the banks of the river – all well executed and create an effective backdrop for preserving the illusion. In contrast, one misses a truly taut plot which is interrupted for too long through the dream and the story of the Persian Prince and becomes as a result more secondary in nature.[23]

Other reviews also lauded the acting and locations while sharing reservations about the storyline.[24]

Ustad next produced *Die Todeskarawane* (*The Caravan of Death*, 1920). According to *Deutsche Lichtspiel-Zeitung*:

The story, which plays out in Baghdad and Isfahan, will also reveal to the audience the secrets of the Tenth of Muharram (the big Shiite festival day). – Carl de Vogt plays Karl May's celebrated character Kara ben Nemsis. [Meinhart Maur] will portray his loyal companion Hadschi Halef Omar. The film, for which big crowd scenes including horseback battles are to be staged, will be realized abroad. The scripts are being prepared by Frau Dr. Droop. She will also direct together with Herr [Muchzsin Bey]. Photography and operation of the company's mobile lighting equipment lie in the hands of Herr [Gustave] Preiss. In order to handle the great technical demands, the company has secured an extensive floodlighting set-up.[25]

Der Kinematograph added, "Extraordinary expenditures are being made on this creation."[26] Lugosi played a Sheik, but nothing else is known of his role.

Production on *Die Todeskarawane* apparently began in May or June of 1920.[27] Strangely, *Der Kinematograph* mentioned it being filmed in October 1920, but that almost certainly referred to retakes or new scenes that didn't require Lugosi.[28] At any rate, Josef Stein directed this six-reel film rather than Droop, who seems to have fallen in love with Carl de Vogt during the summer of 1920. According to *Neue Kino-Rundschau*, "The overall success of the film was marred in art by a lack of effective scenography and sets which a film about the Orient needs to achieve its full effect."[29] By contrast, *Der Film* praised *Die Todeskarawane*'s direction, script, and acting.[30]

The production timeline of Lugosi's third and final Ustad film, *Die Teufelsanbeter* (*The Devil Worshippers*), originally announced as *Bei den Teufelsanbetern*, is also hard to determine. Carl de Vogt and Meinhart Maur reprised their roles from *Die Todeskarawane*. Kläry Lotto also appeared. Lugosi's role is unknown, but

Published in *Lichtbild-Bühne* on July 3, 1920.

Published in *Lichtbild-Bühne* on December 11, 1920.

BECOMING DRACULA

it is possible he played the same Sheik as in *Die Todeskarawane*. A trade publication from late June 1920 mentions:

Der zweite **KARL MAY-**Film

Die Todeskarawane

Filmdrama in 6 Akten

Bearbeitet von: **Erwin Báron**

Regie: **Joseph Stein**

Hauptdarsteller: **Carl de Vogt** / **Meinh. Maur** / **Erwin Báron**

Für Jugendliche genehmigt!

Filmhaus Bruckmann & Co.

BERLIN SW 48, Friedrichstraße 233

Düsseldorf / Frankfurt a. M. / München / Hamburg / Danzig / Leipzig
Kaiser-Wilhelmstr. 32   Zeil 19   Kaufingerstr. 2   Breat-Markstr. 12–14   &.TANN   Handegasse 9

Published in *Lichtbild-Bühne* on December 11, 1920.

The film *Die Teufelsanbeter*, which was adapted for the screen wonderfully by Frau Dr. Marie Luise Droop and is currently being filmed on the studio stages of Jofa, depicts one of the most mysterious of Asia's sects which suffered from horrible persecution in past centuries. Frau Dr. Droop has succeeded in determining the unique theology of these 'men of the devil' or 'extinguishers of light' as they are known with the help of heretofore unknown English source materials. The results of this research which have been utilized dramatically and scenically in the film, should be published in a respected professional journal. The leading role in the film is played by Carl de Vogt. He appears in genuine Meccan garb that Karl May also wore on one of his trips to the Orient. He will also have with him a Henry carbine, the famous American repeater rifle for which American collectors before the war offered to pay 100,000 Marks.[31]

Despite the different release dates of the three Ustad films, it is possible that Josef Stein shot at least some footage for all of them concurrently at Johannisthal. That would have been a cost-saving measure, and, if true, it would clear up some conflicting details about their productions in the industry press.

At any rate, despite their titles, *Die Teufelsanbeter* and *Die Todeskarawane* were not horror films, but rather adventure stories of "exotic" peoples. As for *Old Shatterhand* and *Vom Stamme der Verfluchten*, neither film was made. Ustad expended more money on its initial productions than it made on them, and so the other projects couldn't be financed.[32]

Luna-Film

At the beginning of 1920, *Deutsche Lichtspiel-Zeitung* announced a major change at Luna-Film, the oldest and most prestigious of the German companies that would hire Lugosi:

Dr. Max Maschke, chairman of the German Association of Film Manufacturers, will step down during the course of January as president of Luna-Film, the company

Lugosi in *Die Todeskarawane* (*The Caravan of Death*, 1920).

he founded in 1912. Over these seven years, Dr. Maschke's unflagging creativity and inventiveness have helped raise Luna-Film's profile to that of an industry frontrunner. Taking over Dr. Maschke's position shall be Arthur Wellin, co-owner of the Amboss-Film company, who will join Luna's existing co-president Gustav Schwab in the future management of Dr. Maschke's brainchild.[33]

The new regime "expanded its operations in a most substantial manner."[34] And it pursued several priorities, not least of which was greater international distribution of its features.[35]

Also key to the new strategy was the western genre, which – thanks to writers like Karl May – had proven venerable in Germany long before the rise of cinema. As of January 10, 1920, the trade press announced, "*Leatherstocking, The Last of the Mohicans* and *The Pathfinder*, those dear old pals from our youth, are soon to appear on the screen. Luna-Film has purchased scripts for them adapted from [James Fenimore] Cooper's unforgettable works by Robert Heymann."[36]

In June of 1920, *Film-Kurier* wrote, "In addition to Robert Heymann, great credit is given to Luna-Film, which produced the films with enormous production costs and for having established a new literary apex for the Western film as intermediary of those times, people and cultures."[37] The company hired Erhard Brauchbar to design the exterior sets, as well as Professor Karl Henckel, who helped ensure the accuracy of the "costumes and ethnographic scenery."[38] Log cabins, farmsteads, wooden outhouses and an "entire fort" were constructed near Wünsdorf.[39] Lugosi would play Chingachgook, pretending once again – as he had in his youth in Hungary – to be a Native American.

Lugosi in *Die Teufelsanbeter* (*The Devil Worshippers*, 1921). *(Courtesy of Dennis Phelps)*

Lugosi in *Die Teufelsanbeter* (*The Devil Worshippers*, 1921). *(Courtesy of David Wentink)*

Der Film claimed that shooting didn't begin until August of 1920.[40] On September 4, *Deutsche Lichtspiel-Zeitung* reported that the production was in "full swing."[41] Visiting the shoot, a journalist from *Film-Kurier* reported, "We got to watch an Indian attack, the mass-storming of a fort. The whole thing looked extremely lively...."[42] Russian officers in the Bermondt Army (who had left Russia after the success of the communist revolution) also watched some of the filming. Shooting apparently ended in September, with the film edited by mid-October. By the end of that month, Luna-Film hosted invitation-only previews in Berlin, Hamburg, Wrocław, Leipzig, Düsseldorf, and Munich.

When *Lederstrumpf* went into general release in November, it appeared in two parts, *Der Letzte Mohikaner* (*Last of the Mohicans*) and *Wildtöter* (*The Deerslayer*, aka *Wildtöter und Chingachgook/The Deerslayer and Chingachgook*).[43] *Deutsche Lichtspiel-Zeitung* published the following review:

Before there was a Karl May, J. F. Cooper was writing. His *Leatherstocking* was for many

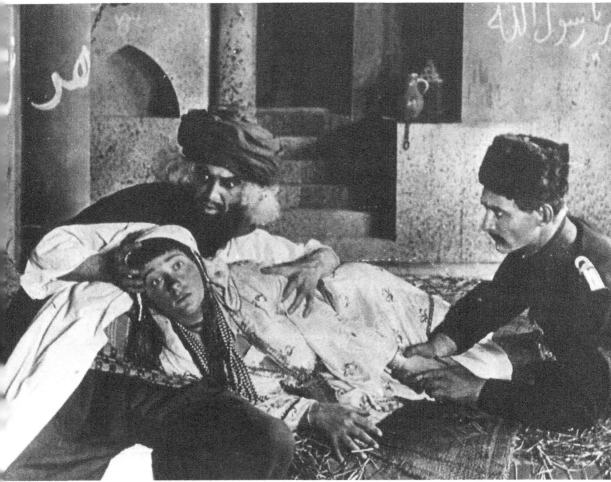

Lugosi in *Die Teufelsanbeter* (*The Devil Worshippers*, 1921). *(Courtesy of David Wentink)*

decades *the* defining book for a youthful generation whose outrage at the perfidy of the Iroquois was equal in measure to its gushing enthusiasm for Deerslayer, Chingachgook and Wah-ta-Wah. Robert Heymann has transformed this standard work about American Indians from the bookshelves of our childhood into a film script that starts out by relating Leatherstocking's youthful escapades – or much rather, bringing them to life in a series of deftly arranged scenes. ... Fortunately, Luna-Film has not relied solely on the profound impact that the book continues to exert to this day, but has also paid special heed to the film's form, ensuring the finesse of its technical and artistic presentation.

Under Arthur Wellin's direction, assured performances are given by Emil [Mamelok] and Bela Lugosi, followed by Margot [Sokolowska], Herta Heden and Erna Rehberger; … and Ernst [Plhak] has photographed all the movie's settings with clarity and verve.[44]

An abbreviated version of *Wildtöter* survives, with its costumes, sets, and location

Gary D. Rhodes | Bill Kaffenberger   307

Lugosi in *Lederstrumpf* (*Leatherstocking*, 1920). *(Courtesy of David Wentink)*

photography remaining impressive. Despite the unfortunate use of redface makeup, Lugosi was well suited to Chingachgook, and not just in appearance. His acting is quite reserved and subtle, not at all of the exaggerated style some critics noticed him using in *Hypnose: Sklaven fremden Willens* (*Hypnosis: Slave of a Foreign Will*).[45]

Going West

While *Der Januskopf* (1920) may have been the most artistic German film in which Lugosi appeared, *Lederstrumpf* was the most publicized and perhaps the most popular with audiences of the time.

But Lugosi left Germany prior to its release, and perhaps even before those previews in late October. He likewise wasn't in the country for the premiere of *Die Teufelsanbeter* in January 1921.[46]

The question remains as to why Lugosi left Berlin when he did. Even though his plan

Lugosi in *Lederstrumpf* (*Leatherstocking*, 1920).

was to immigrate to America, the timing is worth considering. In June 1920, the trade press reported:

> The well-known film actor Bela Lugosi has accepted the leading role in *Die Teufelsanbeter* ... before he devotes himself to founding his own film production company.[47]

Here is crucial information, with Lugosi's plan perhaps inspired by Bruno Decarli, the actor-turned-actor/producer whose departure from Eichberg-Film had opened the door to Lugosi in 1919.

But no Lugosi production company formed. Could his professional disappointment have made him decide to leave Germany in October? Perhaps. In fact, *Die Silbermine* (*The Silver Mine*) may have compounded his feelings. Ernst Klein announced plans to shoot that five-reel western with Lugosi in August 1920, but it never went into production.[48]

Contrary to this information is the fact that Lugosi had enjoyed an extremely busy summer, enough so that he could have confidently anticipated much more work in the months ahead. He might also have performed in German theater productions, given that he knew the language. A fan magazine in 1932 certainly claimed that he temporarily worked "on the Berlin stage."[49]

Saving more money would have allowed for a much easier journey to the United States than he would experience. This is all in addition to the fact his advertisement in *Film-*

Magazin includes movies he made during the summer and early autumn of 1920.[50] Why would Lugosi have bothered buying an advertisement if he already had plans to leave in October?

The exact timing of his departure might have been prompted not by professional reasons, but instead by personal worries. Perhaps a love affair had gone badly in Berlin, whether with Violette Napierska or someone else. Or, perhaps more likely, it was the pain from his failed marriage. In July 1920, he had learned about Ilona Szmik filing for divorce; he may have initially remained in Berlin in hopes of reconciliation. But his mention of moving to America when the two were together in Vienna in 1919 had been one reason she returned to Budapest without him.[51]

Lugosi in *Lederstrumpf* (*Leatherstocking*, 1920).

Regardless, legal proceedings forged ahead and would conclude in November 1920. To remain in Europe might no longer have been emotionally tenable, even in the short term. And so he departed. He departed Germany, with the clear intent to leave the continent, to travel to a new life in America, home of Broadway, home of Hollywood, and home of Chingachgook.

As Cooper writes in his *Leatherstocking Tales*, "Her face, as it encountered the rays of the moon from the east, seemed not unlike a sun rising in the west."

(Endnotes)

1   Kracauer, Siegfried. *From Caligari to Hitler: A Psychological History of the German Film* (Princeton, NJ: Princeton University Press, 1947). See also: Kalbus, Oskar. *Vom Werden deutscher Filmkunst* (Altona-Bahrenfeld: Cigaretten-Bilderdienst, 1935, 2 vols).

2   Göktürk, Deniz. *Künstler, Cowboys, Ingenieure…: Kultur- und mediengeschichtliche Studien zu deutschen Amerika-Texten 1912-1920* (Munich: Wilhelm Fink Verlag, 1998).

3   Advertisement. *Lichtbild-Bühne* 24 July 1920.

4   Some modern sources give the company name for these Lugosi projects as "Dua-Films," rather than "Dua-Film." But Dua-Film GmbH did not officially change its name to Dua-Films GmbH until 18 Sept. 1920, by which time Lugosi was no longer acting in the company's films. See *Berliner Börsen-Zeitung* 21 Sept. 1920. That said, it should be noted that most, if not all, promotional materials for the Lugosi films do bear the later name "Dua-Films." Between the shooting and release of those films, the company name had changed.

5   "Dua-Film." *Der Kinematograph* 8 Aug. 1920.

Lugosi in _Lederstrumpf_ (_Leatherstocking_, 1920). *(Courtesy of John Antosiewicz)*

6   Prior filmographies that list *Der Sklavenhalter von Kansas-City* and *John Hopkins III* as separate films are mistaken. They are different titles for the same film. In addition, filmographies that list the title *Apachenrache. 3. – Die verschwundene Million* (*Apache Revenge 3 – The Disappearing Million*, 1920) as a Lugosi film are also mistaken. It was not an alternate title for *John Hopkins III*. Rather, it was a separate film that definitely did not feature Lugosi, despite its title *Apachenrache 3*, which wrongly makes it appear to be the third installment in the Neff-Bess series.

7   The first *Apachenrache* film, *In den Krallen des Vampirs* (*In the Vampire's Clutches*, 1920), is a distinctly different film than Heinz Sarnow's film *In den Krallen des Vampyrs* (*In the Vampyre's Clutches*, 1919). Given the near-identical title, the two have been conflated in some prior filmographies.

8   "Dua-Film." *Lichtbild-Bühne* 12 Feb. 1921.

9   For more information, see the series of thirteen articles on this subject by Jörg-M. Bönisch and Gerd Hardacker published between 2010 and 2015 in the *Mitteilungen der Karl-May-Gesellschaft*, available at: https://1drv.ms/u/s!Aid5WjzWYR_EhyEf_annJ9WUsh42?e=q3UNsc. Accessed on 10 Dec. 2019.

10   For more information, see Kipp, Rudolf W. "Die Lu-Droop-Story." *Mitteilungen der Karl-May-Gesellschaft* Sept. 1978.

11   "Der Karl May-Verlag." *Der Kinematograph* 10 Mar. 1920.

12   "Karl May im Film." *Film-Kurier* 30 Mar. 1920.

13   "Was die LBB erzählt." *Lichtbild-Bühne* June 1920.

14   *Deutsche Lichtspiel-Zeitung* 12 June 1920.

15   Untitled. *Lichtbild-Bühne* 30 Oct. 1920

16   "Ustad-Film." *Der Kinematograph* 25 July 1920.

17   Untitled. *Lichtbild-Bühne* 4 Sept. 1920.

18   *"Auf den Trümmern des Paradieses."* *Deutsche Lichtspiel-Zeitung* 13 Nov. 1920.

19   Prof. Ernst Stern im Dienste Karl Mays." *Lichtbild-Bühne* 17 July 1920.

20   "Neuheiten-Anzeiger." *Deutsche Lichtspiel-Zeitung* 31 July 1920.

21   Untitled. *Lichtbild-Bühne* 17 July 1920.

22   Untitled. *Lichtbild-Bühne* 9 Oct. 1920.

23   *"Auf den Trümmern des Paradises."* *Der Kinematograph* 14 Nov. 1920.

24   See, for example: *"Auf den Trümmern des Paradieses."* *Lichtbild-Bühne* 13 Nov. 1920 and *"Auf den Trümmern des Paradieses."* Deutsche Lichtspiel-Zeitung* 13 Nov. 1920.

25   *Deutsche Lichtspiel-Zeitung* 15 May 1920.

26   "Ustad-Film." *Der Kinematograph* 8 Aug. 1920.

27   "Was die L.B.B. erzählt." *Lichtbild-Bühne* May 1920.

28   "Ustad-Film." *Der Kinematograph* 10 Oct. 1920.

29   *"Die Todeskarawane."* *Neue Kino-Rundschau* 5 Feb. 1921.

30   *"Die Todeskarawane."* *Der Film* 26 June 1920.

31   *"Die Teufelsanbeter."* *Lichtbild-Bühne* 26 June 1920.

32   See Jörg-M. Bönisch and Gerd Hardacker's articles on this subject, published between 2010 and 2015 in the *Mitteilungen der Karl-May-Gesellschaft.*

33   Untitled. *Deutsche Lichtspiel-Zeitung* 10 Jan. 1920.

34   "Luna-Film Company." *Film-Kurier* 8 Feb. 1920.

35   "Handels-Zeitung." *Deutsche Lichtspiel-Zeitung* 14 Feb. 1920.

36   Untitled. *Deutsche Lichtspiel-Zeitung* 10 Jan. 1920.

37   "Luna-Film." *Lichtbild-Bühne* June 1920.

38   Untitled. *Film-Kurier* 1 Sept. 1920.

39   *"Lederstrumpf,* Cooper & Co." *Film-Kurier* 15 Sept. 1920.

40 "Luna-Film." *Der Kinematograph* 15 Aug. 1920.

41 "Neuheiten-Anzeiger." *Deutsche Lichtspiel-Zeitung* 4 Sept. 1920.

42 *"Lederstrumpf,* Cooper & Co."

43 Articles in *Lichtbild-Bühne* 35 (1920) and *LBB* 43 (1920), as well as a full-page ad in *LBB* 37 (1920) used the title *Wildtöter,* as did an ad in *Film-Kurier* (1 Sept. 1920), an ad in *Der Film* (29 Aug. 1920), and an article in *Der Film* 43 (1920). But a review in *Film-Kurier* (1 Nov. 1920) used the title *Wildtöter und Chingachgook,* as did reviews in *Der Film* 44 and 46 (1920). At times (as in an article in *Der Film* 1 [1920], and a full-page ad in *Der Kinematograph* 688-689 [1920]), *Wildtöter* was referred to as *Der Pfadfinder* (*The Pathfinder*).

44 *"Lederstrumpf."* *Deutsche Lichtspiel-Zeitung* 27 Nov. 1920.

45 *"Hypnose."* *Film-Kurier* 4 Jan. 1920.

46 Untitled. *Deutsche Lichtspiel-Zeitung* 7 Jan. 1921.

47 Untitled. *Lichtbild-Bühne* June 1920.

48 "Luna-Film." *Lichtbild-Bühne* 7 Aug. 1920.

49 Ergenbright, Eric. "The Man Who Knows Too Much!" *Screen Play* July 1932. [In addition, another fan magazine quoted Lugosi as saying "There was an opening for me in a Berlin theater." See Sinclair, John. "Master of Horrors." *Silver Screen* Jan. 1932.]

50 "Béla Lugosi." *Film-Magazin* (Berlin: Reinhold Kühn, 1920).

51 Rhodes, Gary D. Interview with Noémi Saly, 24 May 2006.

Lugosi, crewmember aboard the *Gróf Tisza István* (*Count Stephen Tisza*).
(*Courtesy of John Antosiewicz*)

Chapter 20

Journeys

"How am I to account for all these horrors
when I get to port? When I get to port!
Will that ever be?"
– Bram Stoker, *Dracula*

His passage to America could scarcely have been more difficult, as these words written in yellowing old pages reveal:

> There was unrest among the crew. … He extended sympathy to members of the crew in their claimed unjust treatment. … The captain and the officers got tough and, with some loyal members of the crew, decided to settle the trouble with belaying pins as clubs. … It quickly became a battle royal. … The officers had subdued what they called a mutiny, but they too carried indications that they had been through a battle. [He] was definitely not invited to sit at the captain's table during the voyage. He spent the remainder of his journey nursing scores of bruises and sitting in meditation at the stern of the ship....[1]

This story is not from a biography of Béla Lugosi, but of Nikola Tesla, who immigrated to the United States in 1884. Tesla died in 1943, the same year that Lugosi starred in *The Return of the Vampire* (1943), portraying Armand Tesla, a character whose name may well have been inspired by the famed inventor. Like Nikola Tesla, Lugosi's voyage to America was fraught with troubles, in his case both real and invented.

When he decided to leave for the United States, Lugosi made his way from Germany via Austria to the seaport city of Trieste. Its docks face the Gulf of Trieste, which morphs into the Adriatic Sea, then the Ionian Sea, then the Mediterranean Sea, and finally the Atlantic

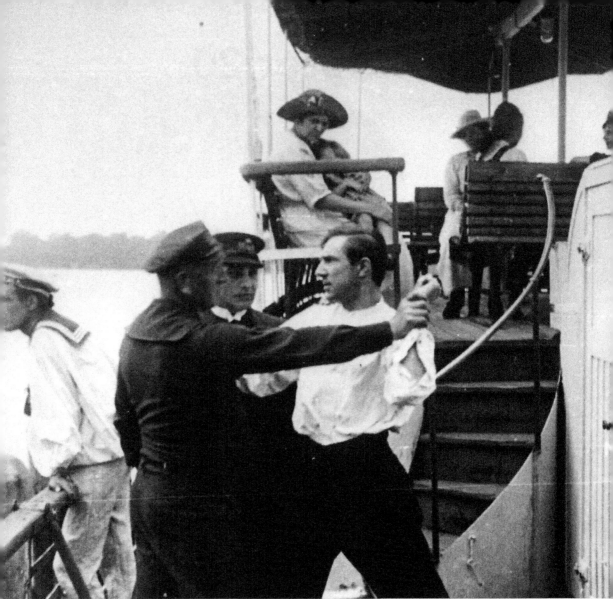

Lugosi fights aboard ship in a scene in *Nat Pinkerton im Kampf* (*Nat Pinkerton in Combat*, 1920).

Ocean.[2] Though once part of the Austro-Hungarian Empire, Trieste was annexed by Italy following World War I.

After arriving in the city by October 9, 1920, Lugosi stayed at the Excelsior Palace Hotel, also known as the "Hotel Excelsior – La Grande Trieste" and the "Ocean Liner Hotel."[3] When opened in 1912, it was touted as "the most important and luxurious hotel in Austria-Hungary."[4] Located very near the docks, the Excelsior apparently remained opulent in 1920.

During his brief sojourn, Lugosi received documents from his lawyer in Hungary. Ilona Szmik's divorce proceedings were nearly finished. The marriage would legally end on November 22, 1920. By that time, though, Lugosi was no longer in Trieste. He was bound for America, in more ways than one.

To secure passage, Lugosi convinced a harbormaster named Luigi Cozzi to help him find employment as a seaman. He invoked his railroad engineering work in Szabadka, but that

Lugosi as Armand Tesla
in *The Return of the
Vampire* (1943).

Lugosi imperiled by the waters in *Der Sklavenhalter von Kansas-City* (*The Slaveholder of Kansas City*, aka *John Hopkins III*, 1920/21).

hardly translated to the skills needed on a freighter. Lugosi's prior experience on the water was probably little more than scenes in a few German films and a couple of cabaret performances aboard the *Auguszta* on the Danube in 1916. Nevertheless, Cozzi agreed to help him, and by October 26, 1920, Lugosi worked on the *Gróf Tisza István* (*Count Stephen Tisza*).

The steel screw steamer had been built in 1904 for the Hungarian-Levant Steamship Company of Budapest for both Danube and continental trade.[5] By 1920, the Levante Soc. di Nav. Marittima of Fiume owned the *Tisza István*. Its manifest claims Lugosi had "shipped or engaged" from Monfalcone, a thriving ship manufacturing center about 19 miles northwest of Trieste.[6] Presumably Lugosi traveled from Trieste to Monfalcone to join the crew.

That he needed to work in order to pay for his journey is not particularly surprising. However, it begs the question of why he would have been staying at a luxurious hotel. Perhaps it was an effort to appear financially sound, even successful, to his attorney and thus to Ilona.[7]

There is also the issue of gaining employment on a ship sailing not for his intended destination of New York, but rather for New Orleans. The *Tisza István* was carrying cargo for the A.K. Miller Company, which a 1922 publication called "one of the oldest in the city engaged in the steamship agency and ship brokerage business."[8] Lugosi's limited resources

Trieste „Excelsior Palace Hotel"

Postcard of the Excelsior Palace Hotel from the era in which Lugosi was in Trieste.

and an intense desire to leave Europe after receiving the divorce papers likely left him with no choice other than to accept work on the *Tisza István*.

Moreover, after fleeing from Hungary, he may not have had proper identification in his posession. In 1932, one fan magazine claimed he left for America without a passport.[9] If true, that would have been an important reason for him to seek employment on a ship rather than purchase even the cheapest passenger ticket. He might also have believed that he could potentially elude customs as a sailor arriving in New Orleans easier than as a passenger arriving at Ellis Island.

The ship departed from the Port of Trieste on October 27, 1920, only one day after Lugosi was hired. Cozzi was kind to help Lugosi, but the ship could also have been in need of a few final crewmembers. Lugosi served as an Apprentice answering to 3rd Officer Paolo Thian. The menial role might have meant that Lugosi received room and board in exchange for labor, but little or no salary.

The ship's destination was Louisiana, though it stopped temporarily at Palermo and then Gibraltar in early November. The total voyage from Italy to America took over five weeks. It was more than long enough for Lugosi to experience major troubles, not unlike those that Nikola Tesla suffered in 1884. But the exact nature of the troubles remains beclouded. In *Dracula*, Stoker writes, "A thin mist began to creep up from the river, and it grew, and grew; till a dense fog enveloped the ship and all around her." In Lugosi's case, the fog builds due to incomplete evidence and what seem to be major exaggerations.

For example, Lugosi gave fan magazine writer Gladys Hall the following account in 1941:

I … embarked as an assistant engineer on a small cargo boat.[10] Our cargo was steel plates. There was a very heavy storm at sea. Our ship turned over on its side and for

Sheet No. _____ 1½/12

LIST OR MANIFEST OF ALIENS EMPLOYED ON THE VESSEL AS MEMBERS OF CREW

Required under Act of Congress of February 5, 1917, to be delivered to the United States immigration officer by the representatives of any vessel having such aliens on board upon arrival at a port of the United States.

Vessel, *Gróf Tisza István*, arriving at *New Orleans*, 1/4, 19_0, from the port of *Fiume*

No. on list	Name in full		Position in ship's company	Shipped or engaged		Whether to be paid off or discharged at port of arrival	Whether able to read	Age	Sex	Race	Nationality	Height	Weight lbs	Physical marks or peculiarities
	Family name	Given name		When	Where									
1	Szabo	Lodovico	captain	24/12 20	Trieste	Yes		32	men	European	Italian	5'8"	173	
2	Vargha	Alexander	1st officer	24/12 20	Venezia			47				5'11"	175	
3	Kaplanek	Hugo	2nd officer	24/12 20	Napoli			28				5'5½"	134	}
4	Thian	Paolo	3rd officer	14/9 19	Brindisi			25				5'8½"	149	
5	Lugosi	Bela	appr.	24/12 20	Monfalcone			38				6'1"	172	

From the manifest of the *Gróf Tisza István* (*Count Stephen Tisza*).

three and a half weeks we were that way. Five weeks it took us to go from Trieste to New Orleans. Spend three and a half weeks turned sidewise upon a raging sea and the mind totters and heaves like the sea beneath....[11]

One press story of 1944 went so far as to claim the *Tisza István* "almost sank several times."[12]

It is quite possible that the ship encountered terrible weather. A number of newspapers reported a storm that had been centered over Bermuda was quickly heading for the Atlantic coast, a storm serious enough to bring shipping to a standstill.[13] The tail end of the storm could be the reason why the *Tisza István* docked in New Orleans later than planned.

Aside from the issue of weather, the ship's cargo was fruit, nuts, and preserves, not steel.[14] That said, when the *Tisza István* departed from New Orleans on December 25, 1920, for the return trip to Italy, it carried "3,810 steel angles, 1,264 bundles [of] steel bars, 560 pieces [of] steel bars, 350 drums of alcohol, 60 barrels of soap stock [and] 18 pieces of pine timber."[15] Perhaps Lugosi thought the return cargo sounded more dramatic when retelling the story, or perhaps his memory was faulty. After all, there is no indication that he helped load the ship's cargo.

In later publicity, Lugosi claimed the ship departed Trieste in December 1920, allowing him to state incorrectly that he was stuck on the ocean on Christmas Day. But he likely did recall the correct timeline, certainly knowing that the tale of Christmas was untrue. Then he added, "I locked myself in my cabin, and the rest is too personal to me to be given to the public."[16]

In a way, it is ironic that the ship was named for someone who had at times been seen as a great Hungarian statesman, but also someone for whom Lugosi likely had great disdain. Tisza was a dualist who placed much faith in the Austro-Hungarian Empire, at least until he was assassinated in October 1918. He had also served as chairman of one of Hungary's largest banks. By contrast, Lugosi had become a member of Kun's communist government, which tried to dramatically remake Tisza's Hungary. Tisza's murderers had in fact been left-wing Hungarian extremists sympathetic to Kun.

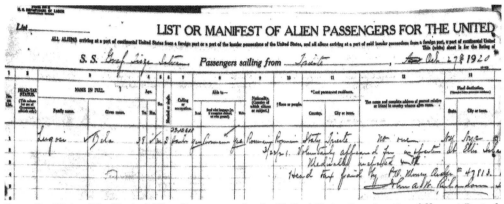

From the *List or Manifest of Alien Passengers for the United States Immigration Officer at Port of Arrival*.

As for those stories "too personal" to tell the public, Lugosi's shipmate Hugó Kaplanek did discuss them with Lugosi's friend Willi Szittja, and he spoke more about storms raging aboard ship than he did those in the skies. Captain Ludovico Szabó, commander of the *Tisza István*, allegedly became incensed with Lugosi's role in the Kun regime, referring to him as "that Bolshevist." In Kaplanek's version of the story, the others aboard ship were royalists who also disliked Lugosi's politics.

Szabó and at least some of his crew even considered throwing Lugosi overboard, but Kaplanek and a crewmember named Felix Hartmann hid Lugosi. They smuggled him food and kept him out of harm's way for the rest of the journey. Once New Orleans was in sight, Hartmann put Lugosi onto a raft and allowed him to reach land safely. Lugosi then told the harbor police he was a political refugee.[17]

Here is a fantastic as well as likely fantastical tale. For example, many of the crewmember names on the manifest appear Italian. A number of others appear to have been German, Hungarian, or Slavic. How many of them would have felt any kind of loyalty to the Austro-Hungarian Empire is unknown. But they might have felt allegiance to their own ship and the man for whom it was named. Tisza's assassination was still major news, especially given that his murderers had been sentenced less than six weeks before Lugosi and the crew set sail.

Then there is the larger issue of anti-communist sentiment. In other words, the crew would not have needed particular loyalties or feelings about Austria-Hungary to be heatedly against Bolshevism. That alone could have made Lugosi unpopular. If Szabó had any or all of the aforementioned reasons to dislike Lugosi, some of his crew might well have adopted the same view, simply to support their captain. And Lugosi might well have felt that he was in greater danger than he was, exaggerating even to himself.

Szittja's tale relied on Kaplanek and Hartmann being aboard ship, and it is quite true that Hartmann's name does not appear in the surviving manifest. However, that might have little meaning. A page of the manifest could be missing, and documents are sometimes incorrect or incomplete. After all, the manifest officially lists the entire crew (including Lugosi) as being of Italian nationality, which is certainly incorrect. And it was Kaplanek who told the story to Szittja; if he was trying to take credit for saving Lugosi, why invent another non-existent person? Moreover, it is evident that a Felix Hartmann did exist and that he knew Lugosi. For the rest of his life, Lugosi kept a photo of Hartmann in his personal archives. His heirs still own it.

What then is the reality of the story that Kaplanek told? Likely there is a bit of truth in it, along with a great deal of exaggeration. Perhaps the captain and some or all of the crew did take a dislike to Lugosi. They might even have been jealous of his tales of success on the stage, in the cinema, and with women of more than one nation. Lugosi could have become something of an outcast. Indeed, the manifest shows the word "discharged" stamped above his name. Might he have been fired, even if his life was not actually under threat? Or was the stamp added later, simply because he disembarked in America?

Portrait of István Tisza.

Whatever the case, the *Tisza István* arrived at the Port of New Orleans on December 4, 1920, having passed through Port Eads, Louisiana, earlier in the day, thus making Lugosi's

The Port of New Orleans, circa 1920.

BECOMING DRACULA

Ellis Island, circa 1920.

total voyage around 39 days.[18] The ship had originally been expected on November 22.[19] The arrival date was then revised to November 28 and again to December 1.[20] Whatever else is true or false about Lugosi's journey, the delay of some twelve days must have been excruciating, particularly for someone who hated ocean travel.

Various persons, including one librarian at the U.S. Department of the Interior, have speculated that Lugosi jumped ship at New Orleans, eluding the captain, crew, and the U.S. Immigration Service.[21] That could be the case, though a *List or Manifest of Alien Passengers for the United States Immigration Officer at Port of Arrival* does record Lugosi as a steerage passenger. Perhaps he spoke briefly with an immigration officer upon arrival before quickly disappearing from view.

According to the passenger manifest, Lugosi was 38 years of age, 6'1" in height, and weighed 172 pounds; his occupation was listed as sailor, his language given as Romanian, and his final destination New York City.[22] The officer who completed the paperwork noted that Lugosi "voluntarily affirmed" he would meet with the Immigration Service in New York.

But Lugosi didn't report to Ellis Island until March 23, 1921.[23] By then, he had been in New York City for over three months, living at least part of the time at a boarding house at 109 West 93rd Street.[24] He likely received a letter from the Immigration Service's New York Headquarters requiring him to undergo primary alien inspection.[25]

Lugosi told the immigration agent at Ellis Island that he was a sailor originally born in Romania. Given that he had been a member of the crew on the *Tisza István*, and his hometown Lugos had become a part of Romania after World War I, his story was essentially correct. He also mentioned he had $100 in his possession, though whether he meant that was the amount he had upon arrival in New Orleans or at the time of the interview is difficult to say.[26]

Over a decade later, a fan magazine claimed that Lugosi had enlisted "several influential countrymen in his case," which helped the U.S. government to "overlook his lack of papers," particularly since he worked as an actor in America from as early as January 1921.[27] Perhaps this is true. Perhaps it is not.

Tales of Lugosi's voyage to America are perhaps more mythical than those of Nikola Tesla. But once again, it is necessary to remember that historical documents like manifests are sometimes incomplete or inaccurate. For example, the immigration officer at Ellis Island officially recorded Lugosi as being "five feet, ten inches" in height.[28] He was actually over six feet tall.

And then there's the fact that the literal definition of the word "myth" means oft-told tales with *or* without an identifiable basis in fact. Whatever embellishments Lugosi and/or Kaplanek and/or Szittja made, some aspects of these maritime stories could be true. In any event, Lugosi had finally made shore; he had finally landed.

As Stoker writes in *Dracula*, "so will end this one more 'mystery of the sea.'"

The story continues in Volume II of:
Becoming Dracula: The Early Years of Bela Lugosi

(Endnotes)

1   John J. O'Neill. *Prodigal Genius: The Life of Nikola Tesla* (New York: Ives Washburn, 1944).

2   "The History of Trieste." *International Centre for Theoretical Physics*. Available at https://www.ictp.it/visit-ictp/about-trieste/triestehistory.aspx#close. Accessed on 19 Jan. 2019.

3   Béla Lugosi/Ilona Smik Divorce Documents. [Available in Catalog Reference HU BFL – VII.2.c – 1920 – 40714 at the Budapest City Archives, Budapest, Hungary.]

4   "La Grande Trieste." Available at https://www.lagrandetrieste.it/economia/architettura/hotel-excelsior/. Accessed on 19 Jan. 2019.

5   "Grof Tisza Istvan [*sic*]." *The Marine Engineer* 1 Dec. 1904.

6   *List or Manifest of Aliens Employed on the Vessel as Members of Crew*. U.S. Department of Labor. New Orleans, 4 Dec. 1920.

7   It is possible Lugosi stayed at the Excelsior for only part of his time in Trieste, largely to retrieve mail at an address he had given in advance to his attorney. Or that he didn't actually stay there at all, but used it only as an address to collect mail.

8   Kendall, John Smith. *History of New Orleans, Volume III* (Chicago: Lewis Publishing Company, 1922).

9   Ergenbright, Eric. "The Man Who Knows Too Much!" *Screen Play* July 1932.

10   Despite his claim to the contrary, Lugosi was not hired as an assistant engineer, but rather as an apprentice.

11   Lugosi, Bela, as told to Gladys Hall, "Memos of a Madman." *Silver Screen* July 1941. Emphasis in original.

12   Finn, Elsie. "Beauty Hung a Hex Sign on Bela Lugosi." *Philadelphia Record* 9 Apr. 1944.

13   "Shipping Stopped By Atlantic Storm." *Augusta Chronicle* (Augusta, GA) 28 Nov. 1920. Warnings about this and other major storms had gone out to shipping interests as early as 16 Nov. 1920. See "Shipping Warned Of A Big Atlantic Storm." *Ocala Evening Star* (Ocala, FL) 16 Nov. 1920. See also "Atlantic Storm Warning." *Houston Post* (Houston, TX) 29 Nov. 1920.

14   "Shipping News." *New Orleans Times-Picayune* (New Orleans, LA) 7 Dec. 1920.

15   "Shipping News." *Beaumont Enterprise* (Beaumont, TX) 26 Dec. 1920; "Exports." *New Orleans Times-Picayune* 24 Dec. 1920.

16   Quoted in Dello Stritto. Frank J. and Gary D. Rhodes, "Strange Cargo: Bela Lugosi's Maiden Voyage to America." *Cult Movies* 28 (1999).

17   For a more detailed discussion of Lugosi's passage across the Atlantic, see: Cremer, Robert *Lugosi: The Man Behind the Cape* (Chicago: Henry Regnery, 1976).

18   "Movement of Ships." *Beaumont Enterprise* 5 Dec. 1920.

19   "Expected Arrivals." *New Orleans Times-Picayune* 13 Nov. 1920; "Expected Arrivals." *New Orleans Times-Picayune* 16 Nov. 1920; "Expected Arrivals." *New Orleans Times-Picayune* 29 Nov. 1920.

20   "Scheduled Arrivals." *New Orleans Item* 20 Nov. 1920; "Scheduled Arrivals." *New Orleans Item* 27 Nov. 1920; "Expected Arrivals." *New Orleans Times-Picayune* 1 Dec. 1920.

21   Moreno, Barry (United States Department of the Interior, Ellis Island). Letter to Gary D. Rhodes, 15 Oct. 1994.

22   *List or Manifest of Alien Passengers for the United States Immigration Officer at Port of Arrival* 4 Dec. 1920. U. S. Department of Labor, Immigration Service, New Orleans, Louisiana, 4 Dec. 1920.

23   *Inspector's Interrogation During Primary Alien Inspection.* Immigration Services. Ellis Island, New York. 23 Mar. 1921.

24   Moreno, letter to Rhodes.

25   Ibid.

26   *Inspector's Interrogation During Primary Alien Inspection.*

27   Ergenbright, Eric. "The Man Who Knows Too Much!" *Screen Play* July 1932.

28   Ibid.

Lugosi, the Hungarian stage actor.

Appendix A

Hungarian Stageography

Researched and compiled by Gary D. Rhodes and Bill Kaffenberger

This catalogue of Béla Lugosi's stage work covers the years prior to his arrival in the United States in late 1920. His stage work after 1920 is chronicled in Volume II of this book.

We gratefully acknowledge the work of Robert Cremer, the first Lugosi biographer to catalogue a Hungarian stageography. Much effort on our behalf has been extended by Országos Színháztörténeti Muzéum és Intézet (Hungarian Theater Museum and Institute), Somogyi Károly Városi és Megyei Könyvtár Szeged (Károly Somogyi City and County Library of Szeged), and the Országos Széchényi Könyvtár Színháztörténeti Tár (National Széchényi Library Theater History Collection). This is in addition to our own extensive research in Hungary (with the assistance of Raymond E. Glew and Mirjam Dénes).

Importantly, we have relied whenever possible on primary sources (including but not limited to playbills, critical reviews, and published reports). Some plays and dates contradict previous sources, and some plays listed in prior stageographies are intentionally absent. We have made these decisions based upon the best available evidence. The result is the most accurate and comprehensive stageography of Lugosi's career in Hungary that has ever been compiled.

Research Notes

Dealing with gaps in Lugosi's timeline as well as misinformation are two of the hurdles we had to overcome. For example, Lugosi's memories about his days in Hungarian theater were inconsistent and at times difficult to verify. For example, he claimed to have played the title role in Edmond Rostand's *Cyrano de Bergerac*, but extensive research has not found any such performance. And in a filmed interview with Jack Mangan in 1951, Lugosi specifically mentioned appearing in Ferenc Molnar's *A Testőr* (*The Guardsman*) and *Liliom* in Hungary, even suggesting he performed in the very first performance of *Liliom*. But we have found no evidence that he ever appeared in any performance of *A Testőr*, and the only known version of *Liliom* with Lugosi was staged in America in 1921.

Could Lugosi have misremembered? That is possible, given that he played the lead role in Molnár's *Az ördög* (*The Devil*) on at least a few occasions, including in 1907, only months after the play had premiered in Budapest. And he certainly appeared repeatedly in Lajos Bíró's very popular play *A sárga liliom* (*The Yellow Lily*). Then again, Lugosi's knowledge of Hungarian theater and the works of Molnár must have been quite in-depth. At any rate, it is extremely important to note that this stageography is a work-in-progress. Further research will likely reveal additions, whether or not they include *Cyrano de Bergerac*, *A Testőr*, or *Liliom*.

Primary sources do confirm that Lugosi's popularity as a stage actor in Hungary was greater than some biographers have believed. He achieved major successes prior to spending the 1910-11 season in Szeged (specifically in Debrecen). Moreover, while his roles at the Nemzeti Színház (National Theater) in Budapest were often minor, as long believed, our research clarifies that he did play larger and sometimes leading roles at that venue. He also played leading and major roles at other Budapest theaters, which are catalogued herein.

A key difficulty in researching Béla Lugosi's theatrical career in Hungary has been making certain that we found and included stage credits for Béla Lugosi and not some other similarly named individual. At times, theatrical playbills and newspaper advertisements in Hungary listed a given actor by surname alone. Careful and extensive primary research helped determine if the "Lugosi" being credited was Béla Lugosi, or instead "Daniel Lugossy," "Irene Lugosi' or "Jenő Lugosi," among others. Likewise, it must be noted that there were other persons in Hungary at the time named Béla Blaskó (Lugosi's given name), and that there was another notable "Béla Lugossy," meaning Béla Földes, who used "Lugossy" as a *nom de plume*. With much diligence and patience, we were able to determine which Lugosi/Lugossy/Blaskó/etc. was which.

The Stageography

We present our findings in chronological order, with further divisions based upon the cities and towns where the plays were staged. We include not only legitimate theater productions, but other known performances as well, such as cabaret shows. When possible, we include the name of the theaters where the shows were staged.

English translations of the play titles are given in parentheticals. In the few cases where no parenthetical appears, it is because the play title needs no translation. For example, *Casanova*, *Hamlet*, *Trilby*, and *Loute* have no translations because they are proper nouns, names that require no alteration. By contrast, proper nouns that require alterations – even if just of diacritical marks – are translated, as in the case of *Manfréd* (*Manfred*). The same is true of titles consisting of two-word names that would be rendered or spoken in Hungarian as last name-then-first name, as opposed to English as first name-then-last name. For example, the Hungarian *Berger Zsiga* would be *Zsiga Berger* in English, just as "Lugosi Béla" would be rendered "Béla Lugosi."

In addition, when known, the genre of the productions – for example, "drama," "comedy," "tragedy," "operetta," etc. – has been provided in parentheticals. In some cases, descriptions for entries of the same play vary slightly depending on the English translations of the specific Hungarian words used. For example, *Pillangókisasszony* (*Madame Butterfly*) is described on one playbill as an "opera," while on another it is called a "musical drama."

We would stress that the "opening night" dates we give are for the *particular* productions catalogued; "opening night" does not refer to a play's premiere, meaning the first time it was ever staged anywhere. Also, when possible, notes and/or critical reviews for given productions accompany the entries.

1901
Budapest

In his book *Színészarcképek* (Újvidék: Forum Nyomda, 1971), Béla Garay wrote that Lugosi traveled from Szabadka to Budapest in September and auditioned for the major theater guild under his given name of Béla Blaskó. According to the September 1, 1901 edition of *Budapesti Hírlap*, fifty candidates auditioned on that day.

Kalocsa

Theatrical producer Lajos Pesti-Ihász hired Lugosi on the basis of the Budapest audition. This was apparently the start of Lugosi's professional acting career. The Pesti-Ihász troupe was headquartered in Kalocsa for the summer and in Szabadka for the regular season. Lugosi most likely started rehearsing late in September and appeared in productions by October.

During his brief tenure in Kalocsa, Lugosi reportedly acted in *A sasok* (*The Eagles*), staged in the town of Baja on October 12. The October 14 edition of *Budapesti Hírlap* wrote, "this was the first performance of this magnificent comedy in the countryside ... full of entertainment, with great enjoyment and with great success ... the actors received great applause." The company also staged *Cyrano de Bergerac*, *A bor* (*The Wine*), and others. However, it is difficult to determine which included Lugosi and what roles he played.

Szabadka

A sasok (*The Eagles*) (Comedy)
Opening Night: November 2 at the Népszínház (Civic Theater). Also staged on November 19.
Author: Rákosi and Guthi.
Role: Unknown.
Note: References indicate Lugosi's involvement in this play, credited with his given name, Béla Blaskó. His name does not appear in the few published reviews, suggesting his role was minor. There were at least thirty other productions staged in Szabadka through December of 1901, many of which likely utilized Lugosi in small roles.

1902
Szabadka

According to Béla Garay, Lugosi remained in Szabadka at least for part of the 1902 theater season. Specific plays are not known. However, theatrical reports published in Budapest newspapers of the time noted that the troupe continued to perform in the area. In addition, *Szamos*, a local newspaper, indicated the troupe would be performing in the county of Szatmár near the end of February.

Budapest

On or around March 27, Lugosi (using the name Béla Blaskó) again auditioned before the judges of the Országos Színész-Egyesület tanácsa (Council of the National Actors' Assocation) in Budapest. According to the *Pesti Hírlap* of April 3, he was one of eight candidates that did not pass the "exams."

Újvidék and Pécs

Historian Dejan Mrkić obtained a copy of a photo of Lugosi allegedly taken while he was performing in the town of Újvidék (now Novi Sad in Serbia), dated to approximately the same time he was with the Szabadka company. While there is no known primary evidence to support this, it is possible given that Újvidék is only 67 miles distant from Szabadka. Other sources mention Lugosi performing in the town of Pécs during this time frame, but no primary evidence has been found to confirm it.

The Provinces

After his unsuccessful audition in Budapest, it seems probable that Lugosi remained with the Pesti-Ihász troupe. By May, the troupe was working in the town of Nagykörű, where they staged a number of productions. The troupe then moved to the town of Makó in approximately June.

Szilágy-Somlyó (at the Népszínház (Civic Theater)] and **Tordá** (at the Tordai Nagy Városháza (Tordá Great Town Hall)]

Sometime late May or June, Lugosi completed his contract with Pesti-Ihász. He then signed with the Nándor Benedek troupe. Benedek was working out of Szilágy-Somlyó (now Şimleu Silvaniei in Romania), presenting plays at the Népszínház (Civic Theater) for a period of six weeks, starting from approximately the second week of May and into late June. It is possible that Lugosi could have appeared in *Ocskay brigadéros* (*Brigadier General Ocskay*) and *Shulamith* (*The Shulamite*) there.

Benedek also staged productions in Tordá at the Tordai Nagy Városháza (Tordá Great Town Hall) from around late June through early August. Lugosi likely appeared in *Nebáncsvirág* (*Touch-Me-Not*) and *Egy görbe nap* (*A Wild Day*) in that town. After Tordá, the troupe moved on to Hátszeg.

Hátszeg (at the Arany-Bárány Restaurant)
Arany Kakas (*The Golden Rooster*) (Farce)
Opening Night: August 7.
Author: Blumenthal and Kadelburg.
Role: Feri, a Waiter
Note: Credited as Géza Lugosi. Sometimes the spelling of this play was rendered *Aranykakas*.

A nagyzás hobortja (*The Delusion of Grandeur*) (Comedy)
Opening Night: August 8.

Author: Gyula Rosen.
Role: Heinrich, a Son and Financial Buyer
Note: Credited as Béla Lugosi.

Egy görbe nap (***A Wild Day***) (Musical Farce)
Opening Night: August 10.
Author: Bors Csicseri.
Role: Nándor Krasznahubay, a Son.
Note: Credited as Géza Lugosi.

Ocskay brigadéros (***Brigadier General Ocskay***) (Historical Drama)
Opening Night: August 24.
Author: Ferenc Herczeg.
Role: Count Königsegg
Note: Credited as Béla Blaskó.

Házasodjunk (***Were Married***) (Musical Farce)
Opening Night: August 25.
Author: Soma Guthi.
Role: Pokykai
Note: Credited as Béla Lugosi.

Note: Nándor Benedek advertised additional plays for August, but playbills for them have not surfaced. Some of these productions likely utilized Lugosi.

Szamosújvár

The troupe arrived in this town at least by the first of September and may have staged plays there prior to September 4.

A nagyzás hobortjai (***The Delusion of Grandeur***) (Comedy)
Opening Night: September 4.
Author: Gyula Rosen.
Role: Lauter, a Major
Note: Credited as Lugosi.

Kurucz féja Dávid (***Stubborn King David***) (Historical Drama)
Opening Night: September 6.
Author: Samu Fényes.
Roles: Notarius and A Deméndi Gelhó (A Fool from Deméndi)
Note: The same advertisement spelled Lugosi's name two different ways, Lugosi and Lugosy.

A bor (*The Wine*) (Historical Drama)
Opening Night: September 7.
Author: Géza Gárdonyi
Role: Kisbiró. A small supporting role.
Note: Credited as Lugosi

Nebáncsvirág (*Touch-Me-Not*) (Operetta)
Opening Night: September 8.
Author: Mailhac and Milhaud.
Role: Gusztáv
Note: Credited as Lugosi.

Shulamith (*The Shulamite*) (Operetta)
Opening Night: September 16.
Author: Abraham Goldfaden.
Role: Ik Tőpap
Note: Credited as Géza Lugosi.

Felhő Klári (*Claire Felho*) (Folk Play)
Opening Night: September 18 at the Korona Színház (Korona Theater).
Author: László Rátkay.
Role: Vendel Csik, a Tailor.
Note: A "folk play" was a specific type of Hungarian production that focused primarily on rural village life and activities.

Benedek's company advertised additional titles for September, but playbills for them have not yet surfaced. Titles included *Házasodjunk* (*We're Married*), with Lugosi perhaps reprising a role he had played earlier in the season. Lugosi likely appeared in most if not all of the September productions.

Transylvania

Lugosi's next contract was with the György Micsey troupe, but it is unclear exactly when he left Benedek. The typical time to change would have been late September or early October, but there are no primary sources available that provide a specific date. In any event, the Micsey troupe operated in the town of Dés for at least part of October before moving on. By December, the troupe was operating primarily out of Nagybánya but traveling throught the entire "Transylvania District," including such towns as Székesfehérvár. Although Lugosi was not listed among the troupe's members in early December, lesser-known players were often not mentioned in newspaper articles. By late December, the troupe was resident in Nagybánya, presenting a number of plays, including *Lotty ezredesei* (*Lotty's Colonels*), *A Peleskei nótárius* (*The Notary from Peleske*) and *A régi szerető* (*The Old Lover*), all of which Lugosi regularly appeared in for Micsey during 1903.

1903

Nagybánya (with the Nemzeti Színeszet [National Actors' Company] under the direction of manager György Micsey)

Micsey's troupe remained in Nagybánya for at least part of January, presenting a variety of plays. On January 1, they staged *Egy görbe nap* (*A Wild Day*) and on January 3, *Loute*, both of which likely included Lugosi. The troupe remained in this town for fourteen days before moving on to Petrozsény and Vajdahunyad, where they performed for approximately one week each. Then they traveled to Déva (now Deva in Romania), opening there with **Casanova** on February 1.

Déva (at the Vigadó Concert Hall)
Kurucz féja Dávid (*Stubborn King David*) (Historical Drama)
Opening Night: February 10.
Author: Samu Fényes.
Role: Antonio Caraffa.

Micsey's troupe had additional plays scheduled for mid-February, but playbills for them have not surfaced. It is likely Lugosi appeared in some if not all of these productions. Additionally, Sándor Enyedi, in his book *A Tragédia a színpadon* (Budapest: Madach Irodlami Társaság, 2008), claims the troupe staged *Az ember tragédiája* (*The Tragedy of Man*) on February 13. It may have been Lugosi's first appearance in that play.

Stuart Máriá (*Mary Stuart*) (Historical Tragedy)
Opening Night: February 26.
Author: Friedrich Schiller
Role: Aubespine. A small supporting role.

Ezeregy éjszaka (*Arabian Nights*) (Comic Operetta)
Opening Night: March 1.
Author: Mátyás Feld
Role: Orias.

A denevér (*The Bat*) (Operetta)
Opening Night: March 3.
Author: Meilhac and Helévy.
Role: Frosch, a Jailer. A small supporting role.
Note: Translated from *Die Fledermaus* by Johann Strauss.

Monna Vanna (Drama)
Opening Night: March 4.
Author: Maurice Maeterlinck.
Role: Marco Colonna. A major supporting role.

Fédora (*Fedora*) (Drama)
Opening Night: March 5.
Author: Victorien Sardou.
Role: Dr. Loreck. A small supporting role.

   Additional plays were staged March 6 through March 11, but the titles and Lugosi's roles are unknown.

Vajdahunyad (at the Vasgyári Terem Hunedoara [Hunedoara Hall in the Iron Factory])
A boszorkányvár (*The Castle of Witches*) (Operetta)
Opening Night: March 12.
Author: Alois Berla. Music by Carl Millöcker.
Role: Kakasdi.
Note: This venue indicates that theaters or concert halls were not always available. In this case, the troupe staged plays in a local iron factory.

Nagyszeben (at the Városi Színház [Municipal Theater]).
   Local advertisements in this city (now Sibiu in Romania) stated that Lugosi's main character would be that of the "conversational *bon vivant*." He was consistently billed as "Béla Lugosi" in this town.

Katalin vagy: a czárnő kegyencze (*Catherine: or The Favorite of the Czarina*) (Operetta)
Opening Night: March 14.
Author: Izor Béldi. Music by Jenő Fehér.
Role: Buranoff.

Tündérszép Ilona és a vasorrú boszorkány (*Helena, the Fairy, and the Witch*)
Opening Night: March 15.
Author: Mátyás Feld
Role: Minister Cockatoo.
Note: Staged at 3:30 p.m.

On a double bill with:

Kurucz féja Dávid (*Stubborn King David*) (Historical Drama)
Opening Night: March 15.

Author: Samu Fényes.
Role: Antonio Caraffa, a Generalissimo.

*A doktor úr (**Mr. Doctor**)* (Musical Comedy)
Opening Night: March 16.
Author: Ferenc Molnár.
Role: Policeman.

*Lotty ezredesei (**Lotty's Colonels**)* (Operetta)
Opening Night: March 17.
Author: Rudyard Stone.
Role: Head Waiter.

*Kéz kezet most (**One Hand Washes the Other**)* (Comedy)
Opening Night: March 18.
Author: Ferenc Herczeg.
Role: Baron Éberle. A major supporting role.

*Orpheus a pokolban (**Orpheus in the Underworld**)* (Operetta)
Opening Night: March 19.
Author: Meilhac and Halévi. Music by Jacques Offenbach.
Role: Mercury.

*Az ember tragédiája (**The Tragedy of Man**)* (Poetic Drama)
Opening Night: March 20. Also staged on March 23.
Author: Imre Madách.
Roles: Scene 5, Athens: Second Member of the People; Scene 7, [One of the] Crusaders: First
Citizen; Scene 9, Paris in 1793: A Marquis.
Note: Lugosi played the same roles on both dates.

*Az asszonyreiment (**The Regiment of Women**)* (Operetta)
Opening Night: March 21.
Author: Ferenc Rajna. Music by Vilmos Rosenzweig.
Role: Buzó.

*Ezeregy éjszaka (**A Thousand and One Nights**)* (Folk Tale)
Opening Night: March 22.
Author: Mátyás Feld.
Role: A Giant.
Note: Staged at 3:30 p.m.

On a double bill with:

A régi szerető (The Old Lover) (Operetta)
Opening Night: March 22.
Author: István Géczy. Music by Iván Hűvös.
Role: Peti, a Farmer.

Egy görbe nap (A Wild Day) (Musical Farce)
Opening Night: March 25.
Author: Adolf Ágai and Tihamér Almási.
Role: Loránd Dicsőffi.

A Peleskei nótárius (The Notary from Peleske) (Musical Farce)
Opening Night: March 25.
Author: Józef Gaál.
Roles: Second German Iron Merchant and the Judge from Tiszafüred.
Note: Staged at 3:30 p.m.

A boszorkányvár (The Castle of Witches) (Operetta)
Opening Night: March 26.
Author: Alois Berla. Music by Carl Millöcker.
Role: Kakasdi.

Monna Vanna (Drama)
Opening Night: March 27.
Author: Maurice Maeterlinck.
Role: Torello, the Lieutenant of Guido.

Casanova (Operetta)
Opening Night: March 28. Also staged on April 2.
Author: Script by Jenő Faragó. Music by Izsó Barna.
Role: A Police Officer.
Note: Lugosi played the same role on both dates.

Hófehérke és 7 törpe (Snow White and the Seven Dwarfs) (Folk Tale)
Opening Night: March 29.
Author: K.A. Görner.
Role: Vervex, a Courtier.
Note: Staged at 3:30 p.m.

On a double bill with:

*A svihákok (**The Cheaters**)* (Comedy)
Opening Night: March 29
Author: Carl Michael Ziehrer.
Role: Krepelka, a Music Conductor.

*Az őrnagy úr (**The Major**)* (Comedy with Songs)
Opening Night: March 30.
Author: Mars and Keroul.
Role: Old Man Filerin.

*Fifin (**Fifi**)* (Operetta)
Opening Night: March 31.
Author and Music: Aurél Schwimmer.
Role: Mr. Hopkins.

*Uriel Acosta (**Uriel da Costa**)*
Opening Night: April 1.
Author: Karl Gutzkow.
Role: Scenes 2 and 3: Ruben, the Son of Acosta

*A postáfiú (**The Messenger Boy**)* (Operetta)
Opening Night: April 3.
Author: Jannes T. Tanner and Alfred Murray. Music by Iván Caryll and Lionel Honkton.
Role: Gascogne, a Journalist.

*Adám és Éva (**Adam and Eve**)*
Opening Night: April 4.
Author: Blume and Toché.
Role: Benoit, a Restaurant Owner.

Székelyudvarhely (at the Uj Színterem [New Theatrical Hall])

The advertisement for the Micsey troupe promised that 24 productions would be staged in this town. However, only twelve playbills feature Lugosi in the cast. Lugosi had previously performed in other titles on the list, but without further evidence, the additional roles cannot be confirmed. Lugosi's billing varied between "Lugossi" and "Lugossy" in this town.

Bacsányi
Opening Night: April 12.
Author: Samu Fényes.
Role: Morin, a French spy.

Note: Billed as Béla Lugossy. The title of the play likely refers to the family name of the protagonist.

Tündérszép Ilona és a vasorrú boszorkány (***Helena, the Fairy, and the Witch***)
Opening Night: April 13.
Author: Mátyás Feld
Role: Minister Cockatoo.
Note: Billed as Béla Lugossy. Afternoon performance at 3:30 p.m.

On a double bill with:

A leszámolás, vagy az elhantolt gyűlölet (***Showdown, or The Buried Hatred***) (Peasant Play)
Opening Night: April 13.
Author: Written by István Géczy. Music by János Hoós.
Role: A Scrivener.
Note: Billed as Béla Lugossi.

A doktor úr (***Mr. Doctor***) (Musical Comedy)
Opening Night: April 14.
Author: Ferenc Molnár.
Role: Policeman Number One.
Note: Billed as Béla Lugossi.

Lotty ezredesei (***Lotty's Colonels***) (Operetta)
Opening Night: April 15.
Author: Rudyard Stone.
Role: Mr. Norvay.
Note: Billed as Béla Lugossy. This play was also known as *Lotti ezredesei.*

Kéz kezet most (***One Hand Washes the Other***) (Comedy)
Opening Night: April 16.
Author: Ferenc Herceg.
Role: Baron Éberle. A major supporting role.
Note: Billed as Béla Lugossy.

A Notre Damei templom harangozója és Eszmeralda, a szép cigányleány (***The Bellringer of Notre Dame and Esmerelda, the Fair Gypsy Girl***) (Drama)
Opening Night: April 17.
Author: Victor Hugo.
Role: Le Rouge, a Beggar.
Note: Billed as Béla Lugossi.

Casanova (Operetta)
Opening Night: April 18.
Author: Jenő Faragó. Music by Izsó Barna.
Role: A Major-Domo.
Note: Billed as Béla Lugossy.

Ezeregy éjszaka (*A Thousand and One Nights*) (Folk Tale)
Opening Night: April 19.
Author: Mátyás Feld.
Role: A Giant.
Note: Billed as Béla Lugossy. Staged at 3:30 p.m.

On a double bill with:

Aranylakodalom (*Golden Wedding*) (Tragedy)
Opening Night: April 19.
Author: László Beöthy and Viktor Rákosi.
Roles: Scene 1, Nyárádi, a Lawyer; Scene 2, a Jurist; Scene 4, a Lieutenant; and scene 6, Nyárádi, a Lawyer.
Note: Billed as both Béla Lugossi and Béla Lugossy on the very same playbill, depending on the character and scene.

Loute
Opening Night: April 20.
Author: Pierre Weber.
Role: Bézu, the Janitor.
Note: Billed as Béla Lugossi.

Monna Vanna (Drama)
Opening Night: April 30.
Author: Maurice Maeterlinck.
Role: Torello, the Lieutenant of Guido.
Note: Billed as Béla Lugosi.

Micsey's circuit also included the towns of Kovászna, Gyulafehérvár, Szombathely, Székesfehérvár, and Veszprém. The troupe had moved on to other provincial towns by the beginning of May, with Sepsiszentgyörgy reportedly being one of them.

Szatmár
Kéz kezet mos (*One Hand Washes the Other*) (Comedy)

Opening Night: May 4 in Szatmár by the Micsey troupe as special guests of the Béla Heves Company.

Author: Ferenc Herczeg.

Role: Baron Éberle. A major supporting role.

Note: Lugosi and the character he played were mentioned in a local review, but there was no critique of his performance.

Bacsányi

Opening Night: May 5.

Author: Samu Fényes.

Role: Although not mentioned in the local newspaper review, it is likely that Lugosi repeated the role of Morin, a French spy.

Adám és Éva (Adam and Eve)

Opening Night: May 7.

Author: Blume and Toché.

Role: Although not mentioned in the local newspaper review, it is likely that Lugosi repeated the role of Benoit, a Restaurant Owner.

A doktor úr (Mr. Doctor) (Musical Comedy)

Opening Night: May 8.

Author: Ferenc Molnár.

Role: Although not mentioned in the local newspaper review, it is likely that Lugosi repeated the role of Policeman Number One.

Fifin (Fifi) (Operetta)

Opening Night: May 9.

Author and Music: Aurél Schwimmer.

Role: Although not mentioned in the local newspaper review, it is likely that Lugosi repeated the role of Mr. Hopkins.

Keszthely and Zalaegerszeg

The troupe staged a variety of productions from May to July. Although cast listings have not yet been found, Lugosi likely reprised roles in the following plays: in Keszthely, *A régi szerető (The Old Lover)* on May 10; in Zalaegerszeg, *Casanova* on May 18, *A doktor úr (Mr. Doctor)* on May 19, *Bacsányi* on May 21, *Fifin (Fifi)* on May 23, *Kéz kezet mos (One Hand Washes the Other)* on May 25, *Az ember tragédiája (The Tragedy of Man)* on May 27, *Adám és Éva (Adam and Eve)* on May 30, *A régi szerető* reprised on May 31, *Loute* on June 2, *Fifin* on June 9 an *Monna Vanna* on June 12; and then returning to Keszthely, *Az ember tragédiája* on June 18, *Az őrnagy úr (The Major)*, *A Notre Damei templom harangozója és Eszmeralda, a szép cigányleány (The Bellringer of Notre Dame and Esmerelda, the Fair Gypsy Girl)*, and *Katalin vagy: a czárnő kegyencze* (**Catherine: or The Favorite of the Czarina**) on various dates. Lugosi likely appeared in additional titles during the busy schedule.

Siófok

By mid-July, the troupe was in the city of Siófok, remaining there until early August. Lugosi likely reprised his role in *A svihákok (The Cheaters)* and probably appeared in additional productions.

Székesfehérvár

The troupe performed in this town in early September. No information is currently available regarding the plays that were staged.

Veszprém (at the Korona-szálló nagyterme [Great Hall of the Korona Hotel])
Casanova (Operetta)
Opening Night: September 9.
Author: Script by Jenő Faragó. Music by Izsó Barna.
Role: Scene 3, Chief Marshal of the Court.
Note: This was Lugosi's final performance for the Micsey troupe. The very next day, he appeared in his first production for Ignácz Krecsányi's troupe in Temesvár.

Temesvár (at the Ferencz Jozsef Városi Színház [Franz Joseph Municipal Theater], under the direction of Ignácz Krecsányi, unless otherwise noted)

Az Amerikai Magyar Színjátszás, a doctoral thesis by Melinda Mendel (Marosvásárhely: Universitatea De Arte Din Marosvásárhely, 2011) and "Lugosi Béla," an article published on the website *Magyar Vagyok* (*I'm Hungarian*), claim that Lugosi attended drama school in Temesvár during the day, financing the classes from his earnings as an actor. While this is an intriguing possibility, there are no known primary sources that validate this claim.

A brief article in Szeged's *Színházi Újság* on 30 Oct. 1910, likely resulting from an interview with Lugosi, indicated that his first major role in Temesvár was as Gida Tarján in *A Dolovai nábob léanya* (**The Daughter of the Nabob of Dolova**). That production thus would have occurred around this time. There is, however, no independent confirmation of it from 1903 sources.

During his time in Temesvár, Lugosi was credited as "Lugossy" in all plays except those with notations herein that indicate otherwise.

A titok (**The Secret**) (Comedy)
Opening Night: September 10.
Author: Pierre Wolff.
Role: Segédszerelmes.

Note: The October 4 edition of *Budapesti Hírlap* indicates that *A titok* was staged for the regular season on October 8, which would mean an additional performance. However, there is no playbill or review currently available to confirm that the October 8 performance actually occurred.

Shulamith (*The Shulamite*) (Operetta)
Opening Night: October 2 at the Budai Nyári Színházban (Budapest Summer Theater) directed by Ignacz Krecsányi in Budapest.
Author: Abraham Goldfaden.
Role: Unknown.
Note: The October 1 edition of *Budapesti Hírlap* lists Lugosi as a member of the cast for the October 2 performance although his role is not specified. For reasons unknown, Krecsányi sent Lugosi to Budapest to fill in for the final week at the Budapest Summer Theater. Between October 1 and 7, it is likely that Lugosi had roles in some other plays at this theater, among them *Bob herceg*.

Bob herceg (*Prince Bob*) (Operetta)
Opening Night: October 11. Also staged on October 12 and November 17.
Author: Jenő Huszka.
Role: Tom, an Older Brother.

Annuska (Comedy)
Opening Night: October 14. Also staged on October 15.
Author: Géza Gárdonyi.
Role: Imre Vas. A major supporting role.

A Gerolsteini nagyhercegnő (*The Grand Duchess of Gerolstein*) (Operetta)
Opening Night: October 17. Also staged on October 18 and November 15.
Author: Meilhac and Halévy.
Role: Baron Grog. Small supporting role.

Pillangókisasszony (*Madame Butterfly*) (Drama)
Opening Night: October 22. Also staged on November 4 and December 10.
Author: David Belasco.
Role: Pinkerton. A major lead role.
Note: The opera version of this production by Puccini did not debut in its final form until May 28, 1904.

A ket foscari (*The Two Foscari*) (Opera)
Opening Night: October 24. Also staged on October 31.
Author: Piave and Verdi.
Role: Barbarigo (sung as a tenor). A supporting role.

Klo-Klo (Operetta)
Opening Night: October 25. Also staged on October 26 and November 8.
Author: Landesberg and Stein.
Role: Police Officer.
Notes: Credited as "Lugossi."

On a double bill with:

A sárga csikó (The Yellow Colt) (Folk Play)
Opening Night: October 25.
Author: Ferenc Csepreghy.
Role: Gazsi. A supporting role.

II Rákóczi Ferencz fogsága (Francis Rákoczi II in Captivity) (Historical Drama)
Opening Night: October 28.
Author: Ede Szigligeti.
Role: Longueval, a Captain. A major supporting role.

A regények (The Romancers) (Comedy)
Opening Night: October 29. Also staged on October 30.
Author: Edmond Rostand.
Role: Second Man. A minor role, essentially a bit part.

Az ember tragédiája (The Tragedy of Man) (Poetic Drama)
Opening Night: November 1. Also staged on November 2.
Author: Imre Madách.
Roles: Second Demagogue and Saint Just. Both were minor roles (6 lines and 3 lines, respectively).

Az egyetlen leány (The One Girl) (Comedy)
Opening Night: November 4. Also staged on December 10.
Author: Sándor Fredro.
Role: Agost Darzinszky.

Annuska (Comedy)
Opening Night: November 7 at the Szegedi Városi Színház (Szeged Repertory Theater). Also staged on November 8.
Author: Géza Gárdonyi.
Role: Imre Vas. A major supporting role.
Note: For reasons that remain unclear, Ignácz Krecsányi sent Lugosi to Szeged as a guest actor to play the role Imre Vas in Szeged. This was a swap with Szeged actor István Rédey, who

performed on the same dates in Temesvár. There is no evidence available that suggests that this was anything more than a one-time event. Lugosi apparently did not return to Szeged until 1910 when he appeared there in *Rómeó és Júlia* (*Romeo and Juliet*).

Reviews: "There was a guest appearance on stage… Béla Lugosi, an actor from Temesvár, played the role of Imre Vas. He is a young actor, whose talent shines through." (*Szeged és Vidéke* 7 Nov. 1903). "All the others… [as well as] the guest actor Lugosi are great." (*Szeged és Vidéke* 8 Nov. 1903).

Bánk Bán (*Bán Bánk*) (Drama)
Opening Night: November 10.
Author: József Katona.
Role: Ottó Berthold. This was a major supporting role.

A reservisták (*The Reservists*)
Opening Night: November 15. Also staged on November 22.
Author: Durn and Chirot.
Role: A Wayfaring Man.

Katalin (*Catherine*)
Opening Night: November 18.
Author: Izor Béldy.
Role: Ivan Buranoff.

San-Toy (Operetta)
Opening Night: November 21. Also staged on November 22 and December 6 and 25.
Author: Morton and Grenbank.
Role: Yen How, a Mandarin.
Note: Lugosi's character sang two songs, *Six Little Wives* and *I Mean to Introduce It Into China*. This would indicate at least a major supporting role.

A drótostót (*The Tinker*) (Operetta)
Opening Night: November 25. Also staged on December 2 and 7.
Author: Franz Lehár.
Role: Girált.

A becsület (*The Honor*) (Drama)
Opening Night: November 27.
Author: József Hevesi.
Role: Kurt.

New-York szépe (*The Belle of New York*) (Musical Comedy)

Opening Night: November 28. Also staged on November 29 and December 27.
Author: Hugh Morton.
Role: Mr. Peeper, a Photographer.

Hófehérke és 7 törpe (***Snow White and the Seven Dwarfs***) (Fairy Tale)
Opening Night: November 29.
Author: K. A. Görner.
Role: Aranyország.

Az édes lányka (***The Sweet Maiden***) (Operetta)
Opening Night: November 30.
Author: Alexander Landesberg and Leo Stein.
Role: Max.
Note: Translated from the German operetta *Das süßes Mädel*.

Nagyzás hóbortja (***The Whim of Grandeur***) (Comedy)
Opening Night: December 1.
Author: Gyula Rosen.
Role: Henrik.

Hannele (***Hannah***) (Drama)
Opening Night: December 3. Also staged on December 4.
Author: Gerhardt and Hauptmann.
Role: Hanke. A small supporting role.

Felhő Klári (***Claire Felho***) (Folk Play)
Opening Night: December 6.
Author: László Rátkay.
Role: Pista Szita.

A svihákok (*The Cheaters)* (Comedy)
Opening Night: December 8. Also staged on December 9.
Author: Carl Michael Ziehrer.
Role: Pelikán. A small supporting role.

La Traviata (***The Fallen Woman***) (Opera)
Opening Night: December 14.
Author: Giuseppe Verdi.
Role: Baron Douphol (a baritone role). A small supporting role.

A Tót leány (***The Slovak Girl***) (Folk Play)
Opening Night: December 20.
Author: Tihamér Almássy.
Role: Csöbör.

A sasok (***The Eagles***) (Comedy)
Opening Night: December 22.
Author: Rákosi and Guthi.
Role: Viktor Sas.

A szökött katona (***The Runaway Soldier***) (Folk Play)
Opening Night: December 25.
Author: Ede Szigligeti.
Role: Valley Auxiliary Officer.

Árgyílus és Tünder Ilona (***Argyil and Ilona the Fairy***) (Folk Play with Songs and Dancing)
Opening Night: December 26.
Author: Ede Szigligeti.
Role: Bajan.

Ejjeli menedékhely (***The Lower Depths***) (Drama)
Opening Night: December 11. Also staged on December 12, 13 and 27.
Author: Maxim Gorky.
Role: Bubnov. A major supporting role.

Trilby (Drama)
Opening Night: December 28. Also staged December 29.
Author: George du Maurier.
Role: Gecko. A major supporting role.
Review: "Béla Lugosi as Svengali's evil henchman was absolutely spellbinding." (*Temesvári Színpad* 29 Dec. 1903).

1904

Temesvár (at the Ferencz Jozsef Városi Színház [Franz Joseph Municipal Theater] under the direction of Ignácz Krecsányi)

A svihákok (***The Cheaters***) (Comedy)
Opening Night: January 1.
Author: Carl Michael Ziehrer.
Role: Pelikán. A small supporting role.

On a double bill with:

*Aranylakodalom (**Golden Wedding**)* (Tragedy)
Opening Night: January 1. Also staged on January 2.
Author: Beöthy and Rákosi.
Role: Bodó.

*Bob herceg (**Prince Bob**)* (Operetta)
Opening Night: January 4. Also staged on January 24, February 21, and March 27.
Author: Jenő Huszka.
Role: Tom, an Older Brother.

*A drótostót (**The Tinker**)* (Operetta)
Opening Night: January 5. Also staged on January 25.
Author: Viktor Léon.
Role: Girált.

*A vigécek (**The Travelling Merchants**)*
Opening Night: January 6. Also staged on January 10.
Author: Albert Kövessy.
Role: Jenő Pásztói.
Note: A literal translation of the title can also be *The Outspoken Men*. The title is apparently a play on words.

*Ejjeli menedékhely (**The Lower Depths**)* (Drama)
Opening Night: January 7. Also staged on February 3 and March 3.
Author: Maxim Gorky.
Role: Bubnov. A major supporting role.

*Tartalékos férj (**Husband in Reserve**)* (Comedy)
Opening Night: January 8. Also staged on January 21.
Author: Rákosi and Guthi.
Role: Oszkár.

Lugosi was scheduled to appear in *Hymfy dalai (**The Songs of Hymfy**)* on January 10 and 11, but for reasons unknown he was replaced by György Fehér.

*Az aranykakas (**The Golden Rooster**)* (Farce)
Opening Night: January 14. Also staged on January 31.
Author: Blumenthal and Kadelburg.
Role: Boros, an Assessor.

A kereszt jelében (**The Sign of the Cross**) (Drama)
Opening Night: January 15.
Author: Wilson Barrett (Translated by Gyula Komor).
Role: Melos, a Messenger.

Az édes lányka (**The Sweet Maiden**) (Operetta)
Opening Night: January 25.
Author: Alexander Landesberg and Leo Stein.
Role: Max.
Note: Translated from the German operetta *Das süßes Mädel*.

Nebáncsvirág (**Touch-Me-Not**) (Operetta)
Opening Night: January 27. Also staged on February 1, 16, 23, 24, and March 2 and 29.
Author: Mailhac and Milhaud.
Roles: Director (March 29) and Moumoute (all other dates).

Folt, amely tisztít (**The Stain That Cleanses**) (Drama)
Opening Night: January 28.
Author: J. A. Echegary.
Role: Julio.

A svihákok (**The Cheaters**) (Operetta)
Opening Night: January 30.
Author: Carl Michael Ziehrer.
Role: Unknown.
Note: Lugosi likely appeared in this play in the role of Pelikán.

Lumpáciusz Vagabundusz, vagy: a három jómadár (**Lumpacious Vagabondus, or: The Jumping Thief**) (Farce)
Opening Night: February 2.
Author: Johann Nestroy
Role: Vidor.

Bibor és Gyász (**Bibor and Gyász**) (Drama)
Opening Night: February 5.
Author: Lajos Hegedüs.
Role: Kaldor.

Otthon (Drama)
Opening Night: February 9.

Author: Hermann Sudermann.
Role: Miksa Wendlovszky.

Egyenlőség (The Admirable Crichton) (Comedy)
Opening Night: February 11. Also staged on Feruary 12, 13, 14, 19, 26, 29, and March 13.
Author: J.M. Barrie.
Role: Lord Brockelhurst. A major supporting role.

Rang és mod (Rank and Style) (Drama)
Opening Night: February 17.
Author: Ede Szigligeti.
Role: Baron Oszkar Eltey. According to Robert Cremer's book *Lugosi: The Man Behind the Cape* (Chicago: Henry Regnery, 1976), which quoted a local Temesvár newspaper, this was a supporting role.
Review: Lugosi was acknowledged as "titillating women with a strong undercurrent of passion seldom experienced on the Temesvár stage." (*Temesvári Színpad* 17 Feb. 1904).

Párisi élet (Parisian Life) (Musical)
Opening Night: February 18. Also staged on February 27.
Author: Meilhac and Halévy.
Role: A Railroad Worker. A small supporting role.

Forgószél kisasszony (The Forgotten Miss) (Musical Farce)
Opening Night: February 20. Also staged on February 21 and 28.
Author: Kratz and Strobitzer.
Role: Police Officer.

Tannhauser (Opera)
Opening Night: March 4. Also staged on March 7, 9, 14, 18, 24 and 28.
Author: Richard Wagner.
Role: Reinmar von Zweta. A small supporting role.

A nagymama (Grandmother) (Operetta)
Opening Night: March 8.
Author: Gergely Csiky.
Role: Kalman. A major supporting role.

Otthon (Drama)
Opening Night: March 9.
Author: Hermann Sudermann.
Role: Miksa Wendlovszky.

***Fédora* (*Fedora*)** (Drama)
Opening Night: March 10.
Author: Victorien Sardou.
Role: Rouvel. Small supporting role.

***A sasok* (*The Eagles*)** (Comedy)
Opening Night: March 11.
Author: Guthi and Rákosi.
Role: Viktor Sas.

***Az egytlen* (*The One Girl*)** (Comedy)
Opening Night: March 17.
Author: Sándor Fredro.
Role: August Davzinszky.

On a double bill with:

***Pillangókisasszony* (*Madame Butterfly*)** (Drama)
Opening Night: March 17.
Author: David Belasco.
Role: Pinkerton. A major leading role.

***Stern Izsák a házaló Zsidó, vagy: egy a mi népünkből*
(*Isaac Stern, The Homeland Jew, is One of Us*)** (Musical Farce)
Opening Night: March 20.
Author: O. F. Berg.
Role: Feri Kertész.

***Pillangókisasszony* (*Madame Butterfly*)** (Musical Drama)
Opening Night: March 27.
Author: Puccini.
Role: Pinkerton.

On a double bill with

***Az egyetlen leány* (*The One Girl*)** (Comedy)
Author: Sándor Fredro.
Role: Agost Darzinszky.

***Csókon szerzett võlogény* (*The Groom Bargained with a Kiss*)**

Opening Night: March 30
Author: József Szigeti
Role: Baranyay Kálmán

A Dolovai nábob leánya (*The Daughter of the Nabob of Dolova*) (Drama)
Opening Night: March 31.
Author: Ferenc Herczeg.
Role: Loránt, a Lieutenant. A supporting role.

A vasgyáros (*The Forge Master*) (Drama)
Opening Night: April 6.
Author: Georges Ohnet.
Role: Dr. Servan. A minor supporting role, no lines.
Note: Translated from the French play *Le Maître des forges*.

A bajusz (*The Mustache*) (Musical Comedy)
Opening Night: April 10.
Author and Music: György Verő.
Role: A Financier.

A kis szökevény (*The Little Fugitive*) (Operetta)
Opening Night: May 1 at the Fovárosi Nyári Színház (City Park Summer Theater) in Budapest.
Also staged on May 2.
Author: Seymour Hicks and Harry Nichols.
Role: Robert Barclay.

A review of surviving playbills for Temesvár for the balance of 1904 and the entire year of 1905 at the National Széchényi Library Theater History Collection uncovered no evidence that Lugosi remained in that city beyond April of 1904.

However, Lugosi definitely accompanied Krecsányi's troupe to an annual summer theater in Budapest. Lugosi appeared in two performances of the operetta *A kis szökevény* (*The Little Fugitive*), but thereafter was no longer listed as part of Krecsányi's roster or in cast lists. By the time the production had a repeat performance ten days later, on May 12, Lugosi had been replaced with an actor named Virányi.

1904-1905 Season
Budapest

The Budapest City Directory for May 1904 through April 1905 confirms that Béla Lugosi, occupation listed as "színész" (actor), was a resident at Kender Street No. 8 in Budapest's District VIII for at least part of that 12-month period. In a story published in the Szeged theatrical journal *Színházi Újság*, Lugosi himself mentioned that he first worked in Budapest just after his time in Temesvár.

It is evident that Lugosi did not work for Károly Polgár during this period, despite indications to the contrary from several historians. A review of the playbills for the 1904-1905 and 1905-1906 seasons for Nagybecskerek (now Zrenjanin in Serbia) – one of Károly Polgár's major towns – revealed absolutely no stage credits attributed to Lugosi. One possibility is Lugosi could have spent the season attending one of the five acting schools in Budapest and might have played minor and bit roles at local theaters.

1905-1906 Season

Lugosi is not listed in the Budapest City Directory for 1905-1906. While that does not prove that he had moved on, it suggests that he did, at least at some point during that 12-month period. So where was he during this season? He may have taken a non-theatrical job for a period of time. However, it seems more likely that Lugosi contracted with one of the at least 31 countryside troupes then operating in Hungary. To narrow down which of these he might have worked for is problematic due to the lack of surviving playbills and advertisements.

Békés

Lugosi eventually moved on to the Béla Polgár Troupe, likely sometime between August and October, at the beginning of the 1906-1907 season. The Béla Polgár Troupe was working in Békés at that time, presenting a number of plays, some of them known to Lugosi from prior seasons. The troupe probably moved on to other cities in Polgár's particular circuit during the final months of 1906.

1907
The Béla Polgár Theater Troupe

The January 17 edition of the *Pesti Hírlap* reported that Polgár's troupe was in Óbecsé (now Bečej in Serbia), where it staged some plays. Then, on February 13, the newspaper indicated that the troupe had moved on to Hajdúböszörmény. Additional towns in Polgár's circuit included Csongrád, Arad, Csanád, Bihar, Hajdú, Érmihályfalva (now Valea lui Mihai in Romania), Szatmár, Munkács (now Mukachevo in the Ukraine), and Sátoraljaújhely. Lugosi would have appeared in plays in these towns. The April 7 edition of *Iparosok Lapja* reported that Polgár put together a 36-person theater company, and specifically named Lugosi as one of its members. *Érmihálvfalván*, named after the Hungarian town in which it was headquartered at the time, announced that productions would be staged over the ensuing 6 to 7 months in the "rural lowlands districts." Included were many popular titles, along with "various novelties."

Nagykároly
Gül Baba (Operetta)
Opening Night: April 6. Also staged on April 8.
Author: Jenő Huszka and Ferenc Martos.
Role: Unknown but likely Spahi, a Pasha.
Note: The setting was in 1608 in the garden of Gül Baba, located in Old Buda.

Helyre asszony (*A Fair Woman*) (Musical Drama)
Opening Night: April 7.
Author: Elek Kada.
Role: Unknown but likely Ali, a Budai Pasha, the leading role.
Note: The title of this play can also be translated as *A Pretty Woman*, *A Witty Woman,* or *A Hardworking Woman*.

János vitéz (*John the Valiant*) (Operetta)
Opening Night: April 9.
Author: Sándor Petőfi (original poem), Károly Bakonyi (dialog), Jenő Heltai (poetry),
 and Kacsóh Pongrác (music).
Role: Unknown but likely one of the smaller roles.

On a double bill with:

Elnémult harangok (*Silent Bells*) (Comedy)
Opening Night: April 9.
Author: Dezső Malonyay and Viktor Rákosi.
Role: Unknown but likely the lead role as Pál Simándi.

A bajusz (*The Mustache*) (Musical Comedy)
Opening Night: April 11.
Author and Music: György Verő.
Role: Unknown but likely Kozári Gábor.

The above information on the performances in Nagykároly, Hungary was published in the April 14 edition of *Békésmegyei Iparosok Lapja*. As previously noted, it is clear that only certain of the originally advertised plays were actually performed. While not indicating his exact roles, the review of the plays noted that Lugosi was one of the top three men in the company acting in these plays.

Az igazgató úr (*The Headmaster*) (Family Comedy)
Opening Night: May 7.
Author: Edward Knobloch and Wilfred T. Coleby.
Role: Jack Strahan, a Teacher. A leading role.

A király (*The King*) (Comedy)
Opening Night: May 18.
Author: Flers, Caillavet, and Aréne.
Role: Grande Marquis Chamanande. A supporting role.

Érmihálfalva

Gül Baba (Operetta)
Opening Night: June 6.
Author: Jenő Huszka and Ferenc Martos.
Role: Unknown but likely Spahi, a Pasha, a role he had portrayed earlier in the season.

A millíardos kisasszony (*Miss Millionaire*) (Operetta)
Opening Night: June 7.
Author: Karl Lindau. Music by Johann Strauss.
Role: Unknown but likely Véri Ákos, a role Lugosi would portray in other towns while with Polgár.

Berger Zsiga (*Zsiga Berger*)
Opening Night: June 11.
Author: Ferenc Révész.
Role: Unknown but likely Endre Szalai, a role Lugosi would portray in other towns on the circuit.
Note: The play title is a male name, a shortened version of Sigismudus Berger.

Helyre asszony (*A Fair Woman*) (Musical Drama)
Opening Night: June 12.
Author: Elek Kada.
Role: Unknown but likely Ali, a Budai Pasha, the leading role, which he had portrayed at other times in Polgár's troupe.

Budapest

Subsequent to appearing in Érmihálfalva, Lugosi once again participated in auditions in Budapest. The June 14 edition of *Az Újság* reported that he ranked among the top individuals who passed the "exams" conducted by the National Actors Association of Hungary. The auditions were to place actors in regional touring companies or with one of the main Budapest theaters. On June 23, the *Pesti Hírlap* reported that Lugosi had renewed his contract with the Béla Polgár Theater Troupe.

Nagyszalontá

Subsequent to the actor auditions, the June 23 edition of *Pesti Hírlap* noted that the Béla Polgár Troupe (with Lugosi) staged plays in Nagyszalontá (now Salonta in Romania) for the balance of June. However, no information has been uncovered regarding specific productions.

Csongrád (at the Nemzeti Színészet [National Theater])
A víg özvegy (*The Merry Widow*) (Operetta)
Opening Night: July 7. Also staged on July 13 and July 26.
Author: Franz Lehár.

Role: Count Daniló Danilovics. This was a major role.

***János vitéz* (*John the Valiant*)** (Musical)
Opening Night: July 8.
Author: Sándor Petőfi (original poem), Károly Bakonyi (dialog), Jenő Heltai (poetry), and Kacsóh Pongrác (music).
Role: Second Yeoman.

***Takarodó* (*Tattoo*)** (Drama)
Opening Night: July 9.
Author: Franz Beyerlein.
Role: Lauffen, a Lieutenant.

***A postás fiu és a huga* (*The Mail Boy and His Sister*)** (Musical Farce)
Opening Night: July 11.
Author: Bernát Buchbinder.
Role: Géza Bodrogi.

***Víg özvegy* (*The Merry Widow*)** (Operetta)
Opening Night: July 13.
Author: Franz Lehár.
Role: Count Daniló Danilovics

***Amit az erdö mesél* (*What the Forest Tells*)** (Folk Play)
Opening Night: July 14.
Author: István Géczi.
Role: Ferenc Suito.

***A tavasz* (*The Spring*)**
Opening Night: July 15.
Author: Lindeas and Wilhelm.
Role: Gál Feri, an Office Manager.

***A baba* (*The Baby*)** (Operetta)
Opening Night: July 16.
Author: Ordönneaux M. Forditotta.
Role: Angelot.

***A szabadkőművesek* (*The Freemasons*)**
Opening Night: July 18.
Author: Carl Laufs and Kurt Kraatz.

Role: Hidas Bálint.

Note: This play is also known as *A páholy vagy: A szabadkőművesek* (*The Box, or: The Freemasons*).

On a double bill with:

Cserelányok (*Replacement Girls*) (Operetta)
Opening Night: July 18. Also staged on July 22.
Author: Maurice Ordenneau.
Role: Felicien, a Lieutenant.

Gül Baba (Operetta)
Opening Night: July 19.
Author: Ferenc Martos.
Role: Spahi, a Pasha.

A kis pajtás (*The Little Friend*)
Opening Night: July 23.
Author: Henri Bernstein.
Role: Jakab Juvenin.

Berger Zsiga (*Zsiga Berger*)
Opening Night: July 24.
Author: Ferenc Révész.
Role: Endre Szalai.

Kikapós férj (A szalmaözvegy) (*Sneaky Husband [The Grass Widower]*) (Musical Farce)
Opening Night: July 25.
Author: Imre Laky. Adaptation by Rudolf Kneisel.
Role: István Gyutacs.
Note: Béla Polgár was featured in the role of Pál Kocor. It was common practice in Hungary for the director or producer of a traveling theater troupe to play an occasional major role in a production.

Víg özvegy (*The Merry Widow*) (Operetta)
Opening Night: July 26.
Author: Franz Lehár.
Role: Count Daniló Danilovics

Bob herceg (*Prince Bob*) (Operetta)
Opening Night: July 29.

Author: Jenő Huszka.
Role: Bodyguard.

On a double bill with:

*A koldus gróf (**The Beggar Earl**)* (Burlesque)
Opening Night: July 29.
Author: Viktor Léon.
Role: Ttrunky.
Note: The spelling of the character is not a typographical error. This odd spelling is exactly the way it appears on the playbill.

*A milliárdos kisasszony (**Miss Millionaire**)* (Operetta)
Opening Night: July 30. Also staged on August 2.
Author: Karl Lindau. Music by Johann Strauss.
Role: Véri Ákos.

*Lumpáciusz Vagabundusz, vagy: a három jómadár (**Lumpacious Vagabondus or: The Jumping Thief**)* (Farce)
Opening Night: July 31.
Author: Johann Nestroy.
Role: Lumpácius. A lead role.
Note: Besides having the title role, Lugosi also portrayed the supporting roles of Ronyvári and Idegen.

*A svihákok (**The Cheaters**)* (Operetta)
Opening Night: August 1.
Author: Carl Michael Ziehrer.
Role: Fritz Blitz.

During the month of August, Polgár also presented *Az ördög (**The Devil**)* and *II Rákóczy Ferencz (**Ferenc Rakosi II**)* and perhaps additional plays. Lugosi's involvement is uncertain although he likely appeared in these as well.

Gyula (staged at the Színészset Békése)

*Víg özvegy (**The Merry Widow**)* (Operetta)
Opening Night: September. Exact date unknown.
Author: Franz Lehár.
Role: Unknown, but likely Count Daniló Danilovics, a lead character.

A tolvaj (*The Thief*) (Drama)
Opening Night: September. Exact date unknown.
Author: Henri Bernstein.
Role: Unknown but likely Richárd Voysin, a leading role.

Gül Baba (Operetta)
Opening Night: September. Exact date unknown.
Author: Ferenc Martos.
Role: Unknown but likely Spahi, a Pasha.

A milliárdos kisasszony (*Miss Millionaire*) (Operetta)
Opening Night: September. Exact date unknown.
Author: Karl Lindau. Music by Johann Strauss.
Role: Unknown but likely Ákos, Secrectary to Ross.

On September 15, *Békés*, a local newspaper, noted that these plays were staged. No reviews or exact dates were published provided, only that the productions had taken place, that an additional six plays were presented, and that Lugosi was one of the actors who appeared in them. It seems likely that they occurred during the period of September 8 through 21. By September 23, 1907, the troupe was performing in Nagyszalonta, after which they moved on to Kalocsa.

Kalocsa (at the Nyári Kaszíno [the Great Hall of the Summer Casino])
Elnémult harangok (*Silent Bells*) (Comedy)
Opening Night: October 16.
Author: Dezső Malonyay and Viktor Rákosi.
Role: Pál Simándi, a Clergyman of the Reformed Church. This was the lead role.

A bajusz (*The Mustache*) (Musical Comedy)
Opening Night: October 18.
Author and Music: György Verő.
Role: Kozári Gábor, the Nephew of the Vice-Chancellor.

A milliárdos kisasszony (*Miss Millionaire*) (Operetta)
Opening Night: October 19. Also staged on October 27 (on a double bill with *János vitéz* [*John the Valiant*]) and November 10 (on a double bill with *Berger Zsiga* [*Zsiga Berger*]).
Author: Karl Lindau. Music by Johann Strauss.
Role: Ákos, Secretary to Ross.

A víg özvegy (*The Merry Widow*) (Operetta)
Opening Night: October 20. Also staged on October 25.

Author: Viktor Léon and Leo Stein. Music by Franz Lehár.
Role: Count Daniló Danilovics. A major role.

A baba (*The Baby*) (Operetta)
Opening Night: October 21. Also staged on October 28.
Author: Maurice Ordonneau. Music by Edmund Audran.
Role: Angelot.
Note: A Hungarian translation of *La Poupée*.

A tolvaj (*The Thief*) (Drama)
Opening Night: October 22.
Author: Henri Bernstein.
Role: Richárd Voysin. This was a lead role.

Gül Baba (Operetta)
Opening Night: October 23.
Author: Ferenc Martos. Music by Jenő Huszka.
Role: Spahi, a Pasha.

Heidelberg diák élet (*Old Heidelberg Life*) (Romantic Drama with Songs)
Opening Night: October 24.
Author: Vilmos Meyer-Förster.
Role: His Excellency Hofmarshall Freiherr von Passarge (a Marshall from the Court). This was
a small supporting role.
Note: At times, this play title was spelled *Heidelbergi diák élet.*

A cigánybáró (The Gypsy Baron) (Operetta)
Opening Night: October 26.
Author: Jókai and Schnitzer. Music by Johann Strauss.
Role: Józsi, a Gypsy.

János vitéz (John the Valiant) (Musical)
Opening Night: October 27.
Author: Sándor Petőfi (original poem), Károly Bakonyi (dialog), Jenő Heltai (poetry),
 and Kacsóh Pongrác (music).
Role: One of the Generals.
Note: Staged at 3:30 p.m.

A sötétség (The Darkness)
Opening Night: October 29.
Author: György Ruttkay.

Role: Istvándy Lajos, Chief Lieutenant of the Hussar.

On a double bill with

A milliárdos kisasszony (*Miss Millionaire*) (Operetta)
Opening Night: October 29
Author: Karl Lindau. Music by Johann Strauss.
Role: Véri Ákos.

Az ördög (*The Devil*) (Drama)
Opening Night: October 31.
Author: Ferenc Molnár.
Role: János, a Painter. This was a lead role.
Note: Béla Polgár starred in the role of the devil.

A molnár és gyermeke (*The Miller and His Children*) (Folk Drama)
Opening Night: November 1.
Author: Ernest Raupach.
Role: The Son of Konrad, a Miller Apprentice.

Leányka (*The Damsel*) (Operetta)
Opening Night: November 2. Also staged on November 8.
Author and Music: György Vérő.
Role: Gáspár, a Farm Manager.
Note: The title can also be translated as *The Little Girl*.

Bob herceg (*Prince Bob*) (Operetta)
Opening Night: November 3.
Author: Ferenc Martos and Károly Bakonyi. Music by Jenő Huszka.
Role: A Grocer named Gipsy.
Note: Staged at 3:30 p.m.

On a double bill with:

Helyre asszony (*A Fair Woman*) (A Peasant Play with Songs)
Opening Night: November 3.
Author: Elek Kada.
Role: Ali, a Budai Pasha. A leading role.
Note: The story takes place in 1606 when Hungary was under Ottoman rule.

Takarodó (*Tattoo*) (Drama)

Opening Night: November 5.

Author: Franz Beyerlein.

Role: Lauffen, a Lieutenant.

Cserelányok (*Replacement Girls*) (Operetta)

Opening Night: November 6.

Author: Maurice Ordonneau. Music by Justin Clérice.

Role: Felicien, a Lieutenant.

Note: A Hungarian translation of the French operetta *Les filles Jackson et cie* (*The Jackson Girls and Company*) (1905).

A nap hőse (*The Hero of the Day*) (Burlesque)

Opening Night: November 7.

Author: Gustav Kadelburg.

Role: Arthur German.

A koldusgróf (*The Beggar Earl*) (Burlesque)

Opening Night: November 9.

Author: Viktor Léon. Music by Leo Aschor.

Role: Ttrunky, a Beggar.

Berger Zsiga (*Zsiga Berger*)

Opening Night: November 10, on a double bill with *A milliárdos kisasszony* (*Miss Millionaire*).

Author: Ferenc Révész.

Role: Endre Szalai, an Office Director.

Cyrano de Bergerac (Historical Romance)

Opening Night: November 12.

Author: Edmond Rostand. Based on the work by Cervantes.

Role: Guiche, an Earl. This was a major supporting role.

Legvitézebb huszár (*The Bravest Hussar*) (Operetta)

Opening Night: November 13.

Author: Ferenc Martos. Music by Viktor Jakobi.

Role: Dőri, a Captain.

Aranylakodalom (*The Golden Wedding*) (Tragedy)

Opening Night: November 14.

Author: László Beöthy and Viktor Rákosi.

Roles: Scene 2: A Jurist; Scene 3: Lajos Kossuth, a Governor; Scen 6: Szaniszló Lubomirszky.

Note: A "László Lugosi" was also listed in the cast.

Kiskunhalas (at the Városi Színház [Municipal Theater])

Lugosi was always credited as Béla Lugosi in this town.

*A víg özvegy (**The Merry Widow**)* (Operetta)
Opening Night: November 16. Also staged on November 29.
Author: Viktor Léon and Leo Stein. Music by Franz Lehár.
Role: Count Daniló Danelovics. A major role.
Review: "The artists who play the main roles, Szidi P. Szepesi in the title role and Lugosi as Danilo, brought the play to triumph with their brilliant acting which would stand out on any famous stages." (*Kiskunhalasi Újság* 27 Nov. 1907).

*Helyre asszony (**A Fair Woman**)* (Musical Drama)
Opening Night: November 17. Also staged on December 8 (on a double bill with *Aranylakodalom [The Golden Wedding]*) and 14.
Author: Elek Kada.
Role: Ali, a Budai Pasha.

*János vitéz (**John the Valiant**)* (Musical)
Opening Night: November 18. Also staged on December 1 on a double bill with *Magdolna (Magdalena)*.
Author: Sándor Petőfi (original poem), Károly Bakonyi (dialog), Jenő Heltai (poetry), and Kacsóh Pongrác (music).
Role: A General.

*A tolvaj (**The Thief**)* (Drama)
Opening Night: November 19.
Author: Henri Bernstein.
Role: Richard Voysin. The leading role.
Review: "Stefi D. Pető and Béla Lugosi, the two young actors, presented the whole art of acting in Act II, and a bright future awaits them if they keep up with this level." (*Kiskunhalasi Újság* 27 Nov. 1907).

*Leányka (**The Damsel**)* (Operetta)
Opening Night: November 20.
Author: György Vérő.
Role: Lugosi likely repeated his role as Gáspár, a Farmer, from earlier in the season.

*A nap hőse (**The Hero of the Day**)* (Burlesque)
Opening Night: November 21.

Author: Gustav Kadelburg.
Role: Lugosi likely repeated his role as Arthur German from earlier in the season.

*A bajusz (**The Mustache**)* (Musical Comedy)
Opening Night: November 22.
Author and Music: György Verö.
Role: Gábor Kozári, the Nephew of the Vice-Chancellor.
Review: "Béla Lugosi played the young and very Hungarian magnate suitably, with his heated speech and typical manner." (*Kiskunhalasi Újság* 27 Nov. 1907).

*A milliárdos kisasszony (**Miss Millionaire**)* (Operetta)
Opening Night: November 23. Also staged on December 2 on a double bill with *A sötétség (**The Darkness**).*
Author: Karl Lindau. Music by Johann Strauss.
Role: Lugosi likely repeated his role as Ákos, Secretary to Ross, from earlier in the season.

*A postás fiu és a huga (**The Mail Boy and His Sister**)* (Musical Farce)
Opening Night: November 24.
Author: Bernát Buchbinder.
Role: Lugosi likely repeated his role as Géza Bodrogi from earlier in the season.
Review: "Lugosi was manly and heated." (*Kiskunhalasi Újság* 27 Nov. 1907).

*Bob herceg (**Prince Bob**)* (Operetta)
Opening Night: November 25.
Author: Jenő Huszka.
Role: Lugosi likely repeated his role as Testör, a Lieutenant, from earlier in the season.

*Elnémult harangok (**Silent Bells**)* (Comedy)
Opening Night: November 26.
Author: Dezső Malonyay and Viktor Rákosi.
Role: Pál Simándi, a Clergyman of the Reformed Church. This was the lead role.
Review: "The audience especially celebrated Lugosi, who played his role with true intimacy and made himself popular with his engagement." (*Kiskunhalasi Újság* 4 Dec. 1907).

*Cserelányok (**Replacement Girls**)* (Operetta)
Opening Night: November 27.
Author: Maurice Ordonneau.
Role: Lugosi likely repeated his role as Felicien, a Lieutenant, from earlier in the season.

*Heidelberg diák élet (**Old Heidelberg Life**)* (Romantic Drama)
Opening Night: November 28.

Author: Vilmos Meyer-Förster.

Role: Lugosi likely repeated his role as His Excellency Hofmarshall Freiherr von Passarge from earlier in the season.

Notes: At times this play was spelled *Heidelbergi diák élet*.

Magdolna (*Magdalena*)

Opening Night: December 1 on a double bill with *János vitéz* (*John the Valiant*).

Author: Unknown.

Role: Unknown.

Note: A review of the performance notes that Lugosi was in the cast. The play may be *Máriá Magdolna* by Hebbel.

A sötétség (*The Darkness*)

Opening Night: December 2 on a double bill with *A milliárdos kisasszony* (*Miss Millionaire*).

Author: György Ruttkay.

Role: Lugosi likely repeated his role as Lajos Istrándy, a Cavalry Officer, from earlier in the season.

A cigánybáró (*The Gypsy Baron*) (Operetta)

Opening Night: December 4.

Author: Jókai and Schnitzer.

Role: Lugosi likely repeated his role as Józsi, a Gypsy, from earlier in the season.

Az ördög (*The Devil*) (Drama)

Opening Night: December 5.

Author: Ferenc Molnár.

Role: Lugosi likely repeated his role as János, a Painter, from earlier in the season.

Legvitézebb huszár (*The Bravest Hussar*) (Operetta)

Opening Night: December 7.

Author: Ferenc Martos.

Role: Lugosi likely repeated his role as Döri, a Captain, from earlier in the season.

Aranylakodalom (*The Golden Wedding*) (Tragedy)

Opening Night: December 8 on a double bill with *Helyre asszony* (*A Fair Woman*).

Author: László Beöthy.

Roles: Lugosi likely repeated his roles Jurátus, Lajos Kossuth, and Lubomirszky from a production earlier in the season.

A koldus gróf (*The Beggar Earl*) (Burlesque)

Opening Night: December 10.

Author: Viktor Léon.

Role: Lugosi likely repeated his role as Ttrunky from earlier in the season.

On a double bill with:

A tavasz (*The Spring*)

Opening Night: December 10.

Author: Lindeas and Wilhelm.

Role: Lugosi likely repeated his role as Gál Feri, an Office Manager, from earlier in the season.

Lumpáciusz Vagabundusz, vagy: a három jómadár (*Lumpacious Vagabondus or: The Jumping Thief*) (Farce)

Opening Night: December 15.

Author: Johann Nestroy.

Role: Lugosi likely repeated his role as Lumpácius from earlier in the season.

A baba (*The Baby*) (Operetta)

Opening Night: December 16.

Author: Maurice Ordenneau.

Role: Lugosi likely repeated his role as Angelot from earlier in the season.

A szabadkőművesek (*The Freemasons*)

Opening Night: December 17.

Author: Carl Laufs and Kurt Kraatz.

Role: Lugosi likely repeated his role as Hidas Bálint from earlier in the season.

Note: This play is also known as *A páholy vagy: A szabadkőművesek* (*The Box, or: The Freemasons*).

Gül Baba (Operetta)

Opening Night: December 18.

Author: Ferenc Martos

Role: Lugosi likely repeated his role as Spahi, a Pasha, from earlier in the season.

Munkács

Kiskun-Halas, a local newspaper, reported on December 25 that the Polgár troupe completed its run on Sunday December 22 and moved on to the town of Munkács. Although the troupe likely worked from December 19 and into the New Year, no known primary evidence lists the play titles or dates.

1908

Munkács and Kisvárda

The Polgár troupe continued its residence in Munkács until the end of February, where they presented a number of plays, with Lugosi likely acting in a number of them. By the first of March, the troupe had moved on to the town of Kisvárda, where they remained for approximately two weeks. No known primary evidence lists the plays.

Sátorljaújhely (at the Városi Színház [Municipal Theater])

The Polgár troupe arrived in this town by March 16 to begin a few days of rehearsals prior to reopening the town theater, which had been dark for some time. Polgár won the contract for a three-week stay, with the first performance staged on March 21. The local newspaper, *Zemplén*, listed Lugosi among the troupe's major players.

Lumpáciusz Vagabundusz, vagy: a három jómadár (*Lumpacious Vagabondus or: The Jumping Thief*) (Farce)
Opening Night: March 22.
Author: Johann Nestroy
Role: Lugosi likely repeated the role of Lumpácius from earlier in the season.
Note: One local newspaper, *Zemplén*, listed *Náni* as the production for the day. Given that two plays were sometimes staged on Sundays – one in the afternoon and one in the evening – that was likely the case here.

Gül Baba (Operetta)
Opening Night: March 24. Also staged on April 1.
Author: Jenő Huszka and Ferenc Martos.
Role: Lugosi likely repeated the role of Spahi, a Pasha, from earlier in the season.

A bajusz (*The Mustache*) (Musical Comedy)
Opening Night: March 27.
Author and Music: György Verö.
Role: Lugosi likely repeated his role as Gábor Kozári from earlier in the season.

A víg özvegy (*The Merry Widow*) (Operetta)
Opening Night: March 28.
Author: Franz Lehár.
Role: Lugosi likely repeated his role as Count Daniló Danilovics from earlier in the season.

Amit az erdő mesél (*What the Forest Tells*) (Folk Play)
Opening Night: March 29.
Author: István Géczi.
Role: Lugosi likely repeated his role as Ferenc Suito from earlier in the season.

Cserelányok (*Replacement Girls*) (Operetta)
Opening Night: March 30.
Author: Maurice Ordonneau.
Role: Lugosi likely repeated his role as Felicien, a Lieutenant, from earlier in the season.

A cigánybáró (*The Gypsy Baron*) (Operetta)
Opening Night: April 3.
Author: Jókai and Schnitzer.
Role: Lugosi likely repeated his role as Józsi, a Gypsy, from earlier in the season.

Bob herceg (*Prince Bob*) (Operetta)
Opening Night: April 4.
Author: Jenő Huszka.
Role: Lugosi likely repeated his role as Testör from earlier in the season.

A nap hőse (*The Hero of the Day*) (Burlesque)
Opening Night: April 7.
Author: Gustav Kadelburg.
Role: Lugosi likely repeated his role as Arthur German from earlier in the season.
Review: "Lugosi played with influence and satisfaction." (*Zemplén* [Sátorljaújhely, Hungary] 8 Apr. 1908).

Nagymihály

The Polgár troupe departed Sátorljaújhely likely on April 13. They staged productions in Nagymihály (now Michalovce in Slovakia) from April 26 through May 1. Further details are unknown.

Other Towns in the Polgár Circuit

Existing newspaper articles indicate the troupe completed the season sometime in September, playing such towns as Munkács, Beregszász (now Berehove in Ukraine), Gyöngyös, Kalocsa, Csongrád, Sárospatak, and Máramarossziget (now Sighetu Marmației in Romania). No known primary source confirms Lugosi's presence with the troupe for the summer season. At any rate, his association with Polgár likely ended by late August.

Debrecen (at the Városi Színház [Municipal Theater] under the direction of Gyula Zilahy, unless otherwise noted)

By September 10, the Gyula Zilahy Troupe announced Lugosi as one of its new members. Local press indicated he had been hired to specialize in "romantic hero" roles. Lugosi could have even worked with this troupe on part or all of its summer circuit prior to the new season in Debrecen.

Throughout Lugosi's time in Debrecen, his billing varied between "Lugosi," "Lugossi," "Lugosy," and "Lugossy." The October 30, 1910 edition of Szeged's *Színházi Újság* claimed that, during his time in Debrecen, Lugosi appeared as Hamlet in *Hamlet*, as Ocskay in *Ocskay brigadéros* (*Brigadier General Ocskay*), as Géza Joász in *A császár katoná* (*The Soldiers of the Emperor*), and as Derion in *A nök barátja* (*The Friend of Women*). However, no known primary source from the Debrecen season confirms any of these roles.

Szigetvári vértanúk (*Martyrs of Szigetvar*) (Historical Drama)
Opening Night: October 6.
Author: Mór Jókai.
Role: Miklós Zrínyi.

Gyimesi vadvirág (*Wildflower of Gyimes*) (Folk Play)
Opening Night: October 29. Also staged on November 22.
Author: István Géczy.
Role: Imre.
Note: Billed as Lugossi.
Review: "Lugosi accomplished his task much less successfully. In some scenes he was rather weak but in some others his acting expressed dramatic strength." (*Debrecini Újság* 30 Oct. 1908).

Manfréd (*Manfred*) (Poetic Drama)
Opening Night: November 7. Also staged on November 8 and 13, and December 15.
Author: Lord Byron.
Role: Manfréd. This was a major role.
Note: The November 5 edition of *Debrecini Újság* stated that "Lugosi" would appear in the title role. Several surviving playbills show Jenő Lugosi in the role of Manfréd. However, that was apparently a printing error. The only "Lugosi" active in Debrecen at the time was Béla Lugosi. Additionally, a review of the November 7 opening night for *Manfréd* (published in the November 15 edition of the weekly Debrecen newspaper *Debreceni Főiskolai Lapok*) makes clear that Béla Lugosi was the actor in the role of Manfréd beginning with the first performance. The playbill of December 15 finally corrected the error.

Folt, amely tisztít (*The Spill That Cleans*) (Drama)
Opening Night: November 14. Staged at the Városi Színház in Nyíregyháza.
Author: Jószef Echegaray
Role: Fernando

A gyermek (*The Child*) (Tragedy)
Opening Night: November 15. Staged at the Városi Színház in Nyíregyháza.
Author: Árpád Abonyi.
Role: Radák, a Soldier.
Note: According to the *Debrezeni Újság* of December 12, this play was also staged in Debrecen on December 13.

*A kék egér (**The Blue Mouse**)* (Comedy)
Opening Night: November 16. Staged at the Városi Színház in Nyíregyháza.
Author: Engel and Horst.
Role: Cézár Róben, a Board Director

*Az ember tragédiája (**The Tragedy of Man**)* (Poetic Drama)
Opening Night: November 29. Also staged on November 30 and December 6.
Author: Imre Madách.
Role: Adam. A lead role.
Review: "We must admit," continues the critic, "that his Danton [one of the personages that Adam assumes] was one of the most iron-willed, most revolutionary and most artistic one that we have ever seen, and this daring inconsistency was quite surprising." (Quoted from *Debrecini Független Újság* 1 Dec. 1908 by Anna Szabó in *Kitűnő kvalifikációi vannak a hősi szerepekre, Lugosi Béla kultusza – debreceni szemmel*).

Simone (Tragedy)
Opening Night: December 16. Also staged on December 17.
Author: Eugène Brieux.
Role: Chantreaux. A small supporting role.

*A Peleskei nótárius (**The Notary of Peleske**)* (Musical Farce)
Opening Night: December 31.
Author: József Gaál.
Role: Othello.
Note: Credited as Béla Lugosi. A small supporting role.

1909
Debrecen (at the Városi Színház [Municipal Theater] under the direction of Gyula Zilahy, unless otherwise noted)

*A Peleskei nótárius (**The Notary of Peleske**)* (Musical Farce)
Opening Night: January 6.
Author: József Gaál.
Role: Othello. A small supporting role.
Note: Billed as Béla Lugosi.

*Rómeó és Júlia (**Romeo and Juliet**)* (Tragedy)
Opening Night: January 8. Also staged January 11, February 7 and 17, and November 1.
Author: Shakespeare.
Roles: Escalus (January 8 and 11) and Romeo (February 7 and 17 and November 1).

Note: The role of Escalus was a small supporting one. However, Lugosi received special billing with his name in bold in the cast list for his appearance as Romeo on February 17.

A szerencse fia (***The Lucky Ones***) (Comedy)
Opening Night: January 15. Also staged on January 16 and 18.
Author: Gábor Drégely.
Role: Márton Szontag, a Teacher.

Szökött katona (***The Runaway Soldier***) (Folk Play)
Opening Night: January 17.
Author: Ede Szigligeti.
Role: Count Monti. A large supporting role.
Note: Billed as Béla Lugosy.

Tell Vilmos (***William Tell***) (Drama)
Opening Night: January 22. Also staged on January 23 and 24, and February 4.
Author: Friedrich Schiller.
Role: William Tell. The lead role.
Note: Billed as Béla Lugosi and Béla Lugossy on the same playbill for this production.
Review: "This grandiose, magnificent play which keeps the whole cast occupied, tests the abilities of the entire company. As announced earlier, the role of William Tell will be played by Lugosi, who is preparing himself ambitiously for this rather tiring but fulfilling role." (*Debreceni Újság* 16 Jan. 1909).

Fédora (***Fedora***) (Drama)
Opening Night: January 29.
Author: Victorien Sardou
Role: De Siriex. A major role.

Csizmadia, mint kísértet (***The Ghostly Bootmaker***) (Folk Play)
Opening Night: January 31. Also staged on February 3 and 9 and March 25 (on a double bill with ***Domi, Az amerikai majom, vagy a serecsen bosszuja*** [***Domi, the American Monkey, or: Revenge on the Saracens***]).
Author: Jószef Szigeti.
Role: Alpári, a Squire.

Izráel (***Israel***) (Drama)
Opening Night: February 5. Also staged on February 6 and 8, and April 6 (at Nyíregyháza).
Author: Henri Bernstein.
Role: De Sallaz, an Earl. Likely a small role.
Note: The May 23 edition of the Nyíregyháza newspaper *Nyírvidék* mentions an additional performance of *Izráel* during the month of May. However, no playbill has surfaced, so it remains

uncertain if the play was performed again that month.

A remény (The Hope) (Drama)
Opening Night: February 11. Also staged on February 12.
Author: Herman Heyersman.
Role: Barend.
Note: Lugosi was replaced by another actor for the February 2 performance due to illness, and by László Tallián for the April 24 performance for reasons unknown.

A gyújtogató (The Firebrand) (Drama)
Opening Night: February 13. Also staged on February 14, 15 and (according to *Debreceni Újság*) 20, March 8, 9 (at Szatmár), 14 and 28 (Érmihályfalva), and April 5 and 7 (both days at Nyíregyháza), 13 and 24 (in Hajduszoboszló), as well as November 27 (in Ungvár).
Author: Herman Heyersman.
Role: The Examiner.
Note: Theater director Gyula Zilahy appeared in multiple roles as the lead in this production, with Lugosi in one of the main supporting roles.
Review: "Béla Lugosi plays his role conscientiously, too." (*Debrecini Újság* 14 Feb. 1909).

Debreczen a holdban (Debrecen on the Moon) (Low Comedy)
Opening Night: February 26. Also staged on February 27, March 1 and 2.
Author: Gyula Than
Role: Unknown.
Note: This was a "low comedy spectacular" that featured a "marching group of street performers … dance medleys … and many interesting dancing groups" in addition to a dramatic presentation, according to the February 20 edition of *Debrecini Újság*, which listed Lugosi among the performers. However, given that playbills for the production did not list Lugosi in the dramatic cast, the nature of his involvement is unknown.

Forradalmi nász (The Revolutionary Wedding) (Drama)
Opening Night: March 4. Also staged on March 5 and 6 and April 8 (at Nyíregyháza).
Author: Sophus Michaëlis.
Role: Darvont.

Hamlet (Tragedy)
Opening Night: March 11.
Author: William Shakespeare.
Role: Claudius, King of Denmark. A major supporting role.
Note: Billed as Béla Lugossy. Popular Hungarian actor Béla Mándoky received above the title billing in the role of Hamlet.

Az ember tragédiája (*The Tragedy of Man*) (Poetic Drama)
Opening Night: March 16 in Szatmár. Also staged on March 17.
Author: Imre Madách.
Role: Adam. The lead role.
Note: Staged by the Debrecni Színház Tagjanak Fellepte (Debrecen Repertory Theater Company). They were special guests of the local theater for these two performances, having been invited by the Béla Heves Társulata (Company). Originally scheduled for March 13 and 14.

Domi, Az amerikai majom, vagy a serecsen bosszuja (*Domi, the American Monkey, or: Revenge on the Saracens*) (Farce)
Opening Night: March 25.
Author: Johann Nestroy.
Role: Dezza Gazatta
Note: This was a special presentation featuring Árpád Dunai, one of the leading actors of the time.

Hajótörés (*Shipwreck*) (Monologue)
Opening Night: March 28 at the theater in the Nemzeti Szálló (National Hotel) at Érmihályfalva.
Author: Unknown.
Role: Monologist.
Note: The playbill that exists for this production does not identify the author of the work; however, it could possibly be based on 1878 French poem by Francois Coppée. In addition to other short presentations on the bill, Lugosi also appeared in *A gyújtogató* (*The Firebrand*).

A falu rossza (*The Evil of the Village*) (Folk Play)
Opening Night: April 11.
Author: Ede Tóth.
Role: County Commissioner. A small supporting role.

Felhő Klári (*Claire Felho*) (Folk Play)
Opening Night: April 12. Also staged on April 25 and December 25.
Author: László Bátkai.
Roles: János Tömjén (April 12 and 25) and András Aba (December 25).

Trilby (Drama with Singing and Dancing)
Opening Night: April 18.
Author: Georges Du Maurier.
Role: Talbot Wynne

A király (*The King*) (Comedy)
Opening Night: April 20. Also staged on April 21, 22 and 29, and October 21.

Author: Flers, Caillavet, and Aréne.
Role: Marquis Chamarande. A supporting role.

A három testőr (***The Three Musketeers***) (Farce)
Opening Night: April 23.
Author: Ferenc Herczeg.
Role: János Nagy.

Fátum (***Fate***) (Drama)
Opening Night: May 3.
Author: István Zairos.
Role: Richárd Zinneburg.

Hivatalnok urak (***The Gentleman Clerk***) (Drama)
Opening Night: May 10. Also staged on May 11 and 12, and October 26.
Author: Imre Földes.
Role: Feleki.

Meztelen nő (***The Bare Woman***) (Drama)
Opening Night: May 13. Also staged on May 14.
Author: Henry Bataille.
Role: Rauchárd. A supporting role.

A tiszteletes úr keservei (***The Reverend's Tribulations***) (Farce)
Opening Night: May 16.
Author: Kneisel.
Role: Zordbereki, a Diocese Counselor.

Summer Theater

A surviving playbill announced May 13 as the start date for the summer season, with an operetta as the first presentation. The playbill also lists over 24 additional productions slated for the summer. Lugosi, billed as "Béla Lugossy," is mentioned as "an actor for roles of the dramatic hero and lover." Included were plays that Lugosi had appeared in during the regular season, including *Izráel (Israel), A szerencse fia (The Lucky Ones), Hivatalnok urak (The Gentleman Clerk), Forradalmi nász (The Revolutionary Wedding), A remény (The Hope), Kék egér (The Blue Mouse), Manfréd (Manfred), A gyújtogató (The Firebrand),* and *Simone*. More than likely Lugosi reprised his earlier roles in at least some of these plays.

On September 1 and again on September 5, the *Budapesti Hírlap* reported that Lugosi (as a member of the Gyula Zilahy Theater Troupe) performed primarily in Nyíregyháza and Máramarossziget during June, July, and August before returning to Debrecen to prepare for the next regular season.

Nyíregyháza

Hivatalnok urak (*The Gentleman Clerk*) (Drama)
Opening Night: May 17.
Author: Imre Földes.
Role: Feleki.

A király (*The King*) (Comedy)
Opening Night: May 18. Also staged on May 27.
Authors: Flers, Caillavet, and Aréne.
Role: A Marquis.
Review: "Irma Bárdos, Lajos Ligeti, Béla Lugosi are pleasing young actors. We think that Béla Lugosi will be absolutely adequate for bigger, more serious roles, too." (*Nyírvidék* [Nyíregyháza, Hungary] 23 May 1909).

A szerencse fia (*The Lucky Ones*) (Comedy)
Opening Night: May 20.
Author: Gábor Drégely.
Role: Márton Szontag, a Teacher.

Forradalmi nász (*The Revolutionary Wedding*) (Drama)
Opening Night: May 21. Also staged on May 25.
Author: Sophus Michaëlis.
Role: Darvont.

A falu rossza (*The Evil of the Village*) (Folk Play)
Opening Night: May 30. Also staged on June 6.
Author: Ede Tóth.
Role: County Commissioner. A small supporting role.

Meztelen nő (*The Bare Woman*) (Drama)
Opening Night: Week of June 1. Exact date uncertain.
Author: Henry Bataille.
Role: Rauchárd. A supporting role.

Rómeó és Júlia (*Romeo and Juliet*) (Tragedy)
Opening Night: Likely on June 9.
Author: William Shakespeare.
Role: Romeo. The lead male role.
Note: A review in *Nyírvidék* on June 13 leaves the date unclear. It was likely June 9 but could have been the day prior.

Hamlet (Tragedy)
Opening Night: June 11.
Author: William Shakespeare.
Role: Claudius, the King of Denmark.
Note: A major supporting role.

A gyújtogató (*The Firebrand*) (Drama)
Opening Night: Possibly June 12.
Author: Herman Heyersman.
Role: Lugosi likely repeated his role as the Examiner, which he had portrayed earlier in the season.
Note: The local newspaper, *Nyírvidék*, referenced a performance of this play in the June 13 edition but did not specify the date.

Az ember tragédiája (*The Tragedy of Man*) (Poetic Drama)
Opening Night: June 13.
Author: Imre Madách.
Role: Adam. Lugosi had the leading role.

One primary source indicates that the troupe remained in Nyíregyháza until late July. However, the local newspaper, *Nyírvidék* ceased reporting on theater activities after the June 30 edition, which suggests the troupe might have moved on to another location. The June 18 edition of *Pesti Hírlap* indicated they would open in Máramarossziget on July 31.

Máramarossziget (at the Máramarossziget Színház [Máramarossziget Theater])

A király (*The King*) (Comedy)
Opening Night: August 2.
Author: Flers, Caillavet, and Aréne.
Role: Lugosi likely repeated his role as the Marquis Chamarande, which he had portrayed earlier in the year.

A kivándorló (*The Emigrant*) (Drama)
Opening Night: Early August, possibly August 3.
Author: Ferenc Herczeg.
Role: Unknown.

Az ember tragédiája (*The Tragedy of Man*) (Poetic Drama)
Opening Night: August 11.
Author: Imre Madách.
Role: Adam.

Note: In his book *A Tragédia a színpadon/The Tragedy on Stage* (Budapest: Madach Irodlami Társaság, 2008), Sándor Enyedi references Lugosi's appearance in the leading role of Adam on this date, citing a review published in the August 19 edition of the local newspaper *Máramaros*.

Margit Néni (Margaret Neni)
Opening Night: August 27.
Author: Bertalan Füzi.
Role: Unknown.

Szegény emberek (The Poor Folk) (Drama)
Opening Night: August 28.
Author: Fyodor Dostoyevsky.
Role: Unknown.
Reviews: "It was very interesting to watch the natural acting style of Béla Lugosi and Aranka Gazdy." (*Budapesti Hírlap* 1 Sept. 1909). "In the play, Aranka Gazdy and Béla Lugosi brought down the house." (*Az Újság* 31 Aug. 1909).

A gyújtogató (The Firebrand) (Drama)
Opening Night: August 29.
Author: Herman Heyersman.
Role: Lugosi likely repeated his role as the Examiner, which he had portrayed earlier in the year.
Note: The September 1 edition of *Budapesti Hírlap* mentions a possible additional performance of the play; however, no other known source confirms it.

Az igazgató úr (The Headmaster) (Family Comedy)
Opening Night: Most likely August 30.
Author: Edward Knoblock and Wilfred T. Coleby.
Role: Unknown

Manfréd (Manfred) (Poetic Drama)
Opening Night: Most likely August 31.
Author: Lord Byron.
Role: Unknown, but perhaps the title role, given that he had played it previously.
Note: In discussing the closing of Gyula Zilahy's summer theater season, the October 5 edition of *Az Újság* mentioned "Béla Lugossy" as having been "… a great and memorable success" in the production of **Manfréd**.

According to the *Pesti Napló* of August 3, the Zilahy Troupe was scheduled to remain in Máramarossziget until September 28.

Debrecen (at the Városi Színház [Municipal Theater] under the direction of Gyula Zilahy, unless otherwise noted)

A tanítónő (The Lady Teacher) (Folk Play)
Opening Night: September 29 to open the new season in Debrecen. Also staged on October 17.
Author: Sándor Bródy.
Role: A Tanitó (Elementary School Teacher). A major role.

A kivándorló (The Emigrant) (Drama)
Opening Night: October 1. Also staged on October 2 and 14.
Author: Ferenc Herczeg.
Role: Hatfaludy, a Prince.
Review: "The audience liked Béla Lugosi in the role of Prince Hatfaludy. He should polish his acting in a few subtle scenes, though." (*Debrecen* 2 Oct. 1909).

Bánk Bán (Bán Bánk) (Drama)
Opening Night: October 6. Also staged on November 14.
Author: József Katona.
Role: Bánk Bán, a Hungarian Lord. A major role.

Kétszerkettő-Öt (2 x 2 = 5) (Satire)
Opening Night: October 15. Also staged on October 16 and 21.
Author: Gustav Wied.
Role: Hugó Jörgensen.

Passe-Partout (The Master Key) (Drama)
Opening Night: October 28. Also staged on October 29 and 30.
Author: Georges Thurner.
Role: Eugénie Régis.
Note: Examining the script indicates this was a major role; however, a review of the play stated this to be a minor role.
Review: "Lugosi exquisitely played this minor dramatic role." (*Debrecen* 29 Oct. 1909).

Rosenkranz és Güldenstern (Rosenkranz and Guildenstern) (Comedy)
Opening Night: November 2.
Author: Michael Klapp.
Role: Albert Libeustein.

Buridán szamara (The Donkeys of Buridan) (Farce)
Opening Night: November 10. Also staged on November 11, 12 and 23 (in Nyíregyháza), and December 19.
Author: Flers and Caillavet.

Role: Lucien De Versannes.

Review: "Lugosi played the role of Lucien fairly but in a slightly colorless way." (*Debrecen*, 10 Nov. 1909).

Iglói diákok (Students of Igló) (Operetta)
Opening Night: November 14. Also staged on November 15, 16, 17 and 26, and December 4, 8 (on a double bill with *Falusi idyll* [*Rural Idyll*]), 9 (on a double bill with *A király házasodik* [*Marriage of the King*]), 12 and 26.
Author: Imre Farkas.
Role: The Director.

A bányász szerencsétlensége (The Miner's Misfortune)
Opening Night: November 27 at the Hungarian Theater in Ungvár.
Author: Unknown.
Role: Monologist.
Note: An article in the local newspaper, *Határszéli Újság* (Ungvár, Hungary, 25 Nov. 1909), indicates that this performance was one of a series of short recitations and sketches in support of *A gyújtogató (The Firebrand)*, in which Lugosi also appeared in the role of The Examiner.
Review: A review in a local newspaper (*Határszéli Újság* 29 Nov. 1909) believed the troupe leaned too much on comedy and not enough on more serious subject matter.

A haramiák (The Robbers) (Drama)
Opening Night: December 2. Also staged on December 3, 4 and 29.
Author: Friedrich Schiller.
Role: Charles Moor. A major role.
Review: "We must admit that the direction of the play is almost flawless, and this holds true to the quality of acting, too. Praise goes, first, to Lugosi, who, this time, played the role of the son of Károly Maximilian, and he did it in a rather artistic way, showing refined nuances. Through his acting today, we could clearly see how his talent grows." (*Debrecen* 3 Dec. 1909).

Falusi idyll (Rural Idyll) (Folk Play)
Opening Night: December 5. Also staged on December 6, 8, 10 and 14.
Author: Menyhért Lengyel.
Role: Bodnár.
Note: The play was originally scheduled for an October 8 opening, but was replaced by a staging of *Válás után (After Divorce)* without Lugosi.

A király házasodik (Marriage of the King) (Historical Comedy)
Opening Night: December 9.
Author: Kálmán Tóth
Role: Lajos I-sö, Hungarian King. A major role.

***A hallottak visszajárnak* (*The Dead Return*)** (Drama)
Opening Night: December 10. Also staged on December 11.
Author: Gábor Oláh.
Role: Géza Hegedüs.
Review: "The performance of Lugosi … was artistic and interesting…." (*Debrecen* 11 Dec. 1909).

***Taifun* (*Typhoon*)** (Drama)
Opening Night: December 15. Also staged on December 16, 17 and 18.
Author: Menyhért Lengyel.
Role: Ottó Lindner. Based on an existing review, this was a large role.
Review: "Lugosi's interpretation of Lindner was interesting." (*Debrecen* 16 Dec. 1909).

***Csöppség* (*The Little One*)** (Comedy)
Opening Night: December 30.
Author: Samu Fényes.
Role: Lenczi.

1910
Debrecen (at the Városi Színház [Municipal Theater] under the direction of Gyula Zilahy, unless otherwise noted)

***Falu rossza* (*The Evil of the Village*)** (Folk Play)
Opening Night: January 2. Also staged on January 25 and 26.
Author: Ede Tóth.
Role: County Commissioner. A small supporting role.
Note: The January 25 and 26 presentations had a start time of 3 p.m. so as not to conflict with the evening shows.

***Taifun* (*Typhoon*)** (Drama)
Opening Night: January 4. Also staged on January 22, 27 (at Nyíregyháza), and March 23.
Author: Menyhért Lengyel.
Role: Ottó Lindner.

***Vigyázz a nőre* (*Take Care of Her*)** (Operetta)
Opening Night: January 6. Also staged on January 7, 8 and 9.
Author: Georges Feydeau.
Role: The Prince.

***Botrány* (*Scandal*)** (Drama)

Opening Night: January 15. Also staged on January 16 and 17, and April 18.
Author: Henry Bataille.
Role: The Prefect.
Note: Gyula Gál, a prominent actor, was the guest star for the April 18 performance.

*Az iglói diákok (**Students of Igló**)* (Operetta)
Opening Night: January 18. Also staged on February 1 and 13, March 5, and May 1, 10 and 12.
Author: Imre Farkas.
Role: The Director.

*A Dolovai nábob leánya (**The Daughter of the Nabob of Dolova**)* (Drama)
Opening Night: January 21. Also staged on February 26, and April 10.
Author: Ferenc Herczeg.
Role: Szentirmay, a Hussar Captain, a supporting role (on January 21 and February 26) and Baron Merlin, a major supporting role (on April 10).

*Gyimesi vadvirág (**Wildflower of Gyimes**)* (Folk Play)
Opening Night: January 23.
Author: István Géczy.
Role: Imre.

*A tanítónő (**The Lady Teacher**)* (Folk Play)
Opening Night: January 24. Also staged on February 25, and April 1 and 17.
Author: Sándor Bródy.
Role: A Tanitó (Elementary School Teacher). A major role.
Note: Emma Somló, a popular member of the Nemzeti Színház (National Theater), was the guest star for the April 17 performance.

*Szent hazugságok (**Holy Lies**)* (Dramolette)
Opening Night: January 26. Also staged January 30.
Author: Zoltán Szatmári.
Role: The Man's Friend.
Note: In Hungarian theater, the "dramolette" was similar to a one-act play.

*Az ördög (**The Devil**)* (Drama)
Opening Night: January 29. Also staged on May 15.
Author: Ferenc Molnár.
Role: László, a supporting role (on January 29) and János, a leading role (on May 15).

*Pillangókisasszony (**Madame Butterfly**)* (Musical Drama)
Opening Night: January 31.

Author: Puccini.
Role: Pinkerton. A major role.

Velencei kalmár (The Merchant of Venice) (Drama)
Opening Night: February 9.
Author: William Shakespeare.
Role: Antonio. A major role.

Tartuffe (aka The Impostor) (Comedy)
Opening Night: February 10.
(Comedy)
Author: Moliére.
Role: Damis, Orgon's son. A small supporting role.

Hálás utókor (The Grateful Posterity) (Satire)
Opening Night: February 11.
Author: Menyhért Lengyel.
Role: Rapolti.
Note: Also performing in a major role was guest actor Jenő Ivánfi, a leading member of the Nemzeti Színház (National Theater) in Budapest. He was also at times a theater director who translated foreign plays into the Hungarian language.

Forradalmi nász (The Revolutionary Wedding) (Drama)
Opening Night: February 17.
Author: Sophus Michaëlis
Role: Marc-Arrán.
Review: "Among male performers, Béla Lugossy had undivided success ... played with such bravura that the audience rewarded him with everlasting applause at the end of the performance, which rarely happens in Debrecen." (*Budapesti Hírlap* 23 Feb. 1910).

Csöppség (A Young Child) (Comedy)
Opening Night: February 18. Also staged on March 6 and May 16.
Author: Samu Fényes.
Role: Lenczi.

Hivatalnok urak (The Gentleman Clerk) (Drama)
Opening Night: February 24.
Author: Imre Földes.
Role: Feleki.

A sasfiók (The Eagle) (Rhymed Drama)

Opening Night: February 27. Also staged on February 28, March 1, 2, 11, 20 and 30, and May 9.
Author: Edmond Rostand.
Role: A Tailor. A small supporting role.
Note: Also known by the title *L'Aiglon*.

Gotterhalte (II. A Kossuth nóta) (*Part II: A Kossuth Song*) (Drama)
Opening Night: March 15. Also staged on March 16.
Author: Adolf Mérei.
Role: A Captain.
Note: Composed by Haydn in 1797, *Gotterhalte* became the Austrian national anthem. It was despised in Hungary. Performances of it were often interrupted at the turn of the twentieth century. The phrase "Kossuth Song" could refer to a song that was sung for helping to recruit soldiers in the Hungarian Revolution of 1848. It might also refer to the primary politician behind the revolution and the war for independence, Lajos Kossuth. This drama seems to have been a response to Haydn's *Gotterhalte*.

Kis czukros (*The Little Chocolatier*) (Comedy)
Opening Night: March 17. Also staged on March 18 and 19.
Author: Paul Gavault.
Role: Hector de Pavézac.
Note: Billed as Béla Lugossi for all three performances.

Csokonai körtől (*The Csokonai Circle*) (Poetry Reading)
Opening Night: March 19.
Author: Various.
Role: Guest Reciter.
Note: Mihály Csokonai was a famous poet from Debrecen. His life and art were celebrated annually at a poetry reading founded in 1890. Lugosi, in his portion of the program, recited poetry written by Sándor Petőfi, Emil Ábrányi and Gyula Szávay. The celebration was held prior to Lugosi's appearance in an encore performance of *Kis czukros* (*The Little Chocolatier*) staged the same day.

Az ördög mátkája (*The Devil's Sweetheart*) (Folk Play)
Opening Night: March 20. Also staged on April 24.
Author: István Géczy.
Role: Andor, the first son.

Czifra nyomorúság (*Coat of Many Miseries*) (Drama)
Opening Night: March 21. Also staged on April 22.
Author: Gergely Csiky.
Role: Gusztav Bálnai, an accountant.

Az ember tragédiája (***The Tragedy of Man***) (Poetic Drama)
Opening Night: March 27. Also staged on April 3 and 4.
Author: Imre Madách.
Role: Adam. The lead role.

Francillon (Comedy)
Opening Night: April 6. Also staged on April 27.
Author: Alexander Dumas.
Role: Stanislas Grandredon. A major supporting role.

A kaméliás hölgy (***Lady of the Camellias***, aka ***Camille***) (Drama)
Opening Night: April 13. Also staged on May 4.
Author: Alexander Dumas.
Role: Armand Duval. The lead role.
Note: Emma Somló, member of the Hungarian Nemzeti Színház (National Theater), was the guest for the April 13 performance.

A sárga csikó (***The Yellow Colt***) (Folk Play)
Opening Night: April 16.
Author: Ferenc Csepreghy.
Role: Gelecséri. A supporting role.
Note: Emma Somló was the guest artist.

Elnémult harangok (***Silent Bells***) (Comedy)
Opening Night: April 19.
Author: Dezső Malonyay and Viktor Rákosi.
Role: Juon.
Note: Gyula Gál was the guest artist in the major role of Tódor Todorescu.

Zách Klára (***Klára Zách***) (Musical Farce)
Opening Night: April 24 (on a double bill with *Az ördög mátkája* [***The Devil's Sweetheart***]). Also staged on April 26.
Author: Sándor Székely.
Role: Róbert Károly, a Hungarian King.

Baccarat (Drama)
Opening Night: May 3.
Author: Henri Bernstein.
Role: Amadeé Lebourg.
Note: Ella G. Kertész and Sándor Góth, a husband and wife team prominent in the Hungarian theater world, were the guest artists for this production.

Folt, amely tisztít (The Stain That Cleans) (Drama)
Opening Night: May 14.
Author: Jószef Echegaray.
Role: Fernando.

Summer Theater

A surviving advertisement entitled *Drámaihős és zerelmes színesz* lists Lugosi as a summer theater performer under the auspices of Gyula Zilahy. Further confirmation of Lugosi's summer theater involvement exists in the form of a similar document entitled *Előleges színházi jelentés*. It advertises a start date of May 15 for Zilahy's productions in "Nyíregyháza and the countryside."

The schedule included the following plays that featured Lugosi earlier in the regular season: *Kétszerkettő-Öt (2 x 2 = 5)*, *Passe-Partout (The Master Key)*, *Buridán Szamara (The Donkeys of Buridan)*, *Falusi idyll (Rural Idyll)*, *Vigyázz a nőre (Take Care of Her)*, *A sasfiók (The Eagle)*, *Kis czukros (The Little Chocolatier)*, *Gotterhalte*, *Zách Klára (Klára Zách)*, *A haramiák (The Robbers)*, *A Dolovai nábob leánya (The Daughter of the Nabob of Dolova)*, *Gyimesi vadvirág (Wildflower of Gyimes)*, *Czifra nyomorúság (Coat of Many Miseries)*, *Az ember trajédiája (The Tragedy of Man)*, *Az ördög mátkája (The Devil's Sweetheart)*, and *Elnémult harangok (Silent Bells)*. More than likely Lugosi reprised his roles in a number of these plays.

On May 8, *Nyírvidék*, the local newspaper, published a brief article on the local summer theater season, stating it would begin around the middle of May. Lugosi was listed as one of the main performers. The June 26 edition of *Nyírvidék* reviewed the plays from the prior week that featured Lugosi.

Nyíregyháza (at the Nyíregyháza Színház [Nyíregyháza Theater])

According to the June 4 edition of *Pesti Hírlap*, the Zilahy troupe arrived in Nyíregyháza by the early part of June to begin their theatrical program there. However, the local newspaper *Nyírvidék* reported that the troupe began their run on May 15.

Izráel (Israel) (Drama)
Opening Night: May 17.
Author: Henri Bernstein.
Role: De Sallaz, an Earl.
Note: This production was scheduled for May 17; however, no playbill or review currently exists confirming that it actually took place in Nyíregyháza on this date.

Kis czukros (The Little Chocolatier) (Comedy)
Opening Night: May 18.
Author: Paul Gavault.
Role: Lugosi likely reprised his role as Hector de Pavézac.

Falusi idyll (***Rural Idyll***) (Folk Play)
Opening Night: May 19.
Author: Menyhért Lengyel.
Role: Lugosi likely reprised his role as Bodnár.

Vigyázz a nőre (***Take Care of Her***) (Operetta)
Opening Night: May 20.
Author: Georges Feydeau.
Role: Lugosi likely reprised his role as the Prince.

Bálkirálynőt (***Take a Bow***)
Opening Night: June 21.
Author: Unknown.
Role: Unknown.

Gyimesi vadvirág (***Wildflower of Gyimes***) (Folk Play)
Opening Night: June 22.
Author: István Géczy.
Role: Unknown.

Az ember trajédiája (***The Tragedy of Man***) (Poetic Drama)
Opening Night: June 23. Also staged on July 2.
Author: Imre Madách.
Role: Adam. The lead role.
Note: Mention of Lugosi's appearance as Adam, the main character, was published in *A Tragédia a Színpadon*, edited by Sándor Enyedi (Budapest: Madách Irodalmi Társág, 1908). Enyedi references a review in the June 26 edition of *Nyírvidék*.

Az ördög mátkája (***The Devil's Sweetheart***) (Folk Play)
Opening Night: June 24.
Author: István Géczy.
Role: Unknown.

Domi, Az amerikai majom, vagy a serecsen bosszuja (***Domi, the American Monkey, or: Revenge on the Saracens***) (Farce)
Opening Night: June 25.
Author: Johann Nestroy.
Role: Lugosi likely reprised his role as Dezza Gazatta.

Elnémult harangok (***Silent Bells***) (Comedy)
Opening Night: June 29.

Author: Dezső Malonyay and Viktor Rákosői.
Role: Lugosi likely reprised his role as Juon.

***Botrány* (*Scandal*)** (Drama)
Opening Night: June 30.
Author: Henry Bataille.
Role: Lugosi likely reprised his role as the Prefect.

Note: According to the July 2 edition of *Pesti Hírlap*, the troupe completed its run in Nyíregyháza on Sunday July 3.

Máramarossziget (at the Máramarossziget Színház [Máramarossziget Theater])

On July 21, *Pesti Napló* reported that, after a two-week break, the troupe opened in Máramarossziget on July 16. The July 19 edition of *Délmagyarország* and the August 13 editions of both *Pesti Napló* and *Pesti Hírlap* stated that the troupe presented additional plays in the town from August 14 through 17 with well-known actor Mihály Kiss as the guest artist. As of late August, Lugosi left the truope. On August 24, *Délmagyarország* announced that Lugosi had switched to the theatrical troupe at Szeged. The August 25 edition of the same publication announced that his debut performance in Szeged would be as Romeo.

***A sasfiók* (*The Eagle*)** (Rhymed Drama)
Opening Night: August 1.
Author: Edmond Rostand.
Role: Unknown
Note: Also known by the title ***L'Aiglon***. Actress Aranka Gazdy, Lugosi's co-star, suffered eye lacerations during the performance due to a shattered mirror.

Szeged (at the Szegedi Városi Színház [Szeged Municipal Theater] under the direction of Aranka Ábray)

Note: Lugosi's billing was generally "Béla Lugossy" during his residency in Szeged, but there were a few ads that listed him as "Lugosy."

***Rómeó és Júlia* (*Romeo and Juliet*)** (Tragedy)
Opening Night: September 2. Also staged on October 9.
Author: William Shakespeare.
Role: Romeo. The lead male role.
Review: "Last night, Béla Lugossy, a new member of the troupe, demonstrated his artistic talent in the role of Romeo, which will undboubtedly destine him as the permanent replacement for Mihály Kertész. The pleasant, handsome actor will certainly become one of the greats, judging by audience reaction to his performance." (*Mai Színlap* [Szeged, Hungary] 2 Sept. 1910).

Az aranyember (*The Golden Man*) (Drama)
Opening Night: September 4.
Author: Mór Jókai.
Role: Major Kadisa. A major supporting role.

On a double bill with:

Az ingyenélők (*The Parasites*) (Folk Play with Singing and Dancing)
Opening Night: September 4. Also staged on September 11.
Author: Pál Vidor.
Role: Pista Balog.

Az obsitos (*The Soldier on Leave*) (Operetta)
Opening Night: September 5. Also staged on September 6, 17, 23 and 25, October 4 and 11,
November 10, and December 7 and 8 (on a double bill with *A sasfiók* [*The Eagles*]).
Author: Kálmán and Bakonyi.
Role: Jóska.
Review: "… Felho, Nyári, I know they are your favorites… Laci Miho was also very cute. A
handsome boy. So is Lugosi. I like the new actors, anyway." (*Szeged és Vidéke* 6 Sept. 1910).

A kaméliás hölgy (*Lady of the Camellias*, aka *Camille*) (Drama)
Opening Night: September 7. Also staged on October 5.
Author: Alexander Dumas.
Role: Armand Duval.
Note: The theatrical magazine *Mai Színlap*, as well as a local newspaper, *Szeged és Vídéke*, listed
Lugosi as portraying Armand Duval for both dates. However, Szeged's *Színházi Újság* credited
Lugosi as portraying György Duval (George Duval).

A Dovolai nábob leánya (*The Daughter of the Nabob of Dolova*) (Drama)
Opening Night: September 8.
Author: Ferenc Herczeg.
Role: Lieutenant Loránt. A supporting role.

Az ördög (*The Devil*) (Drama)
Opening Night: September 9.
Author: Ferenc Molnár.
Role: János, a Painter. The lead role.
Note: The theatrical magazine *Színházi Újság* and the newspaper *Délmagyarország* list
Cygánybáró (*The Gypsy Baron*) without Lugosi as the play scheduled for that day. However, a
surviving playbill shows *Az ördög* with Lugosi as that day's production.

Review: "The other actors… did their best to make this celebratory play as perfect as possible. Despite that, they did not really succeed, but we might blame it on the lack of rehearsals. Lugossy played the role of the painter in a rather wooden manner." (*Délmagyarország* [Csongrád, Hungary] 16 Sept. 1910).

Taifun (Typhoon) (Drama)
Opening Night: September 10.
Author: Menyhért Lengyel.
Role: Ottó Lindner, an Author.

Bilincsek (Shackles) (Drama)
Opening Night: September 16. Also staged on September 24 and 26, and October 30.
Author: Hermann Reichenbach.
Role: Simon. A significant role.
Note: A surviving playbill gives September 10 as the opening night; other sources confirm this was an error. Opening night was in fact September 16.
Reviews: "Lugossy cleverly played the exiled military officer." (*Delmagyarorszag*, 17 Sept. 1910). "Béla Lugosy did his best to make the character of the apostle Simon acceptable." (*Szegedi Napló* 21 Sept. 1910).

A postás fiu és huga (The Mail Boy and His Sister) (Musical Farce)
Opening Night: September 18. Also staged on September 19, October 2 and 26, November 16, and December 31.
Author: Bernát Buchbinder.
Role: Dr. Emil Csipkés.

Amihez minden asszony ért (What Every Woman Knows) (Comedy)
Opening Night: September 20. Also staged on September 21 and November 17.
Author: J.M. Barrie.
Role: John Shand. A major role.
Reviews: "Lugossy played the role of John Shand skillfully and casually." (*Délmagyarország*, 21 Sept. 1910). "… [Almási] and Kende fought for Béla Lugosi. This was [his] first serious, great performance, and we ladies liked it very much. However, the gentlemen's opinion is that he is very stiff, sometimes staggering, and his speech is lifeless, but you know, men are always too critical." (*Szeged és Vidéke* 21 Sept. 1910).

A Szigetvári vértanúk (The Martyrs of Szigetvar) (Tragedy)
Opening Night: October 6. Also staged on November 1.
Author: Mór Jókai.
Role: Confidant Szelim. Based on contemporary reviews, a significant role.
Review: "Béla Lugossy, in the role of Szelim, conveyed the high intelligence and attested

austerity." (*Délmagyarország* 7 Oct. 1910).

A vasgyáros (*The Forge Master*) (Drama)
Opening Night: October 10.
Author: Georges Ohnet.
Role: Prince Blygny. A supporting role.

A kard becsülete (*The Honor of the Sword*) (Social Drama)
Opening Night: October 19. Also staged on October 20 and 27, and November 2 and 27.
Author: Antal Kazaliczky.
Role: Landowner Ernő Rozgonyi. Based on contemporary reviews, a significant role.
Review: "The success of Lugossy was well deserved, who acted the role of Rozgonyi nicely."
(*Mai Színlap* 20 Oct. 1910).

A csikós (*The Cowboy*) (Folk Play)
Opening Night: October 23. Also staged on November 20.
Author: Ede Szigligeti.
Role: Asztolf Ormódi. A supporting role.

A kormánybiztos (*The Government Commissioner*) (Musical Farce)
Opening Night: November 1. Also staged on November 11, 13, 14 and 21, and December 20.
Author: Soma Guthi.
Role: Assemblyman Viznemissza.
Note: The name of Lugosi's character has the literal meaning "the one who does not drink water."

Bánk Bán (*Bán Bánk*) (Drama)
Opening Night: November 12.
Author: Józef Katona.
Role: Ottó Berthold. A major supporting role.
Note: Lugosi was billed above the title and mentioned in the cast listing in *Színhazi Újság* for this major role. Curiously, a local newspaper, *Szeged és Vidéke*, listed Lugosi in a different role, that of "Egy zászlós ur" (An Ensign), with Jenő Janovics in the role of Otto. Prior to the performance, Lugosi recited a poem by Vilmos Sz. Szigethy entitled *Makó Lajos emléke* (*To the Spirit of Lajos Makó*) in honor of deceased producer-director Lajos Makó.

Az orvosok (*The Doctors*) (Satire)
Opening Night: Uncertain.
Author: George Bernard Shaw.
Role: Unknown.
Note: A local newspaper, *Szeged és Vídéke*, announced that Lugosi was to appear in this play during the week of November 13-19. However, no theater listings for that week confirm that the

play was actually staged.

A sasfiók (*The Eagle*) (Drama)
Opening Night: November 23. Also staged on November 24 and December 7 (on a double bill with *Az obsitos* [*The Soldier on Leave*]).
Author: Edmond Rostand.
Role: Frigyes Gentz. A supporting role.

A Balkáni hercegnő (*The Balkan Princess*) (Operetta)
Opening Night: November 25. Also staged on November 26 and 27, and December 11.
Author: Lonsdale and Curzon.
Role: Max Hein.

A balga szűz (*The Foolish Virgin*) (Drama)
Opening Night: November 30. Also staged on December 1, 2, 9 and 14.
Author: Henry Bataille.
Role: Gaston de Charance. A supporting role.
Note: *Szeged és Vídéke* announced an additional performance of this play scheduled for the week of November 13-19; however, no other supporting evidence is available to confirm it took place.

A gyerekasszony (*The Child-Woman*) (Folk Play)
Opening Night: December 6.
Author: József Bokor.
Role: Ferkó Selyem.
Note: Sometimes referred to simply as *Gyerekasszony*.

Egy szegény ifju története (*The Romance of a Poor Young Man*) (Drama)
Opening Night: December 12. Also staged on December 13, 24, and 25.
Author: Octave Feuillet.
Role: De Bevallan. A major supporting role.
Note: Some translations from the French list Lugosi's role as Bevannes rather than De Bevallan. It is the same role.

Karenin Anna (*Anna Karenina*) (Drama)
Opening Night: December 16. Also staged on December 17, 18 and 19.
Author: Guiraud and Tolstoy.
Role: Count Vronsky. The lead male role.
Note: Actor Sándor Góth was brought in as a special attraction and replaced Lugosi in the leading role for the December 27 and 29 performances. Lugosi was not included in the cast on those two days.
Review: "The rather passive role of Vronsky was played by Lugosi with qualities, but from time

to time a certain warmth came through in his recital, which was rather too fast instead of [with] suitable articulation." (*Szegedi Napló* 18 Dec. 1910).

III. Richard (***Richard III***) (Historical Drama)
Opening Night: December 20. Also staged on December 21.
Author: William Shakespeare.
Role: George, the Prince of Clarence. A small supporting role.

A czégér (***The Sign***) (Folk Play with Songs)
Opening Night: December 26.
Author: Ármin Balassa.
Role: Sibi, a Gypsy.
Note: The "sign" in the title refers to the wooden or metal board with the store name on it that hangs above the entryway.

1911
Szeged (at the Városi Színház [Municipal Theater])

Az obsitos (***The Soldier on Leave***) (Operetta)
Opening Night: January 1.
Author: Kálmán and Bakonyi.
Role: Jóska.

A Balkáni herczegnő (***The Balkan Princess***) (Operetta)
Opening Night: January 6.
Author: Lonsdale and Frank Curzon.
Role: Max Hein.

On a double bill with:

A czégér (***The Sign***) (Folk Play with Songs)
Opening Night: January 6. Also staged on January 29.
Author: Ármin Balassa.
Role: Sibi, a Gypsy.

A gyerekasszony (***The Child-Woman***) (Folk Play)
Opening Night: January 8.
Author: József Bokor.
Role: Ferkó Selyem.

On a double bill with:

*Naranczvirág (**Orange Blossom**)* (Musical Play in One Act)
Opening Night: January 8. Also staged on January 9 and 15.
Author: Imre Farkas.
Role: Sidney Clark, a Composer.

*III. Richard (**Richard III**)* (Historical Drama)
Opening Night: January 10.
Author: William Shakespeare.
Role: George, the Duke of Clarence. A small supporting role.

*Megúntam Margitot (**Tired of Margaret**)* (Comedy)
Opening Night: January 14. Also staged on January 16.
Author: Wolf and Corteline.
Role: Lavernie. Based on contemporary reviews, a significant role.
Review: "In the role of the painter, Lavernie, Béla Lugosi was quite likeable, but in the second act he barely knew his role, which would be a great mistake for experienced actors. His onstage speech is sometimes very difficult to understand. If he had more diligence, he would have turned out to be a fair actor." (*Délmagyarország* 15 Jan. 1911).

*A szent liget (**The Sacred Grove**)* (Comedy)
Opening Night: January 20. Also staged on January 21 and 22, February 1 and 3, and April 25.
Author: Flers and Caillaver.
Role: Count Zakuskin. A major role.
Review: "Lugossy plays the bizarre role of the Italian-Russian Count Zakuskin fairly, but with a strange Slovak accent...." (*Délmagyarország* 21 Jan. 1911).

*Karenin Anna (**Anna Karenina**)* (Drama)
Opening Night: January 26. Also staged on April 17 and May 23.
Author: Guiraud and Tolstoy.
Role: Count Vronsky. The lead male role.
Note: On an advertisement for the April 17 performance, Lugosi was credited as Béla Lugosy. The same is true of a May 23 playbill.

*Az ördög (**The Devil**)* (Drama)
Opening Night: February 1.
Author: Ferenc Molnár.
Role: Unknown.
Note: While no playbill is available, the Vasváry Collection, Somogyi Library, Szeged provided a working list of Lugosi performances, which included this production. The specific role was not identified. However, *Színházi Újság* indicates the play for that day was *A Szent Liget (**The Sacred** Grove)*, with Lugosi billed as Lugossy.

A postás fiu és huga (*The Mail Boy and His Sister*) (Musical Farce)
Opening Night: February 2. Also staged on February 26 and 28, and on April 18.
Author: Bernát Buchbinder.
Role: Dr. Emil Csipkés.
Note: The Vasváry Collection, Somogyi Library, Szeged provided a list that includes February 26 as one of the performance dates. However, *Színházi Újság* shows *A medikus* (*The Medic*) staged on that day. Following the February 28 performance, the Szegedi Városi Színház sponsored the annual **A Színház Bal (Theater Masked Ball)** during which the contracted actors, including Lugosi, appeared in various masks that disguised their identities.

A sárga liliom (*The Yellow Lily*) (Folk Play)
Opening Night: February 14. Also staged on February 15, 17 and 22, March 1, 11, 14 and 29, and April 16 and 29.
Author: Lajos Bíró.
Role: The Archduke. A leading role.
Note: In the audience for the March 14 performance was Imré Tóth, director of the Nemzeti Színház in Budapest.
Review: "Lugosi played his first truly suitable role today. His acting was of real quality. This man will probably go very far." (*Délmagyarország* 15 Feb. 1911).

A medikus (*The Medic*) (Drama)
Opening Night: February 25. Also staged on February 26 and 27, and on March 6.
Author: Sándor Bródy.
Role: János, the Medic. Based on contemporary reviews, a significant role.
Review: "Béla Lugosy lent a likeable tone to the figure of the doctor. His firm, clever and slightly virulent appearance was very suitable for the figure of John. He is a worthy artist for whom the many stage appearances are rather beneficial, since they provide him the opportunity of development." (*Szegedi Napló* 26 Feb. 1911).

Lotti ezredesei (*Lotti's Colonels*) (Musical Folk Play)
Opening Night: March 2. Also staged on March 7, and on April 19 and 30.
Author: Rudyard Stone.
Role: Ramanajah.
Review: "Only Béla Lugosy's skillful dances and the funny situations in Act 2 deserve special attention. Loud remarks from the actors and their average moodiness made the play hard to enjoy." (*Színházi Újság* 12 Mar. 1911).

A sasfiók (*The Eagle*) (Drama)
Opening Night: March 4. Also staged on March 19.
Author: Edmond Rostand.
Role: Frigyes Gentz. A supporting role.

Othelló (***Othello***) (Tragedy)
Opening Night: March 9.
Author: William Shakespeare.
Role: Cassio. A major supporting role.

A jómadarak (***The Scoundrels***) (Farce with Dancing Girls)
Opening Night: March 12. Also staged on March 13 and 26.
Author: Gusztáv Raeder.
Role: Sam Bandheim.
Note: The author Raeder commented about the production in a local newspaper, saying: "My little birds, fly to the stage and tweet, dance the coconut dance, the top hat dance, and if possible, dance the pantskirt dance, too, and even do the Lugossy-Lendvay jump and curse in the meantime." (*Szegedi Napló* 12 Mar. 1911). The meaning of his satirical comment is unfortunately lost in translation.

Independence Day Celebration
Opening Day: March 14 at the Klauzál Square in Szeged.
Role: Lugosi gave a speech in support of the ceremony celebrating the Hungarian Revolution of 1848.

Az aranylakodalom (***The Golden Wedding***) (Tragedy)
Opening Night: March 15.
Author: Beöthy and Rákosi.
Roles: Stanislav Lubomirzki and a Law Student.

Robin Orvos (***Dr. Robin***) (Comedy in One Act)
Opening Night: March 16. Also staged on March 17 and May 5.
Author: Gyula Remaray.
Role: Arthur Mallam.

A becstelen (***The Ignominious***) (Drama)
Opening Night: March 18. Also staged on March 30 and 31, and on April 1, 11, 12 and 20.
Author: Andor Garvay.
Role: László Kápolnay. Based on contemporary reviews, a significant role.
Reviews: "Béla Lugosy acted the grotesque role of the husband in a rather tired way, lacking vim and leaving no impression." (*Színházi Újság* 23 Apr. 1911). "The great endeavors were blocked by errors. For example, although the small room of the representative (Lugosi) is stacked with furniture, Lugosi walks up and down in a desparate speed. Would he walk that way in an overfurnished room?" (*Délmagyarország* 12 Apr. 1911). "Béla Lugsy [*sic*] played the role of Kápolnay. His comprehension of the character was shown here and there, but his character was lacking the loose will of the weak-kneed husband." (*Szegedi Napló* 12 Apr. 1911).

A tolvaj (*The Thief*) (Drama)
Opening Night: March 23.
Author: Henri Bernstein.
Role: Fernande Lagardes. A supporting role.
Review: "Béla Lugosy managed to give meaning to the role of Fernande. He used the right voice/tonality and his speech was calm and smart." (*Szegedi Napló* 24 Mar. 1911).

Az Erddélyi-jubileum (The Transylvanian Jubilee)
Opening Night: March 25 at the Kass Café.
Role: Presenter of the theater company laurel.
Note: Lugosi participated in this celebration of Transylvania along with the mayor of Szeged and other artists, journalists and dignitaries.

A víg özvegy (*The Merry Widow*) (Operetta)
Opening Night: March 30.
Author: Franz Lehár.
Role: Count Danilo Danilovics. A major role.

Hamlet (Tragedy)
Opening Night: March 31.
Author: William Shakespeare.
Role: Laertes. A supporting role.

A makrancos hölgy (*The Taming of the Shrew*) (Comedy)
Opening Night: April 2.
Author: William Shakespeare.
Role: Lucentio. A supporting role.

A kaméliás hölgy (*Lady of the Camellias*, aka *Camille*) (Drama)
Opening Night: April 3.
Author: Alexander Dumas.
Role: Armand Duval. A leading role.
Note: The theatrical magazine *Színházi Újság* lists Lugosi's role as György Duval (George Duval); however, the playbill shows him in the leading role of Armand Duval.

A balga szűz (*The Foolish Virgin*) (Drama)
Opening Night: April 4.
Author: Henry Bataille.
Role: Gaston de Charance. A supporting role.

*A boszorkány (**The Sorceress**)* (Drama)
Opening Night: April 5.
Author: Victorien Sardou.
Role: Don Enrique de Palacios. A major role.

*Viola, az alfoldi haramia (**Viola, the Lowland Highwayman**)* (Folk Play)
Opening Night: April 10. Also staged on April 23 (on a double bill with *Délibáb [**The Mirage**]*).
Author: József Szigeti.
Role: Ákos, a Son.

*Délibáb (**aka Fata Morgana** or **The Mirage**)* (Operetta)
Opening Night: April 21. Also staged on April 22, 23 and 28.
Author: Sümegi and Kun.
Role: Béla Pomándy, a Journalist.

*A kivándorló (**The Emmigrant**)* (Drama)
Opening Night: April 27.
Author: Ferenc Herczeg.
Role: Baron Szentgróthy.

*Elnémult harangok (**Silent Bells**)* (Comedy)
Opening Night: April 30.
Author: Rákosi and Malonyay.
Role: Pál Simandy, a Presbyterian minister. A leading role.
Note: In a guest appearance, the famous Hungarian actor Gyula Gál played one of the leading roles. This play was sometimes referred to as *Az elnémult harangok*.

*A botrány (**Scandal**)* (Drama)
Opening Night: May 2.
Author: Henry Bataille.
Role: Artanezzo.

*Bábjáték (**Puppet Show**)* (Comedy)
Opening Night: May 3. Also staged on May 4.
Author: Pierre Wolff.
Role: Marquis Roger de Monclars. A major role.
Review: "Lugossy [stays true to the character] many times, but he very often falls out of character." (*Délmagyarország* 4 May 1911). One advertisement referred to this performance as *A bábjáték*.

*A sárga csikó (**The Yellow Colt**)* (Folk Play)
Opening Night: May 7.

Author: Ferenc Csepreghy.
Role: Peti. A small supporting role.

Trilby (Drama)
Opening Night: May 8.
Author: Potter and Du Maurier.
Role: Prince Rochemartel.

A tanítónő (***The Lady Teacher***) (Folk Play)
Opening Night: May 9.
Author: Sándor Bródy.
Role: The Sheriff. A supporting role.

Az államtitkár úr (***The Secretary of State***) (Comedy)
Opening Night: May 10.
Author: Alexandre Bisson.
Role: Lambertin.

Liszt Ferenc születésének centenáriumi (Franz Liszt Birth Centennial)
Opening Night: May 13.
Author: Various works by Franz Liszt.
Role: Narrator of the Prologue.
Note: For this celebration, Lugosi presented a prologue narration. Along with a variety of other performers, Béla Bartók appeared on the bill and played a selection of Liszt works on the piano.

A zseni (***The Genius***) (Tragic Comedy)
Opening Night: May 14. Also staged on May 15.
Author: Endre Nagy.
Role: Rudolf.
Reviews: "Lugosi was great in the title role. Some of the many actors in the play were more, others were less, successful." (*Délmagyarország* 16 May 1911). "The title role of the play by Endre Nagy is being played by Lugosy. This is a bad choice, since we know that the director is the *genius* of the company." (*Szegedi Napló* 14 May 1911).

A Sabin nők elrablása (***The Rape of the Sabine Women***) (Comedy)
Opening Night: May 17.
Author: Franz and Paul von Schönthan.
Role: Dr. Béla Szilvássy.

Anatol (Drama)
Opening Night: May 20. Also staged on May 21.

Author: Arthur Schnitzler.

Role: Max. One of the leading roles.

Note: Lugosi received top billing, again as Béla Lugossy, in the *Színházi Újság* theater magazine as well as on playbills for this major role. This was his farewell performance in Szeged.

Gyula (Summer Theater at the Gyulai Erkel Ferenc Színkör [Ferenc Erkel Theater Circle in Gyula])

Note: With few exceptions, Lugosi was credited as "Lugossy" in Gyula.

A postás fiu és huga (*The Mail Boy and His Sister*) (Musical Farce)

Opening Night: May 22.

Author: Bernát Buchbinder.

Role: Dr. Emil Csipkés. Based on contemporary reviews, a small role.

Review: "Lugossy did not have an important role this time." (*Békés* 28 May 1911).

Karenin Anna (*Anna Karenina*) (Drama)

Opening Night: May 23 and June 30.

Author: Guiraud and Tolstoy.

Role: Count Vronsky.

Note: The June 30 performance was likely Lugosi's final role in Gyula.

Review: "The appearance of Béla Lugossy almost predestines him for the roles of the heroic lover, while his temperament makes him suitable for intelligent, serious acting. In Anna Karenina he personified Count Vronsky, the noble cavalryman, in an excellent way. His acting reveals talent, which, in full growth, will provide him with a bright future." (*Békés* 28 May 1911).

A kaméliás hölgy (*Lady of the Camellias*, aka *Camille*) (Drama)

Opening Night: May 24 (replaced *Bilincsek* on the schedule). Also staged on May 27.

Author: Alexander Dumas.

Role: Armand Duval. Leading male role.

A gyerekasszony (*The Child-Woman*) (Folk Play)

Opening Night: May 28.

Author: József Bokor.

Role: Selyem Fenkó, Infantry Sergeant (credited as Lugosy).

Narancsvirág (*Orange Blossom*) (Operetta)

Opening Night: May 29.

Author: Imre Farkas.

Role: Sidney Clark.

Review: "Lugosi was great in the role of the composer Sidney Clark." (*Békés* 4 June 1911).

*A zseni (**The Genius**)* (Tragic Comedy)
Opening Night: May 31.
Author: Endre Nagy.
Role: Rudolf.
Review: "Lugosy played the role of the unbearable composer in such a great way as if the role was written especially for him." (*Békés* 4 June 1911).

*A medikus (**The Medic**)* (Drama)
Opening Night: June 3.
Author: Sándor Bródy.
Role: János, the Medic. This was the title role.
Review: "Béla Lugossy personified the self-struggling medician apathetically and coldly, an acting style that suited the role well…." (*Békés* 11 June 1911).

*A sárga csikó (**The Yellow Colt**)* (Folk Play with Songs)
Opening Night: June 4.
Author: Ferenc Csopreghy.
Role: Peti, a Son. A small supporting role.
Note: Credited as Lugosi.

*A kormánybiztos (**The Government Commissioner**)* (Musical Farce)
Opening Night: June 6.
Author: Soma Guthi.
Role: Assemblyman Viznemissza.
Review: "Lugosy played the role of the representative in an exhilarating way." (*Békés* 11 June 1911).

*A Balkáni hercegnő (**The Balkan Princess**)* (Operetta)
Opening Night: June 8.
Author: Lonsdale and Curzon.
Role: Max Hein.
Review: "Despite his calm temperament, Lugosy played the role of the false prince enjoyably." (*Békés* 11 June 1911).

*A balga szűz (**The Foolish Virgin**)* (Drama)
Opening Night: June 9.
Author: Henry Bataille.
Role: Gaston de Charance. A supporting role.

*Lotti ezredesei (**Lottie's Colonels**)* (Musical Folk Play)

Opening Night: June 13.
Author: Rudyard Stone.
Role: Ramajanah, a Rajah.

A csikós (*The Cowboy*) (Musical Folk Play)
Opening Night: June 15.
Author: Ede Szigligeti.
Role: Asztolf Ormódi. A supporting role.

On a double bill with:

A sárga liliom (*The Yellow Lily*) (Folk Play)
Opening Night: June 15.
Author: Lajos Bíró.
Role: The Archduke.
Review: "Tonight, Béla Lugossy played the role of the high prince, which was very suitable for his character, and which he played in an excellent way. His appearance, his gestures were most elegant, thus creating a perfect illusion." (*Békés* 18 June 1911).

Othelló (*Othello*) (Tragedy)
Opening Night: June 17.
Author: William Shakespeare.
Role: Cassio. A major supporting role.

A szent liget (*The Sacred Grove*) (Comedy)
Opening Night: June 20.
Author: Flers and Caillavet.
Role: Count Zakonskine. A major role.
Review: "Lugossy's acting was full of life and skills in the role of the Count." (*Békés* 25 June 1911).

A becstelen (*The Ignominious*) (Drama)
Opening Night: June 23.
Author: Andor Garvay.
Role: László Kápolnay.
Review: "Lugossy … acted with care, and with diligent studies he will become perfectly suitable for complicated roles such as this one." (*Békés* 25 June 1911).

Viola (Drama)
Opening Night: June 25.
Author: József Szigeti.

Role: Ákos
Note: Credited as Lugosy.

*A kis szökevény (**The Little Fugitive**)* (Operetta)
Opening Night: June 26.
Author: Seymour Hicks and Harry Nichols.
Role: Unknown.

*Bábjáték (**Puppet Show**)* (Comedy)
Opening Night: June 27.
Author: Pierre Wolff.
Role: Roger de Monclans. A major role.
Note: Lugosi (credited as Béla Lugossy) was billed above the title on playbills.

*A jómadarak (**The Scoundrels**)* (Musical Farce)
Opening Night: June 29.
Author: Gusztáv Raeder.
Role: Sam Bandheim, a Manager.

The summer season in Gyula reportedly ended on July 2.

Sopron

The September 23-30 issue of *Szíházi Élet* reported that Lugosi had acted in the Hungarian town of Sopron prior to moving to the Budapest. No other known primary sources confirm this report.

Budapest

The August 15 edition of *Pesti Napló* announced that Lugosi signed a contract with the Magyar Színház (Hungarian Theater) in Budapest, founded by Szidi Rákosi and administered by her son László Beöthy. The announcement gave his name as Dezső Lugosi, a stage name that he was no longer using at the time. Some biographers have claimed that Lugosi attended Rákosi's acting academy, either just prior to September of 1911 or earlier in his career. However, the only known reference to a Lugosi at Rákosi's academy was Jenő Lugosi, an actor, comedian and vocalist, who attended between early 1905 and early 1907. It seems previous biographers have simply confused Jenő Lugosi and Béla Lugosi in this regard.

Magyar Színház (Hungarian Theater) (under the direction of László Beöthy unless otherwise noted)

*Karenin Anna (**Anna Karenina**)* (Drama)
Opening Night: September 3. Also staged on September 7, 8, 13, 17 and 24, October 8 (on

a double bill with *Az élet szava* [*The Call of Life*]), 9, 25 and 26, November 2 and 19, and December 10.

Author: Guiraud and Tolstoy.

Role: Count Vronsky. A leading male role.

Note: Mihály Kertész (Michael Curtiz) was in the cast as well.

Review: "Another interesting aspect of tonight's performance was the new [Count Vronsky]: Béla Lugosi, who arrived … a couple of months ago, after leaving Szeged where he had made a great success … the audience greeted him in a warm and friendly way, which he very much deserved." (*Az Újság* [Budapest, Hungary] 1 Nov. 1911). "Lugosi, an actor from Szeged, debuted in the role of Count Vronsky; a tall man with a pleasing voice; a nice, blank canvas, which can be easily turned into something valuable by the director." (*Pesti Hírlap* [Budapest, Hungary] 5 Sept. 1911).

A sárga liliom (*The Yellow Lily*) (Folk Play)

Opening Night: September 18. Also staged on September 20, 22, 26 and 30, October 5, 11, 17 and 28, and November 7, 9 and 25.

Author: Lajos Bíró.

Role: Asztalos Kálmán, a Lawyer, until November 25 when the role changed to the Archduke.

Note: Staged on September 6 and 14 with Mihály Kertész (Michael Curtiz) in the role of Kálmán. Lugosi took over the role of Kálmán on September 18. There is some uncertainty as to Lugosi's involvement on November 9. One source indicated that Kertész substituted as Kálmán on November 9 as well as on the November 19 when the play was on a double bill with *Karenin Anna* (*Anna Karenina*). However, *Budapesti Hírlap* claims Lugosi played Kálmán on November 9. By contrast, *Pesti Napló* advertised an actor named Törza in the role. Then, for reasons unknown, Lugosi played the Archduke instead of Kálman on November 25.

Az élet szava (*The Call of Life*) (Drama)

Opening Night: October 7. Also staged on October 8 (on a double bill with *Karenin Anna* [*Anna Karenina*]), 9, 12, 14, 19, 20 and 29.

Author: Arthur Schnitzler.

Role: Max, a Young Officer. A supporting role.

Review: "Two new actors were introduced, Mária Simonyi and Lugosi, both of them promising young talents." (*Világ* [Budapest, Hungary] 8 Oct. 1911).

1912

Budapest (at the Magyar Színház [Hungarian Theater], under the supervision of László Beöthy with Imré Tóth as theater director unless otherwise noted)

Karenin Anna (*Anna Karenina*) (Drama)

Opening Night: January 7. Also staged on April 14, June 2, August 22, and September 1, 11, 12 and 29.

Author: Guiraud and Tolstoy.
Role: Count Vronsky. The leading male role.

A gésák (*The Geisha*) (Operetta)

Opening Night: April 12 at the Király Színház (Royal Theater). Also staged daily from April 13 through 30, daily from May 1 through 13, May 15, 17, 19, 22 and 26, and daily from June 3 through 11 (at the Magyar Színház). After moving to the Király Színház, staged from June 12 through 15, from 17 through 19, from 24 through 30, and August 24, 27, 29 and 30, and September 1, 3 and 22.
Author: Owen Hall.
Role: Reginald Fairfax, a Navy Lieutenant. The leading male role.

A sárga liliom (*The Yellow Lily*) (Folk Play)

Opening Night: September 5.
Author: Lajos Bíró.
Role: The Archduke.

Föiskolai hallgatók társasága (College Students Society)

Opening Night: November 9 at Westend-kávéház (Westend Coffeehouse).
Role: Guest artist.
Note: The *Budapesti Hírlap* edition of November 9 announced that, "the Society of College Students will hold an artsy night with dancing, at 9 o'clock… at the underground halls of the Café Westend… Klára Küry, Gizella Báthory, Frigyes Tanay, Károly Ferenczy, Sándor Horthy and Béla Lugosi will perform, among others."

Jezus élete, szenvedése és halála (aka *A passziójáték*) (*The Life of Jesus – Suffering and Death, aka The Passion*) (Historical Drama)

Opening Night: December 21 at the Budapesti Színház (Budapest Theater). Also staged daily from December 22 through 31.
Author: Father Hildebrand.
Role: Jesus Christ. The lead role.

1913

Budapest (at the Nemzeti Színház [National Theater], under the direction of Imré Tóth unless otherwise noted)

Jezus élete, szenvedése és halála (aka *A passziójáték*) (*The Life of Jesus – Suffering and Death, aka The Passion*) (Historical Drama)

Opening Night: January 1 at the Budapesti Színház (Budapest Theater). Also staged daily from January 2 through 18, as well as on January 26 and February 2.
Author: Father Hildebrand.

Role: Jesus Christ. The lead role.

A vasgyáros (***The Forge Master***) (Drama)
Opening Night: January 5 (afternoon matinee). Also staged on February 9 and 25, March 24, May 12 and 24, September 14, October 10, and November 23.
Author: Georges Ohnet.
Role: Pontac. Minor supporting role.

Az ember trajédiája (***The Tragedy of Man***) (Poetic Drama)
Opening Night: January 6 (as Catulus). Also staged on January 20, February 9, March 5 (role changed to Plato), 21 (Catulus, Plato and the Marquis from this date forward) and 23, April 13 and 23, May 11, June 13, September 17 and 28, October 14 and 27, and November 9.
Author: Imre Madách.
Roles: Catulus (small supporting role), Plato (minor role), and the Marquis (minor role).
Note: From March 21 onward, Lugosi played three different roles during each performance.

Mary-Ann (Comedy)
Opening Night: February 1 at the Várszínház (Palace Theater). Also staged on February 4 and 16 at the Nemzeti Színház (National Theater).
Author: Israel Zangwill.
Role: O'Gorman, a Journalist. Minor supporting role.

Cyrano de Bergerac (Historical Romance)
Opening Night: February 3. Also staged on May 5 and 18.
Author: Edmond Rostand. Based on the work by Cervantes.
Role: The Second Marquis. Minor supporting role.

Stuart Máriá (***Mary Stuart***) (Historical Tragedy)
Opening Night: February 7 at the Várszínház (Palace Theater). Also staged at the Magyar Színház (Hungarian Theater) on February 19, September 10, and December 15.
Author: Friedrich Schiller.
Role: Count Belliévre. A supporting role.

III. Richard (***Richard III***) (Historical Drama)
Opening Night: February 10.
Author: Shakespeare.
Role: Sir Walter Herbert. Minor supporting role.

Cézár és Kleopátra (***Caesar and Cleopatra***) (Drama)
Opening Night: February 21. Also staged on February 22, 23, 26 and 28, March 2, and at the Várszínház (Palace Theater) on March 19.

Author: George Bernard Shaw.

Role: Achillas, an Egyptian Commander. Minor supporting role.

Review: "As new characters, Béla Lugosi and József Pataki also appeared, rather pleasingly. The whole performance was enjoyable, and it suited the intentions of the play." (*Budapesti Hírlap* 22 Feb. 1913).

Az aranyember (*The Golden Man*) (Drama)

Opening Night: March 3. Also staged on March 30, June 5, September 11, and October 5.

Author: Mór Jókai.

Role: Major Kadisa. A major supporting role.

A szentivánéji álom (*A Midsummer Night's Dream*) (Comedy)

Opening Night: March 4.

Author: William Shakespeare.

Role: Demetrius. A supporting role.

Tartuffe (Comedy)

Opening Night: March 8 at the Várszínház (Palace Theater). Also staged on March 10 at the Nemzeti Színház (National Theater).

Author: Molière.

Role: Valère, Mariane's lover. A supporting role.

Review: "Lugosi, who played the role of Valère, has a lovely figure fitting for the stage and an equally lovely voice. The strongest point of Molière's comedy is the giant, almost fearful impersonator of Tartuffe." (*Budapesti Hírlap* 11 Mar. 1913).

II. Rákóczi Ferencz fogsága (*Francis Rákoczi II in Captivity*) (Historical Drama)

Opening Night: March 15. Also staged September 1.

Author: Ede Szigligeti.

Role: Solári, the Commander of Castle Sarospatak. A minor supporting role.

A boszorkány (*The Sorceress*) (Drama)

Opening Night: March 16. Also staged on March 26, May 19, and October 11.

Author: Victorien Sardou.

Role: Fray Eugenio Calabazas. A small supporting role.

Hamlet (Tragedy)

Opening Night: March 17. Also staged on November 14.

Author: Shakespeare.

Role: Rosenkranz. A supporting role.

A fáklyák (*The Torches*) (Drama)

Opening Night: March 28. Also staged on March 29, 30 and 31 (at the Várszínház (Palace Theater) on this date), April 2, 4, 6, 10 and 19 and May 25.

Author: Henry Bataille.

Role: Hervé, a Taxidermist.

Note: Some playbills listed the character's name as Hedvé. According to a contemporary review, Lugosi had a small role.

Review: "From those with minor roles, Bartos, Lugosi and Gizella Rosos earned recognition through a couple of characteristic words or movements." (*Budapesti Hírlap* 29 Mar. 1913).

Bizánc (Byzantium) (Drama)

Opening Night: April 8.

Author: Ferenc Herczeg.

Role: Folko, a Mercenary from Genoa. A minor supporting role.

Drághy Éva esküje (The Oath of Eva Dragby) (Drama)

Opening Night: April 14.

Author: Gyula Pekár.

Role: Farkas Weér.

A fogadott apa (The Adopted Father) (Comedy)

Opening Night: May 2. Also staged May 3, 4, 6, 11 and 14.

Author: Félix Duquesnel and André Barde.

Role: Gilbert Rivers.

Review: "Lugosi, the new member of the Nemzeti Színház [National Theater] is still immature and slightly provincial. It might have been caused by stage fright or by the role he played but based on this production we cannot predict his future yet." (*Népszava* [Budapest, Hungary] 3 May 1913).

Hernani (Drama)

Opening Night: May 8. Also staged on May 9 and 13, June 6, and October 7 (at the Várszínház [Palace Theater]) and 13.

Author: Victor Hugo.

Role: Courtier Don Sancho. A minor role.

A kegyenc (The Favorite) (Tragedy)

Opening Night: May 16. Also staged on May 18 and 21.

Author: László Teleki.

Role: Senator Marcus. A minor supporting role.

Fauszt (Faust) (Tragedy)

Opening Night: May 22. Also staged on May 23, June 8 and 9, and October 6.

Author: Goethe.

Roles: Michael the Archangel and the First Student. Both are minor roles.

Note: Lugosi appeared in two supporting roles for the entire run of the production, the role of the First Student being the larger of the two.

Endre és Johanna (*Andrew and Joanna*) (Historical Tragedy)

Opening Night: May 28. Also staged on June 1 and October 19.

Author: Jenő Rákosi.

Role: Melazzo. A minor role.

A kaméliás hölgy (*Lady of the Camellias*, aka *Camille*) (Drama)

Opening Night: June 3.

Author: Alexander Dumas.

Role: Varville. A supporting role.

The regular season for the Nemzeti Színház (National Theater) ended on June 16. It is possible that Lugosi appeared in regional summer theater from approximately the middle of June through mid-to-late August, but no evidence has yet surfaced.

Viola (Drama)

Opening Night: September 13. Also staged on September 14, 15, 18, 23 and 26, and October 15 (at the Várszínház [Palace Theater]) and 26.

Author: József Szigeti.

Role: A Liveried Attendant. Reviews indicate this was a small role.

Note: The performance celebrated the centennial of the birth of Baron József Eötvüs.

Bolondok tánca (*Dance of the Fools*) (Comedy)

Opening Night: September 19. Also staged on September 20, 21, 24, 27 and 30.

Author: Leo Birinszki.

Role: Malakov, a Revolutionary.

Note: According to a contemporary publicity piece, Lugosi played "one of the main roles."

Lear király (*King Lear*) (Tragedy)

Opening Night: September 29.

Author: Shakespeare.

Role: A Knight. A minor role.

Az utolsó nap (*The Last Day*) (Drama)

Opening Night: October 3. Also staged on October 4, 5, 8, 26, 29 and 30, and November 2, 5, 7, 11 and 18.

Author: Béla Balázs.

Role: La Spagna, a Painter. Newspaper publicity articles indicate that Lugosi's role was a small one.

Hónapos szoba (*The Monthly Room*) (Comedy)

Opening Night: October 4 at the Vigszínház (Comedy Theater). Also staged on October 10 and 17.

Author: Imre Farkas.

Role: Krajnay.

Note: There is some doubt as to whether it was Béla Lugosi or some other Lugosi (such as Jenő Lugosi or Daniel Lugossy) in this production. Advertisements of the time definitely show "Lugosi" in the role of Krajnay. While it was not unusual for actors to occasionally appear in two different productions on the same day, even at two different theaters, it usually involved plays with at least two different curtain times. In this case, on October 4 and 10, the curtain time was 8 p.m. for both productions. As a result, it is uncertain as to whether Béla Lugosi appeared in both of them.

Az attaché (*The Ambassador's Attaché*) (Comedy)

Opening Night: October 23 at the Várszínház (Palace Theater). Also staged at the Nemzeti Színház (National Theater) on October 28 and November 5, 7, 11 and 15.

Author: Henri Meilhac.

Role: Lucien de Meré. A major role.

A konventbiztos (*The Convention Commissar*) (Drama)

Opening Night: October 24. Also staged on October 25, 26, 29 and 30, and November 2, 5, 7, 9, 11, 18 and 19 (at the Várszínház [Palace Theater]) and December 2 (at the Nemzeti Színház (National Theater).

Author: Pál Farkas.

Role: A Military Lieutenant. Based on newspaper reviews, this was likely a small role.

Essex Gróf (*Count Essex*) (Comedy)

Opening Night: November 8 at the Várszínház (Palace Theater). Also staged on November 17.

Author: Heinrich Laube.

Role: Count Southhampton. A supporting role.

Mária Antónia (*Marie Antoinette*) (Historical Drama)

Opening Night: November 21. Also staged on November 22 through 24, 26, 28 and 30, and December 3, 5, 7, 8, 10, 11, 13, 14, 16, 17, 25, 27 and 29.

Author: Dezső Szomory.

Roles: Breteuille and Saint Priest.

Note: Lugosi performed in two small supporting roles for the entire run of the production.

*Az egyszeri királyfi (**The One-Time Prince**)* (Drama)
Opening Night: December 19. Also staged on December 20, 21, 26, 28 and 30.
Author: Ernő Szép.
Role: A Cowboy.
Note: Some sources describe this play as a "tragic comedy." One review singled out Lugosi and a few other actors "for recognition" in some of the smaller roles.

Monna Vanna (Drama)
Opening Night: December 22.
Author: Maurice Maeterlinck.
Role: Vedio, Prinzivalle's Secretary. A small supporting role.

*Karácsonyi álom (**Christmas Dream**)* (Bethlehem Play)
Opening Night: December 23. Also staged on December 25.
Author: Géza Gárdonyi.
Role: The First Actor.
Note: Lugosi's role was featured in a prologue. Given that the published version of the play does not include a prologue, it may have been written for this particular production.

1914

Budapest (at the Nemzeti Színház [National Theater], under the direction of Imré Tóth unless otherwise noted)

*Éva boszorkány (**Eve, the Sorceress**)* (Comedy)
Opening Night: January 1. Also staged on January 7, February 14 (at the Várszínház (Palace Theater) and 22, and May 8.
Author: Ferenc Herczeg.
Role: Mr. Enzio.

*Az ember trajédiája (**The Tragedy of Man**)* (Poetic Drama)
Opening Night: January 1 (continuing in the three roles of Catulus, Plato and the Marquis). Also staged on February 15, March 1 and 29, April 9, May 1 and 10, and June 16.
Author: Imre Madách.
Roles: Catulus (small supporting role), Plato (minor role), and the Marquis (minor role).

*Mária Antónia (**Marie Antoinette**)* (Historical Drama)
Opening Night: January 2 (continuing in the roles of Breteuille and Saint Priest). Also staged on January 6, 8, 11, 14, 21, 23 and 26, February 3, 13, and 19, March 2, 15, April 7 and 28, May 6, and June 2 and 6.
Author: Dezső Szomory.
Roles: Breteuille and Saint Priest. Small supporting roles.

A fogadott apa (**The Adopted Father**) (Comedy)
Opening Night: January 3 at the Várszínház (Palace Theater). Also staged on January 11 at the Nemzeti Színház (National Theater).
Author: Mór Jókai.
Role: Gilbert Rivers.

A konventbiztos (**The Convention Commissar**) (Drama)
Opening Night: January 4. Also staged on January 28.
Author: Pál Farkas.
Role: Militiaman.

On a double bill with:

Az egyszeri királyfi (**The One-Time Prince**) (Drama)
Opening Night: January 4. Also staged on January 9, 13, 19 and 24, and February 4 (at the Várszínház [Palace Theater]) and 8.
Author: Ernő Szép.
Role: A Cowboy.

Bolondok tánca (**Dance of the Fools**) (Tragic Comedy)
Opening Night: January 5 at the Várszínház (Palace Theater).
Author: Leo Birinszki.
Role: Malakov, a Revolutionary. One of the "main roles" according to a review.

Matyó lakodalom (**The Wedding at the Matyo's**) (Folk Play)
Opening Night: January 16. Also staged on January 17, 18, 20, 22, 25, 26, 27 and 29, February 2, 11, 17, 26 and 28, March 4, 12 and 18, April 12, and May 18.
Author: Sándor Garamszeghy.
Role: Pesta, the Best Man. Based on newspaper reviews, this was likely a small role.

Az aranyember (**The Golden Man**) (Drama)
Opening Night: January 24. Also staged on January 12, 14 and 25, February 4 (at the Várszínház (Palace Theater), March 27, and May 11 and 12.
Author: Mór Jókai.
Role: Major Kadisa. A major supporting role.
Note: The play was staged on January 5. On that date, Béla Náday filled the role of Major Kadisa rather than Lugosi, who did not appear in any role in the first performance.

Macbeth (Tragedy)
Opening Night: January 30. Also staged on January 31, and February 1, 9 and 23.

Author: William Shakespeare.
Role: Angus. A minor role.

A kölcsönkért kastély (*The Borrowed Residence*) (Comedy)
Opening Night: February 6. Also staged on February 7, 8, 10, 12, 15, 16 (at the Várszínház [Palace Theater]), 18, 26 and 28, March 6, 10, 19, 24 and 26, April 10, 12 and 26, and May 19.
Author: Gyula Pekár.
Role: Clausevitz. Publicity articles indicate this was likely a small role.

Aesopus (*Aesop*) (Comedy)
Opening Night: February 20 at the Várszínház (Palace Theater).
Author: Jenő Rákosi.
Role: Dorsus. A small supporting role.

A nők barátja (*The Friend of Women*) (Comedy)
Opening Night: February 24. Also staged on February 27 (at the Várszínház [Palace Theater]) and March 3, 13, 22 and 31, and April 24.
Author: Alexander Dumas.
Role: De Montégre. A major role.
Note: This is the Hungarian version of *L'Ami des femmes* (**1864**).

Fenn az ernyő nincsen kas (*The Tent is Up, but There is No Basket*) (Comedy)
Opening Night: March 7. Also staged on March 11 (at the Várszínház [Palace Theater]).
Author: Ede Szigligeti.
Role: Baron Várkovy. A major role.
Review: "… the youthful charm, the cheerful shallowness of Dezső, and the seriousness of Lugosi made an excellent ensemble, which did not let our attention loose, not even for a moment." (*Budapesti Hírlap* 8 Mar. 1914).

Liliomfi (Comedy)
Opening Night: March 9. Also staged on March 15 and 24, and on April 21.
Author: Ede Szigligeti.
Role: Uracs. A minor role.

Az igazgató úr (*The Headmaster*) (Family Comedy)
Opening Night: March 20. Also staged on March 21, 22, 25, 28 and 30 (at the Várszínház [Palace Theater]).
Author: Edward Knoblock and Wilfred T. Coleby.
Role: Jack Strahan, a Teacher. A major role.
Review: "Lugosi was very sympathetic and intelligent as Strahan." (*Pesti Hírlap* 21 Mar. 1914).

*Lear király (**King Lear**)* (Tragedy)
Opening Night: March 23.
Author: William Shakespeare.
Role: A knight. A minor role.

*Az attaché (**The Ambassador's Attaché**)* (Comedy)
Opening Night: April 1.
Author: Henri Meilhac.
Role: Lucien de Meré. A major supporting role.

*Egy karrier története (**The Story of a Career**)* (Comedy)
Opening Night: April 3. Also staged on April 5, 8, 11, 13, 17, 19 and 23, and May 2, 7, 13, 28 and 30.
Author: József Pakots.
Roles: A Department Counselor (a small role) and Count Nyárády (beginning with April 5).

*III. Richard (**Richard III**)* (Historical Drama)
Opening Night: April 6.
Author: William Shakespeare.
Role: Sir Walter Herbert. A minor role.

*A vasgyáros (**The Forge Master**)* (Drama)
Opening Night: April 13.
Author: Georges Ohnet.
Role: Baron Préfont. A supporting role.

*János király (**King John**)* (Historical Drama)
Opening Night: April 27.
Author: Shakespeare.
Role: Limoges, the Duke of Austria. A small supporting role.

Julius Caesar (Historical Tragedy)
Opening Night: May 4. Also staged on May 11.
Author: Shakespeare.
Role: Cinna. A small supporting role.

*A trónkövetelők (**The Pretenders**)* (Historical Drama)
Opening Night: May 15. Also staged on May 16, 17, 20, 24 and 27.
Author: Ibsen.
Role: Pál Flida, a Nobleman. A small role according to contemporary newspaper reviews.

II. Rákóczi Ferencz fogsága (Francis Rakoczi II in Captivity) (Historical Drama)
Opening Night: May 18.
Author: Ede Szigligeti.
Role: Solari, the Commander of Castle Sarospatak. A minor role.

A bethuliai zsidónő (The Jewish Woman) (Ballet)
Opening Night: May 20 at the Magyar Királya Operahaz (Hungarian Royal Operahouse). Also staged on May 21, 24, 27 and 29.
Author: Mozart.
Role: Holofernes. Contemporary reviews imply this was a major role.
Note: There is no evidence that Lugosi danced in this ballet. He portrayed a dramatic character within the context of the story.

Cyrano de Bergerac (Historical Romance)
Opening Night: May 22. Also staged on May 25 and June 6.
Author: Edmond Rostand. Based on the work by Cervantes.
Role: Second Actor. A minor role with only one line of dialogue.

Monna Vanna (Drama)
Opening Night: May 26.
Author: Maurice Maeterlinck.
Role: Vedio, Prinzivalle's Secretary. A small supporting role.

A Peleskei nótárius (The Notary of Peleske) (Musical Farce)
Opening Night: June 4. Also staged on June 7 and 10.
Author: József Gaál.
Role: Othello. A small supporting role.

Lugosi was originally scheduled to appear in *A Boszorkany* on June 5. However, the play *Mary-Ann*, without Lugosi's participation, replaced it on the schedule.

Fauszt (Faust) (Tragedy)
Opening Night: June 14. Also staged on June 15.
Author: Goethe.
Role: Michael the Archangel and a Student. Minor roles.

Summer Theater

There is no evidence that Lugosi participated in summer theater in 1914. Given that *Pesti Napló* of August 15 reported Lugosi was a Lieutenant in the army, it is unlikely that he acted in any play that year after *Fauszt* on June 15.

1915

Given his military service, Lugosi did not undertake any acting roles in 1915.

1916

Budapest (at the Nemzeti Színház [National Theater], under the direction of Imré Tóth unless otherwise noted)

A fehér szarvas (***The White Stag***)
Opening Night: Spring. Exact date unknown.
Author: Uncertain
Role: Unknown
Note: Lugosi's heirs own a photograph of Lugosi and actress Hella (or Stella) Leitz along with cast members from a possible stage production called ***A fehér szarvas***. The photo is dated "Spring 1916." After being released from the military, Lugosi certainly would have had ample time to appear in a production prior to returning to the Nemzeti Színház (National Theater). Nevertheless, it is uncertain as to whether he appeared in this play and in this time frame.

Stuart Máriá (***Mary Stuart***) (Historical Tragedy)
Opening Night: April 10.
Author: Friedrich Schiller.
Role: Count Belliévre. A supporting role.

Jezus élete, szenvedése és halála (**aka** *A passziójáték*) (***The Life of Jesus – Suffering and Death, aka The Passion***) (Historical Drama)
Note: Most biographers have indicated that Lugosi performed in this production on or about April 15 in Debrecen for the Easter season. However, there is extreme doubt that a Debrecen version took place. A playbill for an entirely different play exists for April 15, as well for both the Western and Orthodox Easter weekends. A careful search of the published Debrecen playbills for the early months of 1916, which cover every day the theater there was active, do not show any performance remotely resembling a Passion play.

Concert for Wounded Soldiers
Opening Night: Cabaret style on April 15 at the Pénzintézetek Hadikórházában (Pensioners Military Hospital).
Role: Guest artist.
Note: An audience of around 1,200, including many convalescing soldiers, watched this show. The program was around two hours in duration and consisted of a concerto and other entertainment.

Hamlet (Tragedy)
Opening Night: April 30. Also staged on May 13 and 25.
Author: William Shakespeare.

Role: Fortinbras, the Prince of Norway. A minor role.

Opening night on a double bill with:

II. Richard (***Richard II***) (Historical Drama)
Opening Night: April 30.
Author: William Shakespeare.
Role: Bagot. A minor role.

Macbeth (Tragedy)
Opening Night: May 2. Also staged on May 16.
Author: William Shakespeare.
Role: Lennox. A small supporting role.

Concert for Wounded Soldiers
Opening Night: May 5 at the XVII. számú helyőrségi körházban (17th Century Garrison Hospital).
Role: Guest Artist.
Note: Lugosi appeared along with opera singers and a violinist.

Othelló (***Othello***) (Tragedy)
Opening Night: May 6. Also staged on October 7 and November 20.
Author: William Shakespeare.
Role: Lodovico. A small supporting role.

Rómeó és Júlia (***Romeo and Juliet***) (Tragedy)
Opening Night: May 10. Also staged on May 17, September 25, November 3 and 19, and December 10 and 27.
Author: William Shakespeare.
Role: Escalus. A small supporting role.

No evidence has been found to establish Lugosi's participation in any summer theater productions for 1916. His documented appearances suggest that he remained in the Budapest area performing in cabarets on Danube cruise ships as well as providing charity entertainment for convalescing soldiers.

Cabaret-Soiree
Opening Night: June 27 on board the Danube boat *Auguszta*.
Role: Guest artist.
Note: A cabaret style entertainment primarily for wounded soldiers from the Wodianerné Katonai Kórház (Wodianer Military Hospital).

Cabaret-Concert

Opening Night: July 22 at the Wodianerné Katonai Kórház (Wodianer Military Hospital).

Role: Guest artist.

Note: A concert and cabaret entertainment for wounded Hungarian soldiers.

Charity Concert for Wounded Soldiers

Opening Night: August 5 at the Red Cross Hospital.

Role: Guest artist.

Note: Lugosi and other entertainers performed for recuperating soldiers.

Concert for Wounded Soldiers

Opening Night: August 10 at the Wodianerné Katonai Kórház (Wodianer Military Hospital).

Role: Guest artist.

Note: A concert and other entertainment for wounded Hungarian soldiers.

Cabaret-Concert

Opening Night: August 15 on board the ship *Auguszta* on a Danube cruise.

Role: Guest Artist.

Note: Open to the general public, this cabaret-style entertainment featured Lugosi (billed as Béla Lugossy) along with other artists.

A szökött katona (The Runaway Soldier) (Drama)

Opening Night: September 17. Also staged on September 21, 24, 27, and on October 6 and 15.

Author: Ede Szigligeti.

Role: Tengeri. A minor role.

Hamlet (Tragedy)

Opening Night: September 23. Also staged on October 23.

Author: William Shakespeare.

Role: Laertes. A supporting role.

IV. Henrik király (Henry the IV Part II) (Drama)

Opening Night: October 11. Also staged on October 13, 15, 18 and 25.

Author: William Shakespeare.

Role: Lord Mowbray. A small supporting role.

Aesopus (Aesop) (Comedy)

Opening Night: October 14.

Author: Jenő Rákosi.

Role: Diodor, the Prince of Samos. A supporting role.

Note: Also known as *Ezópusz*.

A nök barátja (***The Friend of Women***) (Comedy)
Opening Night: October 19. Also staged on October 21, 24 and 31, November 5, and December 14.
Author: Alexander Dumas.
Role: De Montégre. A major role.
Note: This is the Hungarian version of ***L'Ami des femmes* (1864).**

Zsuzsi (***Susie***) (Peasant Comedy)
Opening Night: October 27. Also staged on October 28 and 29, November 2, 4, 7, 9 and 14, and December 16 and 23.
Author: Lajos Barta.
Role: A Young Man. Likely a small role.

Cabaret Concert for Wounded Soldiers
Opening Night: November 3.
Role: Guest artist.
Note: This event for wounded soldiers was performed at a military hospital then located at 25 Molnár Street on the Pest side of the Danube River.

Wodianerné Katonai Kórház (Wodianer Military Hospital)
Opening Day: November 8 in the afternoon.
Role: Guest artist.
Note: This cabaret entertainment was staged in the courtyard of the Budapest City Park.

Don Carlos (Drama)
Opening Night: November 10. Also staged on November 11, 12, 15 and 16.
Author: Friedrich Schiller.
Role: The Duke of Feria. A small supporting role.

Egy szegény ifju története (***The Romance of a Poor Young Man***) (Drama)
Opening Night: November 22. Also staged on December 5, 11 and 31.
Author: Octave Feuillet.
Role: Gaston. A small supporting role.

A három testőr (***The Three Bodyguards***) (Comedy)
Opening Night: December 9.
Author: Ferenc Herczeg.
Role: Cszernay, a Journalist. A small supporting role.

A makrancos hölgy (***The Taming of the Shrew***) (Comedy)

Opening Night: December 19. Also staged on December 28.

Author: William Shakespeare.

Role: Lucentio. A supporting role.

Ünnepi játék (***Festive Games***) (A Festive Play)

Opening Night: December 30.

Author: Ferenc Herczeg.

Role: A Poet.

1917

Budapest (at the Nemzeti Színház [National Theater], under the direction of Imré Tóth unless otherwise noted)

Don Carlos (Drama)

Opening Night: January 2. Also staged on January 7, 15 and 22, February 3, and September 8 and 28.

Author: Friedrich Schiller.

Role: The Duke of Feria. A small supporting role.

A makrancos hölgy (***The Taming of the Shrew***) (Comedy)

Opening Night: January 5. Also staged on January 10, 17 and 28, March 12 and 29, April 13 and 22, May 21, October 8 and 28, November 19, and December 31.

Author: William Shakespeare.

Role: Lucentio. A supporting role.

A nők barátjá (***The Friend of Women***) (Comedy)

Opening Night: January 7. Also staged on January 25, March 21, April 1, May 22, September 11, and December 15.

Author: Alexander Dumas.

Role: De Montégre. A major role.

Note: This is the Hungarian version of ***L'Ami des femmes (1864).***

Hamlet (Tragedy)

Opening Night: January 8. Also staged on March 17, April 16, May 31, September 3, October 1, and December 21.

Author: William Shakespeare.

Role: Laertes. A supporting role.

Kőmives Kelemen (***Clement, the Mason***) (Drama)

Opening Night: January 12. Also staged on January 13 and 14.

Author: Aurél Kárpáti and László Vajda.

Role: The First Mason. A small role.

Az ember tragédiája (***The Tragedy of Man***) (Poetic Drama)
Opening Night: January 19. Also staged on January 26 and 31, February 5 and 16, March 9, April 27 and 30, May 25, September 17, October 15, and November 12.
Author: Imre Madách.
Roles: Catulus (small supporting role), Marquis and The Second Worker (minor roles).

Rómeó és Júlia (***Romeo and Juliet***) (Tragedy)
Opening Night: February 2. Also staged on April 5, September 10 and October 19.
Author: William Shakespeare.
Role: Escalus. A small supporting role.

A hadifogoly (***The Prisoner of War***) (Comedy)
Opening Night: February 9. Also staged on February 10, 11, 15, 18, 22, 25 and 27, March 8, 11, 14, 18, 22 and 27, April 1, 4, 8, 12, 21 and 24, May 3, 8, 17 and 27, September 5, 13 and 29, and November 11.
Author: Sándor Hevesi.
Role: Henri Talmont. Based on contemporary reviews, likely a small role.
Review: "Lugosi is good as Talmont." (*Pesti Napló* 16 Feb. 1917).

Egy szegény ifju története (***The Romance of a Poor Young Man***) (Drama)
Opening Night: February 11. Also staged onApril 29, June 2, and September 6 and 23.
Author: Octave Feuillet.
Role: Gaston. A small supporting role.

A pártütők (***The Insurgents***) (Comedy)
Opening Night: February 12.
Author: Károly Kisfaludy.
Role: Lieutenant Élosdy. Based on contemporary reviews, a significant role.
Review: "Béla Lugosi and György Kürthy were new, but rather talented performers of the well-known and rather stylish play." (*Pesti Napló* 13 Feb. 1917).

IV. Henrik király (***Henry the IV Part II***) (Drama)
Opening Night: February 14. Also staged on December 28.
Author: William Shakespeare.
Role: Lord Mowbray. A small supporting role.

Janos király (***King John***) (Historical Drama)
Opening Night: March 15.
Author: William Shakespeare.

Role: Louis the Dauphin. A small supporting role.

A szentivánáji álom (*A Midsummer Night's Dream*) (Comedy)
Opening Night: March 16.
Author: William Shakespeare.
Role: Demetrius. A supporting role.

A szőkőtt katona (*The Runaway Soldier*) (Folk Play)
Opening Night: March 18.
Author: Mór Jókai.
Role: Tengeri. A minor role.

Hegedű Ferenc jubileuma - Magyar operafesztivál (Ferenc Hegedu Jubilee – Hungarian Opera Festival)
Opening Night: March 28 at the Royal Hungarian Opera House. Also staged on March 29.
Role: Guest Artist.
Note: Reviews from newspapers and theater publications confirm Lugosi's participation. However, it is unclear whether he performed one night or two.

A kaméliás hölgy (*Lady of the Camellias*, aka *Camille*) (Drama)
Opening Night: March 30. Also staged on April 3 and 17, May 2, 11, 18 and 27, June 5, September 22, and October 2.
Author: Alexander Dumas.
Role: Varville. A supporting role.

Zsuzsi (*Susie*) (Peasant Comedy)
Opening Night: April 15.
Author: Lajos Barta.
Role: A Lad. A small role.

Az aranyember (*The Golden Man*) (Drama)
Opening Night: May 7. Also staged on May 28 and December 7, 10, 17 and 25.
Author: Mór Jókai.
Role: Kadisa. A major supporting role.

Máriá Magdolna (*Maria Magdelena*) (Tragedy)
Opening Night: May 19. Also staged on May 20, 24 and 29.
Author: Friedrich Hebbel.
Role: Leonhard. A major supporting role.
Review: "In the role of the cunning 'seducer,' Béla Lugosi was too stiff, rather like an actor who just recites his lines." (*Népsava* 20 May 1917).

A nagymama (*The Grandmother*) (Comedy)
Opening Night: May 26. Also staged on June 3.
Author: Gergely Csiky.
Role: Kálmán Örkényi. A supporting role.

There is no known documentation that Lugosi participated in the summer theater circuit during 1917. It is more likely that the gap in his stage performances was due to film production commitments as well as his honeymoon after his marriage to Ilona Szmik on June 25.

A három testőr (*The Three Bodyguards*) (Comedy)
Opening Night: September 2. Also staged on October 21 and December 31.
Author: Ferenc Herczeg.
Role: Csernay. A small supporting role.

Deréki Antal jubileuma (Jubilee Celebration for Antal Deréki)
Opening Night: September 11 at the Budai Színház (Buda Theater).
Role: Guest artist.
Note: The exact nature of Lugosi's participation in this celebration of the life and art of actor Antal Deréki is unknown.

Lugosi was scheduled to perform in *Stuart Máriá* (*Mary Stuart*) on September 24 and October 22, but for reasons unknown, he was replaced by György Kürthy.

Árva László király (*Lonely King Laszlo*) (Historical Drama)
Opening Night: October 26.
Author: Ferenc Herczeg.
Role: King László. A major role.

1918
Budapest (at the Nemzeti Színház [National Theater], under the direction of Zoltán Ambrus unless otherwise noted)

A hadifogoly (*The Prisoner of War*) (Comedy)
Opening Night: January 1.
Author: Sándor Hevesi.
Role: Henri Talmont. Based on contemporary reviews, likely a small role.

Az aranyember (*The Golden Man*) (Drama)
Opening Night: January 3. Also staged on January 11 and 30, February 11, March 1, and April 1.
Author: Mór Jókai.

Role: Kadisa. A major supporting role.

Rómeó és Júlia (***Romeo and Juliet***) (Tragedy)
Opening Night: January 7.
Author: William Shakespeare.
Role: Escalus. A small supporting role.
Note: While a playbill for this performance exists in the files of the Hungarian National Library Theater History Collection, newspapers of the era report a different play scheduled for that day.

A kaméliás hölgy (***Lady of the Camellias***, **aka** *Camille*) (Drama)
Opening Night: January 10. Also staged on February 3 and April 7, 8, and 27, June 12 and 16, September 24, and October 13.
Author: Alexander Dumas.
Roles: Varville and Armand Duval.
Note: While first playing the smaller role of Varville, Lugosi debuted as Armand Duval for the first time at the Nemzeti Színház (National Theater) starting with the April 7 performance. While no playbill has surfaced for the April 8 performance, a review of it mentioning Lugosi was published in the April 9 edition of *Az Újság*. For an additional show on December 10, Lugosi was replaced at the last minute with another actor.

A hogy tetsik (***As You Like It***) (Pastoral Comedy)
Opening Night: January 18. Also staged on January 19 and 20, February 1, 3, 7, 13 and 17, March 2, 9, 10, 15 and 24, May 30, June 29, September 15, and December 23.
Author: William Shakespeare.
Roles: Jaques (supporting role) and Le Beau (small supporting role).
Note: The play was performed on January 23 as well, but Sándor Garamszeghy replaced Lugosi. For the December 23 performance, Lugosi had himself been a last-minute substitute in the role of Le Beau.

IV. Henrik király (***Henry the IV Part II***) (Historical Drama)
Opening Night: February 4.
Author: William Shakespeare.
Role: Lord Mowbray. A small supporting role.

Don Carlos (Historical Tragedy)
Opening Night: February 20. Also staged on March 18, June 28, and September 16.
Author: Friederich Schiller.
Role: The Duke of Feria. A small supporting role.

Charlotte kisasszony (***Mademoiselle Charlotte***) (Historical Drama)
Opening Night: February 22. Also staged February 23, 24, 26, 28, March 3, 6, 8, 10, 12, 14, 16,

21, 23, 25, 28 and 31, and April 2, 13 and 18.

Author: Menyhért Lengyel.

Role: Pál Cséfalvi. Based on contemporary reviews, likely a supporting role.

Note: Various Budapest newspapers show this play also scheduled for April 23 and 30, May 8, 11 and 19 and June 1, 9 and 15. Those schedules did not include cast lists and the playbills have not yet been found to confirm these dates or Lugosi's involvement.

Árva László király (Lonely King Laszlo) (Historical Drama)

Opening Night: March 13. Also staged on March 19 and 27, April 8, 10 and 22, May 8 and 27, and June 3, 8, 17, and 29, and September 2.

Author: Ferenc Herczeg.

Role: King László. A major role.

Note: Prior to opening night, the original lead player, Árpád Odry, took ill. According to the *Budapesti Hírlap* edition of March 14, Lugosi was promoted to this lead role with good reviews. Lugosi had previously appeared in this part for at least one performance during the autumn of 1917.

Review: "Tonight's performance of the play… was made interesting by two new actors. Instead of Odry, who was on sick leave, Béla Lugosi played László Hunyadi with noble fire and moderate temperament. The enthusiastic applause of the audience confirmed the right choice of director Ambrus and praised the artist's lovely acting." (*Az Újság* 14 Mar. 1918).

Macbeth (Tragedy)

Opening Night: March 22. Also staged on April 11.

Author: William Shakespeare.

Role: Lennox. A small supporting role.

II. Jozsef Császár (Emperor Joseph II) (Drama)

Opening Night: April 5. Also staged on April 6, 7, 8, 12, 15, 17, 19, 21, 24 and 28, May 1, 6, 10, 13, 15, 20, 22, 26, 29 and 31, June 2, 4, 6 and 10, September 3, 11, 20 and 26, October 1, 8 and 16, and November 6 and 14.

Author: Dezső Szomory.

Role: Count Hatzfeld. A small supporting role.

Review: "Lugosi, for whom a great future awaits…." (*Szíházi Élet* [Budapest Hungary] 14-21 Apr. 1918).

Kozonyt Kozonnyel (Donna Dianna) (Musical Comedy)

Opening Night: April 26.

Author: Moreto.

Role: Unknown.

Note: Although subsequent reviews do not specifically mention him, both *Pesti Náplo* and *Pester Lloyd*, in their April 18 editions, announced that "Lugosi" would be among the performers presenting a reprise of this play.

Görögtűz (*Greek Fire*) (Comedy)
Opening Night: May 3. Also staged May 4, 5, 9, 12, 14, 16, 19, 21, 23, 28 and 30, and June 9, 16 and 27.
Author: Sándor Hevesi.
Role: Imre Adorján. Based on contemporary reviews, this was a major role.
Review: "The main role was played by Béla Lugosi, whom we can see in a bigger role again after a very long time; we have seen him excellent in conversation and in love; everyone had to admit that he played exactly what the author had imagined. He was the center of that storm – that hurricane in a glass of water, what's more, in sugary water – which was formed around the question whether the lady should marry, and if she should, whom she should marry." (*Népszava* [Budapest, Hungary] 4 May 1918).

Rómeo és Júlia (*Romeo and Juliet*) (Tragedy)
Opening Night: June 7. Also staged on June 11, 18 and 22, September 6 and 30, and October 14.
Author: William Shakespeare.
Role: Tybalt. A small supporting role.

A makrancos hölgy (*The Taming of the Shrew*) (Comedy)
Opening Night: June 26. Also staged on June 29 and September 10.
Author: William Shakespeare.
Role: Vincentio. A supporting role.
Note: Lucentio was printed on the playbill as Lugosi's role, but was lined through and replaced with Vincentio.

There is no existing documentation that Lugosi participated in the summer theater circuit during 1918. It is more likely that the gap in stage performances was due to film production commitments.

A nök barátja (*The Friend of Women*) (Comedy)
Opening Night: September 7. Also staged on November 29.
Author: Alexander Dumas.
Role: De Montégre. A major role.
Note: This is the Hungarian version of *L'Ami des femmes* (**1864**).

Bizánc (*Byzantium*) (Drama)
Opening Night: September 18. Also staged on November 9.
Author: Ferenc Herczeg.
Role: Ahmed Khan, a Turkish Ambassador. A minor role.

III. Richard (*Richard III*) (Historical Drama)

Opening Night: November 15.
Author: William Shakespeare.
Role: Henry, the Earl of Richmond. A small supporting role.

VIII. Henry (*Henry VIII*) (Historical Drama)
Opening Night: November 24. Also staged on November 27 and December 2 and 28.
Author: William Shakespeare.
Role: Suffolk. A small supporting role.

Bagatelle (*Bagatelle*) (Comedy)
Opening Night: December 20. Also staged on December 29.
Author: Paul Hervieu.
Role: Sarsy.

1919

Budapest (at the Nemzeti Színház [National Theater], under the direction of Zoltán Ambrus unless otherwise noted)

Bagatelle (Comedy)
Opening Night: January 2. Also staged on January 4, 9, 15, 18 and 22.
Author: Paul Hervieu.
Role: Sarsy.

Sancho Panza királysága (*The Kingdom of Sancho Panza*) (Comedy)
Opening Night: January 10. Also staged on January 12, 14, 16, 19, 21 and 23.
Author: Menyhért Lengyel.
Role: The Prince.
Note: Lugosi received top billing in this role.

Othelló (*Othello*) (Tragedy)
Opening Night: January 27. Also staged on February 14.
Author: William Shakespeare.
Role: Lodovico. A small supporting role.

Árva László király (*Lonely King Laszlo*) (Historical Drama)
Opening Night: February 10.
Author: Ferenc Herczeg.
Role: King László. A major role.

A makrancos hölgy (*The Taming of the Shrew*) (Comedy)
Opening Night: March 25.

Author: William Shakespeare.
Role: Lucentio. A supporting role.

A fekete lovas (*The Black Rider*) (Drama)
Opening Night: March 26. Also staged on March 27 and 28.
Author: Ferenc Herczeg.
Role: Baron Leitmaritz.
Note: The March 28 performance is Lugosi's last confirmed stage appearance in Hungary. While no playbill has been found for this Nemzeti Színház (National Theater) production, a review of it mentioning Lugosi's participation was published in the March 23-29 issue of *Színházi Élet*. The March 22 edition of *Világ* also lists Lugosi in the cast. In addition, several Budapest newspapers (*Az Est*, *Budapesti Hírlap*, and *Pesti Napló*) report a three-day schedule for the play at the end of March. However, there is some uncertainty about the date of the opening night. The March 16-22 edition of *Színházi Élet* claimed opening night would be March 24, while the March 4 edition of *Pesti Napló* gave a date of March 21. Moreover, the March 23 edition of *Magyarország* listed an additional performance on March 30; however, that date does not appear in the theater schedules published in other Budapest newspapers.

May Day Celebration
May 1, 1919.
Lugosi was on the entertainment committee for this event. Free admission to theater presentations was available on that day. It is unknown as to whether or not Lugosi appeared in any of the productions. In any event, this was one of his final official acts before fleeing to Vienna.

Lugosi in *Az élet királya*
(*The King of Life*, aka
Élet királya, 1917).

Appendix B

Hungarian and German Filmography

Researched and compiled by Gary D. Rhodes and Bill Kaffenberger

The following filmography is the most complete and accurate catalogue of Lugosi's output based on the best available primary sources. The films are listed in chronological order and divided into categories that denote their country of origin: Hungary and Germany.

Some Hungarian films appearing in previous Lugosi filmographies are absent herein because Lugosi's involvement in them is far too questionable.[1] For example, advertisements in Hungarian trade publications announced that Lugosi would star in the title role of Star Film's *Casanova* (1917). But in the released film, Alfréd Deésy played Casanova; Lugosi wasn't named in any known period cast listings. Lugosi might have appeared in the film in a smaller role, but there is no compelling evidence to that effect.[2]

It is also important to note that *Lili* (Star, 1917) is intentionally excluded. As with *Casanova*, initial ads and announcements claimed Lugosi would appear in the film, playing the character Plinchard at two different stages of his life. But advertisements and reviews for the film's premiere in Budapest indicate that Gusztáv Vándori (aka Gusztáv Vándory) played Plinchard. This is further proven by a number of surviving still photographs of Vándori as Plinchard, including one of the character at an older age. It is possible that Lugosi could have played a smaller role in the film, but there is no known evidence to that effect. At present, *Lili* is too questionable to remain in any Lugosi filmography.[3]

And then there are two Hungarian newsreels in which Lugosi might appear, but there is no evidence other than visual recognition of the onscreen persons. The first was *Az Est-Film* (*The Evening Film*) for the week of September 17-23, 1918. One of its stories covers the funeral of theater and film actress Márta Szentgyörgyi, which took place on September 20, 1918. A mourner looks like Lugosi from one angle, but not as much from another. Moreover, his face is largely obscured and he is seen only briefly. Perhaps it is Lugosi, but perhaps it is not. He likely knew Szentgyörgyi, but there is no known evidence that he attended her funeral.

The second newsreel that might show Lugosi is *Vörös Riport-Film* (*Red Report Film*) for April 29 to May 5, 1919. It depicts a variety of May Day festivities and parade routes filmed on May 1, 1919. Lugosi definitely took part in the event, but whether he appears in this newsreel is another matter. Someone who resembles him marches in the parade with a group of film professionals.

But a high-resolution transfer of the restoration of this newsreel released makes the person in question look less like Lugosi than the version used in the documentary film *Le vampire déchu* (*The Fallen Vampire*, 2007). Similar to the *Az Est-Film* newsreel, there is no documentation or evidence that this person is Lugosi beyond possible visual recognition.

There are also a few German films too questionable to include. For example, Lugosi was announced as an actor in three films for Eichberg-Film's 1919-1920 season: *Jettatore* (*The Jinx*), *Sünden der Eltern* (*Sins of the Parents*), and *Nonne und Tänzerin* (*Nun and Dancer*).[4] A careful examination of period cast listings and censorship records for these films suggests that his appearance in any of them is highly doubtful. Perhaps he appeared in one or more of them in small roles, but there is no evidence to that effect, save for one advertisement that ambiguously implies he appeared in them.

Given that Lugosi played George Corvin in *Der Sklavenhalter von Kansas-City* (*The Slaveholder of Kansas City*, 1920, aka *John Hopkins III*), it is possible he played the same character in the first two *Apachenrache* (*Apache Revenge*) films, *In den Krallen des Vampirs* (*In the Vampire's Clutches*) and *In den Krallen von Gg. Corvin, dem Ausbrecher-König* (*In the Clutches of Geo. Corvin, King of Escapes*, 1920).[5] There is no evidence that he did, but there is no credible, contemporary information on who played Corvin in those two films, both having been produced during Lugosi's time in Germany.

It is also worth noting a few additional titles included in some previous filmographies that are far more spurious, the most absurd being *Nachenschnur des tot* (1919). This is in fact a gibberish title, probably the result of an English speaker fumbling to translate the words *Necklace of the Dead* into German; as is, this alleged German title is a nonsense that would translate back into English as something like "Nape-shoelace of the deads." Here is the most ridiculous German or Hungarian entry ever added to a Lugosi filmography.

At least one Lugosi filmography has included *Diadalmas élet* (*Triumphant Life*, 1923), an obvious error given primary sources that discuss its production. Filmographies have at times also listed *Lulu* (1918) as a Lugosi film. While not impossible given that it was a Phönix film directed by Mihály Kertész produced during the same time frame as when Lugosi appeared in *99-es számú bérkocsi* (*Rental Car Number 99*, aka *99*, 1918) and *Az ezredes* (*The Colonel*, 1918), absolutely no primary sources mention Lugosi's involvement *Lulu*.

While avoiding the aforementioned titles, we do include two films never previously catalogued, *Radmirov Katalin* (*Catherine Radmirov*, 1917) and *Asszonyszívek kalandora* (*The Adventurer of Women's Hearts*). The former should be treated with caution, but enough evidence exists to include it at the present time.[6] The latter was definitely a two-reel Lugosi film, but it could have been an abbreviated version of one of his features at Star.[7]

The films that are listed herein have been checked and double-checked for accuracy against existing copyright records, censorship records, and surviving film trade publications.[8] The Hungarian and German entries are listed by their known release dates or, in some cases, preview dates. Any variances from previous filmographies are intentional and should be seen as corrections. Where possible, additional notes and reviews are given.

Hungary

*Leoni Leo (**Leo Leoni**)*[9] (Adventure Drama)

Star, 1917

Role: Leoni Leo.

Note: Lugosi was billed under the pseudonym Arisztid Olt. Star reportedly previewed the film in August of 1917.

*Álarcosbál (**The Masked Ball**)* (Drama)

Star Film, 1917

Role: René, Secretary to the Prince of Mondero Island.

Note: Lugosi was billed under the pseudonym Arisztid Olt. Previewed at the Uránia in Budapest between October 21 and 28, 1917, before being released on March 11, 1918.

Reviews: "Arisztid Olt played the lovely, warm role of the secretary, and with his superb dynamism he won the appreciation of the audience right away" (*Színházi Élet* [Budapest, Hungary] 10-17 Mar. 1918). "The best Hungarian cinematic actors play in this grandiose, three-act drama, and Annie Goth and Arisztid Olt play the main roles brilliantly" (*Nyírvidék* [Nyíregyháza, Hungary] 11 June 1918).

*Radmirov Katalin (**Catherine Radmirov**)* (Drama)

Star, 1917

Role: Unknown

Note: Previewed at the Uránia in Budapest between October 21 and 28, 1917, before being released on February 4, 1918. Trade announcements for this film did not mention Lugosi, nor did most period credits for the film. However, during the film's run at the Uránia in Szeged in April of 1918, newspaper advertisements listed Arisztid Olt as being in the cast. A brief review in the April 25, 1918, edition of Szeged's *Délmagyarország* not only mentioned Arisztid Olt and costar Annie Góth, but also applauded their performances as being given "with their usual art." By contrast, other reviews of the time mention Góth, but not Lugosi.

*Az élet királya (**The King of Life**)*[10] (Drama)

Star, 1917

Role: Lord Harry Watton.

Note: Lugosi was billed under the pseudonym Arisztid Olt. On numerous occasions, Hungarian film trade publications also referred to this movie as *Dorian Gray*. Previewed at the Uránia in Budapest on October 23, 1917 and then released on January 21, 1918.

Review: "Arisztid Olt played the role of Lord Watton, and his acting was truly artistic" (*Pesti Hírlap* [Budapest, Hungary] 19 Jan. 1919).

*Asszonyszívek kalandora (**The Adventurer of Women's Hearts**)* (Romantic Drama)

Company unknown, ca. 1917

Role: Title character

Note: This was definitely screened, with a descriptive review published in New York in 1922. There is no doubt that Lugosi starred in it. The question is whether the film was a unique production, or whether it was a shortened and retitled version of one of the features he made at Star.

*Nászdal (**Wedding Song**)* (Drama)
Star, 1918
Role: Paul Bertram, a Violinist.
Note: Lugosi was billed under the pseudonym Arisztid Olt. The film's title was sometimes rendered as *A nászdal (The Wedding Song)*. Previewed on February 27, 1918 at the Corso in Budapest before being released on April 8, 1918.
Review: "The main role was played by Arisztid Olt, with mature artistic skills and with elaborate style" (*Világ* [Budapest, Hungary] 7 Apr. 1918).

*A régiséggyűjtő (**The Antiquarian**)* (Comedy)
Star, 1918
Role: Unknown.
Note: Fictional short subject (640 meters). Lugosi was billed under the pseudonym Arisztid Olt. The film previewed at the Corso Theater in Budapest on February 28, 1918, before being released on March 6, 1918.
Review: "The ingenious direction confirms the proven talent of Alfréd Deésy. One can admire Kamilla Hollay's lovely impishness and the cheerful appearance of Arisztid Olt, Norbert Dán and Miklós Ujváry in the main roles." (*Pesti Hírlap* [Budapest, Hungary] 27 Jan. 1918).

*Tavaszi vihar (**Spring Tempest**)* (Drama)
Star, 1918
Role: Renner, a Landowner and Husband.
Note: Lugosi was billed under the pseudonym Arisztid Olt. Previewed at the Corso in Budapest on February 28, 1918, before being released on April 22, 1918.
Review: "… Arisztid Olt sketched the role of the husband with dramatic intimacy and subtle art" (*8 Órai Újság* [Budapest, Hungary] 24 Apr. 1918).

*Küzdelem a létért (**The Struggle for Life**)* (Drama)
Star, 1918
Role: Pál Orlay, an Architect.
Note: Lugosi was billed under the pseudonym Arisztid Olt. Previewed on July 16, 1918 at the Mozgókép-Otthon in Budapest, before being released on September 22, 1918. The film was also advertised and discussed in Hungarian trade publications as *A Leopard (The Leopard)*. Filmographies that list the two titles as separate films are in error.

*99-es számú bérkocsi (**Rental Car Number 99**)* (Crime Drama)
Phönix, 1918

Role: Detective Ward.

Note: Previewed at the Royal-Apolló in Budapest on September 12, 1918, before being released on November 8, 1918.[11] At times, the film's title was rendered simply as *99*. Lugosi was billed as Béla Lugosi.

Az ezredes (The Colonel) (Comedy)

Phönix, 1918

Role: The Colonel.

Note: Premiered at the Omnia in Budapest on December 30, 1918. Lugosi was billed as Béla Lugosi.

Review: "The comical situations of this extremely funny film were unprecedentedly successful. Béla Lugosi, Kläry Lotto, Zoltán Szerémy and László Z. Molnár in the main roles proved again how great their talent for acting is, and they contributed greatly to the success of the film with their superb acting" (*Az Újság* [Budapest, Hungary] 1 Jan. 1919).

Germany

Hypnose: Sklaven fremden Willens (Hypnosis: Slave of a Foreign Will, 1920) (Drama)

Eichberg-Film, 1920

Role: Professor Mors.

Note: After its premiere at the beginning of January 1920, Eichberg deleted *Hypnose* as the film's title, leaving *Sklaven fremden Willens*.

Reviews: "Bela Lugosi, straight out of Budapest, is a welcome newcomer – he possesses decided talent, but must guard against exaggeration" (*Film-Kurier* [Berlin, Germany] 4 Jan. 1920).

Der Tanz auf dem Vulkan (The Dance on the Volcano) (Drama)

Eichberg-Film, 1920

Role: Andre Fleurot.

Note: Released in two parts, *Sybil Joung* (*Sybil Young*) and *Der Tod des Großfürsten* (*The Death of the Grand Duke*). The first part premiered at the Ufa-Filmpalast in late February of 1920. For its American release, the film was shortened and retitled *Daughter of the Night*.

Der Januskopf: eine Tragödie am Rande der Wirklichkeit (The Head of Janus: A Tragedy on the Border of Reality) (Horror)

Lipow Film Co. and Decla-Bioscop AG, 1920

Role: A Butler.

Note: This film was initially known as *Schrecken*, including at a trade preview in April 1920.[12] When it premiered at Berlin's Marmorhaus-Lichtspiele on August 26, 1920, it bore the title *Der Januskopf: eine Tragödie am Rande der Wirklichkeit* (*The Head of Janus: A Tragedy on the Border of Reality*).

Der Fluch der Menschheit (*The Curse of Humanity*) (Action/Adventure)
Eichberg-Film, 1920
Role: Mälzer.
Note: Released in two parts, *Die Tochter der Arbeit* (*The Daughter of Labor*) and *Im Rausche der Milliarden* (*Intoxicated by Billions*). The first part premiered in September of 1920.

Das ganze Sein ist flammend Leid (*The Whole of Being is a Flaming Misery*) (Drama)
Emelka (Münchener Lichtspielkunst AG), 1920
Role: Unknown.
Note: Premiered in September of 1920.

Auf den Trümmern des Paradieses (*On the Ruins of Paradise*) (Drama)
Ustad-Film, 1920
Role: Unknown
Note: Premiered in October 1920 and went into general release in November 1920.

Lederstrumpf (*Leatherstocking*) (Western)
Luna-Film, 1920
Role: Chingachgook.
Note: *Lederstrumpf* appeared in two parts, *Der letzte Mohikaner* (*Last of the Mohicans*) and *Wildtöter* (*The Deerslayer*, aka *Wildtöter und Chingachgook/The Deerslayer and Chingachgook*).[13] After being previewed in October, the film went into general release in November 1920.
Review: "Under Arthur Wellin's direction, assured performances are given by Emil [Mamelok] and Bela Lugosi…" (*Deutsche Lichtspiel-Zeitung* [Munich, Germany] 27 Nov. 1920).

Die Frau im Delphin (*The Woman in the Dolphin*) (Action/Adventure)
Gaci Film (Gamsa-Film und Citograph GmbH), 1920
Role: Tom Bill.
Note: Also known as *Die Frau im Delphin oder 30 Tage auf dem Meeresgrund/The Woman in the Dolphin, or, 30 Days on the Ocean Floor*). First screened in November of 1920.

Die Todeskarawane (*The Caravan of Death*) (Drama)
Ustad-Film, 1920
Role: A Sheik.
Note: Premiered in November 1920.

Nat Pinkerton im Kampf (*Nat Pinkerton in Combat*) (Action/Adventure)
Dua-Film, 1920
Role: A Gang Leader.
Note: Released in two parts, *Das Ende des Artisten Bartolini* (*The End of the Performer Bartolini*) and *Diebesfallen* (*Criminal Traps*). Part two was not released until 1921. Lugosi only appeared in the first part.

Die Teufelsanbeter (*The Devil Worshippers*) (Drama)
Ustad-Film, 1921
Role: A Sheik
Note: Originally announced as *Bei den Teufelsanbetern*. Premiered in January of 1921.

Der Sklavenhalter von Kansas-City (*The Slaveholder of Kansas City*) (Drama)
Dua-Film, 1920/1921
Role: George Corvin.
Note: Screened to the press in November 1920, but the earliest known public screening came in February 1921. Also known as *John Hopkins III*, as well as (in modern sources, albeit erroneously) *Apachenrache. 3. – Die verschwundene Million* (*Apache Revenge 3 – The Disappearing Million*).

Ihre Hoheit die Tänzerin (*Her Highness, the Dancer*) (Drama)
Eichberg-Film, 1923
Role: Unknown.
Note: Eichberg made this film in 1920. Release delayed until February 1923 due to censorship problems.

(Endnotes)

1   In addition to eschewing *Casanova* (1918), we also do not include *Lulu* (1918) or *Diadalmas élet* (*Triumphant Life*, 1923). For our rationale, please see endnotes for Chapter 11.

2   Please see Chapter 11 for a lengthy discussion of *Casanova* (1918).

3   Please see Chapter 11 for a lengthy discussion of *Lili* (1917).

4   Advertisement. *Der Film* 18, 1919.

5   More information on the *Apachenrache* (*Apache Revenge*) films appears in Chapter 19.

6   More information on *Katalin Radmirov* (*Catherine Radmirov*, 1917) appears in Chapter 11.

7   More information on *Asszonyszívek kalandora* (*The Adventurer of Women's Hearts*) appears in Chapter 24, published in Volume II of *Becoming Dracula: The Early Years of Bela Lugosi*.

8   For his Hungarian films, the trades *Mozihét Kino-Woche, Mozgófénykép Híradó, Mozi-Világ*, and *Színházi Élet* have been key sources. For his German films, censorship records and such film publications as *Der Film, Der Kinematograph, Film-Kurier*, and *Lichtbild-Bühne* have been key sources.

9   See *Mozgófénykép Híradó* 19 Aug. 1917 for an ad and a lengthy plot summary.

10 In some Star advertisements, *Az élet királya* was referred to as simply *Élet királya*. See ads in *Mozgófénykép Hiradó* published on 7 Apr. 1918, 14 Apr. 1918, 21 Apr. 1918, and 28 Apr. 1918.

11 Advertisement. *Az Újság* (Budapest, Hungary) 31 Aug. 1918.

12 The film was mentioned by the title *Schrecken* in *Lichtbild-Bühne* 5 (1920), *LBB* 7 (1920), *LBB* 9 (1920), and *LBB* 18 (1920); it was also under the title *Schrecken* in *Film-Kurier* (29 Apr. 1920). Ads using the title *Schrecken* appeared in *Der Kinematograph* 701-702 (1920), *LBB* 21 (1920, three

different ads), *LBB* 21 (1920), *LBB* 23 (1920), *LBB* 25 (1920), and *Film-Kurier* (30 Apr. 1920), among others. An ad for the film as *Der Januskopf* appeared in *Der Film* 36 (1920). An article in *LBB* 35 (1920) used that title, as did a review in *Film-Kurier* (27 Aug. 1920).

13   Articles in *Lichtbild-Bühne* 35 (1920) and *LBB* 43 (1920), as well as a full-page ad in *LBB* 37 (1920) used the title *Wildtöter*, as did an ad in *Film-Kurier* (1 Sept. 1920), an ad in *Der Film* (29 Aug. 1920), and an article in *Der Film* 43 (1920). But a review in *Film-Kurier* (1 Nov. 1920) used the title *Wildtöter und Chingachgook,* as did reviews in *Der Film* 44 and 46 (1920). At times (as in an article in *Der Film,* and a full-page ad in *Der Kinematograph*), *Wildtöter* was referred to as *Der Pfadfinder.*

Index

Hungarian State Police 241-242, 244-245, 252

Hungarian State Superior Gymnasium 23-24, 26

Hunyadi Castle 53

Hyänen der Lust (*Hyenas of Lust*, 1919) 255

Hypnose: Sklaven fremden Willens (*Hypnosis: Slave of a Foreign Will*, 1920) 254-261, 272, 290, 308, 313

Igazgató úr, Az (*The Headmaster*) 63, 124

Ihre Hoheit die Tänzerin (*Her Highness, the Dancer*, 1923) 265, 273

Ilniczky, János 251

In den Krallen des Vampirs (*In the Vampire's Clutches*, 1920) 294-295, 311

Isherwood, Christopher 255, 272

Janowitz, Hans 280-282, 284, 290

Januskopf, Der (*The Head of Janus*) see *Schrecken* (*Terror*, 1920) 275-291

John Hopkins III see *Der Sklavenhalter von Kansas-City* (*The Slaveholder of Kansas City*, 1920) 294-299, 311, 318

Jókai, Mór 48

Juhász, Gyula 93

Kaiser Wilhelm II 203, 255

Kalbus, Oskar 293, 310

Kálmány, Béla 87, 99

Kalocsa, Hungary 42

Kaméliás hölgy (*Lady of the Camellias*) 75, 77, 149

Kaplanek, Hugo 321-322

Kard becsülete (*The Honor of the Sword*) 88

Karenin Anna (*Anna Karenina*) 100, 102-103, 105-107

Karloff, Boris 58-59, 201, 272

Károlyi, Count Mihály 205, 207, 209, 211, 212, 215, 216, 218, 227, 231, 239, 251, 252

Kenessei, József 40

Kertész, Mihály (Michael Curtiz) 79, 80, 84, 170, 171, 172, 173, 176, 190, 209, 217, 224, 232

Kéz kezet mos (*One Hand Washes the Other*) 53

Király Színház (Royal Theater) 58, 105, 110, 115

kis szökevény, A (*The Little Fugitive*) 57

Knevels, Fritz 296

kölcsönkért kastély, A (*The Borrowed Residence*) 128

Kontler, László 105, 215-216, 227, 238

Korda, Michael 216, 234

Korda, Sándor (Alexander) 216, 227, 232

Kornay, Richárd 40,184, 186

Kracauer, Siegfried 257, 265, 272, 273, 277, 289, 293, 310

Krauss, Werner 277

Krecsányi, Iganác 55-57

Kremer, Jenő 84

Krúdy, Gyula 105

Kun, Béla 215-218, 222, 224, 226-229, 231-234, 238, 241-242, 244, 246, 251-253, 320-321

Kurfürstendamm (1920) 284

Kurucz Féja Dávid (*Stubborn King David*) 51-52

Küszer, Vilma 18

Rückert, Ernst 267

Rye, Stellan 281

Sz. Szigethy, Vilmos 92

Saly, Noémi 193-195, 199, 201, 228, 229, 233, 234, 237, 238, 313

Sancho Panza Királysága (The Kingdom of Sancho Panza) 221

Sand, George 164

Sannom, Emilie 268, 270, 271

Sárga csikó (The Yellow Colt) 101

sárga liliom, A (The Yellow Lily) 94, 95, 96, 107-108

sasok, A (The Eagles) 42, 43

Schlegel, Margarete 280, 286

Schreck, Max 288, 293

Schrecken (Terror, 1920) 278, 280-284, 288, 289, 290

Shakespeare 83, 157

Shomer, Robert 98

Siklósi, Iván 172

Silbermine, Die (The Silver Mine) 309

Sirius-Film 283

Szirontai Lhotka, István (Lhotka, Stefan) 162

Sittengeschichte des Kinos (History of Cinema's Morals, 1926)

Sklaven fremden Willens see *Hypnose: Sklaven fremden Willens (Hypnosis: Slave of a Foreign Will, 1920)* 254, 257-261

Sklavenhalter von Kansas-City (The Slaveholder of Kansas City, 1920) 294-299, 311, 318

Somló, Sándor 41

Son of Frankenstein (1939) 36

Sopron, Hungary 103

Star Film Company 158, 159-170, 184-189

Stein, Josef 298, 302, 303

Stevenson, Robert Louis 278, 283

Stifter, Magnus 268, 270, 271, 281

Stoker, Bram 11, 30, 68-69, 183, 257, 288, 315, 319, 324

Strange Case of Dr. Jekyll and Mr. Hyde (1886) 278

Student von Prag, Der (The Student of Prague, 1913) 281

Summer Theater 42, 57, 58, 101, 102, 103, 104, 115

Sybil Joung (Sybil Young, 1920) 259

Szabadka, Hungary (Subotica, Serbia) 28, 38-39, 40, 41, 47, 48, 316

Szabó, Anna Viola 69, 75, 80, 81

Szabo, Captain Ludovico 321

Szalai, Gyula 40

Szatmári, Zoltán 40

Szeged, Hungary 38, 57, 79, 83-98, 101, 184, 185, 186, 187, 193, 207, 231

Szeged Popularity Polls 95

Szegedi Városi Színház (Szeged Municipal Theater) 84

Szerémy, Zoltán 171, 172

Szigetvári Vértanúk (The Martyrs of Szigetbár) 70

Szittja, Willie 321-322, 324

Szmik, Ilona 193-201, 227, 236, 237, 316, 318

Made in the USA
Middletown, DE
16 September 2021